RETAIL
STRATEGY AND STRUCTURE

A Management Approach

RETAIL STRATEGY AND STRUCTURE

A Management Approach

SECOND EDITION

DAVID J. RACHMAN

Baruch School of Business Administration
City College of New York

PRENTICE-HALL, INC., Englewood Cliffs, New Jersey

Library of Congress Cataloging in Publication Data

Rachman, David J
   Retail strategy and structure.

    Bibliography: p.
    1. Retail trade — Management. I. Title
HF5429.R317 1975 658'.91'381 74-14635

Printed in the United States of America

10 9 8 7 6 5 4 3 2 1

Prentice-Hall International, Inc., *London*
Prentice-Hall of Australia, Pty. Ltd., *Sydney*
Prentice-Hall of Canada, Ltd., *Toronto*
Prentice-Hall of India Private Limited, *New Delhi*
Prentice-Hall of Japan, Inc., *Tokyo*

To

BARBARA

Contents

xi

Preface

In writing the second edition of this book I have made some important changes. Perhaps the major change can be found in Part IV, where I have recognized the importance of the control function within the retail firm. In that part I have developed a special chapter on financial control of the firm and collected the chapters on retailing research.

The book has also been improved by the separate treatment of retail selling in Chapter 14. Because retailing is always concerned with change, the second edition reflects many changes from the past few years. The section on consumerism is indicative of this treatment. Lastly, to aid the student to understand the problems of managing a retail firm I have included a number of case studies.

In writing a college text in the business field, the author must take a point of view. My point of view is clearly that of the management of the firm. To keep this consistent I have put the management direction in the form of a question to myself — namely, what should the higher-level management in the firm know about each aspect of its retail operation in order to make decisions? As I approached each subject, I asked myself this question, listed my answers, and proceeded to write the text.

I think it is also possible to generalize about my approach to the subject matter. Possibly one generalization that can be made is that a management approach of necessity should be broad in nature. This division, it would seem to me, can be found in the firm if one compares the role of the supervisor and executive manager. The supervisor is involved with the day-in, day-out task of getting the work done. Little time is allowed for long-range thinking and planning. The supervisor by the nature of his job must be concerned with the details of the job and must be prepared for any eventuality. Executive management, however, must be more concerned with the broader problems of the firm. Though many of the executives at this level are familiar with the details of many of the tasks performed by those under them (since many of these executives have risen through the ranks of lower management), by the nature of their job they must concern themselves with the larger strategy problems of the firm.

My years of studying and working in retailing have shown me that this distinction is particularly true in the retail firm. A good indication of this change from supervision to management can be seen in the growth of the discount firm at the present time. Many of these firms have grown rapidly without the slightest indication of a problem. Others have either gone into bankruptcy or have been forced to merge in order to get the needed management. The problem of most of these firms would seem to me to be that the original owners and entrepreneurs found it difficult to make the transition from owner-operator-direct-supervisory management to the job of leaving this task to others and assuming the major burdens of planning the strategy of the firm.

A second distinction between the management point of view in this text and the supervisory approach is that management must be preoccupied with change in its environment and adaption to change on the part of its organization. This adjustment is a full-time activity to management. It requires a complete understanding of all facets of the business, not, I should add, an understanding of the details of each operation, but its effect and over-all role in terms of the companies' adjustment to change. Thus, management should not be concerned with how to write out an order; or what the terms of this order such as ROG mean; management should be aware mainly of the over-all economies of placing an order with a manufacturer, the structure of the manufacturer's industry, and how consumers view the products they are purchasing. Thus, the major distinction is that management must have change in mind at all times, and must take an overview of the retail management.

The overview includes the third distinguishing mark of executive management in that the firm must make decisions. Most of these decisions again are broad based and are closely related to change and the firm's internal adjustment to change. Hence, a decision to add a skiing department would come under the eye of top executive management. To make this decision, management must understand the consumer trends in the economy (the movement toward affluence and leisure activities) and the relationship of skiing products to the rest of the firm's offerings.

In summary, therefore, this text takes a broad overview of the firm and one particularly related to the management activities of decision making and the role of change in the firm's environment.

A book is essentially the collection and integration of ideas, and in this sense I am obligated to all of the authors quoted throughout the text and hopeful that none have been slighted.

Special thanks go to David Rothchild, my graduate assistant, for his creative work on the cases found at the end of the text. Professor John Lloyd, Monroe Community College, Rochester, N.Y.; Professor John Sullivan, North Shore Community College, Beverly, Mass.; and Professor Sumner M. White, Massachusetts Bay Community College, Wellesley, Mass. deserve acknowledgement for their help

in reviewing the manuscript. In preparing this second edition, I would like to thank
Mrs. Thelma Weil for her typing and manuscript assistance.

Naturally, I take full responsibility for all errors of commission and omission.

David J. Rachman
Great Neck, New York

INTRODUCTION

I

Retailing management like any other business involves making choices. The purpose of this introductory section is to acquaint the reader with the elements of the retail organization that make up management's sphere of influence. In addition, this section points out the different problems faced by the retail firm, particularly in comparison with the manufacturer.

Basically, these first two introductory chapters are intended to acquaint readers with the point of view of the retailer, especially with that of the management of the firm.

Introduction: Essentials of Retailing

1

OBJECTIVES YOU SHOULD MEET

1. *Explain* how retail decision making fashions a store's personality.
2. *Outline* the major divisions of the controllable and uncontrollable factors of the retail management mix.
3. *Define* each of the five areas included in the mix.

Retailing is a vast field of business in the United States. Approximately one out of eight employed persons is engaged in some phase of retailing.

The retail firm varies considerably in size. It ranges from the "mama and papa" grocery store to the large chain organizations. Its management scope also varies. A typical firm may be concerned with the potential business on its block; the potential sales in the city; the larger metropolitan area; the region it serves; or in some cases the national markets it wishes to penetrate. This vast scope makes it difficult to present a complete and all-encompassing textbook on retailing. Therefore, compromises must be made and, in particular, the book must present a viewpoint in the study of this field.

There are numerous approaches to the study of retailing. These approaches, if we are to generalize, are covered in the following list:

Approaches to the Study of Retailing

1. A reliance on economic theory in understanding the management of the retail store
2. The functional study of retail firms
3. The institutional approach
4. The study of management decision making in the retail firms

Though early classical economists like John Stuart Mill and Alfred Marshall attempted to understand the actions of retailers, they were usually confused by retailers. Mill in particular was at a loss to explain the reasons for the different prices he found in European bookstores that were within the same narrow trading area. Even today, students are no doubt aware of the fact that prices of the same merchandise may vary considerably in stores not only in the same trading area but also on the same block. It is not unusual, for example, to find a well-known brand of cigarettes selling for five or ten cents less in a food supermarket than in a small tobacco shop. An economist like Mill, reasoning from a theoretical background of perfect competition, would probably surmise that this could not happen and hence he was confused by what he found in the European bookstores. His conclusion, therefore, was that the retailer acted in an uneconomic manner and probably set prices according to custom.

As economic theory became more sophisticated, economists began to recognize other factors than price and goods among the offerings of retailers. Nonprice factors such as service, location, and exclusivity of merchandise became subjects of attention.

The 1930's and the decades following brought forth numerous articles and a few textbooks purporting to interpret retail actions in terms of economic theory.[1] Though these interpretations have been useful in our understanding of retailing they are limited for a number of reasons. First, it is obvious that many retailers are guided by subjective evaluations rather than by the more exact calculations credited to them by economists. A number of the criticisms simply point out that the retailer is not in a position to know the costs of merchandise sold since all costs in retailing are joint and hence not measurable. By joint, it is meant that each of the thousands of items sold share in the rent, payroll, service expenses, and utilities. Since the products are numerous, it is too expensive, if not physically impossible, to determine these costs. Without this knowledge, the critics ask how actions of retailers can be said to be calculated exactly or described by economic theory.

Second, and more important from the reader's point of view, this understanding of economic theory tells us little about the day-to-day workings of management that can be useful in understanding the problems which beset those concerned with making a decision.

Nevertheless, some useful economic theories have developed and some of these should be made available to the reader.

ꭉ **Functional Study**

The functions of retailing have been the subject of study in many textbooks. This approach recognizes that retailers perform numerous functions and proceeds to examine them in detail. Most books of this nature list the following functions as the basis for their study:

---

[1]For example, Henry Smith, *Retail Distribution* (London: Oxford University Press, 1937); see also the articles in Stanley C. Hollander, *Explorations in Retailing,* M.S.U. Business Studies, Michigan State University, East Lansing, 1959.

1. Buying (including the securing and handling of merchandise)
2. Pricing
3. Promoting (advertising, display)
4. Offering servics
5. Selling (personal salesmanship)
6. Control (including inventory and expense controls)
7. Others (such as choosing locations, design store exterior, and interior layouts)

The functions enumerated above are studied in great detail. A typical textbook of this type will describe the following activities connected with merchandise already purchased:

1. The location of the receiving department
2. Equipment used for receiving
3. Procedures for recording received merchandise
4. Checking procedures
5. Procedures for ticketing merchandise
6. Distribution of merchandise
7. Management organization and responsibility for the performance of this function

A number of excellent textbooks have appeared, and a reader who wants to learn about the workings of a retail firm would be wise to avail himself of this type of text.

ꝫ) The Institutional Approach

The institutional approach examines in detail the many different types of retailers that make up the retailing complex. This approach usually concentrates on the functions and operations of department stores, supermarkets, specialty, and "mama and papa" stores. Another approach might be to study the institution from the point of view of size, such as chains or a single proprietorship.

This approach has been used in many books concerned with the total distribution field. For example, one marketing textbook describes retailers on the basis of the following criteria:

1. Size (small and large stores)
2. Location (urban-rural and regional distribution)
3. Ownership (chain stores, independents, franchises)
4. Method of operations (full-service stores and non-stores — i.e., vending machines)
5. Extent of product lines handled[2]

Though useful, this approach is mainly descriptive. To give it meaning in a *marketing text,* it should be combined with the manufacturer's view of the firm showing the relationship of the retailer to the total distribution system.

---

[2]William J. Stanton, *Fundamentals of Marketing* (New York: McGraw-Hill Book Company, 1971), Chapter 12.

In the past decade many marketing texts have appeared that demonstrate the role of the marketing manager as a decision maker in the manufacturing organization. Admittedly, the acceptance of the "marketing concept," where all major product decisions are made centrally, has spurred this interest in the executive as a decision maker. Prior to the development of this concept, however, marketing decisions were being made despite the fact that academic publications did not delineate this function as a separate area of treatment.

Retailing management too involves decision making, and it is the purpose of this book to explore this concept. To do this one must examine the role of the retail decision maker, and determine the areas within which he can make decisions and the areas that are beyond his scope.

Change and Decision Making

Though great stress will be placed throughout this text on the functions performed by management and particularly those that relate to making the right decision, one should also consider the management function as related to change.

In the abstract sense, the retailer's effort is guided by his environment. Though the environment of the firm will be discussed in later chapters, it is worth noting here that the changing consumer and competition are the prime factors in this regard. In a sense the retailer has three choices in adjusting to his environment. The first and least palatable is that he can simply refuse to adjust to this environment and suffer the consequences; he will then end up either supporting a profitless retail enterprise or closing his doors. In this connection one might suggest that a large number of small enterprises that manage to pay the owner only a meager salary fall into this grouping.

His second choice would seem to be the most logical — adjust to the environment. This is the subject matter of most of this text, i.e., the methods and tools that he can use to make this oftentimes difficult adjustment.

His third choice has social overtones. That is, the retailer may attempt to effect changes in the environment in many different ways. Unlawful pricing arrangements, mergers, false advertising, anti-chain legislation, fair trade pricing, and anti-union activities are all attempts to control the firm's environment and thus in a sense forestall change. The role of government seems to play a prominent part in countervailing retail firms and industries that elect this path.

The history of retailing is replete with firms that have been faced with change. Food retailing has gone through a whole evolution. Following World War I, the bulk of the food business was being done by the independent grocery store. Even the chain food stores at that time and through the 1920's were patterned after the small grocer. However, in the early 1930's, the spacious, self-service supermarket came into being. The consumer response was dramatic. Between 1934 and 1937 the Great Atlantic and Pacific Tea Company closed 933 of its neighborhood units and replaced them with 204 supermarkets. Similarly, Kroger dropped 355 stores and added 33 supermarkets.[3]

Sales at A & P reached the $1 billion mark for the first time by 1930 and increased to over $5 billion by 1965.[4] Surely this performance must be considered outstanding. On the other hand, in recent years A & P has had more than its share of problems. For example, it has experienced a serious profit decline, has lost a sizable share of the food market, suffered a decline in sales between 1970 and 1971, and has been forced to change its top-level management.

The reasons for its problems are many. One major indictment was the firm's reluctance to offer customers trading stamps in spite of obvious consumer interest. After much resistance, A & P finally offered stamps, but only in a limited number of markets. Even the stamp policy suffered from being too late, as stamps became unfashionable in the new consumer movement. Possibly another failure was A & P's reluctance to merge with smaller chains in order to expand in newly developing population centers. The merger movement as a means of expansion has become a conspicuous policy of most major food chains. This failure reduced A & P's size advantages over its competitors. Perhaps the most serious error was a continuation by A & P of its depression-born policy of emphasizing low prices. Though this policy was effective during that period because of the economic conditions, its continuance through the postwar period has had limitations.[5]

At the present time A & P is still trying to solve its problems. In fact it is repeating history in the sense that it is presently converting its stores from the supermarkets of the thirties to low-priced outlets. These outlets, presently dubbed the WEO (Where Economy Originates) Stores, involve converting all stores in the chain, now numbering 4,167 stores.[6] Though it is not exactly clear at this point what services the WEO stores will offer the consumer as they are presently constituted, it is clear that the present range of services and frills will be eliminated. In exchange for the loss of services the customer is offered a price substantially below that of the standard supermarkets and the former A & P stores. Some reports have placed the new A & P markup at approximately 15 per cent, as measured against a former markup exceeding 20 per cent.

The impact of A & P's move was immediately felt by all competitors, and at least one considered it to be an act of desperation on the part of A & P's management.[7]

The list of firms that have had to adjust is endless. Some, however, have not been forced to make such drastic changes as A & P. The J. C. Penney Company is one firm that has adjusted to change. In this case, it was particularly difficult simply because many of the organizational policies were deeply imbedded in the philosophy of the firm — a firm, incidentally, that grew over the years from a small store to a $4 billion corporation specializing in the sale of apparel.

---

[3]Rom J. Markin, "The Supermarket," *Economic and Business Studies Bulletin*, No. 36, Washington State University, Pullman, Washington (January, 1963), p. 15.

[4]Tom Mahoney and Leonard Sloane, *The Great Merchants* (New York: Harper & Row, 1966), pp. 172-177.

[5]David Rachman and Linda Kemp, "Are Retail Profits Declining?" *Journal of Retailing*, Vol. 40, No. 3 (Fall, 1964), pp. 22 and 24.

[6]*The New York Times*, June 21, 1972, p. 59.

[7]*Supermarket News*, June 19, 1972, p. 1. Indications are now growing that the firm has abandoned its low price leadership. *Barron's*, February 11, 1974, p. 3.

As J. C. Penney emerged from the postwar period, the firm chose to ignore some of the important trends in the consumer market. Though the U. S. market experienced a huge increase in consumer credit during the period, J. C. Penney remained a cash store until as late as 1958. It was difficult for Penney's to embark on credit since the founder of the firm was opposed to credit buying on a moralistic ground.[8] However, in recent years the implementation of credit plans has spurred the firm's development and has led to other changes within the organization. For instance, Penney's, almost simultaneously with the introduction of credit, expanded the lines of merchandise to include durable goods, particularly appliances. The introduction of a mail order catalog (similar to Sears, Roebuck's) was a major change in another direction.

Penney's and A & P are only two companies out of thousands. Though some are faced with changes of a less severe nature, it is nonetheless true that management is continually confronted by these challenges. It is management's adaptation to the environment that determines the firm's ability to make profits and survive.

Retail Decision Making

To develop a proper perspective on management problems and the areas of decision making, we have divided our text into five major areas as illustrated in Figure 1-1. These divisions consist of the *controllable* and the *uncontrollable* aspects of the retailing environment. The controllable aspects of this environment are the:

1. Goods and services mix
2. Communication mix
3. Physical distribution mix

The uncontrollable are the:

4. Consumer
5. Restraints, such as competition, economic conditions, and legal and social pressures.

In a sense, the controllable aspects of the mix represent the retailer's effort to meet the needs of the consumer. This effort consists of the tools of retail management, namely, the products and services sold, and the ability of the firm to communicate with the customer and to control the amount and location of its offerings. The effort is hindered by the environment, which includes legal restraints and pressures of competition. The judgment as to the effect of this effort rests with the consumer, who expresses his interest by patronizing the store.

The Controllable Mix   The controllable mix, as we noted above, represents management's effort to meet the needs of the consumer. We examine this area of his mix because the retailer is in a position to manipulate the mix ingredients in any manner he sees fit. For example, he can rely heavily on newspaper advertising and less on services, and can

---

[8] For J. C. Penney's moralistic approach to business, see J. C. Penney, *View from the Ninth Decade* (New York: Thomas Nelson & Sons, 1960).

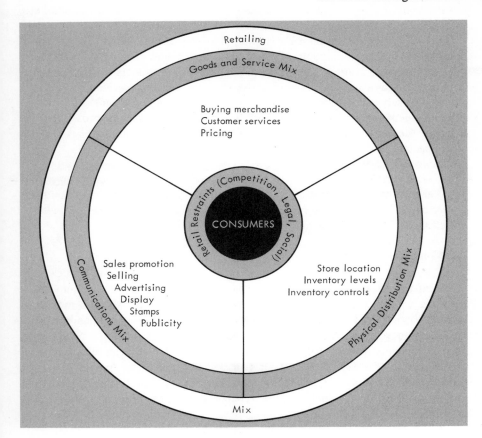

Adapted from William Lazar and Eugene J. Kelley, *Journal of Retailing,* Vol. 37, No. 1 (Spring, 1961), p. 38.

carry a limited assortment of merchandise. Or he can rely on a very limited advertising campaign, and offer the consumer a large variety of services and a wide assortment of merchandise that appeals, for instance, to income groups earning above $6,000 a year. All of these adjustments can be made within certain restrictions that will be discussed later. The point we are making here is that retail firms can control this aspect of their mix and have the authority to implement each choice.

A) The Goods and Services Mix

The consumer's most obvious judgment of a store is usually made on the basis of the types of products and services offered. Some stores, for example, carry only appliances. Others carry furniture or sporting goods as well. Still others carry, in addition to appliances, apparel, housewares, drugs, and photographic supplies. The latter assortment is found typically in the present-day apparel discount firm. The choice of the types of goods to be carried is endless. At some point, however, management makes a choice, and any study of this mix must take into consideration the ingredients that go into making a decision of this nature.

In some cases the consumer's view of the store is colored by the variety of services a firm offers the public. Customers of major department stores have been led to expect a variety of services. Conversely, customers of the postwar phenomenon known as the discount house are accustomed to receiving much less in the way of services. This dichotomy is so instilled in the consumer's mind that he expects a department store to state specifically in its newspaper advertisement that a service such as delivery is not being offered, whereas with a discount house this is not expected.

The firm's commitment to a policy of selling certain types of goods is governed by a whole set of relationships. In essence, however, the firm must be convinced that there exists a local market for most of its offerings. On the other hand, the choice of services is governed not only by the demands of the customers but also by the cost attached to each service.

B) The Communication Mix

All of the efforts at this stage are for naught if the firm cannot communicate its offerings to the consumer. The communication mix includes all sales promotion efforts on behalf of the firm. It includes, in particular, annual expenditures for newspaper advertising. Since most of a firm's promotional budget is expended in this way, a great deal of analysis goes into this effort. Other means of reaching the public include television, radio, direct mail advertising, display, free publicity, and trading stamps. Since so much effort is concentrated on this mix, a detailed evaluation is made not only of the type of expenditure but also of the most profitable level of expenditure.

C) The Physical Distribution Mix

Once the firm has determined the nature of its offerings to the consumer it must make two major determinations. One is the extent of the assortments to be offered, and the other is the exact location of the outlets.

The total amount of goods to be offered the consumer is governed by the amount of money allocated to this endeavor. In addition, the inventory control methods used by the firm ultimately affect the level of the inventory and the assortment of merchandise. All of these controls are governed by the firm's interpretation of the costs, both measurable and unmeasurable, of carrying a level of inventory.

The choice of location and merchandise offered are of course major aspects of the firm's decision-making process. The choice of a location though a direct function of the numerous economic statistics available to the retail firm, is nonetheless intimately related to its evaluation of the type of customer it is trying to reach and the location of this market. The firm's choice of statistics and the emphasis of each is a reflection of the management's interpretation of this market. Thus, management in its evaluation of the total physical distribution mix is primarily concerned both with the size of the inventory and with its location or distribution in the proper outlets.

Store Personality

The results of changing the mix of the store through the efforts of management can be seen in the store personality that is projected to the public. The store personality in a sense is the image the firm projects to the public. If one lives in a community for several months, he soon becomes aware that certain stores sell quality merchandise or the latest fashion merchandise. Some stores sell reasonably priced merchandise that represents good value. Other stores may project an image to the public of terrific values in the sense that prices are low. The latter represents the hope for the WEO stores started by A & P.

There exist various gradations of these personalities in each area. Those who live in Detroit consider that the huge J. L. Hudson store has almost anything in merchandise one could ever need. This firm is comparable to R. H. Macy in New York, Marshall Field in Chicago, Rich's in Atlanta, or the Higbee Company in Cleveland. These stores project a feeling of bigness, in that the shopper is assured that almost any department-store item can be found under their roofs.

Other stores may project a fashion image. That is, if a shopper were to need a fashionable apparel item she would be sure to shop in the fashion-personality store. In New York City one would certainly associate this image with Lord and Taylor's, Bergdorf Goodman, Saks Fifth Avenue, or any number of specialty shops located in the Fifth Avenue area. In Dallas, Neiman Marcus certainly represents such an outlet.

On the other hand, if one were buying film or an appliance one might look for the store with the price personality, most likely a local discount house. In Chicago one might travel to Polk's; in Boston, Lechmere Sales; in New York and several other cities, E. J. Korvette.

Even among smaller stores similar personalities can develop. One, for instance, may have a favorite ice cream parlor or candy store. One may prefer a small menswear store or bookstore. One may have a favorite florist or liquor store. It is well to remember that most of these stores have developed a personality in a deliberate fashion. That is, management has developed a mix in such a way that the personality of the store has been clearly communicated to the local market.

All of the above-mentioned efforts have as their goal the satisfying of consumer wants. It is the firm's expectation that the successful completion of this endeavor will ultimately result in profits, the implication being that the firm has correctly evaluated not only the needs of the consumer but the other restraints that are beyond the firm's control.

In our analysis the consumer is classified as an uncontrollable aspect, in that the retail firm can do little to make the consumer conform to its wishes and desires. In its everyday operations an attempt is made by the firm to meet the needs of the consumer by adjusting the mix in the most profitable way.

The Uncontrollable Environment

The Changing Environment

The consumer is a major unknown simply because he is constantly undergoing change. The change in the consumer is best understood if one recognizes the continuing movement in the direction of population growth and affluence. Perhaps no data support the view of growing affluence more than the fact that in 1970 seven million cars were junked in the U. S. About 70,000 of these cars were abandoned in the streets of New York City alone.[9]

The age of affluence has had a staggering impact on retailing. Its effect will be discussed in greater detail in several chapters. However it can be best summarized by examining three major factors:

1. The population characteristics of the country
2. The total amount of income
3. The distribution of income among persons[10]

Population Growth

The U.S. population growth up to 1970 has been explosive. Perhaps the most dramatic statistic can be seen in the fact that from 1915 to 1950, a span of 35 years, the population increased by approximately 50 million persons. That is, it went from 100 million to 150 million.

From 1950 to 1970, a span of only 20 years, the population increased by another 50 million persons!

There is substantial evidence that the pattern of upward growth may be reversing itself. For instance, a recent comparison of births during 1972 clearly indicates that the number of births may have declined by as much as 10 per cent over the previous years. Should this trend continue, the U.S. could be heading for a zero growth rate in a relatively short period of time, which would have tremendous implications for all segments of society.

In any case the change in the U.S. population has been characterized not only by growth but also by movement. Its movement has been westward nationally and away from rural areas into the city.

Income of the Population

The increase of population does not necessarily mean that a country will prosper. Much evidence can be brought to our attention supporting this view, India being an outstanding example. On the positive side is the tendency for the population to move from the rural areas to the city, positive in that this movement indicates a population moving from lower-paying jobs (rural) to higher-paying city work.

The over-all growth of income in the U.S. has been dramatic. Gross National Product (the total national output of goods and services valued at market prices)

[9]*The Atlantic Monthly,* August, 1972, p. 89. Only Canada, France, Britain, Japan, and Germany have more than seven million cars on the road.

[10]Joseph W. McGuire, *Business and Society* (New York: McGraw-Hill Book Company, 1971), p. 252.

has increased from $100 billion in 1940 to $976 billion in 1970. This more than ninefold growth has been accompanied by a similar increase in family income. Median family income in 1947 was $3,031. By 1971 it exceeded $10,000.

All statistics of this sort, whether they be of consumption or income, have been moving in a similar direction for many years. In all cases they show a growing population accompanied by an ever-increasing income.

Income Sharing

Another important consideration in evaluating the growth of affluence in a society is the sharing of this affluence by all income groups.

Here again one finds a growing sharing among all income groups. For instance, in 1947 over 27 per cent of all families had annual income of under $2,000. By 1970 this group had dwindled to under 4 per cent. Similarly, in 1947 only 2.7 per cent of all families had income of over $10,000. By 1970 almost half of all families had income exceeding this amount.

Although this growth does not mean that poverty has been wiped out in our country, it does mean that much of our society is sharing in the growing affluence.

Though the impact of such growth will be discussed in greater detail in Chapter 5, it would seem obvious that such pronounced changes have had and will continue to have a strong impact on the retailer. By its very nature the age of affluence will constantly cause the retailer to adjust his effort and mix to this changing market.

Consumer Segmentation

Though the retailer is concerned with the economic changes within the economy and particularly with the changes that affect the consumer, it is apparent that not all statistics are of vital interest. This is so because the retailer's interest is in a local rather than a national market, and, in particular, in a segment of this market. It is a rare store that appeals to all consumers. Most, either by deliberate choice or by location, cater to a segment of the total market. Though segments are not mutually exclusive they do exist, and the retailer's ability to delineate each market and cater particularly to its needs represents a major factor in the firm's choice of a mix. It is apparent that the main task of the retailer is to adjust his mix to the needs of the consumer, the major unknown in his retailing formula.

Other Uncontrollable Aspects

Even if the firm is closely attuned to the needs of the customer, there are other restraints or uncontrollable aspects that affect the firm's ability to meet this challenge. We have indicated four other factors, namely, economic conditions, legislation, competition, and social pressures.

It is obvious that changing economic conditions — a sudden shift in the business picture — can greatly affect a particular segment of the retail market. It can alter consumers' earnings or their outlook for the future. In particular, this may have an important bearing on the sales of durable goods at the retail level.

Legislation and court rulings can have a stultifying effect on the retailer's actions. The retailer is affected not only by national legislation but by many municipal and city ordinances. Court rulings usually constitute an important restraint on retail competition. For example, a recent court case sharply curtailed the power of shoe manufacturers to purchase retail outlets and thereby integrate manufacturing and retail distribution.[11]

Social pressures also play a role, particularly in small towns. These pressures may restrict the retailer's tendency to compete based on local "gentlemen's agreements."

The retailer, regardless of his environment, must also consider both the number and the size of his competitors in making adjustments to his environment. For example, a firm may believe that it can still retain its customers without offering delivery services. If within its competitive environs, however, most of his competitors decide to offer this service to customers, the firm may be forced to add delivery services to its offerings.

In effect, the uncontrollable aspects of the retailer's environment act as a major restraining force. In a sense this environment, whether established by law, social pressures, or the whims of the consumer, represents a framework within which the retailer must conduct his business.

Manufacturer and Retailer Contrasted

Throughout this text, at significant points, the manufacturer's and retailer's views are presented and contrasted. It is intended in these sections to demonstrate that even though both marketing institutions have as their goal the making of profits, their opinions as to how this is to be accomplished may at some juncture differ sharply. It is important to understand these differing views since the two institutions rely on each other to accomplish their ends.

SUMMARY

All retail stores develop personalities. The personality of the store is usually not developed by accident; it is fashioned deliberately by the management of the retail enterprise. It is the purpose of this text to study and understand the *retail decision making* that fashions the firm's personality.

Retail decision making includes the controllable factors the retailer deals with, namely, the goods and services, communication, and physical-distribution mixes. These are controllable by management. The results of changing the mix and the management effort can be seen in the store personality projected to the public. Management is also faced with an uncontrollable environment and must adjust its effort to this fact. The uncontrollable environment includes the consumer, competition, economic conditions, and legal and social pressures. Understanding

---

[11] Brown Shoe Company *v.* United States. 30 LW 4561 (S. C., June 25, 1962). See also D. D. Martin, "The Brown Shoe and The New Antimerger Policy," *American Economic Review,* June, 1963, p. 522.

the consumer is a major challenge to retail management, particularly in view of the steady growth of affluence responsible for many changes in consumer behavior.

QUESTIONS

1. What is meant by the retailer's environment? What is its significance?
2. Some authorities refer to competition as the semi-controllable part of the retailer's environment. Explain.
3. To what extent can the operator of a high-priced, prestige apparel store ignore his environment?
4. Decision making is choosing among alternatives. What alternatives does the retailer have in communicating with his customers (see Figure 1-1) in the following types of stores:
a. neighborhood grocery store
b. national shoe chain store
c. gasoline station
5. It is often said that a retailer sells not only goods but many services. Does he actually sell services or offer services? Explain.
6. Describe the personalities of three large stores in your community. From what part of the total mix (goods and service, communication, and physical distribution) do they derive most of their personalities?
7. Discuss the various approaches to the study of retailing.
8. One student claims that all food supermarkets are alike. Another claims they are not. Do you agree or disagree? If you disagree, give examples of differences that exist between two supermarkets in your area. What steps taken by management made the firms different?
9. Supermarkets do not offer services. True or False. Defend your position.
10. List the customer services offered by a department store.
11. List the customer services offered by the corner (small) grocery store.
12. What limitations does legislation place on the retailer?
13. How does the retailer's interest in local markets affect his interest in economic statistics related to the consumer?
14. In what way has the affluence of our society affected the retailer?
15. How does one determine whether or not a society is affluent?

Decision Making
in Retailing

2

OBJECTIVES YOU SHOULD MEET

1. *List* the main functions performed by retail management.
2. *Describe* each function.
3. *Discuss* the importance of setting a firm's objectives.
4. *Distinguish* between strategy and tactics.

Harold Barger in his study of productivity in the field of distribution[1] noted that manufacturing has produced gains during this century far above those found in the retailing field. In studying management, marketing, and economics, it is easy to understand why productivity gains in retailing have not kept up with those in other fields. In particular, one can point to the lack of automation, the lack of scientific engineering talent, the widespread need for personnel, and the reliance on consumers to get the retailing machinery going.

On the other hand, many authorities in this field have noted that retailing has not always lagged in this manner. In fact, there are many management and marketing concepts that have actually been initiated by retail management. Take, for example, two important aspects of the manufacturing field — specialization of work functions and plant layout. The first was pioneered not by Frederick Taylor but by the early department stores, which were quick to see that dividing a large

---

[1] *Distribution's Place in the American Economy Since 1869* (Princeton: Princeton University Press, 1956).

enterprise into departments and concentrating the buying and selling functions into specialized patterns meant a more efficient and profitable way of doing business. In addition, the major large stores were among the first to recognize the importance of merchandise layout. In particular, the self-service, one-story supermarket of the early 1930's was a major innovation in this respect.

Retailing concepts were also ahead of those in other fields during this same period. Today, marketing management seems to be undergoing a major upheaval because of what has been described as the "customer-oriented" approach to problems. From this concept it follows that a business must be conducted on the basis of what the consumer needs and wants rather than what management thinks is best for the consumer. A firm producing a line of products or developing a new product must start with its research function, which will tell the firm what the consumer wants. This type of information will be passed on to the production and promotion departments where it will be turned into a customer-oriented product and distribution program.

This concept, however, is not new to the retailer. Early studies have shown that most managements considered their stores to be purchasing agents for the consumer. In other words, the retailer believed that he had the consumer view of what was needed and wanted, and he would go to any length to buy the products the consumer wanted.

However, a great deal of time has passed since these early concepts were in vogue, and critics of retailing now note a lag in developing new concepts and particularly in increasing productivity. Possibly one of the major drawbacks to a faster rate of development is the retailer's adherence to the belief that to be successful in retailing one must have a flair for merchandise and that retailing is more of an art than a science. To some extent this may be true even today. However, there is another side of the retailing picture that cannot be ignored. Evidence exists that some firms are carefully thinking out their decisions and that some are planning ahead five or ten years.

A glance at Table 18-2 in Chapter 18, listing the sales, profits, and net worth of major retailing firms in the United States, should convince the student that there are well-run retailing organizations and others that leave much to be desired. It is interesting to observe that many of the low-profit producers were not always this way. Many of these firms as recently as ten or fifteen years ago were among the top money-makers in the United States. However, with many, time has taken its toll, and if this list were printed ten years from now some would probably not even be on it.

If we were to investigate the firms on this list that have had deteriorating earnings, we would no doubt find that they have made countless strategic errors, and have done little in the way of what may be called advanced planning and less of what may be called research. We would probably find too that during the postwar era many of the firms with poor earnings were caught unaware by the influx of discount houses, the strong population movement to the suburbs, and the trend in retailing toward "scrambled" merchandising. It is also characteristic of these firms that few personnel within the organization were assigned to the task of planning ahead and relatively few were completely aware of the implications of all of their postwar reactions to competition.

Retail Management   In the manufacturing and the retailing field decision making involves risks. Nevertheless decisions are made, and both successes and failures have been recorded in the business literature. In manufacturing, however, a firm may have access to excellent data, if we are to judge by retailing standards. Take, for example, a decision by a typical soap company. Product A, a detergent bar soap, is considered to be an excellent addition to the company's line of products. Cost accountants immediately determine that if the firm can sell 5,000 bars a month (at 25 cents a unit) the firm can show an excellent profit. In order to determine the acceptability of the product, the firm carefully tests the market for six months by offering samples to potential users. After the preliminary research, the product is distributed and promoted in eight major metropolitan areas of the country. The choice must be made in a deliberate way. The cities may be judged by their income characteristics or other variables that make them typical markets for the firm's other products. During this same test period the price is reduced in some areas and increased in others. It is finally determined that the product can be marketed profitably at the 25-cent price. Thus, the firm goes into a full-scale national marketing program.

At some stage the firm has determined the probability of success of the item. This probability may be stated in crude or in mathematical terms. If crude, it may be simply the "feeling" or judgment of the marketing manager that the product will sell. Or it may be concluded that, allowing for error, the product will have a 70 per cent chance of success. Hence the decision to produce and market the product.

Probability estimates based on such careful research are not available in most retail firms. In a later section we will examine the major differences between the manufacturer and the retailer that affect decision making; suffice it to say at this stage that the many products the retailer offers the consumer preclude the possibility of developing such probabilities.

Yet decisions are made in retailing, and at this stage of our study we shall examine the functions of retail management and its relationship to retail decision making.

The Functions of Retail Management

One should not get the impression that the functions of retail management are different from those of any other organization. Management performs the same functions whether for a manufacturing firm, utility, service organization, or military force.

The following functions are usually attributed to management:

1. Determining the objectives of the firm
2. Planning, including strategy and tactics (decision making)
3. Organizing and coordinating the firm's activities
4. Staffing and assembling other resources
5. Operating and directing the organization
6. Controlling, through analyzing and evaluating performance based on measurements

Most firms have as their major objective the making of money. The word "most" is used deliberately because there are numerous small firms (particularly retail firms) where the owner finds his business to be a way of life rather than a profit-making enterprise. He may think that owning a store gives him a certain freedom and individuality not offered by any job that may be available to him. Actually it may be more profitable for him to sell his business and work for someone else. It may also be true that if he charged his business for his services or in some cases the services of his wife he would be losing money. Nevertheless, there are many small business enterprises that exist in this manner.

The majority of firms, however, have set objectives, one of which is, obviously, to make money. To say this, however, is not enough. A firm's objectives must be more specific, and they should be capable of measurement. They must, of course, be realistic and, in particular, must be well within the firm's capabilities in terms of its environment and the internal controllable factors that make up its total mix. For example, it is unrealistic for General Motors to have as its goal for the next five years an increase in its share of the market from approximately 50 per cent of the automobile business to 95 per cent. Though General Motors may have the capability of achieving this goal, its achievement would probably result in the application of antitrust legislation. Therefore, a firm must develop realistic goals that are well within its capabilities in terms not only of its internal mix but of the external factors that are outside of its control.

Consider the following statement concerning the objectives of the Mark Cross Company, a Fifth Avenue leather goods specialty store catering to high-income groups.

**I. Objectives of the Mark Cross Company
Unpublished paper by Phyllis G. Winkler,
former treasurer of the firm, 1964**

A. Market which we will serve
1. To conduct a leather goods specialty store.
2. To concentrate our efforts towards the customer in the upper-middle or higher income group.
3. To serve the customer who recognizes and is willing to pay for superior quality.
4. To operate a main store at 55th Street and 5th Avenue, a mail order business and such additional branches as deemed advisable by the Board of Directors (outlined in F Objective).

B. Merchandise
1. To concentrate and emphasize and guard zealously the leathergoods classifications which, throughout the competition of more than a hundred years have earned for Mark Cross a distinguished and unique place in the retail world.
2. To provide the highest standards of quality, both in merchandise and service.
3. To be active in the creation or selection of new distinctive styles, functional designs and new items. This will be in line with our history and background as the store which discovered the "wrist watch" and the "thermos bottle" in America.
4. To provide the best in design, material and workmanship and function at the best possible price (this price will be relatively high).

C. *Service*
1. To provide our clientele with the finest service available in any retail establishment. These facilities will also include the maintenance of the merchandise we sell, for as long as it is in existence.

D. *Personnel*
1. To employ in our organization, from "maintenance" to our "Board of Directors" those people who are qualified to carry on the traditions of our company.

E. *Management*
1. To provide management whose main goal is perpetuation of our company and its tradition in a competitive society.
2. To provide management whose goal is an adequate return on the capital invested by our shareholders.

F. *Growth*
1. To constantly seek, investigate and develop additional outlets or branches for the distribution of our merchandise. Growth objectives can be developed only if they are consistent with the quality standard objectives of our business.

G. *Sales Promotion and Advertising*
1. To demonstrate to the public that not only is Mark Cross the finest leather goods store in the world, but that Mark Cross has interesting and exciting items which are not necessarily expensive.
2. To develop Fifth Avenue traffic who may become acquainted with the store.
3. To generate an attitude among our salespeople and staff of excitement, interest and enthusiasm.
4. To re-emphasize the role of Mark Cross as an innovator.
5. To make it clear that in our promotion of novelty items we are not in conflict with our basic philosophy of quality.

The reader will note that the objectives in this statement are set forth in specific terms for those who are entrusted with servicing the customer, selecting the merchandise, and advertising. Thus we see that the overall objectives serve as a guide to the organization, and all other plans must be within the framework of the firm's major objectives.

Once firm goals have been established, management must then engage in planning, which includes the development of strategy and tactics.

Planning the Strategy and Tactics

Planning is decision making since it involves making choices among alternatives. Planning in the retail firm is done not only at the top level but within the separate divisions of the store. For example, though management may determine the size of the promotional budget, each individual buyer may participate in the decision as to the allocation of his own expenditures. Again, though management has established a pricing and marketing objective, it may depend on lower-level management to actually set most of the prices.

As noted above, planning involves decision making. And in the retail store this involves making decisions about the mix that management will present to the public and its relationship to the uncontrollable factors in the external environment. The mix, as noted in Chapter 1, includes the selection of the proper combination of goods and services, communication with the customer, and the proper physical distribution mix. It is the specific purpose of this book to examine the performance, measurement, and development of this function. How well management performs this function is usually the difference between a successful and an unsuccessful store. This raises the question, why are some firms better at decision making than others? Or, to put it more directly, why are some firms better at planning than others?

There are many good reasons. However, to evaluate this better, we should know what is necessary in making a planning decision. One has to have (1) pertinent data; (2) an ability to estimate probabilities.

Pertinent data should not be taken too literally. The firm need not have exact data, but it does need some estimate of the state of the real world. For example, a firm planning a branch store in a section of a metropolitan area must have knowledge concerning the number of customers in the area surrounding the store who will be likely to shop there. It is not enough to know that 10,000 families will be located near the proposed branch. Though this is one statistic, it is more useful to know the number of families with X dollars of income. It may turn out, for example, that only 10 per cent of these families qualify as customers. Unfortunately management does not always have available data and in some cases must rely on incomplete data. Nevertheless, some data are usually better than none.

The second step in making a decision is to have the ability to estimate probabilities. Again, probability estimates rarely approach 100 per cent. However, it is certainly useful for management to know that in six out of ten cases a certain action will prove profitable. Though estimating probabilities takes place at all levels of decisions, it has become increasingly useful and even quantifiable in the development of inventory controls. If, for example, a retailer could know that in placing an order for eight items of a certain unit of merchandise, the chances were that in 95 per cent of the cases the item would arrive on time and the firm would not run out of stock, he would certainly be impressed. This is precisely the direction in which management is going. Later on in this text we will discuss some of the methods for estimating and quantifying these techniques. On the other hand, management is not always in a position to quantify its probabilities. But since planning is merely choosing between alternatives, management must always be in a position to make this choice.

Where exact data is not available, management relies on intuition or past experience to serve as a guide in choosing among alternatives. In some cases this experience may be more reliable even than quantifiable information. The point should be understood, however, that even though management may not have the exact data necessary to make the perfect decision, subjective decisions require that management weigh some probabilities in choosing alternatives.

Strategy and tactics. Strategy is planning. However, in its military implications it is something more than simple planning; it is planning with the "enemy" in mind. In the retailer's case the enemy is plainly his competition.

Tactics refer to the means of attaining a strategic advantage. As an example, a firm may consider it good strategy to emphasize the availability of low-priced clothing to families in the lower-income groups. This strategy may be carried out by using the tactic of direct mail promotion to people residing in a low-income area of the city. To perfect the proper strategy and tactics the firm must have the above-mentioned data and be able to estimate probabilities.

However, all decisions as to the proper strategy must be tempered with a full knowledge of the firm's capabilities. For example, it may be excellent tactics for a firm to plan a major direct mail advertising program to reach income groups that are not ordinarily aware of the offerings of its store. In reality, however, the firm may not have the financial resources or the manpower to conduct such a campaign.

Thus, management is faced with many alternatives and must be aware of the failings of each, the resources of the firm, and the external factors that bear on this problem.

3) Organizing and Coordinating the Firm's Activities

The organizational structure of a firm is the means by which management attains its objectives. Because of the diverse types of enterprises in retailing, therefore, and the diverse goals, the organizational structure varies.

In discussing organizational structure it is implied that somewhere along the line authority to make decisions and perform tasks is delegated. The numerous one-man retailing businesses are, of course, not organized according to this concept: all decision making is retained by one man and therefore the structure of the firm is not a problem.

The larger firm, however, is faced with the problem of organizing and coordinating all its activities. Each executive is delegated certain tasks and powers, and he must coordinate these within the scope management has delegated to him. In addition, all of these tasks must be performed with the firm's goals in mind. It is of primary importance, therefore, that management clearly state the firm's objectives in order to attain maximum organizational efficiency. Specifically, each store manager should be well aware of the firm's objectives in terms of servicing the customer, and of the types of goods to be sold as well as their quality. In addition, the manager should be well aware of the type of consumer the firm plans to reach.

4) Staffing and Assembling Other Resources

Though this book will devote only a small section to personnel and its effect on the retail firm, it is nonetheless a major task of management to staff the firm properly to accomplish its objectives. This implies proper training and development of personnel to step into the numerous management openings that develop over the years. It is particularly important in retailing since a great deal of the firm's money is invested in people and comparatively little in capital equipment.

5) Operating and Directing

Though an executive may have the authority to order people to complete their work, the performance of this function is much more complex than it seems. Good management does not rely on authority to accomplish its objectives but gets people to accomplish their tasks voluntarily and with a minimum of prodding. This is what is meant when it is said that management is leadership.

To attain this enviable position management must instill an appreciation of the firm's goals and traditions. "Managers-to-be" must be taught all there is to know about the organizational relationships within the firm. They must develop a keen understanding of the people they are dealing with and the best way to motivate their subordinates. They must learn, sometimes by experience, what management looks for from the firm's employees.

Control

Though control is listed as the final function of management, it is a continuous and important function. In effect, control tells the retailer whether or not he is achieving his goals and if not why not. In addition, proper controls and measurements tell management where it is failing and indicate the corrective measures that can be taken. In order to measure its achievements management of the retail firm relies on certain measurements and guides. Outstanding among these are budgets, profitability measurements, and consumer surveys which assess the firm's ability to serve the needs of the consumer.

The control function is discussed in the last three chapters, in which the importance of financial controls and research to management is stressed.

The Retailer and Manufacturer

The student of retailing should be aware that the retailer or retailing does not exist independently. It is part of a huge system of interrelationships known as the distribution system. The retailer by definition is the last stage in distribution and in most cases sells directly to the ultimate consumer, who buys the product or products for his own use. Two amendments should be made to this statement. First, some retailers such as department stores do sell products to other institutions or in some cases to manufacturers. This task is usually entrusted to a special department that does not deal with the consuming public. In addition there are many wholesale organizations that sell, as part of their business policy, to the consuming public as well as to other intermediaries. One thinks of plumbing supply houses that sell to plumbers and the consuming public from the same outlet. A second amendment to the above definition is that the retailer is not the only channel member that sells directly to the consuming public. There exist in the distribution system a number of manufacturers that sell directly to the ultimate consumer. This type of organization is called a "direct selling" firm. The manufacturers and distributors of Avon cosmetic products and the equally well-known Fuller Brush Company are examples of firms that have managed to develop this means of reaching the public successfully. Yet the number of firms that have managed to successfully avoid the retailer and sell directly to the ultimate consumer are few. Most of the goods that reach the ultimate consumer are channeled through the retail store.

In addition to the retailer the other major channel members are the wholesaler or middleman and the manufacturer. The wholesaler and his functions will be discussed in a later chapter. However, the role of the manufacturer and his relationship to the retailer will be discussed throughout this book. And any understanding of the distribution system must surely encompass the relationship between retailers and manufacturers.

Though a study of the retailer and retailing is part of many college curriculums, the fact remains that retailers do not exist by themselves. Conversely, though marketing courses are concerned principally with the workings of manufacturers (most of whom sell to retailers or middlemen servicing retailers), from the development of the product to the intensive training needed to develop an adequate sales force, a marketer who has little understanding of the role of the retailer is certainly doomed to failure. This assertion is prompted by the knowledge that both the manufacturer and the retailer are part of a marketing or distribution system. Thus, marketing is concerned with the movement of goods and services from the manufacturer to the ultimate consumer. The study of this movement and particularly the understanding of the relationships and problems must ultimately concern itself with a study of the movement's members — namely, wholesalers, retailers, and manufacturers.

Contrasting the Manufacturer and Retailer

Manufacturers and retailers have a great deal in common. Possibly their greatest joint interest is to sell merchandise at a profit — merchandise that ultimately ends up in the hands of the consumer. This merchandise must please the public in the long run or neither the manufacturer nor the retailer can continue selling to the public. If the manufacturer possesses a product that can be sold profitably and meets the needs of the consuming public then surely the retailer will be interested in selling the product. In addition, the retailer is always mindful of the value of new products, and manufacturers who keep retailers aware of the availability of products are considered to be valuable allies.

In spite of this basic relationship, retailers and manufacturers do have conflicting interests. Even more important, they have different organizational problems that in many cases require a different approach to a marketing solution. Possibly the major area of difference in attitude between retailers and manufacturers is in regard to the products they sell. The manufacturer is concerned primarily with the few products he sells. In performing his marketing activities he is concerned with promoting, properly pricing, and distributing his product. This product is developed from the point of view of a consumer need. When a manufacturer studies his competition, he relates only to firms that carry similar products. His product planning and designing activities are usually concerned only with gaining an edge on his competitors by establishing a product difference. Though it is quite true that his pricing amd some of his design techniques must take into consideration the needs of the retailer, it would not be accurate to state that these are his primary interests. In fact many concerns deliberately attempt to develop a strong consumer demand so that the retailer must carry their products. By successfully attempting this strategy the manufacturer finds that he is in an excellent bargaining position and ultimately offers the retailer a markup or other terms below the usual terms. As a result the distribution system is filled with branded products which the retailer is forced (by consumer demand) to carry but which do not offer him the exclusivity he desires nor for that matter the markup he would ordinarily require. Examples of these are breakfast cereals and many well-known apparel products.

The retailer, on the other hand, is usually not concerned with a product as such. His main concern is with a group of products. For example, the retailer is not concerned with the sale of chairs from the ABC chair company. However, the retailer is concerned with the total volume of sale of all chairs in his furniture department. Though the ABC chair company may represent an important element in the total department sales, the firm is rarely concerned with the individual company contribution. The reason for this attitude is obvious. The retailer offers the public hundreds of products for sale. It is literally impossible for him to maintain even a minimal amount of interest in the offerings of any one manufacturer. The retailer is also interested in the total image projected by his furniture department and more concerned with whether all products fit the image.

Other major differences also exist. In general most manufacturers are concerned with the total national market for their product. Their measurement techniques reflect this. Sales managers of manufacturing companies use national statistics such as Department of Commerce production indicators or buying-power estimates by city, state, or counties compiled by *Sales Management Magazine* to indicate the progress of their company in each major market. These same sources are considered practically useless by retail firms, the obvious reason being that retailing is basically a local business. That is, the individual store's sales and related profit needs can only be met within a short radius of the store's location. Even the large multi-unit retail store measures its well-being by each individual unit in the chain. A location, for example, is chosen on the basis of the individual store's needs and not the national potential of the firm. The management groups within the firm are concerned with the individual store manager's ability to penetrate a local market.

The ability of management to allocate costs to the individual products represents another major area of differences between the manufacturer and the retailer. The manufacturer with his elaborate cost-accounting systems can estimate costs based on a unit volume of sale per product. For example, it is not beyond the ability of General Motors to estimate automobile sales in the coming year, make further estimates as per the cost of materials and handling contained in each product sold, make the appropriate allocation of administrative overhead, and thereby fix a price for each automobile sold. As the year progresses, the estimates will doubtless deviate from the original. At this point adjustments can be made. The retailer, however, is not blessed with such a systematic and elaborate means of estimating costs and allocating overhead. Faced as he is with the sale of thousands of products, any attempt to apply cost estimates to the sale of each product is certainly a hopeless task. In addition to cost estimates, a retailer must allocate the cost of the services he renders to the public to each unit of merchandise sold. Though more will be said in a later chapter concerning this allocation and the method used, suffice it to say at this point that the allocation is probably more arbitrary than the manufacturer's attempts. This conclusion is in line with our previous discussion concerning the firm's inability and unwillingness to concern itself with the individual product. Since the retailer adds mainly distribution costs to the product (rather than changing the form of the product), most of the allocation is in the form of expenses that are not related directly to the product. For example, if a customer enters a department, pays cash for an item, and takes the product directly with him, he may be paying for the cost of maintaining the firm's credit department and elaborate delivery system. Whether or not one agrees that the price of the item would take into consideration these services, one would certainly agree that the allocation of the expense incurred by these services is a difficult if not insurmountable task. Many students of retailing have questioned whether it is even possible to allocate these expenses, and others have recommended that the stores avoid this allocation.

There are still other basic differences between retail and manufacturing firms. Some of these may be attributable to the peculiarities of the organizations. For example, the unsteadiness and vagaries of day-to-day demand, and the need for a great deal of personal service, indicate that the retailer has not participated in the automation revolution as much as have many of the manufacturing firms and other institutions. The implications of this are manifold. First, one must assume that retailing will never match the efficiencies of manufacturers in directing large groups of humans. In addition, with the possible exception of one trend (noted below), the retailer can probably expect little relief in reducing the pressures of rising expenses. On the other hand, the manufacturer will surely be in a position to increase the efficiency of his operations in the years ahead owing to the development and growth of automation.

The view of competitive strategy between retailers and manufacturers varies also. For example, the producer of a product that is considered to be a convenience item will attempt to sell the product in as many outlets as possible. The producer of shopping goods, though not necessarily requiring the same intensive distribution system as the convenience goods manufacturer, may nevertheless require the services of many retailers in the same area. For example, the producers of television sets usually attempt to sell their products to practically all retailers of this item. Conversely, the retailer is always attempting to obtain an item exclusively. This of course is to his advantage in that it ties the customer to him and allows him to substantially ignore competition. This conflict occurs in the sale of both branded and unbranded products.

A similar conflict arises in the attitude of the channels toward resale price maintenance. Though not all retailers are concerned with maintaining fixed prices in all stores, most retailers are. On the other hand, manufacturers as a rule are not concerned with maintaining prices at the retail level. Though many manufacturers are forced to take a public position in favor of maintaining retail prices at the present level, their actions in fact do not support this program. The manufacturer favors competitive prices since the lower the price the more he is able to sell. Retailers (and in particular small retailers) resist price cutting since it limits the differentiation between their firm and larger and more efficient operators.

The nature of retailing also means that the retailer must be more sensitive to competition — probably more so than the manufacturer. Hence, the retailer is concerned with the attributes of competition. Thus, the above-mentioned policies of exclusive franchising have more than a limited appeal to the retailer. Retailers also favor manufacturers who not only prefer a policy of establishing retail prices but also make more than a token attempt to enforce these policies.

Retailers not only have philosophical differences with manufacturers but also can get involved with practical problems on a day-in, day-out basis. For example, one manufacturer aware of the fact that his customers wanted a package that could be easily opened designed a simple tear-open feature on his package. Unfortunately the package of bubble-gum balls was rejected by retailers who simply did not want a package that would invite "free sampling" by children. The retailers were also concerned with spillage onto the display floor when the package was opened.[2]

A producer of instant coffee ran into another packaging problem when he designed an instant coffee in a vacuum can for retailers. The package design was similar to those used for vacuum-packed ground coffee and was intended to impress the consumer with the fact that the instant coffee was as fresh as regular coffee. The problem arose when the retailers found that the round vacuum package would take up considerably more space than competing instant jars. As a result the manufacturer was forced to change his design to meet the shelf-stacking needs of the retailer.

SUMMARY

The main functions performed by retail management include:

1. Determining the objectives of the firm
2. Planning the strategy and tactics
3. Organizing and coordinating the firm's activities
4. Staffing and assembling other resources
5. Operating and directing
6. Controlling the firm

One of the first tasks of management is to clearly determine the objectives of the firm. The objectives should be stated in such a manner as to serve as a guide to all members of the management team.

The second function, which concerns us in most of the ensuing chapters, is the planning of the strategy and tactics of the firm. Here management faces its greatest challenge, the selection of the proper mix to reach its objectives.

Functions 3, 4, and 5 are applicable to all retail firms but are not discussed in any great detail.

The final function, control, includes a study of the accounting and research data necessary to evaluate and measure the retail firm's performance. The proper performance of this function is covered in the final three chapters of this book.

QUESTIONS

1. How do the functions of management in the retail store differ from those performed in the manufacturing firm?

2. Why is store planning sometimes called store decision making? What is decision making?

3. Is a retail firm free to choose its objectives? Why or why not?

---

[2]Walter Gross, "Profitable Listening for Manufacturers and Dealers," *Business Horizons,* December, 1968, p. 35.

4. Comment on the following statement: Manufacturers and retailers have the same goal, to make money. Therefore anything that a manufacturer does to make money automatically benefits the retailer.

5. Choose a local retail store. Write a statement of the firm's objectives as you envision them.

6. A retail firm decides to offer its products in the rural areas of its market. To accomplish this the firm resorts to developing a mail-order catalog. Presently the firm consists of five general-merchandise stores situated in the downtown business districts of three major cities. Does the establishment of the mail-order division represent a change in strategy or tactics?

7. Define and distinguish between strategy and tactics.

8. What is the merchandising strategy of Sears, Roebuck? What tactics do they follow to achieve this strategy?

9. In what ways can legislation restrict the merchandising effort of a liquor store?

10. The objective of a large retail firm is to maximize its profits. Comment.

11. How do the objectives of manufacturers and retailers differ? In what ways are they alike?

12. Why does management have to constantly analyze and evaluate its operation?

THE
UNCONTROLLABLE
FACTORS

II

In this section are presented the major external uncontrollable factors with which retail management must contend in its business environment. The *first is retail competition*. This factor more than any other accounts for the vast changes that are always taking place in retailing, for entry in retailing is relatively easy and numerous competitors can start what look like profitable enterprises.

Legislation represents another aspect of the retailer's environment that he must live with and yet cannot control. Some of the more recent court decisions have made legislation an even more ominous factor to contend with.

Lastly, the retailer must contend with the whim of the *consumer*. For it is the consumer who is the target of the retailer's efforts.

Competition is covered in Chapter 3, legislation in Chapter 4, and the consumer in Chapters 5, 6, and 7.

Competition and the Influence of the Retailer

3

OBJECTIVES YOU SHOULD MEET

1. *Explain* why competition in retailing is intense.
2. *Explain* why in spite of competitive intensity, profits in retailing are comparable to those in manufacturing.
3. *Describe* the average small store.
4. *Illustrate* the "wheel of retailing."

The question, Is retailing competitive?, may seem rather inane to a hard-pressed small retailer who can barely meet his bills at the end of the month. As a matter of fact there are few retailers who would answer that question in the negative. The reason is simply that most of them can name a few local stores that compete directly with them and that represent firms which must be watched constantly.

On the other hand, economists and those interested in the trends of competition would tell us that all businessmen think they are in a competitive industry and spend most of their waking hours worrying about their competition. Nevertheless, economists do recognize varying degrees of competition in all industries. Intensity of competition usually implies that prices will be lower, larger firms will have less control over the prices they set, and, stated in obvious economic terms, the allocation of resources will be the most efficient.

Management View of Competition Role of Competition

Aside from the economist's interest and that of related governmental agencies in the level of competition in retailing, it is extremely important that the firm's management have a complete understanding of the level of competition in its industry. The most obvious reason for understanding competition is its impact on pricing. If a firm has a major advantage over its competitors, this will certainly be reflected in its pricing. However, competition influences all areas affecting the retail firm. It can strongly influence the purchasing habits of the firm and guide its expansion policies, particularly in relation to the location of new outlets.

To fully develop the management point of view in this section, we are going to examine the ease of entry and concentration in retailing, the number of retail firms, management's view of what constitutes competition, the ability of the retail firm to differentiate its product, and the effect of innovation.

Retail Entry and Concentration

On the basis of observation alone, competition in retailing would seem to be unparalleled. In many neighborhoods one sees numerous drugstores and what appears to be an oversupply of food supermarkets and specialty stores. By contrast, in the manufacturing or wholesaling field the number of competitors is considerably smaller. The reasons for this are fairly obvious. In the economist's terms, entry in retailing is easy. That is, it takes little capital to open a small retail store. As a matter of fact, little of the investment made is in capital equipment such as fixtures, machines, and other appliances needed to set up a manufacturing plant. Most of the initial investment in the retail store is in liquid assets — namely, inventories. One expert, for example, noted that a small retailer can commence business with a capital of less than $3,000. Yet even the smallest apparel manufacturer must have a minimum investment of from $10,000 to $20,000. Most large manufacturers of many products require investments that run into the millions. Only the very largest retail stores require this kind of investment.

 Professor Backman has made estimates concerning the investment per worker in retailing versus manufacturing, and has found that investment in retailing averages $5,100 per worker,[1] whereas manufacturing investment approximates $12,000 per worker. The retailing investment consists of inventories, store fixtures, cash registers, and other assets needed to complete the store. The manufacturer requires a plant, tools, and thousands of dollars of inventory and machinery to produce the product. Hence, an entrepreneur starting a retail business needs to invest considerably less per worker than would a manufacturing enterprise.

 The implications of the low entry cost in retailing are obvious. High profits in a retail enterprise almost automatically invite competition. Ease of entry constantly forces profits down. Moreover, few retail firms are in a position to control prices in the market. Accordingly, one would expect the concentration of sales among the large retail firms to be considerably below that in most manufacturing industries. Tables 3-1 and 3-2 confirm this observation. Listed in Table 3-1 are 30 major manufacturing industries. Note that in a significant number of these manufacturing industries sales are concentrated in the hands of four or fewer sellers. The retailing fields tend to show a low concentration ratio (see Table 3-2), and it is the rare retail enterprise indeed that can control sales in any major city.

[1]Jules Backman, "Why Wages Are Lower in Retailing," *The Southern Economic Journal,* Vol. XXIII (January, 1957), pp. 295-305.

Concentration Ratio in 30 Major Manufacturing Industries*   TABLE 3-1

	Percentage Share of Market
Primary aluminum	99
Passenger cars, knocked down or assembled	98
Cigarettes	82
Tin cans and other tinware	80
Synthetic fibers	79
Tires and inner tubes	78
Tractors	67
Aircraft	55
Hot rolled sheet and strip (the leading steel mill product)	53
Copper rolling and drawing	52
Electric motors and generators	48
Plastic materials	45
Meat packing products	39
Flour and meal	38
Farm machinery except tractors	36
Petroleum refining	32
Footwear except rubber	30
Pulp	29
Canned fruits and vegetables	28
Beer and ale	27
Fluid milk	21
Paper and paper board	19
Bread and related products	19
Newspapers	19
Machine tools	18
Cotton broad-woven fabrics	17
Commercial printing	9
Sawmills and planing mills	6
Dresses, unit price	5
Women's suits, coats and skirts	3

*Top four firms in the industry
Source: *Concentration in American Industry:* Report of the Subcommittee on Anti-Trust and Monopoly, Committee on the Judiciary, U.S. Senate, 85th Cong. 1st Sess., 1957, p. 23.

However, merging and acquisition in the retail field continues to take place. As expected, most of the merging occurs among the largest retail firms. For example, between 1951 and 1961 the eight largest department stores in the United States acquired 39 stores.[2] Most of the acquisition of outlets took place among the food chains; during this period the top 16 grocery chains acquired 181 firms through mergers. Most of this merger activity in the grocery field was "market extension" merging; that is, stores were acquired in order to enter new markets.

[2]*Mergers and Superconcentration,* Staff Report of the Senate Committee on Small Business, House of Representatives, 87th Cong., November, 1962, p. 40.

TABLE 3-2   Total Sales of the Four Largest Firms in Food and General Merchandise, 1972 (in millions of dollars)

FOOD STORES	
Great Atlantic & Pacific Tea Company	$ 6,369
Safeway Stores	6,058
Kroger Stores	3,791
Acme Markets, Incorporated	2,025
Total four largest	$18,243
Total all food stores	94,969
Top four as percentage of total	19%
GENERAL MERCHANDISE STORES	
Sears, Roebuck	$ 10,991
Montgomery Ward	3,369
J. C. Penney	5,530
Federated Department Stores	2,665
Total four largest	$22,555
Total all general merchandise, apparel, furniture, and appliance stores	118,094
Top four as percentage of total	19%

Source: *1972, Retail Trade,* U.S. Department of Commerce and Annual Reports.

This technique indicates that many grocery firms believed that further expansion in their present markets was rather limited and that new markets were their only means of attaining new business. The importance of this policy as a means of expanding the market power of the grocery chains is reflected in the fact that one of the few chains to lose in sales volume and suffer reduced profits in the early 1960's, The Great Atlantic and Pacific Tea Company, did not acquire any food stores during this period. The two mergers for this company were vertical in nature, one being a nut company and the other a dairy products firm.

Table 3-3 lists the trends in this direction. It shows for example that the ten leading grocery chains made 197 acquisitions from 1949 to 1968. These acquisitions added over $2 billion to their sales volume.

Profits

From the above analysis and our observations of retailing, it might be concluded that profits are considerably lower for retail firms than for other types of enterprises. Though this observation may be correct for small enterprises, it is decidedly erroneous in the case of the larger retail enterprises. Referring to Table 18-3a, Chapter 18, we see that profits ranged from 0.5 to 9.5 as a percentage of sales and from 3.2 to 45.0 when measured as a return on investment. According to these findings profits in retailing compare favorably with those for manufacturing firms as summarized in Table 3-4. Why the paradox of ease of entry, plentiful competition, and yet respectable profits? The answer is probably twofold.

Year	Total Acquisitions		By 20 Leading Grocery Chains		By 10 Leading Grocery Chains	
	Number of Acquisitions	Sales of Acquired Stores (millions)	Number of Acquisitions	Sales of Acquired Stores (millions)	Number of Acquisitions	Sales of Acquired Stores (millions)
1949	5	$ 66	1	$ 47	1	$ 47
1950	5	4	2	3	1	1
1951	12	28	6	25	5	19
1952	10	71	5	55	4	53
1953	13	88	4	77	2	61
1954	24	76	7	37	4	31
1955	55	559	23	465	15	267
1956	69	450	32	310	20	141
1957	52	319	20	194	14	170
1958	74	517	41	361	27	261
1959	63	319	34	136	14	24
1960	44	307	25	201	10	36
1961	50	518	30	407	16	292
1962	53	306	24	179	14	157
1963	51	568	27	463	16	416
1964	41	312	16	188	8	153
1965	28	558	5	61	3	35
1966	40	539	6	110	3	73
1967	29	[1] 937	2	5	0	0
1968	43	[2] 1,210	6	[3] 68	2	6
Total	760	$7,752	316	$3,392	197	$2,243

[1]Includes grocery stores with sales of $472 million acquired by nonfood store chains.
[2]Includes grocery stores with sales of $590 million acquired by nonfood store companies.
[3]The figure excludes the acquisition of Consolidated Food Stores' Eagle supermarkets by Lucky Stores pursuant to an FTC divestiture order because both chains were among the 11th to 20th size class.
Source: Bureau of Economics, Federal Trade Commission, *Economic Report on Corporate Mergers, 1969,* p. 676.

First, not all retail firms earn the profits listed. It may be recalled from the section discussing the objectives of firms that many smaller retail operators are content to earn a living and rarely earn profits. However, though they earn either marginal or submarginal returns they still remain in business and therefore draw off potential sales and earnings from other, better-established firms.

Second, though retailing is competitive, entrance easy, and the competitors numerous, many firms are still able to isolate themselves in some manner from their competition. This ability is referred to in this text as *firm differentiation.* It refers simply to the firm's ability to isolate its product offerings and location to some extent from those of its competitors. To the extent that it can do this, the retail firm has a chance to administer its prices. The practice of administering prices refers

TABLE 3-4   Rates of Return on Investment in Selected Manufacturing Industries, 1968

Industry	Rate of Return After Taxes (%)
Bakery products	12.2
Tobacco products	13.9
Carpets and rugs	9.7
Paper and allied products	10.5
Petroleum refining	12.3
Tires and inner tubes	12.0
Metal cans	12.3
Motor vehicles	15.8
Electrical machinery	13.7
Office computing and accounting machines	18.6

Source: Adapted from *Federal Trade Commission, Rates of Return in Selected Manufacturing Industries, 1959-1968.*

to the firm's ability to set the market price of a product and particularly to its ability to maintain that price.

Though more will be said about pricing in a later chapter, it should be noted that retailers pre-retail merchandise and hope to maintain these prices through a season. However, as will be noted later, markdowns taken by retailers reflect the amount of competitive pressure or miscalculation on their part. Thus, the more differentiation the firm is able to establish in its trading area (reflected in its ability to administer or maintain its prices), the more profitable the enterprise.

Quantifying Retailing

Retailing is a business of contrasts. Although there are firms that have an annual sales volume of over $1 billion, the average retail store in 1972 reported sales of under $300 a day! Knowledge of the scope of retailing gives us some idea of the difficulty of generalizing about retail problems where the range is so great. In this section firms will be discussed on the basis of sales volume, ownership, and the size of the firm.

Total retail sales in 1971 exceeded $400 billion, or almost tripled the retail sales in 1950. The interesting thing about this increase in sales is that the total number of retail establishments remained approximately the same over this period. How does one explain this paradox? There seem to be two logical explanations.

First, a portion of the increase reflects merely a rise in prices rather than an increase in the number of units sold. From 1950 to 1971 the consumer price index increased by 68 per cent; if we deflate the 1971 sales by this index we find that the increase was only 65 per cent instead of 180 per cent, as seen in Table 3-5. Thus a substantial part of the over-all retail sales increase is illusory.

The second reason for this paradox has to do mainly with the nature of retailing. A retail firm that is growing need not add additional establishments but can simply increase its capacity. In fact, the stores that have been added during this period have been larger. For example, in the past few years the new outlets of the J. C. Penney Company have almost doubled in size over the outlets built in the early

	Retail Sales *(in billions of dollars)*	*Sales Deflated by* *Consumer Price Index* *(in billions of dollars)*
1950	$147	$204
1960	220	248
1971	409	337
(increase 1950/1971)	+ 80%	+ 65

Source: U.S. Department of Commerce

postwar years. The trend toward carrying wider lines of merchandise has caused this development. Many of the newer J. C. Penney stores have started to carry hard lines in addition to the traditional apparel specialty items. The food supermarkets are another example of retail firms that have built larger stores over this same period. The variety chains with their movement into discount operations have also joined this trend. Thus, though the number of retail establishments has not increased, the size of these establishments has increased considerably.

Sales Volume by Types of Stores

As shown in Table 3-6, the largest volume outlets in the U.S. are the food stores. Food stores account for over 20 per cent of all retail sales. This dominance is understandable, as food is a basic commodity that represents more than 20 per cent of the typical family's expenditures.

The second-largest group of retailers is represented by the automobile dealers. The automobile dealer, however, finds that his business can be subject to severe fluctuations in demand, and as shown in this table, his business declined by about 7 per cent between 1969 and 1970. In view of the fact that total retail sales increased during that period by 4 per cent, this decline points up the fact that automobile demand is subject to changing economic conditions.

The third-largest group of retailers is represented by the department stores. Department stores not only account for a substantial proportion of retail sales but affect certain branches of it in a particular way. Department stores are important outlets in the apparel and home furnishings industry, primarily because of their vast expenditures on advertising and displays. In addition, the department store has been able to attract the middle-class housewife, one of the major beneficiaries of the affluent society. As a result of this position in retailing, the department store has participated in the development of the shopping center in the suburban areas of the major cities. Few shopping-center promoters would be able to develop a center without first attracting a major department store.

Ownership

The two main divisions of retail stores by ownership are the independents and the chains. The independent is usually controlled and owned by an individual or small family. As a rule independent stores do not have any outside management,

37

TABLE 3-6   Estimated Sales of All Retail Stores in the United States, by Kind of Business: 1970 and 1969 (in millions of dollars)

Kind of Business	1970	1969	Percent Change
United States, total	364,571	351,633	+4
Food group	81,466	75,866	+7
Eating and drinking places	27,872	25,849	+8
General merchandise group with nonstores	62,867	58,615	+7
General merchandise group without nonstores (except department stores mail order)	56,852	53,083	+7
Department stores and dry goods general merchandise stores	45,962	43,016	+7
Department stores	38,558	36,411	+6
Variety stores	7,056	6,548	+8
Mail order houses (department store merchandise)	3,834	3,519	+9
Apparel group	20,396	20,158	+1
Men's, boys' wear stores	4,683	4,761	−2
Men's, boys' clothing, furnishings	4,591	4,658	−1
Women's apparel, accessory stores	7,710	7,606	+1
Women's ready-to-wear stores	6,608	6,403	+3
Family clothing stores	3,692	3,631	+2
Shoe stores	3,619	3,505	+3
Furniture and appliance group	16,817	16,719	+1
Furniture, home furnishings stores	10,393	10,439	0
Furniture stores	7,748	7,824	−1
Household appliance, TV, radio stores	5,226	5,223	0
Household appliance dealers	3,456	3,536	−2
Lumber, building, hardware, farm equipment group	19,667	19,246	+2
Automotive group	62,847	66,911	−6
Passenger car, other automotive dealers	57,737	62,048	−7
Gasoline service stations	26,504	25,116	+6
Drug and proprietary stores	12,750	11,863	+7
Liquor stores	8,060	7,403	+9

Source. Adapted from: *1970, Retail Trade,* U.S. Department of Commerce, Bureau of the Census.

nor are they influenced by outside stockholders. The typical corner newsstand or candy store is an example. Though a number of the independents do have more than one store, this is unusual.

The chain consists of a group of stores, usually of the same type, managed and operated from a central office. Here again an all-encompassing definition is too narrow. For example, one of the largest department store chains in the country, Federated Department Stores, permits a great deal of local autonomy. In general, however, chain stores are managed centrally and most of the buying is done by buyers many miles from the local markets. Variety and food firms have a tendency toward this mode of operation.

The independent store is by far the more numerous. The latest Census of Retailing reported that independent stores account for approximately nine out of ten retail stores in the United States. Their share of the total retail business, however, is substantially less than their share of the total number of stores. In the most recent census it was reported that independent stores accounted for about 60 per cent of total retail sales. In many fields of retailing, however, the independent store is the mainstay and rarely finds a chain competing; candy stores, gasoline stations, and furniture stores are excellent examples of fields where independents dominate. On the other hand, there are many fields within retailing where the independent does a very small share of the business. For example, among variety stores the chains account for 80 per cent of the total sales, and in the food business for 53 per cent of the total. A number of these comparisons are made in Figure 3-1. Thus the importance of chains varies considerably from one field to another, the two extremes being the candy store and the variety chain.

One should also recognize that the typical independent retail firm is very small. For example, in Table 3-7 one can see that in the latest year for which statistics are available 48.4 per cent of all retail firms had a sales volume of less than $50,000 a year. Assuming that stores are open about 300 days a year, this figure means that almost half the stores in the U.S. have a sales volume of $167 a day!

Though no set rule applies, it is obvious that the chain thrives where the merchandise sold is relatively staple and the local unit can churn up a large volume of business. This is borne out by the statistics. The 1967 census, for example, showed that the average annual sales volume of the individual chain store was five times that of the average independent. Without this huge per-store volume the chain would not be able to support the vast organizational complex needed to service each of its units.

One of the major problems of the chain organization is that the central management is totally removed from the customer. Thus the chain finds it difficult to buy according to the local needs or to meet the whims of the local clientele. Obviously this factor is of limited importance if the products sold are staples and require little knowledge of the local market. In other words, from the consumer's point of view, the products most successfully sold in chains are those calling for little exercise of choice by consumers, as in the case of many grocery products. These tend to be staples that are easily recognizable. Conversely, a high-fashion dress salon would have difficulty attracting the interest of chain management, as the firm would have to cater to the individual whims of the style-conscious female. Supplying this outlet would require a personal knowledge of each market and would hardly lend itself to centralized buying and merchandising.

Size of the Firm

It was noted earlier in this section that concentration in the retail field was relatively low compared to manufacturing. This, however, does not mean that the average retail store is not becoming larger and more important in the distribution of merchandise. The typical retail store (whether a chain or independent) is in fact

FIGURE 3-1   Estimated Sales of Retail Stores of Organizations Operating 11 or More Retail Stores, by Selected Kinds of Business, 1970

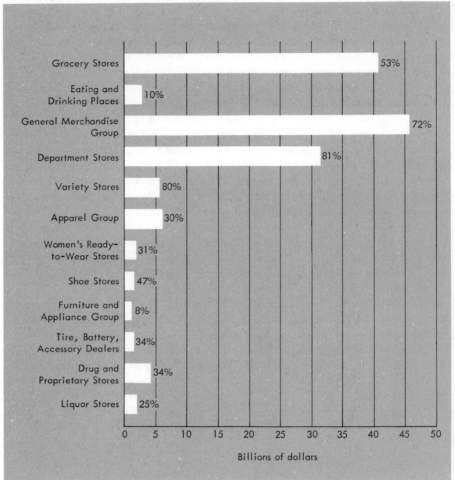

Adapted from *1970, Retail Trade,* U. S. Department of Commerce, Bureau of the Census.

getting larger, though its impact on each type of merchandise varies considerably.

For example, looking again at Table 3-1, one sees that about 3 per cent of the stores in the U.S. had sales of over $1 million or more in the latest census year. However, careful examination of the same table indicates that these stores accounted for 44.4 per cent of all retail sales. Thus, one finds that a small number of large stores account for a sizable proportion of retail sales.

If one examines the content of the share of the market held by establishments with an annual sales volume of over $1 million, this effect becomes clearer (Table 3-8). These stores increased their share of the total retail market by about 6 per cent between 1963 and 1967, but this trend did not apply equally to all the trades. For example, the share of total grocery sales handled by stores selling over a million dollars a year increased from 52.7 per cent in 1963 to 61.3 per cent in 1967.

Full-Year Establishments with Sales of One Million Dollars or More by Selected Kinds of Business — United States, 1967 and 1963   TABLE 3-7

Kind of Business	Sales Amount ($1,000)		Sales Per Cent of All Full-Year Establishments	
	1967	1963	1967	1963
Retail trade, total	132,875,627	89,096,247	44.4	38.4
Building materials, hardware, and farm equipment dealers	4,113,592	2,365,211	24.6	16.8
Building materials and supply stores	2,875,953	1,810,938	30.9	22.2
Hardware stores	234,760	150,500	8.6	6.1
Farm equipment dealers	1,002,879	403,773	21.4	11.5
General merchandise group stores	34,596,162	21,851,304	81.3	75.0
Department stores	31,224,812	19,578,453	98.8	97.6
Variety stores	1,516,320	867,443	28.5	19.7
Miscellaneous general merchandise stores	1,855,030	1,405,738	33.1	29.9
Food stores	38,735,376	26,484,373	57.2	48.8
Grocery stores	38,473,751	26,405,316	61.3	52.7
Automotive dealers	37,233,285	27,903,202	68.9	63.9
Motor vehicle dealers	36,370,061	27,554,947	77.0	70.1
Tire, battery, and accessory dealers	370,399	186,115	9.0	5.8
Miscellaneous automotive dealers	492,825	165,440	18.4	11.3
Apparel and accessory stores	3,523,393	2,429,380	21.6	17.9
Women's ready-to-wear stores	1,539,880	1,184,025	29.3	27.8
Women's accessory and specialty stores	126,969	115,059	14.4	12.4
Furriers and fur shops	42,484	19,604	18.9	10.7
Men's and boys' clothing and furnishings stores	629,968	(D)	19.1	(D)
Family clothing stores	1,023,620	646,928	33.6	24.6
Furniture, home furnishings, and equipment stores	2,713,492	1,356,128	19.1	12.9
Furniture stores	1,485,090	828,606	23.2	16.2
Home furnishings stores	192,080	101,216	10.1	7.3
Household appliance stores	574,756	295,587	19.5	12.9
Radio, television, and music stores	461,566	127,719	15.8	7.8
Eating and drinking places	1,709,725	816,388	7.6	4.9
Drug stores and proprietary stores	1,796,933	788,852	17.0	9.7

41

TABLE 3-7   Continued

Kind of Business	Sales Amount ($1,000)		Per Cent of All Full-Year Establishments	
	1967	1963	1967	1963
Miscellaneous retail stores	4,423,509	2,353,706	16.7	11.6
Liquor stores	974,796	457,576	15.1	9.3
Jewelry stores	297,960	126,372	13.8	8.5
Fuel and ice dealers	723,238	537,122	20.7	16.5
Nonstore retailers	3,588,986	2,700,967	48.2	45.4

D: Withheld to avoid disclosure.
Source: Same as Table 3-6.

TABLE 3-8   Sales Size — United States: 1963 to 1967

Sales Size of Establishment	Type of Establishment as Per Cent of All Full-Year Establishments		Sales as Per Cent of All Full-Year Establishments	
	1967	1963	1967	1963
With annual sales of:				
$5,000,000 or more	.3	.2	14.7	11.6
$2,000,000 to $4,999,000	1.0	.7	15.8	13.1
$1,000,000 to $1,999,000	1.8	1.5	13.9	13.8
$500,000 to $999,000	3.3	2.8	12.8	13.0
$300,000 to $499,000	4.4	3.8	9.4	9.4
$100,000 to $299,000	21.5	20.0	20.1	21.8
$50,000 to $99,000	19.3	21.5	7.6	10.0
Less than $50,000	48.4	49.5	5.7	7.3

Source: *Census of Business, Retail Trade,* vol. I, 1967, U.S. Department of Commerce, Bureau of the Census.

In this same table one can see that department stores, automotive dealers and grocery stores (supermarkets) accounted for $107 billion of the total $132 billion in sales by stores in this grouping. On the other hand, there are relatively few large stores among liquor, jewelry, appliance, and drug stores.

There is, of course, a reason for the increase in size in the food supermarkets. The sharp postwar increase in automobile shopping, particularly in the suburbs, has given rise to larger stores on sites that can accommodate parking. The trend toward one-stop shopping, which has forced food stores to carry other items as well, has tended to increase the size of the store and, more important, its sales volume.

Workable Competition

In spite of all the statistics on competition and the size of the average retail enterprise, the retailer has to determine for himself who his competitors are. On the surface this question may seem to be easily answerable. Like most things in retailing it is more complex.

For the small store a competitor may be nothing more than the nearest store on his block. For example the small food store would perhaps rightfully consider that his major competitor is a small food store across the street. Should he consider the A & P food store on his block a competitor?

Before answering that question let us present the case of the buyer of men's clothing for a major department store and ask the same question: Who are his competitors?

One answer would certainly be other department stores. Should he also consider some of the smaller specialty stores as being competitors? The answer here is not obvious and requires further study.

As a general rule the buyer in the department store is concerned with other department stores, for several reasons. First, as the other department stores spend large sums of money on advertising, they are able to communicate to the public any competitive edge they may have. The smaller store is more dependent on word-of-mouth advertising, a much slower and less dynamic way to reach a market. Thus large stores are direct threats to each other on a daily basis. As a result they read each other's ads and adjust their techniques and merchandise to these efforts.

Secondly, it is more likely that the large stores compete at many different locations in the area. That is, they have suburban, shopping-center, and downtown stores, whereas many of the smaller stores have only one or two locations.

Lastly, the department store may be so much larger than the smaller store that little would be gained by it in terms of sales volume by their competing.

In the case of the grocery store, the small firm would most likely compete against the other small food firm but would tend to ignore the A & P, simply because the difference in size means that they do not compete at the same level. In addition, the small store usually attracts customers who shop there on the basis of services not found in the large supermarket chains. For instance, the small store may be open on Sunday, may maintain longer shopping hours during the day; or may take phone orders and provide a delivery service. In a sense, therefore, the small food stores compete with the A & P by offering services that the larger firm does not wish to provide. However, on a day-to-day basis the small store would not and could not compete with the larger firm on price or merchandise assortment.

As a general rule, therefore, stores regard as workable competitors those firms that operate on the same level as they do. Those that maintain large stores, large advertising budgets, and large staffs consider themselves to be in competition; in effect, they watch each other. Those that operate on a much more limited scale tend to regard as their competitors any stores in similar circumstances.

Differentiation

A retail firm has numerous ways of differentiating its offerings. The most obvious way is to offer unique products and services to the consumer. The tendency of firms to obtain exclusive products, develop fashion products, or import merchandise has to do with this strategy. Large retailers who offer consumers free delivery services, gift wrapping, and gift consultation services are deliberately attempting to accomplish the same goals. The development by firms of both a product assortment and service offerings is discussed in a separate section of this text.

Possibly the most important and unassailable method of differentiation is to choose a key location. An excellent location in many cases offers a firm a differential advantage that is unbeatable. The location of the Macy's store at 34th Street and Broadway in New York (where many major subways meet) epitomizes the advantage of a good location. This aspect and the bigness of firms (economies of scale) as differentiating factors are discussed in the section entitled "The Physical Distribution Mix."

Large expenditures and unique methods of advertising by certain retailers also offer a special means of differentiating products. Most large retailers have a sizable advertising budget which allows them to maintain their advantage over smaller retail firms. It is more difficult, however, for these firms to gain advantage over competitors of similar size except in the style of the ad. In this endeavor the ability of the firm to instill credibility and attract the reader are more important in the long run.

In addition to advertising, some firms have maintained an advantage by using media that are relatively expensive to develop and require many years of nurturing. Mail-order firms in particular have developed this differentiating factor in their communication with the consumer. The total communication function and its related tendencies are discussed in the section of the book entitled "The Communication Mix."

Innovation

Over the years retail firms devise ways of doing business that eventually give them a differential advantage over their competitors. In the daily competitive complex in which they function, they are constantly striving to improve their operations. As a consequence many firms develop unique services or unusual merchandise offerings that have the effect of improving their market position. However, it has been observed that at the same time many firms become over-organized, less efficient, and, ultimately, easy targets for new entrants into the industry. One well-known observer of retailing observed this phenomenon some time ago when he commented on cycles in retail development with these words:

> *Stage 1* "... they catch the attention of the consumer by distributing merchandise at low prices because of a low overhead."
> *Stage 2* "... trading up" ... the merchandise handled.
> *Stage 3* "Competition in services of all kinds ..."[3]

In effect, this same observer has discerned the "wheel of retailing," i.e., that firms go through a growth cycle and finally reach a decline in their ability to meet all market contingencies. The prime example of how this cycle has worked in the past is the food supermarket. Originally the supermarket came upon the American

---

[3]Malcolm P. McNair, "Trends in Large-Scale Retailing," *Harvard Business Review,* Vol. 10, No. 1 (October, 1931), p. 39.

scene as a low-price innovator. During the 1930's the supermarket so effectively overcame the independent and small grocery store that a wave of anti-chain protest backed by legislation swept the country.[4] The early supermarkets were born in warehouses on the outskirts of eastern cities. They originally gave the appearance of being low-cost operations because they lacked the decor of today's supermarkets. Eventually, from these operations large chains developed, based on the principles of self-service, wide assortments, and few services offered to the customer.

Throughout the years, however, these firms have started to increase their offerings to the customer. Many have developed a large "nonfood" business. The services offered to customers since the 1930's have also changed somewhat. Today the supermarkets feature large parking spaces and are much more attractive than their forerunners. In addition, they have added trading stamps to their list of promotional activities.

Supermarkets seem to be at a stage in their growth where a new competitor may enter the field. In fact some observers are carefully watching the recent combining of the discount firm with the food supermarket, and believe it poses a serious threat to the established large food chains. However, most of this competition is in the future. Yet there is evidence that the heyday of this innovator of some thirty years ago is over. For example, profits among the food chains have leveled off during the postwar period, as has the share of the total food market held by the chains. The growth of the food chains during this same period has been maintained only by a rash of mergers. As noted in a previous section, the failure on the part of some well-known chains to participate in this merger activity has cost them dearly.

Possibly the most striking thing about the entrance of an innovator into the retailing field is that it disrupts many of the differential advantages of the more traditional type of outlet. This disruption has caused these firms to do either of the following: (1) copy the innovator's method of conducting his business, or (2) concentrate even more on differential advantages.

An illustration of this is the department store harassed by the growth of the appliance discount firm following World War II. The majority of department stores were forced to reduce their prices in the appliance department in order to meet this competition.[5] Some of the major stores simply discontinued the sale of appliances and concentrated their managerial talents on the upgrading of their remaining departments.

SUMMARY

Competition affects all areas of the retail firm. To understand competition one should understand several important determinants of its level and intensity.

Entry in retailing is relatively easy, and concentration is not as great as in most areas of manufacturing. However, to remain large many firms have merged over the

---

[4]For a historical treatment of this period, see Godfrey M. Lebhar, *Chain Stores in America* (New York: Chain Stores Publishing Corp., 1963).

[5]For example, the cumulative markup in the appliance department of the large department store declined from 36.0 per cent in 1947 to 27.7 per cent in 1960. See *Merchandising and Operating Reports of Department and Specialty Stores,* National Retail Merchants' Association.

past 20 years. In spite of the competition profits in retailing are at least comparable to those of manufacturing, mainly because of the ability of the retail firm to differentiate itself from its competitors.

In terms of the size and number of retail firms it must be remembered that the typical retail firm is small and has an average sales volume of less than $200 a day. Though retail sales are calculated to have increased by 180 per cent since 1950, when deflated this figure amounts to an increase of about 65 per cent. The largest volume of business is done by food stores, followed by automobile dealers and department stores.

Though the independent stores are the most numerous by far, the chain store was on the average five times as large as the independent. Chains accounted for a substantial proportion of the business among grocery, variety, and department stores. The importance of bigness is further supported by the statistics that though stores with a sales volume of over $1 million per year comprised only 3 per cent of all outlets, they accounted for over 44 per cent of all retail sales.

In spite of all the statistics, stores regard as their workable competitors those firms that operate on the same size level as they do. That is, those firms that have large advertising budgets and possess several locations look at similar stores as competitors. The small retailer looks upon other small retailers as competitors.

Stores maintain their competitive edge through differentiating their product mix. There is some evidence that retailers go through a growth cycle that eventually makes them victims of innovators. This cycle is sometimes referred to as the "wheel of retailing."

QUESTIONS

1. Why haven't liquor stores grown dramatically? Why have they tended to be independently owned?

2. Mr. Smith, the owner of a chain of stores, has observed that whenever he rebuilds one of his present stores he adds an additional 5,000 square feet of selling space. He notes that this move always increases sales volume. Why is this so? Why don't all stores do this?

3. In spite of the tendency toward large supermarkets and their accompanying increase in sales, the small independent grocer survives. Is it possible in the future that this outlet will eventually pass from the American scene? Why or why not?

4. Why is concentration low in retailing? Why is concentration high in the automobile industry? Is concentration high or low in the apparel industry? Why?

5. What is meant by the "wheel of retailing"? Apply this concept to the development of the department store.

6. Are costs higher or lower in the retail chain? Support your answer.

7. What advantages does the independent store have over the chain organization?

8. Choose a major department store or chain in your city. How does it attempt to differentiate its offerings? How successful is it?

9. How does the corner drugstore differentiate its offerings to the public?

10. Offer five reasons why retail firms merge.

11. Color television represents a recent product innovation by manufacturing firms. Does this product innovation affect retail firms? If so, in what ways?

12. Discuss in detail a recent retail innovation in your city.

13. Why is investment per worker low in retailing as compared to most manufacturing?

14. What is meant by workable competition? How does it differ from theoretical competition?

15. Whom does the store manager of an F. W. Woolworth store consider to be his competitor?

Legal Restraints
and Consumerism

4

OBJECTIVES YOU SHOULD MEET

1. *List* the 5 types of legislation encountered by the retailer.
2. *Show* how the Robinson-Patman Act and Fair Trade Laws restrict the retailer.
3. *Define* the term "consumerism."
4. *Cite* the recent history of consumerism.

Restraints, both legal and social, affect all areas of the retailer's effort. Pricing, advertising, competition, and the products carried (plus the location of his distribution systems) are affected by these restraints.

To take a simple example, the so-called fair trade laws represent restrictions on the prices that can be set by retailers. Because minimum prices are set by the manufacturer under this legislation, a retailer cannot adjust his prices on products "fair traded." Thus, the more efficient retailer, or the retailer that offers the consumers fewer services, is unable to pass along the savings to the consumer. Specifically, a department store offering numerous services and a food supermarket or self-service discount firm charge the same price on fair trade items, though the department store usually has a much higher expense structure than the other two types of stores.

In this chapter, five types of legislative and social restraints will be discussed. The first are laws that attempt to attack bigness by means of special assessments.

[1]This chapter draws heavily on three sources: Stanley Hollander, *Restraints Upon Retail Competition* (East Lansing, Mich.: Michigan State University, 1965); Joe S. Bain, *Industrial Organization* (New York: John Wiley and Sons, Inc., 1959); and *Manual of Federal Trade Regulations,* ed. by James J. Bliss and Ira M. Millstein (New York: National Retail Merchants' Association, 1963).

The second is legislation that attempts to limit price discrimination in favor of large buyers of merchandise for resale. The third set of laws are those directly concerned with regulating retail prices — fair trade laws and a number of minor laws, namely unfair trade practice acts and minimum markup laws. The fourth section is concerned with restrictions on promotional activities of retailers; in particular, the various advertising controls will be discussed in detail. The fifth set of laws are the numerous local ordinances that restrict the practices of retailers. The last section is a discussion of social pressures and consumerism, the latter the most recent potent force affecting the retailer.

Legislation

Up to this point our study has covered one of the two major uncontrollable factors in the retailer's environment, namely, competition. The other, the consumer, is covered in the next three chapters. Though both are essentially beyond the retailer's control, each can, to a limited extent, be controlled. For example, a retail food chain can build so many food outlets in a given area that it thereby restricts the entry of other firms. Though this is admittedly a rare occurrence, in theoretical terms it is possible. Again, though the consumer is considered to be an uncontrollable part of the retailer's environment, certain elements of control do occur. For example, a powerful advertising campaign can have the long-run effect of attracting consumers into a store the prices of whose products are not commensurate with their value. In support of this are the many articles and studies that have been written on consumer ignorance or discrimination at the retail level. However, for all practical purposes, both the consumer and the competition are an uncontrollable part of the retailer's environment.

The third factor in the retailer's uncontrollable environment, legal restraints and social pressures, is completely uncontrollable. The retailer must adhere to the prevailing laws and local customs, and in fact he can do little to change these pressures on his own. In a sense by joining associations he can attempt to change the laws or influence the writing of new laws. However, this usually results in all of his competitors being treated similarly and hence he fails to attain an advantage. As an individual, he is in the position of having little influence in bringing about changes in legislation.

Background

In the pages that follow, much will be said concerning the many levels of legislation that restrict the operations of the retailer and his relations with the public and his suppliers. Most legislation has arisen out of conflict — conflict between the retailer and the consumer; the retailer and other retailers; the retailer and his suppliers.

Conflicts between the consumer and the retailer arise out of the basic psychological relationship of the seller's trying to impress the buyer with the value of his goods. Much of this conflict arises when the seller is overenthusiastic about his merchandise. His enthusiasm may be reflected in his indulgence in exaggerated praise of his store or products. Or, instead of mere indulgence, his exaggeration may be a deliberate attempt to defraud the public.

Within the bounds of the retailer's relationship with other retailers and vendors, three types of conflict exist — among horizontal, intertype, and vertical competitors.[2] "Horizontal" refers to retailers of the same type, "Intertype" refers to competition among retailers carrying approximately the same type of merchandise, but using different methods of distribution; an example might be the discount house and the department store. "Vertical" is conflict and competition recognized in the relationship of the retailer with his suppliers: the haggling over prices between a food retailer and a major supplier of canned vegetables represents this kind of competitive conflict.

Much of the legislation is aimed at controlling the conflicts that arise in interactions. For example, chain store taxes, mentioned below, were brought about by intertype conflicts that arose because of the growth and development of food chains and their entry into areas where independent grocery stores had existed for many years. Much of the Robinson-Patman Act is concerned with large retail firms gaining unfair advantages over smaller firms. The act attempts to control the relationship between the manufacturer and the retailer by setting up agencies to police the provisions of the act. Regardless of its success the act recognized that many retailers, through pure economic power, were able to secure favorable prices and terms.

How does legislation develop in a democratic society? It comes about when people in conflict organize their economic power and convert it into dynamic political power. Thus, druggists in order to protect themselves against intertype conflict (in the form of discounters) have been a strong force in the passing of fair trade or price maintenance legislation. Just as workers have recognized their group affiliation and have expressed it in unionization, retailers have also achieved such cohesion — whether on the national, state, or local level.

Direct Impact of Legislation on the Retailer

Though all retailers are affected by the various laws in effect on a local, state, or national level, perhaps the most dramatic impact of legislation can be found in the liquor store. This outlet in most states is affected by all kinds of legislation, because of the nature of the products sold. As noted by many analysts, the free dispensing of liquor has been strongly opposed by religious groups of many faiths, their view being that low-priced liquor can cause the break-up of families or have a deleterious effect on the individual's moral character. Rightly or wrongly, the legislators are usually aware of this powerful lobby when they consider a change in the liquor laws.

New York State laws would seem to be typical of the type of regulations that the retailer must cope with. Some of the major regulations are:

1. Laws that restrict the types of products the retailer must carry in a liquor store in New York State. For instance, a liquor store in New York may not carry beer or food products.

2. Laws restricting the age of the buyer. Buyers of liquor in New York State must be over 18 years of age.

[2]Joseph Cornwall Palamountain, Jr., *The Politics of Distribution* (Cambridge, Mass.: Harvard University Press, 1955), p. 24.

3. Laws that restrict the price that may be charged at the retail level. Prices of wine are price fixed by the state. Prices of hard liquor must be marked up a minimum of 12 per cent.

4. Laws restricting the wholesale price. Distillers selling in New York State must match the lowest price they charge in any of the other 49 states in selling to wholesalers.

5. Laws that restrict the selling hours. Stores must close on stipulated holidays and are not allowed to sell liquor on Sunday.

6. Laws restricting advertising. Stores are not allowed to advertise selling prices in newspapers.

7. Laws setting license requirements. In order to sell liquor one must obtain a state license.

8. Laws affecting store locations. Store must be located a stipulated distance from churches and schools.

Special Assessments

Laws restricting the entrance of competition have been enforced at various levels throughout most of this century. Ordinances at the local level and licensing legislation have always been a favored device of retail businessmen to restrict competition. For example, licenses have been used to restrict the number of barbers and pharmacists at both the state and the local level. One survey showed that approximately seventy-five such professions were licensed by one or more states in 1952.[3]

Possibly the most deliberate attempt to restrict the number of competitors were the chain store taxes levied on chains in each state. The taxes were punitive in the sense that they required each chain to pay a progressive tax based on the number of stores operating in that state. In some cases the state levied taxes on the stores both within and outside of the taxing state. These taxes were levied in twenty-nine states, and as of 1960 fourteen states still maintained the tax.[4] Minimum taxes per store ranged from $100, to $750.[5] It is the consensus of analysts that this tax did not hinder to any noticeable extent the growth of chain stores.

The idea of chain store taxes originated during the 1920's and 1930's when depressed business conditions and the growth of chains caused a sales and profit squeeze on the more numerous independent stores. These laws were aimed particularly at the food chains that were growing at a rapid rate, particularly during the 1930's. Coincident with these laws some of the smaller cities started "buy local" campaigns; that is, they encouraged consumers to purchase their food products from the local independent. Here again, these campaigns failed simply because the lower prices of the chains overcame any chauvinistic appeals by the local merchants.

Restrictions On "Bigness"

The Sherman Anti-Trust Act of 1890 represented the first attempt by the government to control big business and particularly restraint of trade. Sections 1

Restrictive
Laws

---

[3]Hollander, *op. cit.,* p. 30.
[4]Hollander, *op. cit.,* p. 31.
[5]Bain, *op. cit.,* p. 564.

and 2 were especially important in that they condemned monopoly and conspiracies in restraint of such trade. The ineffectiveness of this act soon became apparent, and in 1914 Congress passed the Clayton Act, which recognized in more specific terms some of the restraints on trade. Section 2 was concerned with price discrimination; Section 3 with tying and exclusive agreements; and Section 7 with the acquisition of stock by one corporation in another. The key phrase of the act is the words "... where the effect of such discrimination may be substantially to lessen competition or tend to create a monopoly in any line of commerce...." This phrase, of course, is subject to interpretation, and the strength of the law has rested on Court interpretation.

In 1936 Congress amended the Clayton Act (Section 2) in response to the competition of chain stores and, in particular, to their abuse of buying power, which resulted in a great deal of price discrimination at the wholesale level. In many cases threats by chains to buy from other manufacturers resulted in what the Congress considered to be discriminatory concessions. This amendment, known as the Robinson-Patman Act, attempted to eliminate these price concessions.

The Robinson-Patman Act did accomplish a number of things. First, it strengthened the Federal Trade Commission. Set up in 1914 under the Clayton Act, the commission had lacked sufficient authority to prosecute many of the violations. Under the Robinson-Patman Act, it gained in stature. Whereas the Clayton Act was concerned with injury to competition, Congress saw fit under the amendment to recognize injury to individuals. Instead of dealing only with a monopolist's impact on the total industry, the act concerned itself with individual purchasers.

In addition, the Federal Trade Commission was given the power to establish limits on quantity discounts, forbid brokerage allowances to all except independent brokers, forbid promotional allowances (such as cooperative advertising) except where available to all competitors on proportionally equal terms.[6] The forbidding of brokerage allowances was a direct result of an investigation of the activities of a wholly owned brokerage subsidiary of the Great Atlantic and Pacific Tea Company. This firm acted as a broker on behalf of the A & P and eventually returned the brokerage commission to the company.

The impact of this act is open to question. In one sense it made companies more aware that the government was watching them; hence flagrant violations were eliminated in most cases. On the other hand, the growth of mass distribution has continued despite this act. The reasons for this phenomenon are simple. The success of these stores was not based simply on receiving price concessions. Their ability to offer the consumer lower prices through self-service, centralize tasks, reduce advertising costs per store through economies of scale, and generally collect top management under one roof all played a vital role. In addition, the large-scale retailers had other ways of avoiding the provisions of the act.

One of their first steps toward avoidance was to develop specification buying. Thus, retail firms in a sense would develop their own products and go into the market and ask manufacturers to supply these products to their specifications. If this was not in line with the retailer's way of doing business, the firm would simply contract for the manufacturer's entire output and hence avoid his offering different

---

[6]Marshall C. Howard, *Legal Aspects of Marketing* (New York: McGraw-Hill Book Company, 1964, p. 8.

prices to similar firms. As a last resort the firm could simply purchase its own manufacturing facilities and avoid all of the technical problems of the act.[7] In a previous chapter it was noted that A & P, one of the intended victims of the act, purchased a nut and a dairy products company. As a result, consumers received comparable products at a lower retail price.

Regulating Prices

Organizations of small retailers have been after both the state and federal government to pass legislation enabling the manufacturer to establish a retail price for his product, in the hope of eliminating price competition at the retail level. Many vigorous battles have taken place in both the Congress and the various state legislatures within the past thirty-five years. Most recently Congress has held hearings on a fair trade act under the name of the Quality Stabilization Act, which in essence allows the manufacturer to control the retail price of his product.

California was the first state to pass fair trade legislation. Two problems ensued concerning this legislation. In the first place such legislation violated the Sherman Anti-Trust Act, as in effect it restricted competition. Its restriction on price competition included the so-called non-signer clause. According to this clause all resellers of products are subject to an agreement signed with one retailer in a state. This problem was overcome by the passage of two laws: the Miller-Tydings Act of 1937 and the McGuire-Keogh Act of 1952. The first amended the Sherman Act and exempted these price-fixing agreements; the second exempted the non-signer clause from the same Sherman Act.

The second problem revolves around state fair trade acts. Though these acts have been somewhat effective, they have been unable to control sales that originate outside the state. As the buyer takes title to goods in the state where it is sold, many mail order firms and distributors found that they were not governed by price-fixing agreements.

One other problem that has developed in the past few years is that the non-signer clauses have been under fire in many states and have not proven to be effective. Thus, a manufacturer must show a great deal of vigor to enforce any of his fair trade contracts.

Why do manufacturers participate in such agreements at the retail level? The answer is manifold. However, the major reason is to keep their small, independent customers happy. In addition, pre-fixed prices and margins mean that the retailer will probably emphasize one manufacturer's product in preference to others. In recent years one advocate of maintaining retail prices has been the Revlon Company. This policy, however, has forced the company to spend thousands of dollars to obtain court orders and for general policing of all types of retailers.

Of course, a company that wants to maintain prices at the retail level need not resort to fair trade pricing. It can simply control the distribution of its products, making certain that price cutters do not obtain its products. The Magnavox Company, a manufacturer of television and radio products, is an example of a company that controls the sale of its products to retailers. As a result this firm gets special preference in many of the traditional outlets that compete against the

---

[7]Bain, *op. cit.,* pp. 572-573.

price-cutting discount houses. On the other hand, the Magnavox Company is faced with the problem of limited distribution since most television and radio sets are sold through the numerous specialty and discount houses that engage in price cutting.

Yet many manufacturers do attempt to maintain retail prices. Professor Hollander estimates that the proportion of total goods sold that is "fair traded" is around 10 per cent.

Does fair trade actually help the small retailer? The answer to this question is difficult to come by. Theoretically, it would seem that fixed pricing is a small retailer's dream since he does not have to compete on the basis of price. It would also seem that retailers in fair trade states would probably fare better and be less likely to fail. Statistics do not support this observation, however.

In Table 4-1 we see that the drugstores in the fair trade states have not done any better than those in states not having fair trade laws. For instance, in the most recent year failures and bankruptcies in states having fair trade laws seem to be much the higher.

TABLE 4-1   Fair-Trade and Non-Fair-Trade Area Statistics

| | *Line Percentage of Total* | | | |
| | *1958* | | *1954* | |
Item	*Fair-Trade States*	*Non-Fair-Trade States*	*Fair-Trade States*	*Non-Fair-Trade States*
1. Population	62.1	37.9	82.7	17.3
2. Retail Stores	62.2	37.8	83.1	16.9
3. Retail Sales	62.65	37.35	82.2	17.8
4. Drugstores	61.3	38.7	80.9	19.1
5. Drugstore Sales	61.4	38.6	79.7	20.3
6. Merchant Bankruptcies	62.2	37.8	83.9	16.1
7. Retail Store Failures	73.3	26.7	89.8	10.2
8. Drugstore Failures	67.9	32.1	82.6	17.4

Source: Adapted from Steward Munro Lee, "The Impact of Fair-Trade Laws on Retailing," *Journal of Retailing,* Vol. 41, No. 1 (Spring, 1965).

One thing seems sure, however, and that is that fair trade laws are evaded by most retailers. Aside from the shipments from out of state, retailers can give discounts to choice customers, over-allowances on trade-ins and extra trading stamps in lieu of a direct cash discount. These are just a few of the gimmicks that can be used to overcome resale price maintenance.

More important, however, is the belief among most opponents of these bills that fair trade is simply a device for helping the less efficient retailers and is against the public interest in the sense that it probably means higher prices to the consuming public. Thus, most efforts toward enforcement and the development of new legislation are usually halfhearted.

Many states have attempted to control retail prices by simply setting minimum markup standards. Though the laws vary from state to state, they make it illegal to sell certain specified products below cost. The problem arises as to what represents costs. Costs always include the purchase cost of the merchandise to the retailer and an additional margin sufficient to cover his costs of doing business. If his costs of doing business are below this minimum markup, he is allowed to sell below the minimum standards.

These laws are presently on the books in 42 states. However, in 11 of these states they apply only to the sale of cigarettes. Of the remaining 31 state laws, 5 have been declared unconstitutional. The laws came about as an attempt to stop the chain stores from selling "loss-leader" merchandise, which was a particularly effective weapon against the independent store. (Loss-leader selling refers to pricing items below cost in order to attract customers to a store.) These laws, however, had little impact on reducing the amount of loss-leader selling or stifling the growth of chains.

The reason for their failure was obvious. First, the minimum markup standards were in most cases so low that a sizeable reduction in price could be made without violating the law. Second, the law could only be applied to comparable merchandise. Therefore, only branded merchandise had to adhere to these controls; a host of other merchandise would have to be investigated and its applicability to the law decided on an individual basis.

Promotion and Communication Restraints

Communication in the retail store refers mainly to the various ways in which the retailer communicates with the consumer. The retailer's ability to communicate with the consumer and his persuasive powers govern his ability to make profits. If the consumer can be convinced that the retailer is selling him goods and services with a high value at a price that is particularly attractive, then he will purchase the merchandise and perhaps remain a customer.

Newspaper advertising and in-store displays are the main ways of communicating these values to the consumer. However, their powers of persuasion and the results attained oftentimes tempt retailers to exaggerate the values of the merchandise they are offering for sale. Early in the twentieth century the government recognized the tendency of many retail firms to deceive the public and eventually passed the Federal Trade Commission Act of 1914. Though this act was not aimed specifically at retailers, eventually many of the cases and powers of the commission came under this act. Particularly since World War II the commission has taken a much more militant attitude toward deceptive retail advertising.

The powers of the Federal Trade Commission (FTC) derive from Section 5 of the act, which makes it unlawful for any firm to engage in "any unfair method of competition or unfair or deceptive act or practice in commerce." Obviously misleading advertising and mislabeling of products come under this section. Mislabeling became so blatant that it was recognized that further legislation was needed to enhance the powers of the FTC. Hence, many acts were passed, aimed specifically at the most obvious product violations of the Federal Trade Commission Act. Two of the most recent were the Fur Products Labeling Act and the Textile Fiber Products Identification Act (discussed below).

⑴ Misleading Advertising

Misleading advertising takes one of two forms: *deceptive price advertising* or *misleading information* concerning the status of the seller or the type of product being sold.

Price advertising has become a major center of controversy throughout the postwar period. The activity of the FTC in this area of business has increased tremendously, and decisions and discussions have been of such a nature as to appear in the news columns of many daily newspapers on a regular basis. This is in direct contrast with the prewar period, when this type of activity in Washington was almost unknown to the public.

Two reasons can be offered for this change. First, the resale price maintenance contracts were invalidated by many states. For example, by 1963 the Supreme Courts of twenty states had declared the state fair trade laws to be unenforceable.[8] The lack of enforcement at this level meant in effect that retailers could refer to the fair trade price as a list price, regardless of whether or not it was an actual market price. Second, the postwar period saw an enormous increase in discount houses with their ever-present emphasis on price competition. Their growth throughout this period has forced other more traditional retailers to meet price competition, particularly advertised prices. In addition, the increasing awareness of discount competition by the traditional stores and their attempts to meet this competition have led the discount firms to exaggerate their price savings claims even more. Thus, the FTC has been swamped with reports of price violations during this period.

Forms of Deceptive Price Advertising

False advertising of merchandise can take many forms. For example, a recent advertiser of perfumes failed to state that the product he was selling was not the well-known perfume but a cologne. Thus, a large price differential was hidden by a lack of proper identification of the merchandise being sold.[9]

Possibly one of the knottiest problems that has arisen involves the use of such terms as "originally," "suggested retail price," "usually," and "regularly." For example, a product such as a television set may be advertised as follows:

21-inch Television Set Black and White
Originally $199 Our Price — $129

The question arises as to the meaning of the term "originally." If the store had been selling the television set at the higher price ($199), then the use of the term "originally" is perfectly correct. More likely, however, the firm has never sold this set at the higher price since this price represents a list price or the manufacturer's

---

[8] Bliss and Millstein, *op. cit.,* p. 75.
[9] Bliss and Millstein, *op. cit.,* p. 43.

suggested retail price. On the other hand, if a retail firm in the retailer's immediate area had been selling this television set at the list price then the retailer would be perfectly correct in advertising the product as a discount from the original value.

"Two for one" sales have come under the scrutiny of the FTC. Here again the above rules for "originally" and other similar terms apply. Thus, the comparative price for both items must refer to the prices charged in the customary course of the firm's business or must be the customary price in the same trading area.

Deceptive Advertising

Aside from challenging misleading price advertising, the FTC has taken an interest in other forms of false and misleading advertising. Most recently it has started to discourage the use of such terms as "wholesale price," "sold directly from the factory to you," and similar terms that imply a price well below the usual retail price. The extent of FTC enforcement can be seen in a recent case where the commission forced a discount chain to drop the name "Mills" from the company name Atlantic Mills, since the use of the name "Mills" implied that the customer was dealing directly with the manufacturer of the merchandise. As the chain was not engaged in manufacturing, the FTC believed that the title was misleading. An interesting aspect of the case is that the firm had used this name for a number of years before the FTC decided to prosecute the case.

Bait Advertising

Bait advertising is an insincere offer to sell a product or service which the advertiser, in truth, does not intend or want to sell.[10] The use of this technique has become quite common among certain types of promotional stores. Typically, a promotional appliance store may advertise a 21-inch black-and-white television set at a price of $79.95 on a given day. The firm has no intention of selling this product and many of the salesmen in the store jokingly refer to the product as being "nailed down." Why then does a retail firm advertise without intent to sell the product?

The answer lies in the development of many successful, though controversial, sales techniques. In the usual case the customer enters the store fully intending to purchase a low-priced television set. He is approached by the salesman and is immediately discouraged from buying the product. In some cases the salesman may even go so far as to refuse to show or demonstrate the product. In other cases because of disparaging remarks about the product and a refusal to offer guarantees or credit terms, the sale may be deliberately lost. Coincidental with the disparaging remarks about the advertised product the salesman may demonstrate another product which he claims has many advantages over the advertised item. This technique, known as the "switch," deliberately attempts to sell the customer a product that is, for all intents and purposes, a better profit maker for the retailer than the advertised item.[11]

---

[10]"Guide Against Bait Advertising," *Federal Trade Commission,* November 24, 1959, p. 1.
[11]For a further development of this tactic, see Alfred Oxenfeldt, "Customer Types and Salesman Tactics in Appliance Selling," *Journal of Retailing,* Vol. 39, No. 4 (Winter 1963-1964), p. 13.

There are many variations of this selling and advertising technique. For example, in the automobile field many car dealers will take orders for automobiles at prices they know they cannot possibly deliver. However, when the delivery date arrives, the customer is informed that the automobile has arrived with expensive accessory equipment and is presented with an automobile that he can either take or leave. It has been found among many of the automobile dealers that the customer is most likely to take the automobile since he has already waited a number of weeks for delivery.

The FTC is, of course, opposed to bait advertising and "switch" selling techniques. In guides that they offer to businessmen they make the following statement: "No advertisement containing an offer to sell a product should be published when the offer is not a bona fide effort to sell the advertised product."[12]

Deceptive Labeling

In addition to misleading advertising, the government through the FTC has seen fit to restrict labeling practices in all types of retail firms. Many of the abuses in labeling have arisen within certain product lines. For example, in recent years the price wars in the tire field have prompted the FTC to issue Tire Advertising Guides (May 20, 1958). The FTC also managed to prod Congress into passing legislation to control some of the more blatant labeling practices. It should be noted that many of these practices were aimed at the supplier of the merchandise rather than the retailer, who was often unable to correctly determine the materials that went into the finished product. Two of these acts, discussed below, are concerned with furs and textile products.

Fur Products Labeling Act

This act covers practically all middlemen and retailers of fur products. For many years it was a practice to simply call a product by its broad species name, though the animal might be found in various parts of the world, and the quality of the fur differ according to origin. In addition many of these fur products used other skins for trimming that were of an inferior quality. The regulation as it finally passed Congress contained controls on the labeling of these products. For example, the act insisted that certain required information be on all labels. Thus, if the product is dyed, bleached, or otherwise artificially colored then the label must state this. Where the fur piece is composed of pieces or used fur, the customer must be informed of this in both the advertising and labeling. The country of origin must also be printed on the label. Great pains were taken in the act to insure exact definitions of terms. For example, the term "Persian Lamb" may be used only to describe the skin of the young lamb of the Karakul breed of sheep or top-cross breed of such sheep, having hair formed in a certain way.

All in all, the act has greatly decreased the retailers' latitude in advertising and labeling fur products.

---

[12] Bliss and Millstein, *op. cit.*, p. 162.

The Textile Fiber Products Identification Act is similar to the Fur Products Labeling Act in that it attempts to control misleading advertising and labeling. Under this act each apparel product must contain the following basic information:

1. The generic names and the percentages of fiber content contained in each textile product. Example: 55 per cent Dacron and 45 per cent Wool.
2. The name of the manufacturer.
3. The name of the country where the product was manufactured.

Here again the act goes into great detail. For example, many textile products use trim or ornamentation. Often this trim contains material not in the rest of the product. The Act, therefore, in order to keep the labeling problem reasonable, allows manufacturers to ignore this additional material (which may be inserted only for strengthening purposes). However, in all of the above cases they must mention the term "Exclusive of Ornamentation" directly below the listing of the fiber content of the product, provided the additional fiber does not exceed 5 per cent of the total fiber weight.

Other Regulations

In this section we have attempted to cover a number of the major restrictions on retailing; the retailer is also faced with numerous local and state restrictions. For example, the many restrictions on Sunday openings for retail firms vary from state to state and municipality to municipality, and the actual workings of these laws vary tremendously. Each state and municipality allows certain retail establishments to remain open. For example, many food stores, restaurants, and drugstores are allowed to keep their businesses operating on Sunday. On the other hand, the local liquor store is probably forced to close on Sunday — and on many of the national, state, and local holidays. Yet, in spite of these restrictions, it has been found that more and more retail establishments have been opening on Sunday, particularly in areas of the country where discount houses have located.

Zoning ordinances have always been used to restrict entrance into retailing. Typically, shopping centers have been kept out of many cities through this technique. Where zoning restrictions fail, local merchants may insist that the city rigidly enforce fire laws which can keep many types of retailing establishments out of an area. In one particular city in Eastern Maryland, the local motel owner kept a large competing motel out of his city by simply getting the city government to refuse to build additional sewerage lines to the new property.

All in all, the retailer is faced with many legislative and court-determined restrictions on his operations.

Aside from the foregoing legislative restrictions, retailers are faced in many cases with social pressures that restrict their ability to compete and set prices at the level they desire. William T. Kelley pointed out in his study of Collegeville that retailers

*Social
Pressures*

experience a great deal of social pressure in a small city.[13] For example, he found that prices charged by Collegeville retailers were appreciably higher for most items than those found in a city twenty miles away. The tendency, he noted, was not to charge outrageously high prices but to adhere to the manufacturer's suggested or "fair trade" prices.

In further studying this city, Professor Kelley found that there were many reasons for this situation. Possibly the major reason was what he called "solidarity." That is, though there was no overt collusion among the local merchants, there did exist a relationship that helped keep out intruders and at the same time maintain the local price structure. As a matter of fact, it was found that there was a general sentiment against any price cutting by not only the merchants in the city but many of the townspeople. In effect, what this study brings out is that many of the retailers in a small town stand the chance of being socially ostracized if they do not adhere to the rigid price policies of the city.

Obviously, this situation cannot take place where a number of outside stores or promotional discount firms enter the market. However, in many of these small cities, the national price-cutting chain is unwilling to enter the market simply because their break-even volume cannot be attained in cities of this size.

Consumerism

A somewhat paralegal force that has developed in the past five years is referred to as "consumerism." Though consumerism is still in an evolutionary stage, its force has become so powerful that it is affecting all levels of business. Though no definition can adequately describe consumerism at this time, it nevertheless has certain characteristics. First and foremost, as a social force, it represents consumer groups. Second, it is usually viewed by businessmen as being somewhat anti-business. Third, its means of operation is to call public attention to its activities.

If one were to define consumerism, one might suggest the following: *Consumerism is the term that describes efforts by organized groups to call attention to business activities that are seen to be detrimental to the best interests of the consumers they represent.*

Effect of Consumerism

Within a few short years, consumerism has had a strong effect on legislation and the actions of many retail firms. Laws establishing unit pricing[14] (presently in effect in New York City and the State of Massachusetts) setting safety standards for automobiles or establishing pollution controls in industrial areas are all direct or indirect results of the growing tide of consumerism.

History of Consumerism

The history of consumerism has yet to be written. However, it is clear to many observers that several happenings have had a direct effect on the growth of this movement.

---

[13]"Small-Town Monopoly, A Case Study," *Journal of Retailing,* Summer, 1965, p. 63.

[14]This law requires that the food-store operator show clearly the price by weight, volume, or other unit of measure on each item of merchandise sold.

Perhaps the basis for the growth of consumerism is in the early civil-rights marches and campaigns launched in the South and in many northern cities. Though not directly related, several phenomena developed from these activities that gave impetus to the consumer movement.

The first aspect was the *activism* seen in the marches through the streets of Montgomery, Alabama, and many other cities. Though this phenomenon was not particularly new in the rest of the world, it was a rather recent addition to the American scene.

The second aspect was the *challenging of authority* through many useful devices such as boycotts, again a phenomenon of the civil-rights movement. The challenge to authority took place through the ignoring of local laws against demonstrations and a willingness to go to jail in defiance of laws considered to be unjust. Boycotting occurred wherever the movement found it useful to boycott merchants and thus cause a local economic crisis.

The civil-rights tactics were used by other activists in the consumerism cause. For example, in the early sixties a large group of Denver housewives successfully used the economic boycott and marches to challenge high prices and the use of trading stamps in Denver supermarkets.

Naderism

The challenge to authority was probably best demonstrated by the growth in stature of Ralph Nader. Nader came into national prominence upon the publication of his book *UNSAFE AT ANY SPEED,* which pointed out that many American cars were unsafe and that most car manufacturers had little interest in car safety. As a result of Nader's challenge to the authority of some of America's largest business interests, the Congress and many states passed and established auto safety standards, and the end of this impact is still not in sight.

Though Naderism started in the area of car safety, it is branching out into all areas in which there is a feeling that consumer or public interest is at issue. Thus the work of the Federal Trade Commission and all other federal agencies is being carefully scrutinized by people closely associated with this movement.

Other Developments

Consumerism is developing and growing in many ways. On the local level one finds groups challenging the credit policies of stores and banks. Many groups have banded together to challenge the rate structure of the telephone and electric-power companies.

The cities and states have taken more interest in the growth of this movement and have started to enforce and plan legal techniques to protect the consumer. For instance, in New York State an installment contract with a seller of merchandise does not take effect until three days after it is signed. Thus, if a door-to-door salesman sells a consumer a product on an installment basis, the consumer need not carry out the terms of the contract if within the prescribed time limits he notifies the selling firm of his intent not to honor the agreement. This law was passed in order to avoid the problems that ensued when people signed a contract, only to find out at a later date that they had not known what they were signing.

On a national level one finds several changes. First is the fact that the President has been forced to recognize the growth and challenges of consumerism by appointing a consumer advisor. Presently, under the Nixon Administration, Mrs. Virginia Knauer holds that post.

Second, Congress has recognized consumerism as a political challenge, and many have taken up the cry. For instance, hearings have been held in Washington by various Congressmen investigating the pricing policies of food chains in ghetto areas of the major cities. Congress recently enacted a credit bill that makes it mandatory for firms charging interest to indicate the annual rate on each bill to the recipient.[15]

The aggressiveness of many of the participants in these hearings can be seen in the testimony of Robert B. Choate who testified before the Subcommittee on the Consumer Committee on Commerce of the U.S. Senate.[16] His testimony was based on a study he prepared, including the chart shown in Figure 4-1, in which he indicated the nutrient content of the 60 major cereals marketed in the U.S. He also noted the cost per ounce to the consumer. One can see that the cost per ounce is not necessarily related to the nutritional value of the product. For instance, his study indicated that the cost per ounce for the top 20 brands with the highest nutritional value was 3.8 cents; 4.5 cents for the middle 20, and 4.4 cents for the bottom 20. Aside from the cost relationship to nutrition, Mr. Choate presented several other important observations. First, was the fact that over 50 of the 60 cereals are sugar-frosted, sugar-coated or sweetened at the factory. This, he believes, has serious consequences for children's teeth.

Most importantly, he points out that the cereals being touted by many of the companies on television rank low nutritionally. Of the nine Kellogg "television" cereals he observed that only two are in the top 20 nutritionally. Of the cereals promoted by other major cereal manufacturers on Saturday morning shows (each with a budget exceeding $500,000) none are in the top nine nutritionally and, he adds, all contain sugar. One of the major advertisers (but not a Saturday advertiser), Wheaties, ranks 29th nutritionally. Though many of Kellogg's products rank low nutritionally, the company has attained 43 per cent of the cereal market. Its best sellers, Kellogg's Corn Flakes (9 per cent of the market), Rice Krispies (5 per cent), and Sugar Frosted Flakes (5 per cent), rank 38th, 39th, and last nutritionally.

The testimony of Mr. Choate received widespread publicity and caused some change in the retail buying habits of many families. In addition many of the firms added nutrients to their cereal lines.

The recent ban by the Federal Trade Commission on television advertising of cigarettes would seem to be an extension of the consumerism effect. One might also note that the environment and pollutants, whether waste from a factory or no-deposit bottles scarring the countryside, are prime targets for this continuing force.

---

[15] *Consumer Credit Cost Disclosure,* Public Law 90-321, May 29, 1968.
[16] "The Seduction of the Innocent," July 23, 1970.

Rating Chart: Cumulative Nutrient Content of Dry Breakfast Cereals*   FIGURE 4-1

	100 200 300 400 500 600 700 800	Cost Per Ounce
1. Kellogg's Product 19		5.4¢
2. General Mills Kaboom		5.6
3. General Mills Total		5.1
4. Nabisco 100% Bran		2.4
5. Quaker Oats Life		3.7
6. General Foods Fortified Oat Flakes		3.6
7. Kellogg's Special K		5.6
8. General Foods Super Sugar Crisp		3.4
9. Kellogg's Sugar Smacks		4.5
10. Kellogg's 40% Bran Flakes		3.1
11. Quaker Oats Quake		5.6
12. Quaker Oats Quisp		5.6
13. Kellogg's Raisin Bran		2.9
14. General Foods Bran Flakes		2.7
15. General Foods Raisin Bran		2.9
16. General Foods Bran and Prune Flakes		4.2
17. Ralston Purina Wheat Chex		3.0
18. Ralston Purina Raisin Bran Chex		2.8
19. Kellogg's All Bran		2.5
20. Kellogg's Bran Buds		2.2
21. Kellogg's Froot Loops		5.6
22. Kellogg's Apple Jacks		5.9
23. Quaker Oats Puffed Wheat		7.4
24. General Mills Clackers		4.3
25. General Mills Cheerios		4.1
60. Kellogg's Sugar Frosted Flakes		4.1

Legend: ■ Protein   ≡ Calcium   ▦ Iron   ▨ Niacin, Thiamine (B_1), Riboflavin (B_2)
▨ Vitamin A   ☐ Vitamin C   ▦ Vitamin D

*The sum of percentages of minimum daily requirements in nine nutrient categories. Adapted from Robert B. Choate and Associates, 1346 Connecticut Avenue, N. W., Washington, D. C. 20036, June, 1970.

Impact of Consumerism

The growth of consumerism has had a direct impact on government on all levels. Much of this action has affected both legal and quasilegal actions of governmental bodies.

On a national level the impact on the federal government has grown substantially. The government's reaction has been both direct and indirect.

Directly, the consumer movement has resulted in the federal government's passing laws and establishing important guidelines for business that will hopefully aid the consumer. The laws have ranged from federal government control over consumer information on credit to forcing automobile dealers to post manufacturers' suggested list prices on all new automobiles. As noted, the establishment of a Presidential advisor on consumer affairs represents direct government action.

Indirectly, the government action has been just as persuasive taking the form of Congressional hearings that expose the failings of many companies to deal with serious consumer problems. For example, in May of 1971 the Senate held hearings concerning the maintenance costs of automobiles. Much of the testimony revolved around the fact that American consumers spend millions of dollars on parts and maintenance. One witness was Ralph Nader.

The federal government also uses many of its directives and publicity devices on the consumer's behalf. For example, recently the Federal Drug Administration (FDA) announced that swordfish has such a high mercury content that it is judged to be dangerous. The FDA has taken the position that mercury in food can cause tumors and mouth ulcers, produce birth defects, cause kidney disease, and affect the central nervous system.

In recent months the FDA has started a program of reexamining drugs now on the market, to determine whether they are as effective as the manufacturers and the physicians using the drugs believe. This action derives from a law passed in 1962 that gave the FDA the power to determine both the effectiveness and the safety of drugs on the market.

The government has also engaged special study groups to examine problems related to the consumer. For example, the government recently established a National Commission on Product Safety. After many months of study, this commission reported that many products pose unacceptable risks for the consumer. Some of these are listed in Table 4-2. They range all the way from architectural glass to the wringer washing machine. Some, of course, represent small product markets; but as in the case of television sets, publication of hazard warnings can be damaging to markets that represent major industries.

Many of these reports uncover damaging information. For example, the *National Commission on Product Safety* had this to say about glass bottles:

> . . . we find that glass bottles used for carbonated beverages present an unreasonable risk to consumers. When one of these bottles fails, the glass under internal pressure bursts into splinters. Because of this pressure, bottles of carbonated drinks are more hazardous than those containing inert beverages.
>
> Although explosions are the most dramatic cause of injury from glass bottles, they are not the most common. Insurance companies reported more claims related to glass bottles than to any other consumer product.
>
> . . . Responses to our inquiries from the six largest bottlers indicate that 5,000 to 7,000 injuries are reported annually. Hospital records confirm that glass bottles consistently rank high among products connected with injuries treated in emergency clinics.

In most cases in which the commission reports point an accusing finger at an industry, the firms in that industry may take action in order to avoid government restrictions. Many times the industry responds by setting up minimum industry standards to overcome publicized product failings. Though this may not have been the industry practice in previous years, with the growth of the consumer movement, many industries are reluctant to ignore such reports.

State and Local Levels

On the state and local levels approaches similar to that of the federal government are used. Many states have attempted to aid the consumer by concentrating on the

Product	Hazard
Architectural glass	Insufficient use of safety glazing
Color television sets	Fires resulting from high voltages
Fireworks	Explosion, fire
Floor furnaces	Floor grate temperatures of 300-400 F
Glass bottles	Weak or thin glass that explodes or shatters
High-rise bicycles	Poor stability, unsafe design features
Hot-water vaporizers	Easily upset, spilling scalding water
Household chemicals	Petroleum distillates, caustics, and corrosives found in dishwasher detergents, furniture polishes, drain and toilet bowl cleaners
Infant furniture	Bars on cribs, easily-toppled highchairs
Ladders	Lack of nonslip feet, treads, end tips; sharp corners
Power tools	Lack of hoods, guards; shock hazards
Protective headgear	Lack of standards for sport and motorcycle helmets
Rotary lawnmowers	Lack of guards, hoods; failure to meet industry's own safety standards
Toys	Electrical, mechanical, and thermal hazards; deafening noise
Unvented gas heaters	Carbon monoxide
Wringer washing machines	Lack of safety-release mechanism long available for use

Source: *Business Week,* July 4, 1970, page 37.

powers of the state's top law official (usually the attorney general). This official has the power to conduct investigations of consumer complaints and advise the legislature on needed legislation. The law officer has the power to institute legal proceedings against corrupt firms and stop firms from conducting business in his state, if in his opinion they are defrauding the consumer.

At the local or citywide level, many consumer affairs departments have been instituted to help alert the consumer to business practices considered detrimental. New York City, in recent years, has established just such a department that presently is actively engaged in many programs on behalf of the consumer. Many of these practices are publicized by this department, which calls attention to short-weighting, misleading packaging, and high-fat content in hamburgers sold in retail stores.

At the county level a commission on consumer affairs checked out the availability and price marking of advertised specials in department, discount, and appliance stores in Nassau County, a suburban area of New York City.

In their study of advertised items they found:

1. Approximately 22 per cent of the advertised items were not visible to the public or were not available in the store.

2. Approximately 21 per cent of the advertised items were overpriced in the store.

Of the 89 stores checked, 83 stores failed to have all advertised merchandise visible, available, and properly marked at the advertised price! Though the commission did not reveal the names of the stores involved, it should be pointed out that practically all the major stores in New York City have branches in Nassau County.

Not all campaigns for consumerism are waged by governmental bodies. For example, in recent months the Allstate Insurance Company (owned by Sears, Roebuck) has waged a strong and well-publicized campaign to get American car manufacturers to produce cars with bumpers that will absorb punishment. In these ads Allstate has noted that a collision at five miles per hour can cause extensive car damage. The firm goes on to state that they will automatically reduce insurance premiums for anyone buying a car that will absorb the impact of a collision at speeds of ten miles per hour.

Cost of Consumerism

From the retail firm's point of view, consumerism can be costly. In some cases, many steps necessary to meet the demands of consumer groups can increase costs substantially. Many of these changes can result in higher prices and thus, in effect, the consumer may end up paying for consumerism.

In Table 4-3, one sees the results of a recent study of the cost of establishing a unit-pricing system in food chains. In this table, one can see that stores with a sales volume of up to $100,000 in chains with 20 or fewer stores incurred costs that exceeded 4 per cent of sales. In chain stores having 90 or more firms, one sees that the costs dropped dramatically. In the very large-sales-volume stores, that is, those with sales exceeding $2 million, the cost for the largest chain dropped to less than 1 per cent. One should also note that regardless of the sales volume, those chains with 20 or fewer stores incurred the highest cost of unit pricing in all volume groups. In essence, therefore, this study indicates that the smaller grocery chains incurred the highest cost in order to carry out unit pricing.

Other important points are raised in this study. It was noted that only about half the consumers perceived and understood unit pricing; most importantly, those least

TABLE 4-3   Direct Costs of Unit Pricing as a Per Cent of Sales by Size of Store and Organization

Sales Volume of Store	Number of Stores in Chain			
	20	40	60	90
Less than $100,000	4.15	3.61	3.43	3.31
$100-150,000	2.49	2.16	2.06	1.98
$150-300,000	1.38	1.20	1.14	1.10
$300-500,000	.78	.68	.64	.62
$500-1,000,000	.42	.36	.34	.33
$1,000-2,000,000	.21	.18	.17	.17
More than $2,000,000	.12	.10	.099	.095

Source: *Search, Agriculture,* Agricultural Economics 2, Cornell University Agricultural Experiment Station, New York State College of Agriculture, Ithaca, New York, p.9.

likely to understand are the disadvantaged groups, who are held to need the most help.

Those opposed to consumerism point out that if many of the consumer pressures are acted upon by business, the consumer may end up paying a high price for the results. In addition, many feel that the steps taken may not help those most in need of such protection.

Impact on Retailing

The growth of the consumerism movement has had a direct effect on the retailer. It has not only focused interest and publicity on the retailer but also caused an increase in new legislation at all levels of government. For instance the study cited earlier of "advertised specials" was conducted to implement a local Nassau County law passed on February 18, 1970, titled the "Unfair Trade Practices Law." Consumerism has caused a marked rise in the enactment of such laws.

The growth of this movement has also caused the stores to take heed of their advertising claims and the quality of their products. Retailers previously, in many instances could feel free to engage in questionable practices without fear of confronting any law. But with the passage of laws that force the retailer to divulge the cost of credit or give the consumer the right to see his credit-report files, the pendulum has swung in the direction of the consumer.

A recent ruling by the Supreme Court concerning a Florida repossession law continued this trend. In this case a retail store repossessed a gas stove and stereo set from a Mrs. Fuentes.[17] This customer had purchased the items by signing an installment agreement considered a typical contract, signed by millions of consumers. After making payments of $300 (the total cost was $500, plus a $100 finance charge), she refused to pay further when she became embroiled with the store over the servicing of the stove. The store obtained a writ against her, and the sheriff immediately seized the property without a hearing. At that time this procedure was permissible. However, the U.S. Supreme Court, when faced with the evidence in the case, ordered that all statutes of this kind should be struck down. The court was seemingly impressed with the fact that Mrs. Fuentes' merchandise was seized before she was allowed to confront the store in court. The decision made it more difficult for merchants to seize property without offering the consumer a day in court.

SUMMARY

One of the major restraints faced by the retailer is the complex of legislation at all levels of government. In addition the retailer must deal with the problems of social pressures and the most recent and dynamic force, consumerism.

Several sets of laws limit the retailer. The first set concerns restrictions on bigness through special assessments, such as chain-store taxes and licensing requirements set up at the state level. The second set of laws attempts to limit price concessions granted to large firms. These laws at the federal level include the

---

[17] *The New York Times,* August 7, 1972, p. 39.

Sherman Anti-Trust Act, the Clayton Act, and the Robinson-Patman Act.

The third set of laws is concerned with regulating prices. Here one considers fair trade laws, minimum markup laws, and laws restricting the use of "loss leaders."

The fourth set of laws is concerned with restraints on promotional activities of retailers, namely, advertising restraints. This includes restrictions on bait advertising and on the labeling of merchandise.

The last group of laws includes local ordinances respecting Sunday closings and other limitations on hours.

Social pressures and consumerism are powerful forces at the local level. The pressures from the local merchants to restrict innovative behavior on the part of other retailers are one form of social pressure that is widely exercised, particularly in small towns. However the most potent form of social pressure that has arisen in years is the consumerism movement. This movement has fostered the publicizing of activities that are considered to be detrimental to consumers. In addition it has spurred the proliferation of many new laws aimed at helping the consumer.

Epilogue   Prior to 1974, when writing about business, one could assume unlimited availability of land, labor, and capital. To build a new store called for a decision as to whether the return would be adequate to compensate the firm for the investment in land, labor, and capital. Since 1974 decision makers cannot accept as valid the theory of unlimited availability. Anyone asked to make such a decision now would *not* assume capital (defined as machinery, equipment, and energy) to be available without limit. The shortage of energy in the form of oil, as well as its spiraling cost, could act as a significant factor in determining the success of retail firms of the future.

Retailers have reacted to the energy shortage in a variety of ways. Some of the proposals are:[18]

> Dimming of store lighting
> Reduction of window display lighting
> Cutting back on Christmas lights and outdoor displays
> Lowering thermostats
> Using computers to regulate energy consumption

The situation has also influenced the type of goods sold. One finds, for instance, that sales of sweaters, blankets and fireplace accessories have soared.[19] Shopping centers have also been affected by the energy shortage. Gasoline shortages are bound to discourage shoppers and employees from driving long distances to distant regional shopping centers. Shoppers could start car pooling or maybe more realistically driving to centers with a friend. In regard to the employees of a large regional shopping center whose daily presence is required, the management may have to consider busing workers from a central staging area.

A question arises as to whether shoppers will stay away or whether the reverse will prevail with shoppers continuing to drive to the large distant center because of the large selection and variety of goods found there. The latter would eliminate the

---

[18] *The New York Times,* December 6, 1973.
[19] *Wall Street Journal,* December 19, 1973.

need for a second trip elsewhere. With gas short in supply, consumers will be less likely to drive from shopping center to shopping center in pursuit of a difficult to locate item.

A continued energy crisis could effect a great change in consumers' habits. Will shoppers become increasingly purposeful and less inclined toward impulse buying? If obtaining gas for the car becomes difficult, fewer shopping expeditions will be made "just to pass the time." Shopping for convenience goods then will also become more thoughtful with needs determining what will be purchased. Items forgotten or not available will in many cases be done without until the next planned-for shopping excursion.

Shopping in the city gains in appeal, when one can use public transportation to get there and the efficient mass transit systems to get around within the city. Some cities, New York among them, have special buses to facilitate shopping. A single fee enables the shopper to board and get off as many times as needed along the designated shopping routes. Perhaps some of these factors will help the downtown stores experience a revival.

QUESTIONS

1. How do the minimum markup laws differ from fair trade laws?

2. What are some problems in determining whether or not a food chain retailer has violated a minimum markup law when he sells a quart of milk at 25 cents, or 3 cents above his purchase price?

3. Visualize problems that might be faced by General Motors if the company attempted to establish fair trade prices on the Buick automobile.

4. It is now a general practice for brokers to receive a commission or salary only from the seller. This practice was determined by the outcome of the A & P case. Explain.

5. With what types of intertype competition is the local candy store owner faced?

6. In what types of vertical conflict would this same candy store get involved?

7. Based on Table 4-1, why haven't stores in fair trade states done as well as those in non fair-trade states?

8. Take a daily newspaper and examine both display and classified advertising. Choose some questionable price comparisons and present them in class. Why are they questionable?

9. Is loss-leader advertising legal?

10. List some forms of misleading advertising.

11. What is meant by the term "usually sold at this price"? What is meant by the term "originally sold at this price"?

12. Examine the labels of a recently purchased apparel garment. Does it meet the specifications of the Textile Fiber Products Identification Act?

13. The ad reads: *Two for one sale – 2 items for $1 – Save 40%.* Is this ad legal? If so, under what conditions is it legal?

14. Are the restraints in this chapter equally applicable to the large and small retailer?

15. Why have large firms continued to grow in spite of these restraints?

16. Define "consumerism." Is it anti-business?

17. How has consumerism affected the retailer?

The Consumer

5

OBJECTIVES YOU SHOULD MEET

1. *Describe* how consumers balance their gains from shopping against their own investment.
2. *Cite* five important quantitative statistics that can help the retailer identify a market.
3. *Show* how changes in each of the five statistics have affected certain retailers.
4. *Define* "life cycle."

The retailer is constantly examining and developing theories about the shopping habits of consumers. In essence, it is the job of retail management to identify the consumer and relate this identification to the customer to whom he wishes to sell. For example, a department store may find that its chief customer is the low-income city dweller. It is, therefore, incumbent upon management:

1. To estimate the *size* of *this* audience within shopping distance of each outlet, that is, to quantify the market.
2. To determine the *psychological appeals* that will attract this kind of customer; in effect, why they buy particular products.
3. To understand the *peculiar shopping habits* of this group; in effect, where they purchase different types of goods.

Following the above sequence, this chapter will examine the quantitative statistics of the consumer market, such as per capita income and disposable income. In Chapter 6 the psychology of the consumer as it relates to retailing is discussed at some length; in particular, the motivational makeup of the individual consumer. Chapter 7 seeks to identify the consumer groups with which the retail firm is concerned.

Figure 5-1 presents a summary of the consumer's attempts to obtain certain gains from shopping.

Consumer Shopping Gains and Investment   **FIGURE 5-1**

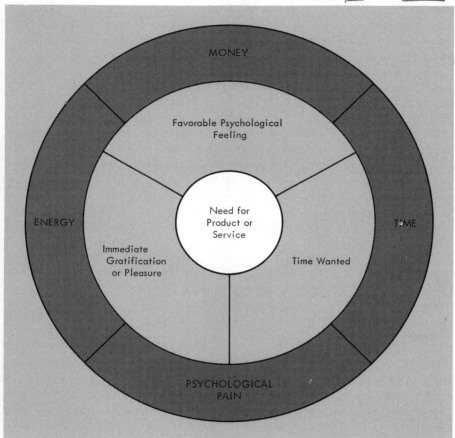

The consumer's shopping problems are indicated in the inner part of the circle, the most obvious being that the consumer in her shopping efforts is interested in obtaining a *product* or *service*. The product may be furniture, an automobile, apparel, or some everyday survival good such as food. In terms of services the consumer may have a need for a travel agent or a cleaning establishment.

Though the consumer may be able to obtain these items, she may find a second problem, namely, obtaining the product or service at the *time wanted*. Thus, she may need almost immediate delivery on a bathing suit during the summer season. Or she may need something at a time it is not usually available, such as food on Sunday.

Even if the product is available when she wants it, the consumer always wants *immediate gratification* or pleasure from whatever she has purchased. The product she has purchased must meet her standards for gratification. If she orders an automobile, it must be received in good working order. If she purchases furniture, she wants it to arrive undamaged. If a travel agent plans a trip for her, it must meet her standards.

Last, the consumer must attain a *favorable psychological feeling* in dealing with the retailer. The retailer must match the feeling of self-esteem possessed by the shopper. The status of the store must impart to the customer a sense of belonging. In more mundane terms, the shopper must feel *pleased* after dealing with the retailer. As we are well aware, shopping is a major psychological activity for the individual, as important perhaps as work.

In attaining these gains the consumer would like to limit her own investment of *money, time, energy* and *psychological pain.* One assumes she wants to pay the *least amount of money,* as by definition she is thereby obtaining the greatest value for herself.

The consumer would also like to expend the least amount of *time* necessary to obtain the goods or services, and she may prefer to shop over the phone or through a catalog. On the other hand, time may be so limited that she may want to obtain the goods or services in a nearby convenience store.

Closely aligned with time is the consumer's wish to limit the *energy* expended in fulfilling her shopping needs. The energy expended may be limited from a practical point of view by shopping in nearby stores or in stores whose parking and store layout afford particular ease.

Last, the consumer would like to reduce the *psychological pain* attached to shopping, which includes reducing uncertainty and thereby lessening the risk of frustration. The shopper prefers stores that carry wide stocks of goods or offer extensive services.

Patronage Motives

One can conclude from the above that although a consumer wishes to obtain a product with as little investment as possible, her decision involves choosing a store, for most products are purchased in a store. The complex reasons behind the selection of a particular store are usually referred to as the *patronage motives* of a shopper.

The motives involved in the selection of a store to purchase a particular product is an area of study of primary interest to most retail firms. The motives of a consumer may range from a convenient location, a rather simple motive, to the status of the store, a more complex concept.

In any case, the retailer is concerned not only with the choice of products by a consumer but also her selection of a store, her patronage motives. This aspect of consumer motivation will be dealt with in Chapter 6.

The
Consumer
Market

It is axiomatic that retailers follow the population, for population makes up the retailer's market. A market, says one author, can be defined as "people with needs to satisfy, the money to spend and the willingness to spend it."[1] Therefore, though

[1]William J. Stanton, *Fundamentals of Marketing* (New York: McGraw-Hill Book Co., 1964), p. 76.

retailers must shift with the population, the particular type of retailer is determined by the characteristics of this same population.

In contrast to manufacturers, most retailers are not interested in the total national market. As will be noted in a later chapter, they are concerned with the area surrounding their store. In the case of a chain of stores they may be concerned with the total market in a metropolitan area. Most manufacturers are interested in the total U.S. market and do not place strong emphasis on a local trading area.

Although the retailer's main interest is in the trading area near his store, he is greatly affected by the changes taking place in the total consumer market.[2] Consider, for example, the general tendency during the postwar years for the population to move to the suburbs. This national trend has affected practically every metropolitan area in the country. Although the velocity of the movement varies, it has had repercussions on local retail markets and the thinking of management from coast to coast. It has spurred the development of shopping centers and highway retailing, and any retailer would be foolhardy to ignore this trend.

The most important statistical changes in the markets are those in *population characteristics, income,* and *expenditure tendencies.* These will be covered in the following sections.

As noted above, population is the major component of a retailing market. It is incumbent upon management to measure not only the size of this market but the specific characteristics such as age, movement, and family formation. The retailer should be concerned both the present status of the population and with the trends within each characteristic.

Population

U.S. Population

The population of the United States, by any standards, has been increasing at a rapid rate. By 1950 the population had reached 151 million; twenty years later it was 204 million, an increase of about 35 per cent. Between 1960 and 1970 the population growth was 12.7 per cent (Table 5-1). Should this rate of growth continue, it is expected that by 1980 the total population will exceed 236 million.

However, there is growing evidence that the U.S. population growth will start leveling off rather abruptly during the seventies. Preliminary data from the 1970 *Census of Population* seems to indicate that the number of births is declining rapidly. For example, a comparison of the first nine months of 1972 with the previous year indicates births have declined by 9 per cent. Population by the end of 1973 reached 211 million, an indication that the 1980 population estimates of 236 million, will not be met.

City Population

Though the over-all increase in population has been impressive, the growth has

---

[2]Chapter 18 outlines some of the techniques retailers can use to obtain data on their local trading areas.

TABLE 5-1   Total U.S. Population 1920-1970

Year	Population (in millions)	Percentage Increase
1920	106	—
1930	123	16.0
1940	132	6.8
1950	151	14.4
1960	181	19.9
1970*	204	12.7

Source: U.S. Department of Commerce, Bureau of the Census.
*1973 population 211 million.

affected each city differently. For example, many cities experienced a decline between 1950 and 1960 in their central city population (i.e., population within the city limits as contrasted with the metropolitan area, which is referred to as the city trading area and includes the suburbs). Specifically, 18 per cent of the major metropolitan areas of the country had central city population losses exceeding 5,000 between 1950 and 1960. In contrast 16 metropolitan areas of the country had central city population gains exceeding 100,000. In this latter grouping a geographical pattern has evolved; most of the central city increases have taken place in the fast-growing western states.[3]

This trend has continued through the sixties. As seen in Table 5-2, population within the central cities increased by 1.5 per cent between 1960 and 1970. Outside the central cities, the increase has been 33.5 per cent, a phenomenal growth rate. By 1970, of the approximately 65 per cent of the population living in the large metropolitan areas, about 55 per cent resided in the suburbs.

This trend has meant that many cities in the United States have experienced a change in downtown shopping patterns. As downtown for the first half of the century represented the center of retail trade in the major cities, and the most valuable property, these changes have been particularly important to both commercial and governmental structures in these cities. In general, the eastern cities experienced a decline in downtown retail sales resulting in the closing of many major downtown stores. For example, since World War II Philadelphia has witnessed the closing of two major department stores; and Boston two also. New York has had a number of major closings, and a few surviving department stores have been forced to either shift their major stores to other locations (i.e., Ohrbach's) or operate stores in the downtown area at a break-even point or at a loss. This trend has also hurt many of the small cities throughout the country.

Suburban Growth

Between 1950 and 1960 almost two-thirds of the U.S. population growth took place in the suburbs. For the first time, the population surrounding the central

[3]United States Department of Commerce, *Changing Metropolitan Markets, 1950–1960* (Washington, D.C., November, 1961), pp. 15, 19.

Population Distribution by Metropolitan-Nonmetropolitan Residence: 1970 and 1960　　**TABLE 5-2**

Area of Residence[1]	1970		1960		Change, 1960-1970	
	Number	Per Cent Distri-bution	Number	Per Cent Distri-bution	Number	Per Cent
Population United States	202,534	100.0	178,677	100.0	23,857	13.4
Metropolitan areas	131,519	64.9	112,367	62.9	19,152	17.0
Inside central cities	58,635	29.0	57,785	32.3	850	1.5
Outside central cities	72,883	36.0	54,582	30.5	18,301	33.5
Nonmetro-politan areas	71,015	35.1	66,310	37.1	4,705	7.1

[1]Outside central cities is commonly called the suburbs.
Source: Adapted from *Current Population Reports, Special Studies, Social and Economic Characteristics of the Population in Metropolitan Areas: 1970 and 1960*, U.S. Department of Commerce, Bureau of the Census, 1971.

cities about equaled that within the corporate limits.[4] In many metropolitan areas the farther away a community is from the central city the higher the rate of population growth. An example of this is seen in Figure 5-2, which shows a computed regression line for the Boston metropolitan area: the cities farthest from central Boston experienced population growth rates averaging well over 40 per cent during the 1950's.

As seen in Table 5-2, this trend continued through the sixties. By 1970 the population in the suburban areas had now exceeded the central city population. This movement will no doubt continue through the seventies, but at a lower rate.

The impact of this movement on retailing has been phenomenal. It has shifted the retailing emphasis from the downtown business districts to the suburban communities, and has changed the whole composition of the retail market. The suburbanite usually resides in his own home and moves around in his own automobile — two facts which have had a major impact on the retailer. For example, home ownership in the suburbs has caused an increase in the demand for home furnishings, simply because a home is more spacious than a city apartment and requires not only more furnishings but more tools and equipment in order to maintain the property.

Possibly even more significant is the reliance of the suburban dweller on the automobile. The automobile encouraged many retailers to develop highway outlets (usually not serviced by public transportation) and eventually to open new areas of retail competition. As the postwar period progressed, numerous shopping centers and free-standing highway units developed and competed directly with the well-established downtown business district.

[4]*Changing Metropolitan Markets, op. cit.,* p. 19.

FIGURE 5-2 Correlation between City Population Changes and Miles from the Center of Boston, 1950-1960

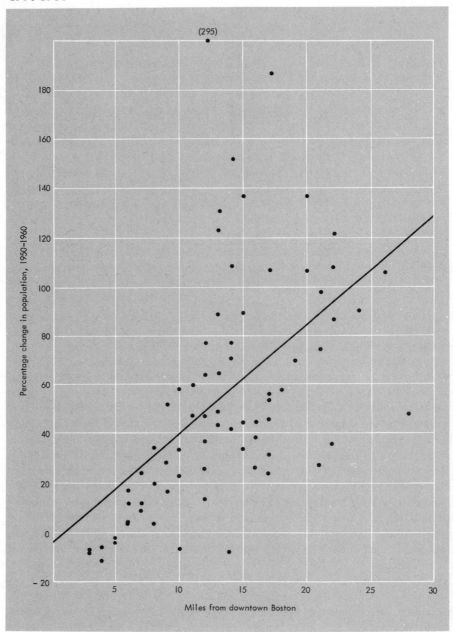

Adapted from David J. Rachman, "A Study of the Environmental Forces and Internal Organizational Factors Affecting Price Making in Apparel Discount Firms in Boston." Unpublished Doctoral Dissertation, New York University, 1965, p. 48.

Though the United States population has been growing at a rapid rate this growth has not been uniform in all sections of the country, particularly in recent years. The eastern states and some of the western and midwestern states have lagged behind the rest of the country. On the other hand, the Far West has experienced population gains far exceeding the national average.

Along with the growth and mobility of the population, there have been changes in *age* composition and in *employment* characteristics. Both of these factors put constant pressure on the retailer to adapt.

Population Character- istics

Age Characteristics

Of increasing interest to retailers has been the changing age composition of the U.S. population. In particular, a retailer is concerned with the present state of the population and the projections for the future.

Table 5-3 lists changes in the age composition. As indicated, the late teens and early adult markets seem to contain a high element of growth, up until 1980. The older age groups also seem to indicate an area of substantial growth, and the youngest age groups will perhaps decrease during this coming ten-year period.

Per Cent Distribution of Population by Age 1960-1980   **TABLE 5-3**

	0-14 Years	*15-29 Years*	*30-44 Years*	*45-64 Years*	*65 Years and Over*
1980[1]	25.1%	27.0%	18.8%	19.0%	10.1%
1970	28.3	24.5	16.9	20.5	9.8
1960	31.0	19.7	20.0	20.0	9.2

[1] Low series estimate.
Source: Bureau of the Census.

To retailers these population changes mean that there will be a greater demand for certain types of products in the future. If these changes occur, they could even affect the goods and services mix of retail stores. For instance, in a later discussion concerning the demand for boys' wear it will be observed that some men's wear stores have been considering the addition of a teen-age department. Careful study of these figures would seem to indicate that demand for boys' apparel will remain at high levels in the year to come. A similar forecast can be made for the sale of apparel, cosmetics, phonograph records, and jewelry. Manufacturers in the years to come will tend to develop product lines in keeping with the population characteristics of a growing youth market.

The market for those at the other end of the life cycle, particularly those over 65 years of age, has also been increasing. Projection on this market seems to indicate that its size will continue to increase in the years ahead. The "senior market" has many implications for retailers. Both retailing and manufacturing businesses will probably consider developing enterprises that appeal to this substantial segment of the population. Some service and retail firms have already considered this market, which is characterized by fixed low-income families and survivors. For example, the movie houses have been offering discounts to those in these age categories. Though retail stores find it more difficult to develop discount lines for senior citizens, they have been aware of the importance of carrying products such as health foods and cosmetics that appeal directly to such groups.

In any case, the growth of these groups within the total population means that the retailer must not only carry the products that are needed but develop promotional appeals that are meaningful to these segments.

Employment Characteristics

As one might expect, along with the population increase the total labor force has also increased. Much more important from the retailer's point of view, the work force contains a significant number of female workers. In 1940 there were approximately 14 million females in the total U.S. work force; by 1970 this number had increased to approximately 31 million (see Table 5-4). More significant perhaps is the fact that in 1940 about a half of the female work force consisted of single girls; by 1970 this proportion had decreased to less than 23 per cent. During the same period, the number of married women in the work force increased from slightly more than 36 per cent to over 63 per cent (the balance, composed of widows or divorced women, remained at approximately 15 per cent throughout).

This change is of major significance to both the manufacturer and the retailer. The retailer finds that the typical married working female has problems peculiar to her status. For example, she has less time to shop, since she is taking care of her family in addition to working. At the same time, her income has increased substantially; therefore, her shopping habits will probably change drastically from her pre-work period.

Further development of this point may provide more insight into some of the changes faced by the retailer. The most immediate change is the customer's interest in one-stop shopping, prompted by her limited shopping opportunities. This has given an impetus to the growth of shopping centers, and, in addition, to the proliferation of items sold in food stores, variety stores, and department stores.

Aside from shopping convenience in terms of variety and location, the working wife has a predilection for store services, particularly services that help to speed up her shopping. Thus it is not surprising that mail order shopping is on the increase.

One study seems to support the view that working wives may have different shopping habits and attitudes toward products. In this study, it was found that working women (1) make fewer trips to the grocery store per week than nonworking women and (2) working women tend to be more brand-loyal than nonworking women.[5]

---

[5]Beverlee B. Anderson, *"Working Women vs. Non-Working Women; A Comparison of Shopping Behaviors,"* paper presented at Fall Educators Conference, American Marketing Association, Houston, Texas, August, 1972.

Marital Status of Women in the Labor Force, 1940-70   TABLE 5-4

| | Female Labor Force (in 1,000's) | | | | | Per Cent Distribution of Female Labor Force | | |
| | | | Married | | Wid-owed or Di-vorced | | | Wid-owed or Di-vorced |
Year	Total	Single	Total	Husband Present		Single	Married	
1940	13,840	6,710	5,040	4,200	2,090	48.5%	36.4%	15.1%
1950	17,795	5,621	9,273	8,550	2,901	31.6	52.1	16.3
1960	22,516	5,401	13,485	12,253	3,629	24.0	59.9	16.1
1970	31,233	6,965	19,799	18,377	4,469	22.3	63.4	14.3

Source: U.S. Department of Commerce Bureau of the Census.

Other Factors

A retail firm must also be concerned with other characteristics of the population. Religion, education, race, family formation, and family size are all factors that may eventually determine the way in which the local retailer manages his business. Religion is surely an influential factor in certain major metropolitan areas. The market for kosher food in New York City, the high level of fish sales during Lent, the demands of the Italian population for "old world" delicacies, all represent markets to be dealt with by any food retailing firm.

The recent interest of the retailer, particularly those with major outlets in the downtown area of a sprawling metropolis, in the Negro market also points to the need for a thorough understanding of the characteristics of the population.

Though it is axiomatic that retailers follow the market, it is also a principle that retailers will follow a market only if they are convinced that the consumer has sufficient buying power. Thus, the retailer must be aware of the income characteristics of the local population.

Income characteristics are not the only factor that the retailer must relate to his decision making. He must also note the trends in the makeup of family income. For example, he must be aware of the amount of family income available for discretionary buying and the trends in consumer debt (a demand-building factor for buying), and of course he must be alert to per capita income levels and particularly to any important shifts.

The most important factors in demand, therefore, are personal income, disposable income, and discretionary income.

These may be defined as follows:

Personal Income The income to individuals in the form of wages and salaries, proprietors' and rental income, personal interest, social security, and related benefits.

Disposable Income Personal income less taxes — federal, state, and local.

Discretionary Income Income which may be spent or saved without consideration of current need or prior commitment.[6]

---

[6]*A Graphic Guide to Consumer Markets* (New York: National Industrial Conference Board, Inc., 1965), pp. 24 and 28.

Personal Income and Disposable Income[7]

Both personal and disposable income have been on the rise during the postwar period. Figure 5-3 shows the naturally close relationship between these two statistics. Obviously, a rise in personal income represents an important indicant for all business segments of the economy. Though there has been a rapid rise in personal income nationally the gains have not been uniform throughout the country. Some indication of this variation can be gained by examining per capita income in each of the fifty states (Figure 5-4). The range from a low of $2,766 in Mississippi to a high of $6,000 in the District of Columbia dramatizes this inequality. On the local level the retailer may find an even greater disparity. For example, within the state of Maryland the per capita income in the Eastern Shore region is considerably below the average for the state as a whole.

Though the above indicators of income are pertinent to the retail firm, disposable income data may be even more relevant. For this is the consumer's after-tax income, which becomes increasingly important in light of the rising local and state tax rates. The increase in tax rates is indicated by the fact that disposable income has risen at a slightly lower rate than personal income. To the retailer disposable income denotes the consumer's financial ability to purchase the retailer's offerings. Disposable income is particularly important to food retailers and general merchandise outlets.

Discretionary Income

Discretionary income represents, in effect, the amount of money available for spending on luxuries. In actuality, the consumer with discretionary income can either save his money or choose to spend it on goods and services. Consumers with large amounts of discretionary income make excellent markets for luxurious cars, jewelry, furs, boats, and better homes. In Figure 5-3 one can see that discretionary income has been increasing at a rapid rate. In 1970 it reached a peak of $300 billion.

Consumer
Expenditures

Though higher incomes result in higher levels of expenditures, it is important to the retailer that he be aware of the trend of these expenditures. For example, retail firms should be alerted to whether the consumer is spending more of his income on goods or on services.[8] This point is particularly important in that most of the retailer's business derives from the sale of goods; therefore, tendencies toward consumer spending in the area of services could portend problems for the retailer. Though more will be said on this topic in the trends chapter, it is sufficient to note here that the pattern of spending on services by the consumer has caused many

---

[7]For the application of these statistics to forecasting, see Chapter 15.

[8]Services are defined as "activities, benefits, or satisfactions which are offered for sale or are provided in connection with the sale of goods." "Marketing Definition," Report of Definitions Committee, American Marketing Association, Chicago, 1960. Retailers offer consumers services in the sense of the latter part of the definition. These services are covered in the major section of the book. The development of small firms selling services is not covered in this text. It would not be incorrect to state, however, that most of the service firms (aside from public utilities) are small retail firms, and many of the concepts offered in this book apply to these businesses.

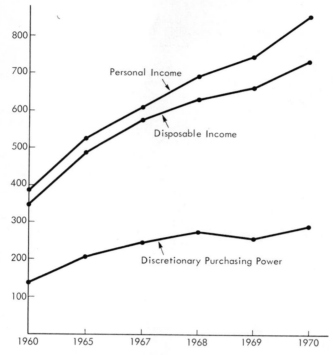

Source: U. S. Department of Commerce.

retail firms to adjust their offerings. As a result some firms are now selling life insurance and travel plans and offering rental services to many of their customers.

Many retail firms are also concerned with the expenditure patterns within income groups and at various stages of the life cycle. For example, they are interested to know the amount of family income that goes toward the purchase of food and clothing. The obvious interest in consumer expenditures derives from two special needs of the retailer: (1) estimating the market for a new store location and making short-run forecasts; (2) forecasting shifting population changes within his present market.

Forecasting

In developing sales forecasts for a new location the retail firm must be able to project the expenditure patterns of those within the confines of its market. Techniques for making these projections are covered in Chapter 15. Briefly, a food store planning an additional outlet in an area not only must know the size of the market and the income of potential customers, but must be aware of the food expenditure patterns within each of the income groups. Knowledge of this will enable the firm to make a more accurate forecast.

It would also seem useful for a firm to base its annual forecasts somewhat on the expenditure patterns of the families within its present market.

81

FIGURE 5-4   Per Capita Personal Income, 1971

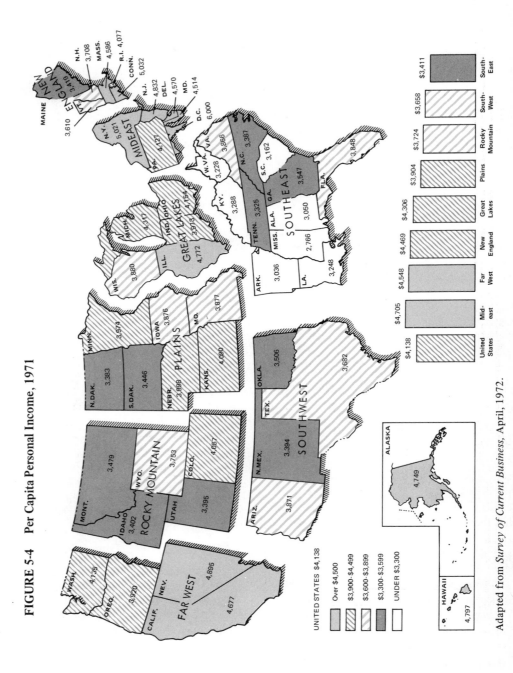

UNITED STATES $4,138

Over $4,500
$3,900-$4,499
$3,600-$3,899
$3,300-$3,599
UNDER $3,300

Adapted from *Survey of Current Business*, April, 1972.

82

Unfortunately for the retail firm, the population is constantly shifting. This was pointed out in an earlier section. As these shifts take place, the retailer must be in a position to study the spending patterns of the new groups and, if necessary, adjust his retailing mix. One particular shift that has been taking place in the major urban areas is the tendency for low-income families to move into the downtown business area. As will be shown in a later section of this chapter, these lower-income families have distinctively different spending patterns than the so-called middle-class family. Whether this particular theory applies to each and every area of the country is not of concern here. What is important to note is that through careful study of the expenditure patterns of these groups, coincident with the other means of obtaining knowledge, the retailer is in a position to evaluate these changes.

Expenditure Patterns

Table 5-5 lists the expenditure patterns of consumers between 1950 and 1970. It shows that consumer expenditures have increased in all spending sectors. Of more significance, however, is the fact that many of these areas have increased at a rate considerably below the average. For example, expenditures for food and tobacco have increased by 2½ times over this period of time, whereas expenditures for housing have quadrupled. When one examines these in relation to total expenditures, the changes become more apparent. Thus we see that the share of food and tobacco expenditures declined from 30.4 per cent in 1950 to a low of 23.2 per cent in 1970. Though actual expenditures on food and tobacco increased during this period, they declined as a proportion of total consumption expenditures. A similar situation is found in expenditures for clothing, accessories, and jewelry.

"Trading Up"

These increases in income and the changing consumption patterns have had an important effect on the sale and distribution of goods. As might be expected, many consumers are tending to "trade up." That is, they are buying more elaborate goods and larger models. Figure 5-5 indicates the extent of this upgrading since 1955 in purchases in three major expenditure areas: housing, food, and automobiles. This exhibit shows that the demand for large houses and houses with two or more baths has increased dramatically during this period. Trading up in food consumption has also progressed at a similar rate. Specifically, the consumption of lard has declined and a notable shift to the more expensive shortening has occurred; similarly the demand for beef has increased, whereas the consumption of potatoes has declined.

These changes have taken place in all sectors of the economy and have affected the operations of both retail stores and manufacturing firms. For example, the tendency to purchase pre-mixed and gourmet food has affected the assortment of goods offered by the retailer. The interest in gourmet foods has caused manufacturers to consider new outlets, and they have found a ready market for their canned products in the department stores. Manufacturers of specialized and imported candy delicacies have also found the department store to be an excellent outlet. The various imported and gourmet soups have had similar success in the department store. Conversely, pre-mixed cocktails and many of the frozen

TABLE 5-5 Personal Consumption Expenditures 1950-1970 (in billions of dollars and as a Per Cent of Total Expenditures)

Type of Product	1950	1960	1970
Total consumption	$191.0	$325.2	$615.8
Food, beverages and tobacco	58.1	87.5	142.9
Clothing, accessories and jewelry	23.7	33.0	62.3
Personal care	2.4	5.3	10.1
Housing	21.3	46.3	91.2
Household operations	29.5	46.9	85.6
Medical care expenses	8.8	19.1	47.3
Personal business	6.9	15.0	35.5
Transportation	24.7	43.1	77.9
Recreation	11.1	18.3	39.0
Private education and research	1.6	3.7	10.4
Religious and welfare activities	2.3	4.7	8.8
Foreign travel and other, net	.6	2.2	4.8
Total	100.0%	100.0%	100.0%
Food, beverages, and tobacco	30.4%	26.9%	23.2%
Clothing, accessories, and jewelry	12.4	10.2	10.1
Personal care	1.3	1.6	1.6
Housing	11.1	14.2	14.8
Household operations	15.4	14.4	13.9
Medical care expenses	4.6	5.9	7.7
Personal business	3.6	4.6	5.8
Transportation	12.9	13.3	12.6
Recreation	5.8	5.6	6.3
Private education and research	0.8	1.1	1.7
Religious and welfare activities	1.2	1.5	1.4
Foreign travel and other, net	0.3	0.7	0.8

Source: Department of Commerce

out-of-season fruits have found a substantial outlet in the food supermarket. These stores have been forced to increase not only the space offered to such items but also their freezer capacity considerably above the 1955 level.

Family Income and Expenditures

In spite of the great increase in all levels of income, there is still a large differential between the lowest-income groups and the highest (Figure 5-6). In 1970, for example, approximately 19.3 per cent of U.S. families had an annual income below $5,000. This group includes the retired and the low-income families found in many of the major urban areas of the country. They represent segments of the market that can barely maintain a decent standard of living; their after-tax (disposable) income covers mainly food, shelter, and clothing.

SIGNS OF TRADING UP ARE FOUND IN:

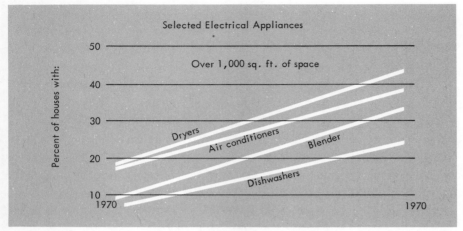

Selected Electrical Appliances

Over 1,000 sq. ft. of space

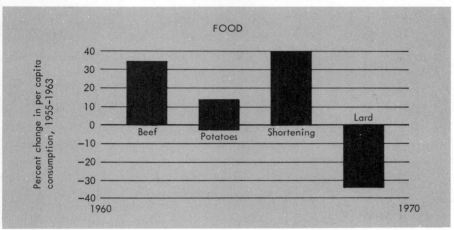

FOOD

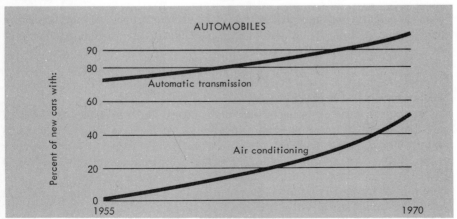

AUTOMOBILES

Adapted from *Business in Brief,* The Chase Manhattan Bank, New York, No. 64 (Sept.-Oct., 1965) and U. S. Department of Commerce.

85

FIGURE 5-6   The Changing Income Period

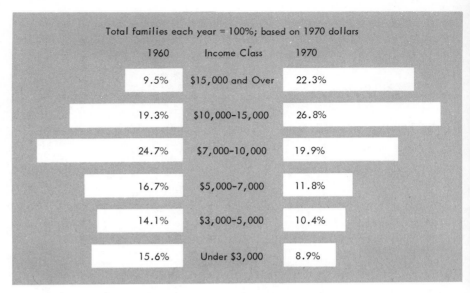

Total families each year = 100%; based on 1970 dollars

1960	Income Class	1970
9.5%	$15,000 and Over	22.3%
19.3%	$10,000–15,000	26.8%
24.7%	$7,000–10,000	19.9%
16.7%	$5,000–7,000	11.8%
14.1%	$3,000–5,000	10.4%
15.6%	Under $3,000	8.9%

Adapted from *A Guide to Consumer Markets, 1972-1973*, The Conference Board, 1972.

The most spectacular change in family income has taken place among the middle-income groups. In 1970 over 58.5 per cent of all families in the United States had a family income of from $5,000 to $15,000 a year. Among these groups the spending patterns vary considerably, and a great deal of their money can be used for luxury items. Though most retail firms are concerned with this group, the national chains are particularly interested in this income category. For example, one large mail order company, in analyzing areas in terms of their market, counts only those customers earning below $15,000. In general, those earning above $10,000 are categorized by most retail firms as a market for luxury products. Families in this income category account for the largest proportion of discretionary spending in the economy.

As observed in the previous sections, rising incomes appear to be a permanent characteristic of our economy. And though total expenditure patterns are helpful in understanding and determining trends in the economy, it is equally important that information be available on patterns of spending within income classes. If spending patterns change as incomes rise, they will most certainly affect any short- or long-run forecast made by a retailer.

Do spending patterns change as income increases? Table 5-6 indicates that in all major spending categories absolute expenditures do increase with an increase in income. For example, families earning pre-tax incomes below $3,000 annually spend $600 for food. This amount is roughly half of the national average for all groups. At the extreme end of the scale families earning over $15,000 a year spend more than twice as much for food as the national average and four times as much as the low-income family.

In other expenditure groups the evidence is similar. Expenditures for clothing

Expenditures for Current Consumption*	Total	Under $3,000	$3,000- 5,000	$5,000- 7,500	$7,500- 10,000	$10,000- 15,000	$15,000- & Over
	100.0%	100.0%	100.0%	100.0%	100.0%	100.0%	100.0%
Food, total	24.4%	29.4%	26.3%	24.8%	23.9%	22.7%	20.0%
Alcoholic beverages	1.6	1.0	1.4	1.5	1.7	1.6	1.9
Tobacco	1.8	2.1	2.2	2.0	1.8	1.5	1.1
Housing and household operations	24.0	30.3	25.1	23.8	22.9	21.8	23.7
House furnishings and equipment	5.2	4.1	4.8	5.3	5.5	5.5	5.4
Clothing and accessories	10.2	7.1	9.0	9.9	10.6	11.5	12.2
Transportation	15.2	8.6	14.5	16.0	16.1	16.7	14.9
Medical care	6.6	8.5	7.0	6.6	6.3	6.2	6.1
Personal care	2.9	3.0	3.1	2.9	2.9	2.8	2.5
Recreation and equipment	4.0	2.3	3.4	3.8	4.3	4.8	4.7
Reading and education	1.9	1.3	1.4	1.7	1.9	2.5	3.5
Other expenditures	2.2	2.3	1.8	1.7	2.2	2.3	4.0
Food, total	$1,259	$ 600	$1,015	$1,318	$1,624	$1,970	$ 2,550
Alcoholic beverages	81	21	55	81	117	152	242
Tobacco	93	42	84	105	123	126	134
Housing and household operations	1,236	620	968	1,263	1,552	1,889	3,002
House furnishings and equipment	269	83	185	284	376	476	690
Clothing and accessories	525	145	348	528	720	1,001	1,550
Transportation	781	176	560	848	1,093	1,450	1,891
Medical care	342	174	269	350	425	539	771
Personal care	148	61	118	156	194	241	312
Recreation and equipment	205	48	133	201	291	419	597
Reading and education	100	26	55	88	126	215	440

TABLE 5-6 Continued

Expenditures for Current Consumption*	Total	Under $3,000	$3,000-5,000	$5,000-7,500	$7,500-10,000	$10,000-15,000	$15,000-& Over
Other expenditure	113	47	69	93	147	201	508
Total	$5,152	$2,043	$3,859	$5,315	$6,788	$8,679	$12,687

*Totals vary slightly due to rounding.
Source: National Industrial Conference Board, *Expenditure Patterns of the American Family, 1965.*

and accessories indicate that families with incomes above $15,000 a year spend over ten times as much as the lowest-income group. Upper-middle-income families ($7,000–$10,000) spend twice as much as the lowest-income families but only half as much as the highest.

It should be emphasized that these figures represent absolute expenditures. As shown in the table, the proportional expenditures by each income group show a different picture, at least in certain categories. Expenditures for food, for example, are shown to be a declining share as family income increases. On the other hand, the percentage expenditures for clothing show an increase at the upper income levels. Expenditures for housing and medical care remain relatively stable, particularly at the middle- and high-income levels.

Life Cycle

The family life cycle (FLC) refers to the relationship of families, the age of their children, and their expenditure patterns. Users of this measurement point to the fact that families with young children are forced to spend a large part of their income in certain ways. As the children get older, the family spending patterns change, particularly after children leave the household.

The use of store services by customers can also be related to the family life cycle. In Table 5-7, an analysis of the use of credit accounts related to the type of store is presented. The data seem to indicate that families without children tend to have credit accounts in high prestige and full-line department stores. Conversely, fewer maintain charge accounts at chain and discount stores.

Are FLC expenditure studies more accurate for analytical projections than other measurements of family expenditures such as the age of the head of the household? Figure 5-7 seems to indicate that they are subject to question. The curves on this chart on home ownership show a steady rise through the early years of life. However, the FLC curve shows a much sharper drop in home ownership toward the end ("6" representing older married, no children; "7" older single). The reason for this difference lies in the fact that older single people are usually widows and widowers who tend to give up their homes. Age of the family head is not related to this fact, as widowhood can take place at any age. The relevant fact, therefore, is not age.[9] Thus the FLC is questionable for some types of projections.

[9]John B. Lansing and Leslie Kish, *op. cit.*, pp. 512-519.

| Demographic Characteristic | Credit Patronage by Type of Store (in per cent) | | | | |
	High Prestige Department Store	Full-Line Department Store	Chain Store	Discount Store	Total
Life Cycle Stage					
Children's Ages					
Under 6 only	14.3%	31.4%	51.2%	3.1%	100.0%
Under 6 and 6-17	13.4	33.0	51.6	2.0	100.0
6-17 only	15.3	34.5	48.5	1.7	100.0
No children — Head					
under 45 yrs.	18.8	33.8	45.9	1.5	100.0
No children — Head					
over 45 yrs.	22.1	39.2	38.2	0.5	100.0
Unclassified	23.2	39.6	37.2	0.0	100.0

Source: Adapted from Ben M. Enis and Keith K. Cox, "Demographic Analysis of Store Patronage Patterns: Uses and Pitfalls," paper presented at the American Marketing Association educators' conference, Denver, Colorado, August 29, 1969.

Implications

The implications of the above expenditure statistics are many. For instance, it was noted that as income increases families tend to spend less proportionately on food and more on other items in the budget. This, of course, has particular connotations for the future of the food store, for it seems to imply that the share of the consumer's dollar in food retailing will continue to decline. In view of this trend it is understandable that food stores have been augmenting their offerings to the consumer by selling many non-food items. As noted earlier, one finds phonograph records, many houseware items, and the like being sold in food stores. Expanding product lines is not the only way a retailer can meet the shifting patterns of consumer expenditures. The retailer can in some cases improve the quality of the merchandise sold and the services, and by doing so can, hopefully, sell goods at higher prices. Thereby the retailer can hope to capture a much larger share of the consumer dollar. For example, stores selling popular-priced dresses may shift to more fashionable, higher-priced merchandise. On a lower level, the variety chain in recent years has attempted to change its image from a low-priced outlet selling mainly convenience goods (such as notions, candy, yarn, etc.) to a popular-priced junior department store. These statistics reveal other tendencies that are of increasing importance to retail management. Looking back at Table 5-6 we see an increase in expenditures for services as family income rises. Increased expenditures for education, recreation, and travel represent a trend in this direction. It is for this reason that some general merchandise firms have entered the travel field, rent-a-car business, and numerous other related activities.

89

FIGURE 5-7   Family Life Cycle and Age as Predictors of Home Ownership

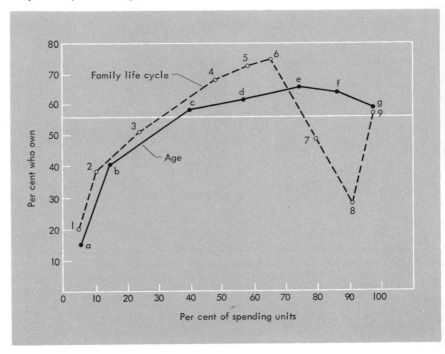

PROPORTION OF SPENDING UNITS WITH EACH CHARACTERISTIC

Age of Head of Spending Unit	Own Home	Stage in the Life Cycle of the Family	Own Home
(a) 18–24	15.4%	(1) Young single	20.2%
(b) 25–34	43.0	(2) Young married, no children	37.3
(c) 35–44	58.7		
(d) 45–54	61.4	(3) Young married, youngest child under six	52.5
(e) 55–64	65.9		
(f) 65 and over	63.4	(4) Young married, youngest child six or older	66.7
(g) Not ascertained	57.5		
		(5) Older married, children	69.9
		(6) Older married, no children	71.4
		(7) Older single	49.2
		(8) Others	27.1
		(9) Not ascertained	56.3

Adapted from John B. Lansing and Leslie Kish, "Family Life Cycle as an Independent Variable," *American Sociological Review*, Vol. 22, No. 5 (October, 1957), pp. 514-515.

The retailer has as his major goal selling products to the consumer. To direct his efforts properly the retailer must study the consumer from the point of view of:

1. the size of the market.
2. psychological appeals that attract this market.
3. the peculiar shopping habits of the consumer that make up this market.

On the other hand, the consumer faces shopping problems. He is interested in obtaining needed goods and services, when wanted, with favorable psychological results. These gains are balanced against the consumer's desire to limit his investment in money, time, energy, and psychological pain. To overcome these problems the shopper selects a store. From the retailer's point of view, understanding the consumer's selection of a store involves an understanding of the patronage motivation.

The quantative aspect of the consumer market consists of studies of population growth and movements, age, and employment. Other factors include income and expenditure patterns. The following important points have been discussed:

1. Population is growing rapidly with a strong geographical movement to the western part of the U.S. and the suburbs.

2. The age of the population seems to contain several areas of growth, particularly the late teens, early adult, and senior citizen categories.

3. The major change among the work force is the continued growth of the number of married female workers.

4. Personal and disposable income have been rising rapidly in our economy. In particular, the huge rise in the middle-income groups is of continued interest to the retail chains.

5. Rapidly rising expenditures are indicative of the rise in income classes. The consumer is spending more on housing and automobiles. Even expenditures for food, which have not risen as rapidly as other expenses, have experienced changing patterns of expenditures toward more expensive types of food. As a family moves from one income level to another, its patterns also change. Thus as family income increases, the proportion it spends on food decreases, and yet the amount rises.[10] Expenditure patterns are also affected by the stage in the life cycle.

QUESTIONS

1. Ernest Engel, a German statistician, developed certain generalizations concerning consumption expenditures in 1857. These generalizations are as follows:
   a. As family income increases, a smaller percentage is spent on food.
   b. As family income increases, approximately the same percentage is spent on clothing.

---

[10]With the recent rapid rise in the cost of food, there is some indication that the proportion expended for food will increase slightly. However, the increase will only be modest in that consumers have been trading down by buying cheaper cuts of meats and buying lower priced staples. Some major chains are capitalizing on this trend by offering lower priced house brands. See *Barron's,* February 11, 1974, pp. 3 and 16.

c. As family income increases, the proportion allotted to housing and household operation remains the same.

d. As family income increases, an increasing proportion is spent on other items (education, recreation, medical care, etc.).

Are Engel's generalizations still valid today?

2. Indicate the significance of distinguishing between absolute and relative increases in consumer expenditures.

3. What is meant by a patronage motive? Relate this definition to the view that consumers attempt to limit the time and energy they invest in shopping.

4. Why should a retailer be aware of population shifts to the suburbs? How does this shift affect the outlook of the:

   a. food chain
   b. variety store
   c. department store
   d. firm selling house to house

5. How does the life cycle affect consumer expenditures? Relate your interpretation directly to a family with two children at home and a family with two children married and living away from home.

6. Why does per capita income differ by state (see Figure 5-4)?

7. List some major economic changes that have occurred in the past fifteen years in your city. Relate some of these changes to problems that have developed for retail firms.

8. How have female employment patterns affected the role of the downtown department store? Relate this directly to the goods and services offered.

9. How can the level of education in a community affect the effort of the local retailer?

10. Working from your findings in Question 7, predict what businesses will fail by 1980 if these trends should continue?

11. John's Bargain Stores is a chain of small stores selling closeout merchandise in low-income areas of some major eastern cities. How do you account for the continued growth of these stores?

12. Name some product groups that will continue to expand if per capita income grows at its present rate.

13. What departments would you suggest that Sears, Roebuck add in the next fifteen years if present consumer expenditure trends continue?

14. Determine the possibilities of developing a high-fashion specialty store catering to women in your city. In evaluating this possibility pay close attention to location and income changes.

15. It has been often stated that suburbanites develop different spending patterns than residents of downtown. Assuming this is true, how do you account for the differences? In what specific expenditures might one find these differences?

Consumer

Motivation

6

OBJECTIVES YOU SHOULD MEET

1. *Explain* how the retailer and manufacturer differ in their need to understand consumer motivation.
2. *Distinguish* between basic needs and hierarchy needs.
3. *Define* safety, social, and ego needs.
4. *Distinguish* between rational and unconscious motivation.
5. *Relate* cognition and learning to the retail firm.

The efforts of retailers are directed at selling goods and services to the consumer. In this chapter we shall outline the motivational responses of the consumer in relation to the retail firm. We are concerned here particularly with individual motivation.

Manufacturing and Retailing Views on Motivation

Before discussing the psychology of the consumer it is well to understand that the retailer and the manufacturer emphasize different aspects of consumer motivation. Both are interested in why people buy. However, the retailer is interested in a more general evaluation than the manufacturer. To illustrate this point: The manufacturer selling instant coffee is concerned with the purchase of *his* product. He may ask: How does the consumer envision my product in relationship to my competitors' products? Is the purchase of coffee related to status? If so, what status level does my product appeal to? Are people sold on the basis of rational predilections? Does the whole concept of instant coffee undermine the

Human
Behavior and
Motivation

93

maternal instinct in our society? The manufacturer is concerned with the image of his product and the buying motives behind the purchase. The food store in which the instant coffee is sold is less concerned with product motivation. From the retail firm's point of view, little is gained by this kind of examination. Nevertheless, the retailer is interested in consumer motivation, that is, why the customer shops in his store. His questions are of a different nature. He will ask: What is the motivation of people shopping in our food store? Do we appeal to certain classes? Are are appealing to the right motives? Is our present campaign geared to this audience? The retail firm, then, is concerned with the motivation of groups toward an organization, whereas the manufacturer is more concerned with product motivation.

This dichotomy is not necessarily mutually exclusive. Certainly the image of General Motors is as overwhelming as that of any of its products. And certainly the Cadillac agency develops its main impression in the community on the basis of the product it carries, rather than any of the services it performs for the buyer.

On the other hand, stores as a group may have a distinct image in the mind of the consumer. Tiffany's, Neiman-Marcus, Macy's, and Saks Fifth Avenue are just a few stores that bring to mind a strong impression — whether or not you have shopped in them. Stores attempt to develop this image. Manufacturers, on the other hand, may as a marketing strategy "play down" the importance of the firm and "play up" the product.

However, the retail firm is not solely concerned with patronage motives. Within the firm, particularly in general merchandise stores, the manager of a department must concern himself with understanding buying motives in relation to a wide classification of merchandise. For example, the buyer of boys' wear must understand the motivations of both the pre-teen boy and the teenager toward the purchase of this product classification. Lack of understanding of customers can result in serious errors in retailing. Take the question of whether a boys' department should be located near, or separate from, the men's department, a question of major concern to management for many years. Without offering a solution, management would agree that to decide properly one must know the motivation of the boy as a customer. What motivates him to shop at a certain store? Does he like to shop with his father or in imitation of his father? Or does he prefer to shop with his peers? Does his social status reflect his buying behavior? Most would agree that answers to these questions would constitute a major step toward solving the problem.

It has been said that all behavior has a history. Certainly the shopper has a long history of individual responses to other human beings and, in the case of retailing, a long list of interactions with salespeople and store owners. These reactions form a basis for subsequent responses of consumers toward firms, and no doubt impede the development of some types of outlets. An example of a type of retail outlet that has had a slow development in terms of its retail sales is the vending machine. At present most vending machines are limited to the sale of convenience merchandise with a great emphasis on confectionary items. One of the factors restraining their growth, or so we have been led to believe, has been their inability to develop a device that will accept paper money. If this were accomplished, according to many observers, higher-priced items could be sold through vending machines. Recently, however, bill-changing machines have been developed, but, except for a few isolated instances, consumers are still reluctant to patronize vending machines. The most plausible answer, as pointed out by a research firm, is that the consumer, because of his previous experiences with mechanically deficient nickel and dime vending machines, is understandable reluctant to try his luck with large-denomination currency.

Aside from this learned behavior the consumer is controlled by his inner drives, which can be traced mainly to his physical and psychological makeup. The following sections will discuss the aspects of human behavior that determine consumer motivation.

Human Behavior[1]

Motivation is simply an impulse or urge to attain some goal-object or goal; for example, it may be simply the urge for food when hungry (goal-object), or the striving to become a medical doctor (goal). Motivation, however, is only one aspect of human behavior. *Cognition* and *learning* are the other determinants of human behavior. Cognition refers to all mental phenomena: perception, memory, judging, thinking, etc. Learning as a process is a more active part of consumer behavior and is based on actual experiences of the individual. By definition, learning refers to changes in behavior that occur through time and is relative to a set of external conditions. However, this reaction is related to the striving for satisfaction of individual needs and to the influence of the cognitive processes. In the following three sections these three aspects of human behavior will be examined closely.

Motivation

The understanding of consumer motivation requires a knowledge of man's needs, both basic physiological and higher-level psychological needs.

For our purposes, however, motivation must be related to the retail firm.

Basic Motivation[2]

Motivation is initiated through needs. However, many of the basic needs in our society are well taken care of and are of only academic interest in tracing behavior and relating it to a business situation. Nevertheless, the retailer is concerned with *basic needs* because they offer him unlimited opportunities for developing appeals, particularly in his communications with the consumer. Some of these are hunger, thirst, air-getting, temperature regulation, and sex. Psychologists now recognize that man has a hierarchy of needs over and above his basic drives. At this higher level he has *safety needs, social needs,* and *ego needs.*[3] Though not all of these levels are easily understood in terms of the retailer, some aspects can be analyzed in this

---

[1]The organization of this section is based mainly on James A. Bayton, "Motivation, Cognition, Learning – Basic Factors in Consumer Behavior," *Journal of Marketing,* Vol. XXII, No. 30, (January, 1958), pp. 282–289.

[2]The section on drives and basic needs is partially drawn from Edward L. Brink and William T. Kelley, *The Management of Promotion* (Englewood Cliffs, N.J.: Prentice-Hall, Inc., 1963), Chapter 5.

[3]Douglas McGregor, *The Human Side of Enterprise* (New York: McGraw-Hill Book Company, Inc., 1960), pp. 36-40.

connection. In particular, the safety and social needs are applicable to a retailer's understanding of the consumer.

Basic Drives

The wants that derive from these drives are basic to human behavior. However, it must be remembered that in our society a drive of this nature may no longer be a prime motive. For example, hunger and thirst are fulfilled to a greater extent in our society than in other parts of the world. The dwindling share of consumer expenditures allotted for food is an indicant of satisfaction. Yet new food-marketing concepts have been widely accepted by the consumer. The growth of gourmet food lines, particularly in department stores, indicates a basic consumer interest in achieving higher levels of satisfaction. The interest consumers have shown in home deliveries of food products and particularly in food freezer plans is another factor supporting the view that habits acquired to satisfy basic drives can be altered under favorable auspices.

Retailers can appeal to other visceral drives. A soda-mat (featuring as many as 40 soda-vending machines) located in a summer resort is a direct attempt to satisfy the strongest visceral drive, thirst.[4]

Other Drives

Aside from the basic drives and needs, man has, as noted above, other, higher needs that tend to dominate his behavior. But these needs tend to come into focus only when the lower physiological needs are satisfied. Since in our affluent society the basic drives of people are for the most part well satisfied, we shall turn to the hierarchy of higher needs[5], which are defined as:

> *Safety Needs:* Man's need for protection against danger, threat, and deprivation.
>
> *Social Needs:* Man's need for belonging, for association, for acceptance by his fellows, for giving and receiving friendship and love.
>
> *Egotistic Needs:* Man's need for self-esteem and needs that relate to his reputation, i.e., the need for status, recognition, appreciation, for the deserved respect of his fellows.

According to psychologists, these categories not only delineate a higher level of man's needs but also indicate the order in which man seeks to satisfy them. Thus, when physiological needs are reasonably well satisfied, needs at the next highest level (safety) dominate a person's behavior. When the person has fulfilled this need sufficiently, he then assumes more interest in the next level, namely, social needs. The last level — egotistic — is, as has been pointed out by a number of authors, one that is rarely fulfilled.

What do the three higher-level needs mean to management? As demonstrated earlier, the basic needs of human beings offer rational themes for advertising and

---

[4]Brink and Kelley, *op. cit.,* p. 89.
[5]McGregor, *op. cit.,* p. 37.

for all commmunication with consumers. The higher levels would seem to offer fewer possibilities; yet possibilities do exist. Safety needs would seem to be fulfilled by individual products rather than by the image projected by a retail store. For example, intangible products such as life insurance or medical insurance would seem to offer opportunities for a marketing man to develop a meaningful strategy aimed at the demands of people concerned with this need. On the other hand, both the social and egotistical needs of people offer more promise in developing a retail strategy. Social needs refer to the consumer as he functions in a group. Certainly, these groups are of interest to the retailer, particularly as they affect shopping habits. Group relationships in general and how they affect the firm are covered to some extent in Chapter 7.

It is interesting to note that the last set of needs — the egotistical — is of greatest interest to the retailer. This is because status is a prime factor here; and status can be symbolized by the store one shops in and in another sense can afford. Status naturally varies according to one's life goals or levels of aspiration. If the consumer feels that his aspirations (or goals) are met by shopping in a particular store, then his association with this store will continue for a long time to come.

In choosing these life goals, individuals differ considerably. Most either lower or raise their goals depending on their successes or failure. In psychological experiments it has been shown that even those with minimum qualifications will raise their goals to higher levels as they achieve success. Many individuals set their goals in terms of income and status. And a sure indicator of status is to have the means to shop at stores that cater to higher income levels. In one sense the retailer stamps certain individuals as having attained status and therewith a certain level in their aspirations or goals. Consumers understand this and are no more perplexed by it than by the motivation of a person buying a Cadillac. Certainly, we buy this product because of its excellent mechanical features.

On the other hand, many customers have low levels of aspiration. It has been noted that many "blue-collar" occupational groups are unimpressed by the possibility of moving into higher management positions. Firms dealing with this general occupational group must adjust any offerings to this type of "conservative" outlook.

Identifying Patronage Motives

Though consumer motivation is of basic interest to the retailer, not all shoppers at a store are motivated by a strong psychological need. For instance, if consumer A buys food at the B chain store, he may do so because it is near his house. Though his basic motivation may be traced simply to his hunger needs, knowing this is of little value to the firm. His interpretation of what the store offers him in terms of convenience and prices may be the most important reasons for shopping at the store, from the standpoint of the retailer. On the other hand, in a department store *status* as a basic motivation for shopping may be of the highest importance. Status, of course, is related to higher egotistic human needs.

Since almost all consumers will offer seemingly rational motives for shopping at a particular store, differentiating between basic motivation and rational, conscious reasons is a primary task. Table 6-1 lists the department-store characteristics that

TABLE 6-1 **Relative Importance of Various Characteristics of Department Stores as Factors Influencing Consumers' Choices of Places to Shop**

Characteristic	Mean Importance Rating
High quality	1.50*
Honest advertising	1.60
Good values	1.63
Reliability	1.77
Consistent quality	1.80
Availability of salesclerks	1.80
Friendly salesclerks	1.83
Merchandise easy to find	1.90
Reputation	2.00
Large Selection	2.00
Clearly marked merchandise	2.03
Return goods privilege	2.10
Good dress department	2.13
Fashion and style in merchandise	2.17
Parking	2.17
Good billing	2.27
Bargains at sales	2.27
Easy to reach store	2.40
Close to public transportation	2.56
Low prices	2.60
Informative advertising	2.62
Wide aisles	2.72
Large number of departments	2.73
Delivery	2.93
No traffic hazards	2.97
Courteous telephone operators	3.10
Charge accounts	3.20
Near other stores	3.40
Modern building	3.73
Window displays	4.00
Type of customers	4.03
Place to eat	4.21
Employee relations	4.53
Good restaurant	4.59
Trading stamps	4.67

*Highest Ranking
Source: F. E. Brown and George Fisk, "Department Stores and Discount Houses: Who Dies Next?" *Journal of Retailing,* Fall, 1965.

influence consumers' choices. Most research studies will turn up what seem like rational patronage motives, and a retailer must pay attention to these. In one sense these motives represent the store's projected image and indicate the success of the firm's effort to communicate with the customer and in particular to satisfy the consumer's needs. The listing of these motives, however, does not necessarily mean that the retailer must concern himself with each factor. Featuring the third item in the table, "good values," may overcome any deficiency the store may have. On the other hand, it is well known that a customer rarely has only one motive for shopping in a store. For example, a shopper may shop at department store A because of low prices, friendly salesclerks, and the availability of excellent parking. Less frequently she may shop at department store B because of the occasional bargains it offers and its excellent location. In the latter case, the shopping is sporadic, as bargain sales are conducted on a less than regular basis. Knowing these motives a retailer can direct his effort toward the individual motivations of most of his customers. In the case of store B, assuming our shopper's motivation is similar to that of a large proportion of customers, it is incumbent upon management to maintain a bargain image.

How trustworthy are these motives offered by the consumer? No doubt a great deal of reliance can be placed on a study that indicates the rational motives of consumers. However, most retailers are aware that rational motives are not always the best indicators of a consumer's feeling. Nor in fact are consumers aware of their motivation; psychology tells us much about unconscious motives. An unconscious motive by definition refers to a motive of which the person is unaware. For example, a young man may admire a young woman because he believes her to be what he admires in a woman. This is the conscious and rational reason. Unconsciously, however (and perhaps totally unbeknown to him) he admires her because she resembles his mother. All unconscious motives represent repressed feelings, that is, unpleasant things that are put out of mind or in the unconscious. Hence, a shopper with feelings of guilt concerning wealth (which may be based on unpleasant family associations with wealth) may tend to shop in low-status stores. Upon being interviewed this shopper may well offer "low prices" or "convenient location" as more rational reasons. This type of individual may be found doing social work or following intellectual pursuits. Another shopper may completely avoid shopping at stores where trading stamps are given for many reasons not discernible from simple interviewing. A person brought up under a strong Protestant ethic (even having discarded this philosophy) may view stamps as representing "something for nothing" and they may be repugnant to that person's unconscious.

Cognition

How does the consumer satisfy the drives we have outlined above? One way is by going out and searching for satisfying products and services. He becomes aware of these ways through his senses; however, these perceptions are also influenced by his experiences. Perception (or cognition) has been defined as "the process of becoming aware of objects, qualities, or relations by way of the sense organs. . . . What is perceived is influenced by . . . experience. . . ."[6]

A consumer's choice of objects and the like is strongly influenced, therefore, by the mental processes related to his perception of the object he is considering. In evaluating products the consumer in a typical supermarket is faced with many choices. His decisions in this case are based on how he perceives the product and his

---

[6]Ernest R. Hilgard, *Introduction to Psychology,* 2nd ed. (New York: Harcourt, Brace & Company, 1957), p. 587.

understanding of the meaning of the product in relationship to his goals and drives. His memory may play a part, and his past experiences, if applicable, may also help him to arrive at a decision. The consumer's evaluation of the product he is considering may be made on the basis of its outward appearance, the information contained on the label of the product, its color, its smell, and the appeal of the displays that promote the product. If the manufacturer of the product can identify the determinants that go into developing the cognitive image of his product, he can attempt to improve this image and can, through research, evaluate its impact.

Similarly, the consumer perceives a store through his cognitive powers. For example, a consumer may find that she is relaxed and comfortable in shopping in department store A, whereas she does not get this same feeling when she shops in A's competitor. What characteristics of store A are crucial in developing her image of the firm?

In Table 6-2 are listed the major cognitive determinants of a store image.[7] Though there are twenty-nine determinants listed, they can be classified into six major groups: the location of the store, the suitability of the merchandise, the values offered, the store services, the congeniality, and the post-transaction satisfaction. The last item is of particular importance since the consumer, if pleased, will have developed a favorable learning experience and will continue to buy at that store. If, as noted in the next section, this favorable experience is multiplied, the consumer may reach the stage of having formed a shopping habit which is almost automatic in its operation.

Learning

After purchasing a product at a particular store the consumer has on the surface satisfied a need. If the customer is completely satisfied with the product and services the firm offers, this process will no doubt be repeated many times. Each succeeding purchase reinforces the conviction that this store and the products it sells are a vehicle to satisfying needs. Where this process is continued for a long period of time the consumer develops shopping habits; habits that are directly related to the learning process.

On the other hand, the consumer may be dissatisfied with both the goods and the services purchased from the retailer. Instead of satisfaction of needs and desires the shopper encounters what is called frustration. Frustration also involves learning in that this experience, if repeated often enough, will induce the consumer to consider other means of satisfying wants.

Habits

The automatic reaction of a person to a stimulus constitutes a habit. Habits are formed through learning and experience. In encountering similar situations a person learns to respond in the same manner. Habits differ from instincts in that habits are learned. However, they do not depend on the thinking process, but involve the repetition of an automatic response to a stimulus.

Habit is an important determinant of consumer patronage. Consumers do develop shopping habits that are automatic, and are without regard to rationality.

---

[7]For a little different approach to measuring image see F. Ronald Stephenson, "Identifying Determinants of Retail Patronage," *Journal of Marketing* (July, 1969), p. 57.

Determinants of Cognitive Dimensions of Store Image   TABLE 6-2

Cognitive Dimension	Determinants
Locational convenience	Access routes
	Traffic barriers
	Traveling time
	Parking availability on arrival
Merchandise suitability	Number of brands stocked
	Quality of lines stocked
	Breadth of assortment
	Depth of assortment
	Number of outstanding departments within store
Value for price	Price of particular item (Z) in a particular store
	Price of item (Z) in competing store
	Price of particular item (Z) in particular store on sale day
	Prices of substitute products in substitute stores
	Trading stamps and patronage discounts in kind
Sales effort and store services	Courtesy of sales clerks
	Helpfulness of sales clerks
	Advertising, reliability, usefulness
	Billing procedures, adequacy of credit arrangements
	Delivery promptness and care
	Restaurant, eating facilities
Congeniality of store	Store layout
	Store decor and attractiveness of merchandise display
	Class of customers
	Store traffic and congestion
Post-transaction satisfaction	Satisfaction with merchandise in use
	Satisfaction with returns and adjustments
	Satisfaction with price paid
	Satisfaction with shopping experience in store
	Satisfaction with accessibility to store

Source: George Fisk, "A Conceptual Model for Studying Customer Image," *Journal of Retailing,* Winter 1961-1962,

As noted above, habits are derived from our previous experience. And in some cases the experiences may be based on the shopping habits of a member or members of the immediate family. For example, a newlywed may shop mainly at stores patronized by her mother. The choice of these outlets may be practically unquestioned by the shopper, and the retailer has only to maintain his basic services and goods to retain this customer's goodwill.

Habits operate in strange ways. For example, the food chains have failed in some measure to attract the housewife to their meat departments. A sizable proportion of meat shopping is still done in the butcher shop. It is the belief of some experts that the food chain stores are faced with the need of changing shopping habits early in life. Some say that a simple transfer of this habit from mother to daughter seems most probable in the sale of meat.

Thus patronage habits are formed at various stages in the life of the consumer. Once they are set they are difficult to change.

Frustration

A frustrating event is one in which goal-directed activity is blocked, slowed up, or otherwise interfered with.[8] Shoppers are often faced with frustrating circumstances that affect their shopping habits. There are many indications of consumer reactions to frustration that have changed some major shopping patterns.

Do consumers encounter a great deal of frustration in their everyday shopping? What forms do their reactions take? Consumers do encounter such frustration. An author recently attempted to measure the extent of this frustration, and in particular to indicate whether it varies by income class and occupation, the theory being that the higher the social class the more sensitive the buyer is to failures in a store's services and goods.

In Table 6-3 it can be seen that the higher the shopper's income, the more likely the frustration. It is interesting to note in the table that the highest area of frustration among the upper-income groups is in fact the lowest area of frustration for the lower-income groups. This would seem to indicate that not all groups react the same to frustrating situations in a typical retail store.

What do these customers do when they are frustrated? In theory they have three choices. First, they may continue shopping at this store and in effect do nothing. Second, they can simply take out their resentment on the store personnel in a face-to-face encounter. As any salesperson can tell you, this happens often. Third, they can take their business elsewhere. This certainly occurs but to what extent is not clear. However, one motivation research disciple suggests that the recent growth of the discount house can be partially attributed to the consumer's need to punish the traditional store for its many years of "poor service, arrogance, and out-datedness of other sales operations."[9]

SUMMARY

In their striving to understand consumer motivation both manufacturers and retailers are interested in different and sometimes contrasting aspects. The manufacturer is mainly interested in the consumer's attitude toward his product. The retailer is primarily concerned with patronage motives. Once the consumer is in the store, however, the retailer is interested in monitoring the consumer's behavior with respect to classes of merchandise, such as boys' wear.

Understanding the motivation of the consumer, that is, the urge to attain some goal-object, requires an understanding of both the physiological and psychological

---

[8] Hilgard, *op. cit.,* p. 176.

[9] Speech by Ernest Dichter, "Bargain Yes – Insults NO," given at the Second Discount Management Congress, New York City, June 6, 1962.

100 = Extreme Frustration

	Income $0-$5,999	Income $6,000-$11,999
Must return several times to shopping center to get what you want.	71.0	80.9
Advertised goods out of stock before you get to store.	64.3	75.8
Store out of weight or texture of clothes you desire.	67.0	71.9
Store out of color you desire.	56.3	90.6
Clerks slow to serve you.	68.7	75.0
Clerks pounce on you as soon as you enter.	71.3	78.5
Clerks sell aggressively.	73.0	85.2

Source: Charles J. Collazzo, Jr., "Effects of Income Upon Shopping Attitudes and Frustrations," *Journal of Retailing,* Spring, 1965.

needs of the consumer. Among the physiological are the basic needs such as food, thirst, and sex. Among the psychological needs are safety needs (need for protection against danger); social needs (more need for belonging); and egotistic needs (the need for self-esteem).

These drives are translated by the consumer through his cognitive powers or senses. How he perceives a store or a product determines how well it meets his needs. An important aspect for a retailer is to identify these cognitive dimensions such as location, value, merchandise suitability, and the like.

Over a period of time the satisfied customer may develop a habit, namely, shopping at the same store. This habit is *learned,* a process that usually develops over time. Conversely, a consumer could find his shopping experiences frustrating and thus learn to avoid a given store.

QUESTIONS

1. What is meant by a "hierarchy" of needs?
2. Manufacturers and retailers emphasize different aspects of human behavior. Why is this so?
3. What are the *three* major determinants of human behavior? Describe each.
4. Define and relate to human behavior in terms of retailing:
   a. frustration
   b. habits
   c. unconscious motives
5. Is the retail firm concerned solely with patronage motives? Why or why not?
6. Describe some probable decisions concerning human behavior that must be made by a manager or owner of a:
   a. food supermarket
   b. candy store
   c. newsstand

    d. men's apparel department in a large department store

    e. appliance discount house

  7. If Table 6-1 represented variety stores, what would be the top five characteristics influencing the consumer's choice of places to shop?

  8. What role do habits play in the development of patronage motives?

  9. Referring to Table 6-3, explain why higher-income groups seem to be much more frustrated about their shopping experiences than do other income groups.

10. Develop some advertising appeals for a department store based on the findings in Table 6-1.

11. What are rationalized motives? Some view rationalized motives offered by the consumer as being misleading. Why is this so?

12. List some major cognitive determinants for a:

    a. product

    b. department store

13. List some recent frustrating experiences you or a member of your family have had as a result of a shopping excursion. How have these experiences affected your shopping patterns?

14. Why is the consumer referred to as an uncontrollable factor in the environment of the retail store?

15. Of the six major determinants of store image (see Table 6-2) how would you rank location in reference to a:

    a. food store

    b. department store

    c. jewelry store

    d. restaurant

    e. drug store

Why?

Group
Behavior
and
Market
Segmentation

7

OBJECTIVES YOU SHOULD MEET

1. *Explain* the role of groups and segments to the retailer.
2. *Distinguish* between demographic and social-personality groups.
3. *Illustrate* a demographic characteristic that can identify a segment for a retail store.
4. *Illustrate* a social-personality characteristic that can identify a segment for a retail store.

In the two previous chapters the customer has been studied from the point of view of the *quantitative* and *psychological* information that is available to us. However, much of this information exists in a vacuum and cannot be useful unless it can be applied to large segments of the population. For example, though it is easily understandable that the individual consumer reacts to shopping frustration, the question from an operational point of view is whether there are enough of these consumers to constitute a meaningful market? Or, if it can be shown that families and their expenditure patterns vary according to the family life cycle, the problem then arises as to whether there exists a group large enough to constitute a market at a given stage in this cycle. Our problem, therefore, in this chapter is to direct our thinking to group segmentation of a market. In particular, we are concerned with the bases for segmenting markets and the types of groups that constitute a meaningful market for a retail firm's products.

A word of caution should be extended. It is important to recognize that, though there is evidence that groups exist and influence behavior, not all patronage is based on reference to groups. In fact, most purchasing probably does not involve group reference. Certainly a good deal of food shopping is based more on convenience than on any social-group influences. It is more than likely, however, that much of the shopping in specialty stores and department stores is influenced by groups.

Though these segments or groups will be discussed in detail, nevertheless there are cases where firms *do not* find it necessary to segment their offerings in the strict interpretation of the term. This deviation is known as the "shotgun" approach to retail strategy.

It can be applied to a large number of retail firms that have little interest in selling to a segment of the retail market. Quite a few take the view that all consumers are potential purchasers at their store. There is some support for this in retail studies which report that many food supermarkets are patronized by *all* income groups and social classes. This view may prevail in stores that have a weak image in the mind of the consumer. Such stores may offer the consumer wide price ranges and assortments. This type of store may also be found in small cities where *all* segments must be induced to shop in a store in order for it to maintain a profitable business.

Retailers opposed to the shotgun approach are aware of the problems of reaching a certain segment of the market. One of the obstacles they face is the fact that the major medium of communication, the newspaper, reaches the total market. Manufacturing firms, on the other hand, have a much easier task if they wish to reach certain segments of the market because of the nature of their business. For example, the manufacturer can advertise in media that accent his strategy. A manufacturer of a face cream that aids in the curing of teen-age skin disorders would naturally run a promotional campaign in teen-age magazines, or patronize radio stations that have a large teen-age following, or even advertise in school papers that are read by this group. Thus, a manufacturer is able to direct a good deal of his effort directly to a segment of the total market for goods and services.

Retailers, however, find it difficult to develop such a program. The first problem is that retailers rarely find magazine advertising within their budgetary limits. In addition, retailers are prone to favor newspaper advertising because it reaches their immediate audience, whereas a magazine involves a great deal of wasted circulation. More important, however, is the idea presented in an earlier section that retailers

are not concerned with the individual product, but with all the products sold whether in a department or within the entire store. In the example of teen-age cosmetics, the strategy of the retail firm would be to develop a local image as the place to shop for such cosmetics.

The smaller retail firms have an even more difficult problem, as management is limited to an audience immediately surrounding the store. It is therefore incumbent upon management to attain as much volume as possible from this limited trading area. This would be particularly true, for example, for the small corner grocery store. In spite of this limitation, however, many stores of this type have become successful by segmenting their audience into groups that are attracted by a liberal credit policy or speedy delivery service in spite of the higher prices.

Identifying Segments

Because of the vast number of competitors faced by the retail store, the well-managed firm must have a clear idea as to the segment of the consumer market it hopes to attract. As an example of the problems posed by competition, consider the independent men's wear retail store in almost any metropolitan area.

Competition may range from the men's wear department in the department store, to the men's wear chain store, the national mail order firm, the large apparel specialty chain (J. C. Penney), and the numerous independent (small and large) men's wear stores. If all of the smaller stores were to use the shotgun approach, they would be under great economic pressure. It is more than likely that these stores carefully cultivate a segment of the local market. For example, one firm may offer custom tailoring combined with easy credit terms, in the hope of attracting the fastidious dresser.

Though this may seem to be a plausible means of maintaining a profitable enterprise, it is usual to find that more than one firm is vying for the same segments. In addition, the firms will overlap even in markets where they do not concentrate their efforts. The major problem for the firm, then, is to determine where *most* of its potential customers come from and how they can be profitably attracted to the firm.

As an illustration of this concept, consider Figure 7-1. This probability distribution is based on the demographic characteristic of *location*. As interpreted in this diagram, the market is divided into major twin-directional four-mile segments. The highest probability of attracting consumers is within a location of one mile (in each direction) from the store. In fact, though the probabilities

107
*Group
Behavior
and
Market
Segmentation*

Total Potential Market Segment Based on Location Characteristics   **FIGURE 7-1**

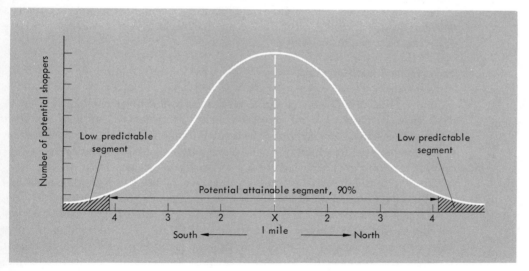

decrease, most of the customers of this store are estimated to come from a distance up to four miles. Beyond this distance, the probability becomes distinctly lower — approximately 10 per cent of the total market studied. It is within the 90 per cent group, therefore, that the store hopes to obtain most of its customers and thus become a profitable enterprise, and it is this group that must be studied carefully. Nevertheless, the firm cannot totally ignore those beyond the four-mile limit, as these customers can be a profitable addition. And for that matter stores do attract many people from outside their trading zone. However, this group represents additional business to the store and is not a group at which the firm should or would aim its promotional effort.

Location as a characteristic is just one of many that can be studied in much the same manner. Perhaps the firm measures its segment of the market in terms of income. Thus, families with annual incomes ranging from $5,000 to $10,000 may be defined as the potential market for a large specialty store selling appliances. The management of the firm may be aware that many of the customers on any given day have annual incomes exceeding their target market by a considerable margin. However, management's view will not be altered by this fact since the target segment of income is the market that helps to guide the total effort of the firm. It not only affects over-all policy but guides the buying policies of every buyer in the firm. Should the firm continue using this segment as the target of its total effort, it would serve as a guide in choosing any additional sites for a branch store.

The challenge to management is how to identify these segments — a task that is difficult but at the same time crucial to the long-run profitability of the firm. In essence, market segmentation in retailing refers to the attempt of the store to identify the major markets for its goods and services.

Market segments for purposes of retail management can be grouped into two broad categories: *demographic* and *social-personality groups*. Included in the demographic are many characteristics noted in Chapter 5, such as family income, expenditures, age, location, stage in life cycle, and so on. Social-personality characteristics include such relevant factors as status among friends and community and dominant personality characteristics, such as extravagant, value-conscious, price-conscious, and many others.

1) Demographic Characteristics

Among retailers demographic characteristics are by far the more important. Even retail firms concentrating on social-personality characteristics of their markets would still be forced to take into consideration meaningful demographic indicators in the community. The retail firm must always be assured of a plentiful supply of consumers with a minimum family income. Demographic characteristics loom large in choosing a site for a new store. The location of the population becomes an important ingredient in the determination of the value of a given retail site.

The task of management is to select those demographic characteristics that are relevant in the determination of the market. Thus, the firm that appeals to the fashion-conscious shopper will probably look for income characteristics, suburban locations, and stages in the life cycle that most nearly fit the needs of this firm. Hence, a high-priced women's specialty shop may choose a location in a small but exclusive suburban community rather than a large shopping center that cuts across all income groups.

2) Social-Personality Characteristics

Almost everybody is a member of a social group, whether small or large. Institutional groups such as the church, state, and organized labor are important in our society. Some of these memberships may be formal, as in bridge clubs, hobby

109
*Group
Behavior
and
Market
Segmentation*

groups, fraternal organizations; neighbors, friends, and family relationships are among the less formal associations.

As Americans live in a highly industrialized and mobile society, they tend to have memberships in many groups, some of them conflicting. Take the case of a college professor. Through his occupation he belongs to the academic world and identifies with this group in many ways. His mode of living and his leisure-time activities tend to be governed by reference to this group. Strong influences are continually exerted upon him by the specialized journals he reads and the communications from colleagues and the hierarchy of his world. Other literature that he reads and television programs that he watches may be directly related to this world. Within the professor's family there may be a teenager who lives in a somewhat different world — one which revolves around his friends and his attempt to achieve status and recognition with reference to peer groups. Hence, the clothes he wears, how he spends his allowance, and the like may be related to these groups.

It will be recalled from the previous chapter that man has a hierarchy of needs. One level is related directly to his membership in groups, namely, the fulfillment of his social needs. The other level refers to man's egotistical needs. We have already noted that the fulfillment of man's egotistic needs is closely related to the desire for status. Man is constantly striving to improve his status and thereby gain self-respect. Though this is a complex matter, part of this process can be achieved through shopping at stores and purchasing products that denote status.

The customer's choices of a store and products are influenced strongly by his social and personality characteristics. If, for example, his upbringing and maturation have imbued him with a particularly strong interest in price, he may shop in stores that make strong price appeals.

The problem of the retailer is to determine whether a particular type of customer exists in sufficient numbers to support his store.

Choice of Segments

There are in fact hundreds of different segments within the consumer market that a retailer can appeal to. Among these, however, there are considerably fewer that can support a firm. To illustrate, there is a segment of the market that is neurotically concerned with price. This group will spend hours shopping for convenience merchandise. Theoretically, it spends close to all its waking hours thinking about ways of reducing the next expenditure. It is no doubt possible to study this group, learn something of its shopping habits, and make a direct appeal to this neurosis. However, this group does not exist in sufficient numbers to make such an appeal profitable.

Most retailers believe that their appeal must be to groups that are relatively compact, that live in their trading area, and that exist in such numbers as to constitute a profitable market. Hence, in retailing the firm's appeal must be as broad-based as possible yet narrow enough to give management, and particularly lower management, direction in planning.

Though much has been said above concerning the demographic and social-personality segments of the market, the fact is that most classification of markets in retailing involves a choice and awareness of demographic characteristics. Thus, retailers choose markets and locations and aim their efforts at segments of the market that meet some sort of statistical average. On the other hand, there is a growing awareness among retail firms, particularly among the newer entrants into retailing, that catering to an economy-conscious consumer can prove to be a profitable business decision.

While personality characteristics are reasonable means of measuring segments of the market, in most cases the retailer thinks first in terms of demographic characteristics in isolating his market and second in terms of personality types. Rarely does he skip the first category.

Demographic Segments Illustrated

Though many of the demographic segments were illustrated in Chapter 5, it should be remembered that it is one thing to isolate a statistic and another thing to turn it into a useful classification that will give direction to the firm's merchandising program. In some instances a characteristic such as income can give direction to the total store program; but among other firms it may be relevant only to a particular department. For instance, income would seem to be a more meaningful statistic to the fine jewelry department than to the house dress department in a department store. Conversely, the number of teen-age boys in an area can be a relevant statistic to the buyer of boys' apparel and yet be almost meaningless to the rest of the store.

As stores put so much emphasis on the proximity of their market, it is understandable that since 1950 stores have favored market segments located in the suburban reaches of the metropolitan area. Another important demographic statistic, income, relates to this choice, because most suburban dwellers have higher family incomes than those who remain in the city.

This fact is demonstrated in Table 7-1, in which one sees that both the median and the mean incomes of families living outside the central city are substantially more than those of their counterparts within the city. It also indicates that the income in these areas between 1960 and 1970 is growing faster. Specifically, incomes outside the central city are increasing at a rate of 3 per cent annually compared with a little over 2 per cent a year inside the central city.

Every major city from coast to coast has stores that deliberately pursue the market that earns an above-average income. It has been said that department stores are mainly interested in middle-income families. In all major areas, there are stores that appeal mainly to higher-income groups. Saks Fifth Avenue (in both New York and California), Tiffany's (New York) and Neiman Marcus (Dallas) represent the type of store that caters to this market.

Conversely, John's Bargain Stores are an excellent example of how a diametrically opposed reaction to the demographic characteristic of income can also result in a successful operation. John's, an eastern variety-store operation, represents an interesting phenomenon that relies heavily on the income characteristics and location of its consumer markets. As a policy, John's stores offer the customer closeout and lower-priced merchandise in their hundreds of outlets. These stores as a practice do not carry regular supplies of staple merchandise. Nor do they carry a basic stock. The firm is also unusual in that its locations are invariably the

Income Characteristics of Families in Metropolitan Areas (Income in 1969 dollars,   **TABLE 7-1**
number of families in thousands, family data as of March 1970 and April 1960)

| | | 1970 Metropolitan Areas | | | 1960 Metropolitan Areas | |
| | | Inside Central Cities | Outside Central Cities | | Inside Central Cities | Outside Central Cities |
Income	Total			Total		
Median Income	$10,261	$ 9,157	$11,003	$ 7,880	$ 7,417	$ 8,351
Change 1960/1970	30%	23%	32%			
Mean Income	11,506	10,450	12,348	9,202	8,634	9,806
Change 1960/1970	25%	21%	26%			

Source: Adapted and computed from "Social and Economic Characteristics of the Population in Metropolitan and Non-Metropolitan Areas: 1970 and 1960," *U.S. Department of Commerce, Bureau of the Census,* June 24, 1971, p. 3.

lower-class neighborhoods, areas deserted by the middle-class family. In fact, these stores are usually located in areas where conventional retailers have long ago closed up shop.[1] Thus, location is chosen on the basis of income levels; the stores serve a community where fashion plays a minor role but income is so low that response to bargains is usually dramatic.

Many other types of stores are related to demographic characteristics. Some outstanding examples are the franchised gasoline station or ice cream store. The latter, in particular, is concerned with two major demographic factors that can be identified: (1) the size of the population in the immediate area; (2) the proportion of that population passing the proposed site. The gasoline station is concerned with passing traffic also. However, its concern is with automobile rather than pedestrian traffic.

Demographic Characteristics and Store Types

Can demographic characteristics be used to identify significant segments of a retail store? One study seems to indicate that large segments of a store market can be identified by: (1) income; (2) life cycle; and (3) residence. In a study of downtown shoppers in two major metropolitan areas, Professor Rich observed that if one categorizes department stores into three major groups — high-fashion, price-appeal, and broad-appeal stores — large segments of the shoppers in these firms can be identified by these three demographic characteristics.

In Figure 7-2, middle-income groups account for 60 per cent of the shoppers in the price-appeal stores. This same group represents about 43 per cent of the shoppers in the high-fashion department store. According to this same analysis, shoppers in the "no children" life cycle stage represent 52 per cent of the shoppers in the typical high-fashion store. This same group represents only one quarter of the shoppers in the department stores with a broad appeal. Analysis by type of residence shows major differences between city and suburban residents regarding store preferences. City dwellers prefer broad-appeal department stores, whereas suburban residents are more likely to shop in downtown high-fashion stores.

---

[1]Frank Schlesinger, "John's Bargain Stores," *The New York Retailer,* April, 1963, p. 14.

FIGURE 7-2 Downtown Store Types and Customer Characteristics

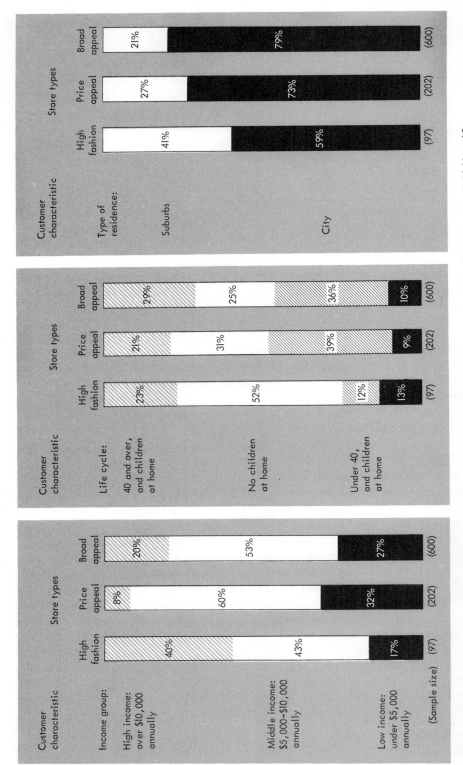

Adapted from Stuart U. Rich and Bernard D. Portis, "The 'Imageries' of Department Stores," *Journal of Marketing,* April, 1964, p. 13.

113
*Group
Behavior
and
Market
Segmentation*

To sum up, this study supports the view that demographic characteristics can be used to identify significant segments of the consumer market.

Psychological and Personality Segmentation Illustrated

Most stores are aware of the psychological image they convey to the public. Much of this image is developed by means of the locations they choose, the prices they charge, the goods and services they offer and the means by which they promote themselves to the buying public. As a direct result of this effort, each store takes on a distinct personality in the minds of the consumer. This personality eventually determines the type of shopper that will be attracted to the store.

In the following sections a number of stores and their personalities will be discussed. First, however, it must be remembered that general shopping areas have also developed personalities. For example, as noted above, the downtown area of the city still attracts the fashion-conscious female shopper. The downtown shopper's concern is with the styling and fashion goods with a particular emphasis on newness. Many of these shoppers are interested in being first. This attitude does not fit any one income group exclusively. Admittedly, however, it is more appealing to the higher-income families. Nevertheless, the demographic characteristic of income is not a true measure of the total market for fashion goods. The psychological effect of the shoppers' attitude toward change and aesthetics seems more applicable than a quantitative measurement.

As further evidence of the different personality types, consider the data presented in Table 7-2. Here one sees a comparison of different life-style characteristics of furniture shoppers patronizing both furniture and department stores.

Because of the scaling technique used, low values show a higher association with the life-style factor. For example, the score of 1.65 for furniture store shoppers indicates they are more fashion conscious than department store shoppers who have a mean of 1.78. Furniture store shoppers tend to be more conservative as measured by the mean of −.04 versus .08 for department stores. Conversely the furniture store shopper (variable 3) is not so careful a shopper as the department store shopper.

Altogether, however, this table indicates several life-style variables that can be used to identify customer groups.

In a similar comparison made between shoppers for stereo equipment in specialty stores and in department stores, one study indicated that shoppers in the specialty store:

1. are less likely to perceive risk in purchasing in these stores;
2. had more self confidence;
3. were more likely to be opinion leaders;[2]

These differences are particularly important in that it was noted in the study that the occupational and income levels of these groups of shoppers were similar.

[2]Joseph F. Dash, "Store Choice: An Investigation of the Characteristics of Consumers Who Bought Audio Equipment from a Specialty Retailer Versus A Department Store," unpublished doctoral dissertation, Bernard M. Baruch College, City University of New York, 1973.

TABLE 7-2 Tables of Comparative Means for Two Types of Retail Outlets and Fifteen Life-Style Variables.

	Variable	Department Store	Furniture Store
1.	Fashion conscious*	1.78	1.65
2.	Poor housekeeper	− .81	− .79
3.	Careful shopper*	1.80	1.93
4.	Disinterest in community affairs*	−1.84	−1.98
5.	Appreciation of the arts	2.12	2.11
6.	Sports spectator	2.87	2.77
7.	Do-it-yourself homemaker	1.96	1.94
8.	Conservative shopper	− .08	− .04
9.	Child oriented	1.08	1.06
10.	Modern thinker	−1.55	−1.60
11.	Energetic	.71	.65
12.	Weight conscious	1.93	1.97
13.	Sports participant	2.23	2.23
14.	Socialite	1.83	1.77
15.	Self-centered	− .24	− .27

*Means are significantly different at .10 level.
Source: Walter S. Good and Otto Suchsland, "Consumer Life Styles and Their Relationship to Market Behavior Regarding Household Furniture," Research Bulletin 26, Michigan State University, Agricultural Experiment Station, p. 27.

Thus, the social-personality characteristics discriminated between the two groups of shoppers.

Men's Wear Stores — Secure Personality

An interesting contrast and demonstration of the usefulness and development of the psychological-personality concept of store image can be found in certain types of men's wear retail stores.

The first distinct type is the favorite of nationally branded manufacturers. This store carries only branded products. Arrow shirts, Hickok belts, Botany suits, Freeman shoes, all represent brands that are featured, advertised, and promoted by the retailers. The psychological appeal is to the consumer who is relatively insecure in choosing merchandise. For this individual nationally branded products instill confidence that culminates in a sale. The retailer, in effect, is saying in his promotion to the public, "confidence for sale here," and he emphasizes the quality and the dignity involved in carrying well-known, well-established products in his store. In direct contrast is the men's wear retail store that does not carry any nationally branded products. This firm appeals to the consumer who is more secure in his choice of products. Still other stores are reluctant to make a definitive merchandising decision and therefore carry both national brands and private brands. However, most of these stores tend to emphasize one or the other and end up attracting either the insecure or secure customer.

The higher-priced men's specialty stores usually carry their own private apparel merchandise. Their reasoning is that higher-income customers have more confidence in their own ability to choose the products they want. Though no definitive study is available, it is known that many of the lower-income groups in the large cities prefer to purchase branded products.

115
*Group
Behavior
and
Market
Segmentation*

Discount Stores — Economical Personality

Throughout the past twenty years, the United States has experienced a phenomenal growth in discount houses. Stores doing business under this banner have a great source of appeal to the price-conscious consumer. If we were to judge the size of the price-conscious audience simply by the growth in this kind of retailing, we would conclude that a sizable portion of the American population falls into this grouping. On the other hand, many authorities who have studied discounting suggest that the early development of stores like E. J. Korvette, and Polks (Chicago), and chains like Zayres, was partly the result of a game played by many upper-class Americans. This game was usually played on a Saturday night when invited guests would announce the prices they had paid for well-known branded products. The victor, of course, was the one who obtained the lowest price in his shopping throughout the week.

In any case, the growth of the discount store has reinforced the view that most areas contain enough economy-oriented consumers to make this an important segment of a market.

Department Stores — Status-Conscious Group

In terms of status, the majority of general merchandise firms make direct appeals to certain high-, middle-, and low-status consumers. These stores through their advertising, pricing policies, products, and locations develop a personality that appeals to large segments of the market.

Two interesting and contrasting types of stores are Sears, Roebuck and Marshall Field. The typical Sears store usually attracts a "blue-collar" or a lower-status shopper. One authority suggests that the lower-status shopper looks at goods from a functional point of view: she wants the store to reflect her values of economy, practicality, and dependability.[3] In addition, Sears shoppers are likely to shop as a family.

In direct contrast, the shopper at Marshall Field (a downtown Chicago department store) is quite willing to shop alone.[4] Sears' merchandising policies and appeals are almost the opposite of those of Marshall Field. The Marshall Field environment includes a respect and restraint from the salesclerk that would probably be interpreted by the Sears customer as much too formal.[5] The Sears emphasis on savings might also be distasteful to the Marshall Field shopper.

As Sears is one of Chicago's largest stores, an easy explanation of its success would be that it has shown an ability to attract a high proportion of this type of

[3]Pierre Martineau, "The Personality of the Retail Store," *Harvard Business Review,* January-February, 1958, p. 50.

[4]*Idem.*

[5]*Idem.*

shopper. However, identification of the shopper and the image the store engenders is not a sufficient explanation for its success. It is more than likely that the values mentioned above — economy, dependability, and practicality — are all reinforced by the firm's policies. One analyst suggests that Sears' apparent success is due to its ability to appeal to four different market segments corresponding to four different value conceptions held by women. For these women, value means:[6]

1. A willingness to pay a little more for a quality product.
2. Merchandise on sale.
3. Merchandise sold at the lowest possible price.
4. Merchandise sold as seconds.

Furniture Stores — Authority Types

Furniture stores represent several types of outlets that seem to attract distinctive segments of the consumer market. These three classes of stores are:[7]

1. Those selling what is commonly called "borax."
2. Those stores selling fashionable furniture with an emphasis on fairly standard items.
3. Those stores selling high-fashion furniture and offering complete decorator services.

The salesmen in these outlets are well aware of the distinctive customers that they attract. Professor Tucker describes the different personalities assumed by salesmen in each of these outlets. In the first store he suggests that the salesman is usually forceful, dynamic, and somewhat brusque with the customer. He is likely to make it clear to the customer that he has superior information (though in actuality he may not) and acts the part of the authority figure. As his own social status is not much above the customer's (he is working in a store that deals with low-status groups, which reflects on his status), he delights in attaining "small social triumphs" over his customer, even at the risk of losing a sale. In spite of this attitude, the customer still relies on the salesman's recommendation simply because he himself lacks the self-confidence to make decisions.

The salesman in the second firm is more likely to be friendly and show more respect for his customers' opinions. He usually cannot play the expert because his customer may have superior knowledge. His approach to selling therefore is to discuss unrelated factors, mainly to determine the customer's occupation and social status. His job is to take himself out of the role of salesman and become a friend of his customer.

The third type of store features a salesman who does have superior knowledge. His sales talk is concerned with aesthetic considerations instead of with the construction of the furniture; and in some cases he may refuse to sell a certain fabric or piece of furniture with the simple explanation: "It is just not for you."

---

[6] Daniel Yankelovich, "New Criteria for Market Segmentation," *Harvard Business Review,* March-April, 1964, p. 88.

[7] W. T. Tucker, *The Social Context of Economic Behavior* (New York: Holt, Rinehart and Winston, 1964), p. 74.

Any refusal on the customer's part implies that he is lacking in taste or simply cannot afford the furniture in the store.

117
*Group
Behavior
and
Market
Segmentation*

Clearly, these stores do attract different segments of the market, and the firm reacts accordingly. It is important to remember that these customer types, though identifiable to some extent by income, can also be classified by social-personality characteristics.

SUMMARY

We have concentrated in the previous two chapters on the quantitative aspects of the retailer's market (i.e., population, income, and expenditure) and the motivational aspects of the individual consumer's behavior.

However the retailer does not deal with either the individual or large population groups. His main interest is usually in sizeable groups and segments of a market. Successful firms are characterized by their ability to identify a segment of the market and concentrate their efforts in that direction.

Major segments can be grouped into two brand categories: demographic and social-personality groups. Demographic segments are those identified through quantitative statistics, such as higher-income groups in suburban areas. Social-personality segments are illustrated by the men's store appealing to the secure personality, discounters appealing to the economical personality, and department stores appealing to status-conscious groups. The furniture store illustrates the fact that outlets in the same retailing industry can engage in different appeals. Among these stores we have identified the "borax" outlet, the fashion furniture store, and the high-fashion decorator outlet. In each of these stores the salesman has a different job to perform.

QUESTIONS

1. Define demographic and social-personality factors. What are their distinguishing characteristics?
2. Under what conditions would a firm use more than one *demographic* factor to identify a target segment?
3. List some articles sold by retailers that have status significance to the purchaser.
4. List five stores in your community that have a status appeal – either high or low.
5. Discuss the pros and cons of using the "shotgun" approach as a strategy for a jewelry store.
6. In what ways can age affect the choice of a store?
7. Relate brand-buying behavior to personality characteristics of consumers in:
   a. a food chain
   b. a small retail food store
8. Do you agree with one author that low prices account for the appeal and most of the success of the discount store?

9. The statement is made that the middle-class Marshall Field shopper is more likely to shop alone than the "blue-collar" housewife. Do you agree or disagree? Discuss the reasons for your answer.

10. In planning to open a variety store in a suburban area, what demographic information would management be interested in? Would your suggestions be altered if they were considering opening a chain food supermarket? If so, in what way?

11. Discuss the possible characteristics that would tend to identify a target segment for the following types of retail and service firms:

   a. women's high-fashion specialty store
   b. basement department of a department store
   c. franchised donut shop
   d. employment agency
   e. restaurant featuring French food and fine wines

12. In question 11 above, demonstrate how the characteristics identified for the women's high-fashion specialty store act concurrently with the policies of the firm relating to promotion, pricing, distribution of goods, and services offered.

13. As noted in Table 7-1, why do families in the suburbs have higher income than those inside the central cities?

14. How can the income differential noted in Table 7-1 affect the supermarket?

THE
CONTROLLABLE
FACTORS
III

Up to this point this book has been concerned with the major *uncontrollable aspects* of the retailer's environment. In a sense the reader has been presented with a picture of retail management looking outward at its environment.

In the rest of the study the controllable aspects of the retail firm will be examined in detail. It must be remembered that these three major divisions — *goods and services, communication,* and *physical distribution* — are the areas of management for which choices are made, strategies developed, and tactics selected — all, of course, with an eye to the environment outside the retail establishment.

INTRODUCTION TO
THE GOODS AND SERVICES MIX

Retailers sell products and services. Their choice of what products to sell and what services to offer covers a major area of decision making.

This section on the goods and services mix is divided into four chapters. The first is concerned with the organization of the buying function and the selection by the retail firm of new products and assortments. The second chapter is concerned with the institutions and the economic pressures that help to establish the terms of the purchase. The third chapter is concerned with the types of services offered by the retailer and their cost. The last chapter is devoted to the pricing of the merchandise by the retail firm.

Introduction
to
Buying

8

OBJECTIVES YOU SHOULD MEET

1. *Distinguish* between the uncontrollable and the controllable aspects of the retailer's environment.

2. *What* is meant by the *goods and services* mix?

3. *Distinguish* among the three general ways retail firms organize for buying.

4. *Define* buying committee and specification buying.

5. *Specify* the conditions under which a firm goes into specification buying.

6. *Indicate* how a firm evaluates new products.

7. *Distinguish* between adding to the *depth* and adding to the *width* of a store merchandise line.

The J. C. Penney Company is one of the largest retail firms in the world. In the year ending January 31, 1973, sales of this company were over $5 billion. At the closing of their year total assets of the company were $2,153,679,745. Of these assets about 50 per cent are made up by the total merchandise inventories in the firm.[1]

The huge investment of its assets in inventories by the J. C. Penney Company is not unusual in the typical retail firm. The retail firms' investment in inventories indicates clearly the concern of retailers with the control of its stock.

Management is concerned both with the buying of stock and with the control of its present inventories. The managerial means (both techniques and organizational methods) of controlling inventories in the retail store will be discussed in subsequent chapters. Because retail decision making at the top and at lower levels is

---

[1] J. C. Penney Company, Inc., 1973 Annual Report.

concerned primarily with choosing the merchandise for sale and because poor decisions in this area are usually costly regardless of the level of sophistication a firm may reach in its inventory control methods, the subject matter of this section deals with what a retailer should stock and in particular *on what basis these decisions can be made.* These decisions must be based on the firm's knowledge of consumer buying habits in relation to various types of goods. For example, management must ask: Are the products puchased basically a consumer convenience or does the consumer spend considerable time shopping and comparing prices? Or, Is the purchase of this product a direct function of traffic and exposure? Management that has the answers to questions such as these has a basis for sound merchandising decision making.

Sometimes the answers to these questions are obvious, at other times, obscure. For example, cigarette sales are closely related to exposure and traffic. Hence, they are found at checkout counters in supermarkets and are sold at many heavily traveled thoroughfares such as commuter terminals and the first floor of major office buildings. On the other hand, furniture stores or the furniture department of a general merchandise store are rarely situated in heavily trafficked areas. Between these extremes are a large number of durable and nondurable products whose relationship to traffic and exposure varies.

The retail firm, however, not only sells the customer goods but in most cases offers services. Therefore, management must be in a position to choose the right services as well as the right goods. In the next few chapters we will discuss the means firms use to evaluate and select the proper goods and services mix.

Organizing for Selecting Merchandise

Three general ways of organizing for buying exist in the retail field: the owner-buyer, central buying, and decentralized buying.

Owner-Buyer

The owner-buyer arrangement is found in the small retail firm. Here the owner purchases the merchandise and with his employees engages in the sale of it. As this type of buying arrangement allows the owner little time in the marketplace, great reliance is placed on wholesalers or, in the case of fashion merchandise, buying representatives. Or the owner may place his orders for merchandise through salesmen of the wholesaler or manufacturer who make regular calls.

Centralized Buying

The larger multi-unit retail outlet has two distinct choices in organizing its buying function. It can leave the buying to the individual units or it can concentrate all of its buying efforts at a central point. The latter technique is the most widely used among the larger chains. There are many advantages to central buying, the most obvious of which are the economies of scale that accrue to the firm. By purchasing merchandise centrally the firm can qualify for discounts that are unavailable to smaller competitors. In addition, centralizing the paperwork and distribution helps to maintain a better control over the money spent on building up individual stores.

Centralized buying has its problems, however. For instance, it may mean buying for a store whose customers are totally unfamiliar to the buyer in the central office. In addition, the huge amount of central paperwork may cause delays and errors and, in particular, duplication, since a great deal of the centralized function is performed again at the individual store. This problem is overcome in some instances by having the vendor drop ship to a designated store even though the merchandise is purchased centrally.

A sketch of the typical centralized buying organization is presented in Figure 8-1. In this chart five major management functions are shown. The main role is performed by the buyer, who determines what items will be bought and, together with the merchandise manager, how much and when.

One Type of Central Buying Organization   **FIGURE 8-1**

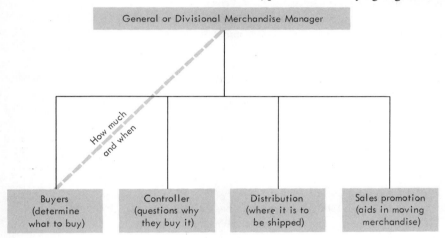

The remaining functions — *control, distribution,* and *sales promotion* — are dependent on the buyer first purchasing the merchandise. The control function, as noted in Figure 8-1, questions the buyer's decision to buy. The essential aspect of this function is to examine the expenditure carefully in terms of its timing, cost, and ultimate destination. A good controller would also question the terms of the purchase. His job is to make sure that the buyer is staying within reasonable financial limits.

Distribution is concerned with allocating the orders to the various stores based on their needs. Within the past ten years distribution has become increasingly important because of the proliferation of branch stores. This function determines not only how the merchandise is to be distributed but also the method of transportation to be used.

The last function, that of sales promotion, is also planned at this stage. The performance of this function is covered elsewhere in this book, as is physical distribution. Sales promotion has become a vital force in helping the individual units to plan their promotional activities and in alerting these firms to the attributes of the merchandise that is going to be purchased.

Committee Buying. Though centralized buying in most firms is done by an individual, major food chains are strong advocates of committee buying.

The Committee within a chain food store is made up of all levels of management. Table 8-1 is a listing of the job titles that are usually represented on the typical buying committee. As can be seen from this listing, almost all members of the committee represent top executive positions. Moreover, no one executive makes a final decision. In most cases, decisions are made on the basis of a consensus of the group. Though each committee operates in a different manner, certain procedures are followed by most firms. As a rule the committee is concerned with new products. However, in many cases the committee receives turnover and individual product reports and hence is in an excellent position to make decisions concerning the addition of a product line or in some cases the dropping of a product line.

TABLE 8-1   Job Titles Represented on Buying Committees

Job Title	By Store %
Merchandising manager	59
Advertising manager	44
Sales manager	30
Branch/division head	23
Purchasing director	21
Over-all department supervisor	21
Over-all department merchandising manager	20
Store supervisor/district manager	20
General/operating manager	17
Executive officer	9
Sales promotion manager	3
Warehouse/transportation manager	3
Store manager	2
Accountant	2
Personnel	1

Source: Howard L. Gordon, "How Important is the Chain Store Buying Committee?," *Journal of Marketing,* Vol. 25, No. 3 (January, 1961).

All products are screened prior to their presentation to the food committee by an organization executive, usually called the buyer. The buyer listens to and evaluates presentations by manufacturers' representatives or salesmen and collects the necessary information, presenting it to the committee at the weekly or biweekly meeting. On the basis of the information presented the committee makes its decisions.

There are exceptions to this technique. A & P does not maintain such an arrangement. All new items must be approved by buyers and an executive officer. Approval at this level does not automatically constitute acceptance. Once approved, however, the goods can then be offered to the firm's nearly 40 operating divisions, scattered throughout the United States.[2]

The weakness in the committee buying system, besides the psychological problems implicit in group relationships, is the fact that the manufacturer rarely gets an opportunity to present his product directly to the committee. In effect, he is dependent on the committee's representative to present his product in a favorable manner. Conversely, the effectiveness of the committee is dependent on the caliber of the buyer who presents the information.

Decentralized Buying

Decentralization occurs when a multi-unit firm allows each store to purchase merchandise separately. Most large chains have units each of which does a certain amount of decentralized buying, that is, the units themselves purchase from local vendors to fill in stocks of staple merchandise. Similarly department stores have had to face the postwar problem of buying for several branches. Traditionally these stores have maintained separate buying staffs for similar-sized units located in other metropolitan areas. Some idea of the relationship between the downtown store and the branches can be seen in Figure 8-2. In both department and specialty stores the trend has been steady upward. For instance, in 1964 branch stores owned by department stores accounted for 47.4 per cent of total firm sales. In the latest year the branches accounted for almost two thirds of total firm sales. Federated Department Stores, the largest department store chain in the United States, noted that their branch stores produced 61.2 per cent of the firm's volume in 1971.[3]

The branches of department stores are usually located in the same metropolitan area, and the individual branch store has a sales volume considerably below that of the main store. The downtown store can either assume the buying duties for each branch or supply each branch with buying personnel. Most firms have done the former, though many have allowed the management staff of the branch to buy a considerable amount of merchandise locally.

The choice of centralizing or decentralizing the buying depends a great deal on the type of merchandise sold and the trading area of the firm. A firm selling staple merchandise that requires little knowledge of fashion on the part of the buyer would respond well to centralized buying. Conversely, a firm selling fashion merchandise would find it more difficult to purchase centrally as consumer taste may vary considerably within the same metropolitan area. In the case of the specialty chain store, consumer taste may vary from one section of the country to another.

It has become an established practice among most centrally organized firms to allow the local units an opportunity to purchase some merchandise directly to cater to the needs of special segments of the consuming public. A typical example might be found in the food field, in a branch store serving an Italian-American group whose tastes would not be met by the central buying office. The firm usually has a policy of buying these items locally for the store or simply leasing the department involved to a local operator.

---

[2]*The Marketing Structure for Selected Processed Food Products* (Washington, D.C.: Pan American Union), p. 23.

[3]Federated Department Stores, Inc., *1971 Annual Report*, p. 2.

FIGURE 8-2   Branch Stores Contribution, Percentage of Total Company Sales

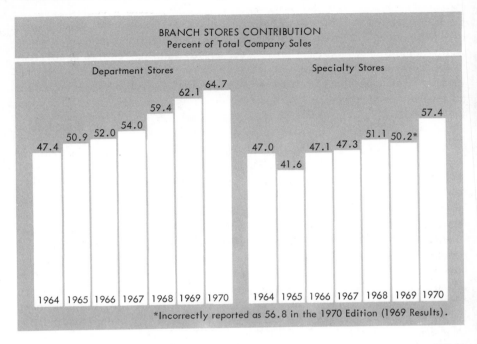

Adapted from *Financial and Operating Results of Department and Specialty Stores of 1970,* Controllers' Congress, National Retail Merchants Association, 1971.

Specification Buying

A retail firm has two ways of obtaining goods for its customers. First, the firm can simply buy from accredited manufacturers (or their representatives) in the field — manufacturers, incidentally, over which the firm has little control and rarely the opportunity to influence the product offered. This group includes most of the suppliers of retail stores and is the subject of much of our later discussion.

The other means of obtaining merchandise is buying by *specification*. Here the retailer has control over the product produced and in some cases may be directly involved in its manufacture. Specification buying takes place when the buyer asks for a change in the product offered by a vendor.[4] This may be simply a request by the buyer for a minor change in a product already manufactured. Or, on the other hand the retail firm may completely document the type of product to be produced. In between, we have variations. For example, in the fashion apparel field a buyer may request a change regarding the collar on a woman's dress, or Macy's may request a specific size of package for its private-label product. A furniture store may request wrought-iron legs on a dinette set, rather than aluminum. All these represent examples of buying by specification.

Specification buying differs considerably among firms. However, there are certain basic characteristics present in all buying of this sort. First, the retailer starts with an idea as to his needs, in other words, the type of product he believes his

_____

[4]See John W. Wingate and Joseph S. Friedlander, *The Management of Retail Buying,* 3rd ed. (Englewood Cliffs, N.J.: Prentice-Hall, 1963), p. 273.

customers will buy. Otherwise he could simply purchase the product on the open market. Second, the supplier or manufacturer usually seeks a contract, which specifies the amount to be purchased and in some cases the profit attached to each item. Third, the item to be sold is usually (but not always) priced to sell below a national brand product.

The agreements among retailers and suppliers vary. Where the retailer seeks out a supplier the contract is for a certain stipulated length of time, and the retailer has limited rights in terms of letting the manufacturer determine how he shall produce the product. On the other hand, there are many cases where the manufacturer has a direct financial interest in the vendor and therefore has more working knowledge of the firm's operation. For example, in recent years Sears, Roebuck assembled a group of apparel suppliers and formed the Kellwood Corporation, which is to supply Sears with much of its apparel and sporting goods needs. Sears in forming this corporation retained a 25 per cent interest in it. The dependence of the Kellwood Corporation on Sears' business gives Sears, even without the large stockholdings, a strong voice in the firm's management.

When should a retail firm go into specification buying? There is no simple answer, but usually a combination of five characteristics should be present.[5]

1. *Sufficient Volume Potential.* To interest a supplier to convert his plant to making a specific product, the sales volume potential must be considerable.

2. *Possibility of Developing New Features.* Products to which new features can be added are ordinarily good candidates for specification buying. By adding a feature, the firm is able to offer the customer additional value for her money.

3. *Possibility of Improvement in Quality.* A product may be improved in quality over the competing national brand through specification buying. Buying a shoe that has an all-leather lining (as opposed to the usual leather-cloth combination) represents an example of quality specification buying.

4. *Potential Cost Reduction.* By placing large orders with certain firms, it is possible to secure price reductions that would not be available on a well-known national product. In most cases the application of the Robinson-Patman Act would preclude a large retail firm from obtaining a sizeable price concession unavailable to its competition. By simply specifying the purchase of a similar product with a lesser-known manufacturer, considerable savings can be had in the marketplace.

5. *Possible Savings in Better Supplier Location.* By choosing a supplier that can produce to specification near the firm's outlets, considerable reductions in transportation and inventory requirements can be obtained.

Private and National Brands

The above details of specification buying are best understood if we differentiate the two types of brands available to the retailer, namely, private and national brands.

National brand is simply another name for a brand product that has been promoted by a manufacturer. This product is usually recognized by the consumer because of the large promotional campaign behind its development. In some cases, however, major retail firms such as Sears and A & P have developed brands that

[5]William T. Kelley, "Specification Buying by the Large-Scale Retailer: An Aspect of Vertical Integration," *Journal of Marketing,* Vol. XVIII, No. 3 (January, 1954), pp. 263-264.

have achieved national status. Nevertheless, the term "national brand" usually refers to a manufacturer-owned product.

The importance of private brands varies by the type of outlet and the character of the products sold. For instance, W. T. Grant private brands account for *60 per cent of sales.*[6] The Grant junior department stores now have yearly sales exceeding $1.5 billion.

U.S. grocery stores report private brands account for about 22 per cent of sales of frozen and refrigerated goods; 2 per cent of health and beauty aids and about 13 per cent of dry groceries and household supplies.[7]

The extent to which a firm will strive to obtain a private brand is seen in the marketing of Sears Coldspot refrigerator. The refrigerator is manufactured by the largest producer of appliances in Europe, ZANUSSI. This company manufactures the Sears refrigerator in the Italian Alps under the Coldspot name.[8]

Sears in particular, in recent years, has been advertising many of its private brands on television and thus giving them national exposure. Ads for All-State tires and batteries are featured in their advertising program.

By now it should be clear that specification buying is usually engaged in by large retail firms interested in developing their own private brands, which are not available for sale in competing outlets.[9] As a matter of fact this seems to be the major reason for retailers' carrying unbranded products.

Other advantages also accrue to the retailer carrying private brand merchandise. For example, by developing his own brands he allows himself the option of choosing his own resources, the implication being that he can switch from firm to firm in order to get the best values for his money. In addition, the fact that he can switch suppliers gives his firm a superior bargaining position. Another major advantage is that he can maintain a flexible pricing system. If he carries manufacturers' brands he is usually tied to a standard list price or markup policy. Even if the manufacturer allows him to set his own retail prices, the chances are slim that he will be able to set prices above the industrywide markups simply because of the pressures of competition. Thus, his price flexibility is limited to a downward movement.

Yet many retail firms carry manufacturers' brands in large quantities. Their major reason for doing this is that many of these products are pre-sold. For example, Dole probably sells more than half of all the canned pineapple in the United States. Obviously, most major food retailers are forced to carry this product because of consumer demand. Carrying branded products provides other advantages to the retail firm. These products may have a higher turnover, help offset a store's lack of promotional activities (particularly in small retail outlets), and help the retailer maintain a standard quality in his merchandise offerings.

However, the effectiveness of brands varies considerably, as can be seen in Table 8-2. For example, the range for Heinz catsup is from a low of 11.7 per cent of the market in Honolulu to a high of 71.8 per cent of the market in the Duluth

---

[6] *The Discount Merchandiser,* February, 1970, p. 16.

[7] *Progressive Grocer,* July, 1972, p. 40.

[8] *Forbes,* May 1, 1971, p. 24.

[9] One recent exception to this is the announcement by R. H. Macy that its private brand drug products will be merchandised nationally through other retail outlets.

TABLE 8-2 Brand Preferences for Catsup in Selected Cities

Percentage of Households in Each City Preferring Various Brands

Brand	Honolulu	Long Beach	Salt Lake City	Wichita	St. Paul	Duluth-Superior, Minnesota	Milwaukee	Chicago	Indianapolis	Fort Wayne, Indiana
Heinz	11.7	26.4	23.0	34.0	65.3	71.8	43.0	46.0	28.0	43.5
Del Monte	63.6	26.9	31.2	26.0	9.9	6.9	16.0	10.0	13.3	21.4
Hunt's	19.1	28.8	6.0	—	14.5	8.9	6.0	10.0	—	7.1
Snider	—	8.0	7.9	—	2.8	4.7	7.0	10.0	—	6.4
Libby's	1.4	—	—	5.0	—	—	—	—	—	—
Dole	2.4	—	—	—	—	—	—	—	—	—
Springfield	—	2.9	—	—	—	—	—	—	—	—
S.S. Pierce	—	—	18.8	—	—	—	—	—	—	—
Brooks	—	—	—	8.0	—	—	—	—	13.0	4.8
IGA	—	—	—	7.0	—	—	—	—	—	—
Red Owl	—	—	—	—	9.9	3.0	—	—	—	—
Ann Page (A & P)	—	—	—	—	—	—	6.0	7.0	3.7	—
Stokely	—	—	—	—	—	—	—	—	20.9	—
Other Brands	1.8	7.0	13.1	20.0	—	4.7	22.0	17.0	21.1	16.8
Total	100.0	100.0	100.0	100.0	101.4[1]	100.0	100.0	100.0	100.0	100.0

[1]Total adds to more than 100 per cent due to sample duplication.
Source: *The Marketing Structure For Selected Processed Food Products, op. cit.,* p. 17.

129

area. This points up one of the major problems of retailers in choosing brands — making a determination of the relative strength of a manufacturer's brand. This problem can only be solved through experience and testing. The much larger decision as to whether to carry a national brand or develop a private brand product is closely related to the following factors.[10]

1. Whether the manufacturers' brands are strongly entrenched in a market.

2. Whether a dependable quality and quantity are available at a reasonable price in order to insure a dependable source of supply. This can be further insured if the retailer does his own manufacturing or processing. For example, the Daitch Shopwell stores, a food chain in the New York area, process many of their own dairy products and compete directly with many of the nationally branded products.

3. Whether the manufacturers' brands are overpriced.

4. Whether the promotion of a private brand would be too costly.

5. Whether a well-established market for the product exists.

6. Whether consumer is able to recognize the value easily.

These conditions, singly or in combination, must be weighed in making a decision. For example, it is doubtful that a retailer would develop a private brand where the already available national brands have almost 100 per cent consumer acceptance.

Buying Decisions

The actual buying of the merchandise is made by the owner in the case of small stores and the lower management levels in the case of large retail firms. In the larger stores the buying decision can be made formally (through committee efforts) or informally through the efforts of a single individual with the aid of an assistant. The latter is the procedure followed in most firms.

In the following sections, the major elements that enter into a buying decision in all types of retail outlets are covered.

Evaluating Merchandise Lines

Most stores by the very nature of their business are obliged to carry certain types of merchandise classifications. One would expect an ice cream parlor to carry ice cream. One would be surprised if an ice cream parlor carried apparel or a stationery store food products. However, one cannot be sure what products will be found in a drugstore. In New Orleans or Baltimore a drugstore is a major outlet for liquor. In New York City the drugstore may be a place to buy lunch, purchase tobacco products, or examine a variety of merchandise items ranging from clocks to thermos bottles. Ed Gold came up with the following examples of what we shall call "scrambled merchandise."[11] Pointing out that Grand Union food stores now carry apparel, he characterized this as selling everything from "tuna to trousers."

In Torrance, California a food store using over 25% of its space for non-foods; a drug store owned by Sears, Roebuck; E. J. Korvette, the

---

[10]E. Jerome McCarthy, *Basic Marketing* (Homewood, Ill: Richard D. Irwin, Inc., 1960), p. 270.

[11]*The Dynamics of Retailing* (New York: Fairchild Publications, Inc., 1963).

famed discounter, entering the "appetizing" field in their store in West Orange, New Jersey; and lastly, a general merchandise store built by a major oil company. The store, air conditioned, features a garden center, gifts, flowers.

This trend has been particularly striking in the food field. Food supermarkets have been most aware of the increasing tendency of consumers to purchase what is usually referred to as non-food items in supermarkets. One study noted that 6.1 per cent of the sales of food stores were accounted for by non-food sales. Health and beauty aids accounted for over 50 per cent of the non-food sales; housewares 2 per cent; soft goods 7 per cent; and magazines and books 5 per cent.[12]

Table 8-3 lists the various lines of non-food products carried by grocery stores. They range from fresh flowers to school supplies. The most widely sold fall into the categories of stationery, apparel, and houseware supplies.

Percentage of Food Stores Carrying Various Non-food Lines, 1971.   TABLE 8-3

Lines	*Stores Stocking Item*
Panty hose	94%
Housewares	88
School supplies	86
Stationery	76
Magazines	68
Toys	65
Soft goods (other than panty hose)	56
Camera film and supplies	52
Home sewing	51
Beer	50
Books	43
Garden supplies	37
Phono records	32
Wine	32
Fresh flowers	20
Liquor	12

Source: Adopted from *Progressive Grocer,* April, 1972, p. 80.

This tendency has resulted in a closer examination of consumer shopping patterns and a reevaluation of the kinds of products a firm can offer to a potential customer. In addition, many other variables have to be considered such as competition, availability of store space, and availability of personnel. As an illustration of the elements involved in determining what goods to offer, consider a furniture firm that is contemplating the addition of appliances to its line of products. These are a few of the factors that the firm must take into account.

1. Appliance selling is highly competitive, as the dominance of brands makes price comparisons relatively easy.

---

[12]*Progressive Grocer,* April, 1972, p. 101.

2. Appliance selling requires the use of easy credit. In many cases the stores must make credit arrangements for the customer.

3. Appliance selling requires employing well-qualified salesmen and the use of incentive compensation plans.

4. Appliance selling requires that a retailer make delivery arrangements for the consumer.

5. Appliance selling usually requires that a retailer have established floor planning (credit) arrangements with distributors or manufacturers.

These factors must be considered by retailers in making a decision. Obviously if the firm cannot make financial arrangements for the consumer or with distributors, it cannot carry appliances. If the firm cannot make delivery arrangements or is disinclined to get involved with customer delivery, the chance of running a successful appliance department is practically nil. At this stage there are probably a number of other questions concerning the sale of appliances that one can think of to ask management. However, such specific criteria must be preceded by more basic considerations. Almost all major decisions as to the development of new product lines are concerned at the start with three general factors:

1. The reactions of consumers to the new product line in the present store environment.

2. The prospects of profit.

3. Competition (related to the above).

Applied to the decision involved in adding appliances to the present offerings of a single-line furniture store, the first consideration, as noted, would be the consumer's reaction to shopping for appliances in a furniture store. We might theorize that the consumer would expect to see appliances displayed in a furniture store because both products appeal to those interested in home furnishings. Therefore, our decision would be positive on this score.

The second question, the additional profits that would accrue from carrying a product line of appliances, might indeed be tricky to handle as it would involve an evaluation of competition and an appraisal of the lines of appliances that should be stocked. However, if we assume that the store can obtain an exclusive franchise (and the nearest similar franchised dealer is across town) we might envision a substantial profit.

In evaluating profit potential, present furniture profits would have to be compared with the potential profits expected from appliances. But even if it is found that appliances do not compare favorably with furniture in terms of dollar profits, the firm may still consider carrying the product line, as anything appliances add over and above variable costs would help to cover the store's fixed costs. More will be said on this subject when we come to the chapter on pricing. It is sufficient to note at this stage that marginal pricing is involved in this decision.

Lastly, no decision can be made without considering competition. Obviously, if two or three appliance stores are located on the same block, management may consider the situation too competitive and the chances of attaining a profit too limited. On the other hand, management may feel that the exclusivity of a line may give the store an edge in competition. In addition, management may believe that the very presence of a number of appliance stores on the same block may act as a magnet to shoppers looking for appliances and furthermore that this very competition may be the source of developing potential customers and exposing them to the furniture offerings of the store.

It is not too often that a firm must consider making a major decision about its product offerings. Usually, decisions to increase the product offerings have to do with minor additions and as a result many are made on the lower management levels.

Width and Depth of the Assortment

The width of the assortment to be offered to the customer can be divided into two levels of decision making: (1) the addition (or subtraction) of lines of merchandise to the store — e.g., a men's shoe store adds a line of shoe polish; and (2) the addition of more depth to the present lines — e.g., increasing the number of brands, sizes, or colors.

Judgments as to the addition of new lines of merchandise to be offered depend a great deal on the subjective evaluation of management concerning the nature of the market and how willing customers are to travel the necessary distance to find the kind of merchandise they want. As a rule, the minimum number of items necessary to attract a customer to a store increases with the customer's distance from that store. Theoretically, a customer would be willing to travel a good distance to a store only if there were reasonable assurance that the merchandise shopped for would be found at this outlet.[13] Since customers do not shop for the total offerings of the store, it follows that consumers judge individual product groups in relationship to the distance traveled. Thus, if a consumer has the feeling of a low probability of success in shopping for a television set at store A, he will undoubtedly shop at a competitor of store A where the probability is much greater. From the point of view of management, judgments must be made as to the relationship of the variety they should carry and the distance the customer is willing to travel. Though this is basically a subjective judgment, it can be verified to a limited extent through market research.

Figure 8-3 illustrates this concept. In essence, it shows that though consumer Y is willing to travel a certain distance to shop for variety X, by increasing variety X to X' the retailer can increase his market to Y'. Obviously, a point of diminishing returns sets in, and in this case it is unlikely that customers will increase if he adds to his variety beyond X'. Just where to draw this line is a crucial management judgment.

Decision making involving depth of assortment — in terms of such factors as size or colors — concerns the individual department more than it does the top-level merchandising executives. At the department store level, the buyer would more than likely make the decisions. His decisions would relate to many basic problems. For instance, should he carry a wing-tipped men's shoe and, if so, in what colors? At what point should he restrict the number of hosiery brands he offers the consumer? How many sizes of men's shoes shall he stock? All these require a decision on his part.

---

[13] Martin Zober, *Marketing Management* (John Wiley and Sons, Inc., New York, 1964), p. 131.

FIGURE 8-3   Width of Assortment Related to Distance Customer Must Travel

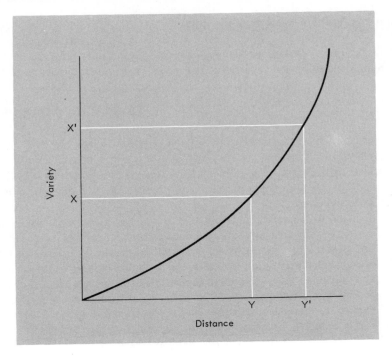

Adapted from Zober, idem.

The decision is not made easily. One problem in most stores is that there is limited space. For instance if he is the food buyer for a chain of supermarkets he is aware that at some point it becomes uneconomical to add more depth to his present lines. It becomes uneconomical because at some point his returns from the addition of factors will begin to diminish. This comes about because the addition of colors, sizes, and the like can reach a point where additional sales are acquired by diminishing the sales of other lines within the same department.

Figure 8-4 illustrates this point. The product illustrated here could be the previously mentioned wing-tipped shoes. The first color sells at the rate of four pairs per week. The addition of a second color raises the sales of the shoes to seven. Two additional colors bring the total sales to a peak of ten. A fifth color results in no additional sales. The buyer, knowing or sensing this, would restrict his offerings to four colors.

This figure is illustrated in table form on the opposite page.

This illustration could be based on dollar gross profit, dollar net profit, dollar contribution to overhead, or a number of other measurements. In any case, it is the task of the buyer to identify the point at which further inventory investment becomes uneconomical.

Choosing New Products   How does a buyer finally decide what product to buy? In general, his decision reflects his subjective evaluation of the product's worth to the consumer. This may

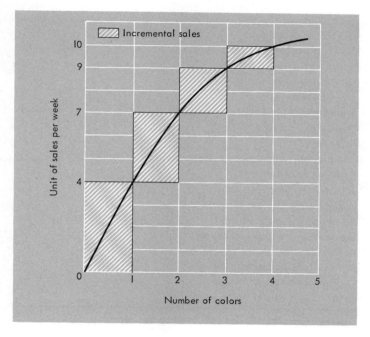

Adapted from Wingate, op. cit., p. 152.

(1) Number of Colors	Total Sales Per Week	(2) Incremental Sales
1	4	4
2	7	3
3	9	2
4	10	1
5	10	0

be based simply on past sales experience with the product or on no experience, since many of his evaluations are made for new products.

How does a firm evaluate new products? What particular attributes of a product should a buyer consider before offering it to his customers? The major attribute of course is its sales appeal; in other words, its implicit value to the customer. A product that does not pass this test is surely a candidate for rejection. However, there are many other features a firm can consider in making a judgment. Table 8-4 presents some of the characteristics a food chain might evaluate in choosing new products.

Rarely would a product be rated high for a majority of these features. Probably only a few of them would be considered pertinent. In addition, some of these factors would not apply to each product. For example, it is unlikely that cooperative advertising ranks high in the sale of unbranded exotic fruits. On the

TABLE 8-4 Food Chain's Evaluation of Factors Affecting the Choice of a New Product

	Rank
Usefulness of product	1
Does not duplicate an existing item	2
Product profitability	3
Advertising support	4
Gross margin	5
Appearance of package	6
Quality of package	7
Retail price	8
Good experience with manufacturer's other products	9
Reputation of supplier	10
Test market results	11
Introductory allowance	12
Advertising allowance	13
Amount of shelf space occupied	14
Deals offered	15
In-store merchandising support	16
Competitor's action on new item	17
Item well-presented by salesman	18

Source: "The Selection and Introduction of New Items, A Study of Retailer Attitudes," *The Food Trade Marketing Council Report to the Industry,* No. 5, September, 1964, p. 15.

other hand, it may well be the decisive factor in purchasing a new coffee product.

Many other instances can be offered. It would be unlikely that a new brand of frozen orange juice would get a response if the markup was below the norm for the regular frozen orange products. Conversely, a lower cost (which might result in a higher markup but not necessarily so) might induce the buying committee to offer this product to the consumers for the first time.

Consider the actions of a buying committee in its evaluation of the following products:[14]

A blue and perfumed liquid starch, which had been rejected at a previous meeting, was now accepted in view of the fact that consumer demand caused some store managers to ask for its reconsideration. To make room for the product, a competitor's product was discontinued.

A chiffon-pie mix was accepted because it was the view of the committee that there was no product like it in the store. The committee accepted the product in only the lemon and chocolate flavors, rejecting strawberry and butterscotch, feeling that space limitations and the seasonality of the product might cause some problems.

The committee also accepted a cheddar-cheese product with toothpicks included, feeling that the manufacturer of the product had a reputation for unique merchandising ideas. The committee felt, however, that the planned promotional

[14]Donald G. Hileman and Leonard A. Rosenstein, "Deliberations of a Chain Grocery Buying Committee," *Journal of Marketing,* Jan., 1961, pp. 52-55.

campaign (one advertisement in Life Magazine) was inadequate. The committee accepted the offer of the manufacturer to guarantee the sales of the product and provide a demonstrator in each store for two days.

The committee rejected four products — a coffeecake mix, sliced apple thins, rootbeer candy, and a pine-oil disinfectant — because it felt each of these products offered nothing new and had little in advertising support.

The committee after considerable debate rejected the purchase of a toothpaste that offered a low price on two tubes on the basis that the nationally accepted brands offered a greater advertising allowance and also used national advertising more extensively.

Would a guaranteed sale item automatically get acceptance? The answer, as many firms have found out, is not necessarily. Though there is little risk to the food chain in purchasing this item, management may well decide that the limited space in the food store should be taken up with faster-selling products of the same group which would yield a larger profit over the long run.

Just how a buyer or a committee decides exactly what merchandise to offer the customer depends on many factors — not the least of which, as we noted above, may be merely a subjective feeling. One is reminded of the experience during the postwar period of a major television manufacturer who, in spite of adverse findings based on a scientific market research study, decided to produce and market a small-sized television set. This happened to result in the firm's greatest success in the postwar period. The decision was based purely on a subjective feeling by the marketing executive, a feeling based on many years of experience. In some cases this may be a better way to make a product decision, although a buyer should usually consider all the available factors.

What Goods To Buy

The firm's choice of the major types of goods to carry is of course one of the main decisions to be made at the top organizational level of the firm. This basic decision serves as a guide to the lower management echelons (usually the buying staff) who are in the position of actually choosing the units of merchandise to be offered to the public.

The top-level and lower-level decisions are delineated in Figure 8-5. The first task of management is, as we noted earlier in the chapter, to choose the general types of products to be sold in the store. This decision may be a simple one: Are we going to sell soft or durable merchandise? Naturally, in most cases the decision was made many years ago by the firm's founders. However, as noted elsewhere in the text, management is always adding new types of products and there decisions are made on the same basis as a decision to start a store. Once the basic decision is made to carry, let us say, durable merchandise, the second-level decision as to the general line of products follows. The firm shown in Figure 8-5 decided to carry only television sets and major appliances. In addition, the general price levels based on the firm's objectives are decided at this level.

After completing the primary and second-level decisions, the decisions as to specific products are made, usually at the buyer or merchandising levels. This decision involves choosing the brands, sizes, colors, and materials of products to be stocked by the department. There are three restraints on the buyer at this stage:

FIGURE 8-5   Delineation of Top-level and Lower-level Management Decisions as to What Goods to Buy

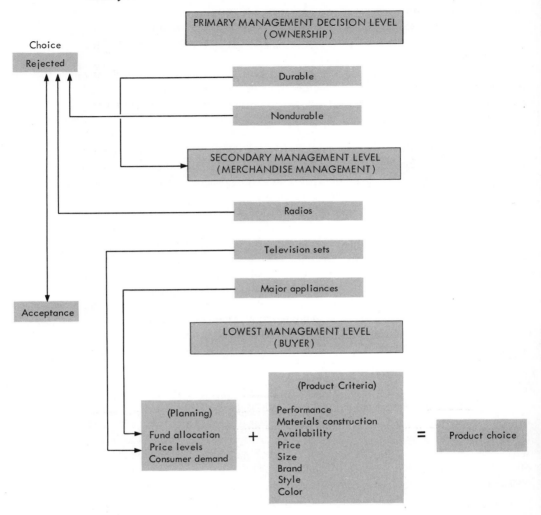

1. The dollar budget he is allotted;
2. The price levels of the products established by management with regard to the store objectives and goals; and
3. The buyer's understanding of the demand aspects of the products he sells.

The dollar budget and its implications will be discussed in Chapter 17. The pricing levels and the demand implications of the goods and services are covered in the chapters in this section.

A word should be said here about the buyer's evaluation of the demand aspects. As will be noted later, the buyer looks for the consumer information concerning demand. However, many buyers rely on their own intuition to make these determinations. And in the case of "high-fashion" merchandise, buyers often set the style patterns for their customers. One observer in his study of specialty stores called this type of intuitive judgment "creative arrogance," emphasizing the fact that many buying judgments were far removed from customer information.

Evaluating Specific Types of Goods

Retail firms are concerned with selling goods. Some of the stores restrict their offerings of products to one type of merchandise. Each type of product sold by the firm is looked upon differently by the consumer. As a result, the demand (over-all) and the intra-store competition vary considerably for each.

It is not the purpose of this chapter to evaluate each and every product the retailer may sell. However, we will discuss the major store divisions of goods and the implications of carrying each type of merchandise.

A retailer may divide his offerings into two major types of goods: shopping and convenience goods. Shopping goods are those goods a consumer spends time and effort in purchasing. Appliances, automobiles, and furniture dominate this group of merchandise. Convenience goods are those goods the consumer buys in nearby outlets and rarely spends much time shopping for. Food, cigarettes, and low-priced apparel products dominate this group.

It should be remembered that these two divisions of goods are not mutually exclusive. There is a large gray area. For example, apparel merchandise can be either shopping goods or convenience goods, depending on its price and availability. An expensive fashion garment may be a shopping good, whereas a child's blouse may not be. In addition, marketing experts have defined a *third* type of product sold in specialty stores and called "specialty goods." These products are usually higher-priced shopping goods. However, customers are apt to shop in these stores because of the wide selection offered them. Stores selling hi-fi equipment, photographic supplies, gourmet foods, and men's clothing represent this type of specialty outlet.

The point has been made that these broad classifications of merchandise are not mutually exclusive; it is still worthwhile to define our terms at this stage.

Shopping goods.[15] "Those consumers' goods which the customer, in the process of selecting a purchase, characteristically compares on such bases as suitability, quality, price, and style."

Convenience goods. "Those consumers' goods which the customer usually purchases frequently, immediately, and with a minimum of effort in comparison and buying."

Specialty goods. "Those consumers' goods with unique characteristics and/or brand identification, for which a significant group of buyers are habitually willing to make a special purchasing effort."

It will be noted that in each of these definitions there is an assumption concerning the consumer's reaction to merchandise offered. However, though we will generalize concerning some of the product lines, we should quickly add that individual consumers react quite differently to the same product area. In many

---

[15]All definitions are from "Marketing Definitions," compiled by the Committee on Definitions of the American Marketing Association, 1960.

cases what is a convenience good to one shopper may be a shopping good to another. Yet, in order to make decisions, management must generalize about the shopper. Management's understanding of consumer reaction to these product offerings is therefore basic to making the proper decision.

The value of the above definitions as an aid to developing a retail strategy lies in their ability to interpret how the consumer views shopping for goods. For as noted above, consumers are capable of viewing the same goods differently. It is also obvious that these definitions are not mutually exclusive and overlap greatly.

Attempts have been made to make these definitions more meaningful. One writer suggests that specialty goods cannot be distinguished from shopping or convenience goods.[16] Holten's definitions of shopping and convenience goods revolve around the consumers' evaluation of the probable gain from price and quality comparisons relative to the cost of shopping. Thus a convenience good can only be called so if the "majority of consumers view it as a convenience good."[17]

It should also be remembered, however, that though consumers react to goods, these goods are sold in retail stores. Thus, the patronage motives of consumers must also be considered along with their views of the goods. In fact, patronage motives (see Chapter 6) may be more important than product motives. Therefore, in buying a shopping good, a consumer with a strong patronage preference will be more inclined to buy the product sold by this particular retailer. Conversely, a consumer with a strong preference for a certain brand product (whether it be a convenience, shopping, or specialty good) is likely to choose the nearest store carrying this product.

One author has suggested that the problem of goods versus patronage motives is an important consideration and offers a means of classifying a retailer's market. By defining behavior in terms of product motives cross-classified by patronage motives, he distinguishes different segments of the market.[18]

In any case, when one realizes that many shopping goods are purchased in convenience stores and convenience goods in shopping goods stores, the possible strategies and combinations are endless. The retailer must be aware of their implications.

In retailing the problem raised by the consumers' motives affects at least three areas of decision making. The first is the location of the firm. For example, where should a children's wear store be located? If management is convinced that shoppers are mainly interested in convenience, rather than brands, it may regard a children's wear store as appealing to the convenience shopper! This decision obviously narrows the site selection process.

The second decision area affected by a definition of the types of goods sold and consumer patronage motives is the width and depth of the assortments. Thus, if management believes that the consumer is willing to accept substitutes (brands or non-branded), the width and depth of the assortment will be affected accordingly. Conversely, if the consumer is attached to one brand of a specialty good, but may

[16] Richard H. Holten, "The Distinction Between Convenience Goods, Shopping Goods, and Specialty Goods," *Journal of Marketing,* Vol. 23, No. 1 (July, 1958), p. 56.

[17] *Idem.*

[18] Louis Bucklin, "Retail Strategy and the Classification of Consumer Goods," *Journal of Marketing,* Vol. 27, No. 1 (January, 1963), pp. 50-55.

make a selection among a manageable number, the choice of assortments is thereby given more precise direction.

The third decision area affected by management's interpretation and definition of goods sold is the location of merchandise within the store. For example, within the department store, management usually places convenience goods on the main floor and shopping and specialty goods on the floors above. On the other hand, management's view of what constitutes convenience goods varies from store to store, indicating differences of opinion. In addition, many of these firms place what one might call shopping goods on the first floor, probably out of concern for other factors. Thus, they concur with Professor Bucklin who suggests that some products belong to a group called the convenience-shopping goods classification, meaning that the consumer selects his purchase from among assortments carried by the most accessible store and location.[19]

Consumer Reaction to Product Groups

A retailer is concerned mainly with *his* customers and *their* reactions. Though a retailer has a tendency to think in terms of his individual store customers, nevertheless he is affected by the over-all consumer demand, in particular the buying power of the consumers in his area. For example, his store would be affected by changes in the business cycle, particularly in the sale of appliances as will be illustrated below. The income level of consumers in his area will of course affect the demand for his goods, particularly if he is selling luxury products such as boats or fur coats.

Some of the reaction of consumers to products sold in stores can be seen in Table 8-5. Here one sees the change in personal consumption expenditures for each 1 per cent rise in disposable personal income. One finds that the total consumption of apparel rises at a slower rate than the rise in disposable income. Men's and Boys' apparel seems to be particularly inelastic (or slow to rise). Conversely, the rate of expenditures for automobiles, radio and TV, drugs, and household appliances rises more rapidly than most other items.

In the chapter on research we will point out some ways in which the retailer can evaluate the consumer's reaction to his store. In this section we shall generalize further about the peculiar properties of certain product lines, concentrating on two types of merchandise — appliances, both small and major, and apparel merchandise. Appliances fall into the category of shopping goods. Apparel, however, cannot be classified in such an exact manner. Low-priced children's apparel can probably be called convenience merchandise, high-style apparel may be shopping goods, and all apparel categories are available in specialty shops.

These products will be viewed from the point of view of (1) the effect of the business cycle on their sales; (2) the increasing demand for these products when income rises.

Appliances and Allied Durable Products

Over-all consumer demand for appliances is related to many things. It is strongly influenced by income structure, new family developments, and new housing

---

[19]*Ibid.*, p. 53.

TABLE 8-5 The Discretionary Effects of Rising Income
(Income-sensitivity ratios, based on years 1955-1970)

Item	Income Elasticity[1]	Item	Income Elasticity[1]
Total Expenditures[2]	.97	Semidurable house-furnishings	1.29
Food at home	.62	Household supplies	.96
Restaurant meals	.51		
Alcoholic beverages	.77	Personal care services	.76
Tobacco	.45	Toilet articles, preparations	1.50
Women's, children's apparel	1.01	Medical care services	1.16
Men's, boys' apparel	.91	Drugs, supplies	1.49
Footwear	.59	Automobile purchases	1.33
Shelter	1.16	Tires, tubes, accessories	1.72
Household operation services	1.06	Gasoline and oil	1.05
		Transportation services	.56
Furniture	.78		
Household appliances	1.43	Sporting goods, toys	1.71
Radio, TV, etc.	2.21	Foreign travel	1.61
China, glassware, utensils	1.22	Higher education	1.55

[1] Percentage change in personal consumption expenditures for each 1% rise in real disposable personal income
[2] Personal consumption expenditures
Source: *A Guide to Consumer Markets 1972/1973,* The Conference Board, 1972, p. 170

construction. In addition, innovations can certainly play a major role in the demand for these products.

Apart from direct influences, economists believe that the business cycle has an indirect influence on demand for these products. Analysis of some early postwar recessions seems to bear this out. These recessions, it may be recalled, took place at a time when consumers were "goods-starved" because of World War II. In spite of this overwhelming demand, it was observed that during the 1948–1949 recession output of kitchen appliances fell by 19.4 per cent, refrigerators by 9.4 per cent, and radios by 31.6 per cent. Similar declines took place in the 1953–1954 recession. The over-all decline in industrial production in 1948–1949 was only 5.4 per cent.[20] Thus, we see that the retailer specializing in the sale of appliances and related merchandise is faced with the vagaries of the business cycle. Though an individual retailer may be able to increase appliance sales at a time when the economy is heading downward, it is unlikely that he will be very successful.

In light of the above knowledge, can we say what the immediate impact on appliance sales would be if consumers experience an increase in disposable income? What would happen, for example, if disposable income increased by one per cent?

[20] Jules Backman, *The Economics of the Electrical Machinery Industry* (New York: New York University Press, 1962), p. 9.

A more eloquent economic term would be — Is the demand for appliances elastic or inelastic?[21] Studies of this relationship have been made. It has been found that with an increase of one per cent in disposable income, sales of major appliances will tend to increase by slightly less than that amount.[22] Thus demand for appliances is elastic and changing economic conditions may have a strong effect on the demand for appliances.

There are other characteristics of appliances that a retailer must take into consideration. First, the product itself has a long life. Therefore, repeat customers for the same product are mainly long run. Second, brands have made inroads in this field. The impact of brands makes it easier for the consumer to compare value and this can ultimately have a depressing effect on prices, particularly in the absence of fair trade laws. It has been the experience of retailers in this field that consumers are responsive to lower price.

Under these circumstances, it can be theorized that eventually many firms specializing in the sale of appliances are forced into expanding their offerings by carrying other lines of products in addition to appliances, or by buying only price-protected appliance lines (why is this so?). A good illustration of the growth of the protected line during the postwar period is the Magnavox Company, which offers protected television and radio franchises throughout the country. The movement into expanding product lines is probably best illustrated by the early postwar appliance and television discounters, who moved gradually into soft goods and other related product lines over the years.

Apparel Products

As might be expected, consumer demand for apparel products differs considerably from the demand for appliances. Apparel demand is relatively inelastic, that is, lower prices do not cause large increases in sales. Nor does an increase in consumer affluence. One study observed that during the postwar period a 10 per cent increase in personal disposable income resulted in only a 5 per cent rise in sales of clothing and shoes.

There are many reasons for this. For one thing, apparel is usually purchased as needed. This is particularly true in the sale of children's clothing and less so in the sale of women's better dresses. Nevertheless, it is a rare family that stocks up on clothing as soon as prices fall.

The lack of established brands or, more accurately, the minor importance of brands no doubt keeps consumers from recognizing values (that is, products sold at a low traditional markup), as in the case of appliances. This may have a mitigating effect on demand. On the other hand, consumer buying according to need has the effect of tempering fluctuations, and hence makes apparel expenditures less responsive to the ups and downs of the business cycle.

---

[21] Though elasticity usually refers to the degree of buyer response to changes in prices, in this section it is also referring to the well-recognized belief that the elasticity of a product line is either intensified or reduced when business conditions change. See Ralph Cassady, Jr., *Competition and Price Making in Food Retailing* (New York: The Ronald Press Company, 1962), pp. 31 and 32.

[22] Louis J. Paradiso and Mabel A. Smith, "Consumer Purchasing and Income Patterns," *Survey of Current Business,* March, 1959, p. 25.

Even though, as we noted, over-all apparel expenditures tend to be relatively constant, people in higher income groups do spend more money on apparel. Table 5-6 (see Chapter 5), a cross-sectional analysis of the expenditure patterns of various consumer income groups, showed that apparel expenditures relative to total expenditures do rise as income rises. Yet the actual increases are relatively stable in all groups earning over $3,000 a year. This observation seems to be in line with what we have discussed concerning the inelasticity of apparel expenditures in the total economy.

Though demand for apparel is relatively inelastic, that is, a decrease in prices will not bring about a sharp upturn in apparel purchases, it does not necessarily follow that the level of retail prices is unimportant. As noted earlier, the consumer indifference to brands (as compared to the brand value in the television set industry) leads to the conclusion that apparel products have a high rate of substitutability; that is, the consumer does not distinguish between brands as readily as in the purchasing of other types of merchandise. We might, for example, find that a consumer shopping for a boy's shirt would be likely to choose a store first; price, second; and last, brand name. Shopping behavior of this type indicates that apparel purchasing (particularly in its less fashionable aspects) approaches the economists' view of perfect competition. The lack of differentiation on the part of retailing also means that price and other retail promotional activities can serve to shift large sections of the consuming public to a particular store.

This is not to say that apparel manufacturers are unable to establish franchises. Many do; however, their ability to control sizable segments of the market is limited since brands are not a prime factor in consumer purchasing.

Imported Goods

Table 8-6 gives an indication of the amount of merchandise imported into this country.[23] Even without specific data one is well aware of the vast increase in clothing, radios (particularly transistor), and photographic equipment entering the United States from the Orient; the sizable amount of imported British and French apparel, gourmet foods from other European countries, and the ever-present foreign automobiles traversing our highways. Many of these products have a prestige appeal to the consumer. Others meet the needs of consumers who are continually searching for products that are different.

From the retailer's point of view, buying in foreign markets offers an opportunity to be different from competitors. The larger stores, by setting up international buying offices and sponsoring buying trips to foreign countries, are more likely to take advantage of these sources. Smaller firms may simply use U.S. importers to obtain similar merchandise.

Aside from the uniqueness of a great deal of foreign merchandise, it usually has a price advantage over U.S. manufactured goods. For example, custom-tailored Hong Kong clothing is usually sold at lower prices in the United States than

---

[23]One organization estimates that 10 per cent of all consumer goods sold in the United States are imported from foreign suppliers. "The Future of Retailing," 1972, Bureau of Advertising, American Newspaper Publishing Association, p. 24.

Coffee	$ 1,160
Meat and preparations	1,014
Textiles	1,135
Automobiles and parts	5,067
Watches and clocks	184
Toys, games, and sporting goods	427
Glass, glassware, and pottery	338
Clothing	1,267
Footwear	629
Photographic equipment	115
Total imports for consumption	$39,963

Source: Adapted from Statistical Abstract, 1971, pp. 777-778.

mass-produced clothing. Japanese photographic equipment has a similar price advantage.

On the other hand, a great deal of foreign merchandise may be priced much higher than U.S. goods. French dresses of an original design, well-engineered Japanese television sets (Sony), and Rolls Royce automobiles are all products that command higher prices in U.S. markets. Nevertheless, most imported merchandise has a great price appeal to the consuming public. Savings in the manufacture of foreign products are particularly marked where labor is a large element in the cost of production.

The growth of these markets was further spurred by the increasing pressure on large retailers to obtain profitable merchandise. Firms have found that they can buy foreign imports at lower prices and sell them at a markup above that of competitive products supplied by U.S. manufacturers.

Fashion

Selling apparel and goods that are considered to be fashionable is a means whereby a retailer can differentiate his offerings. Where does fashion in apparel begin and what is its role in retailing? Fashion begins in the apparel field with dress designers in some of the European capitals, particularly Paris and Rome. These capitals have for years been the centers for developing the latest dress designs. Though marketing experts do not agree completely on their influence on the American fashion markets, it is no doubt true that they do influence the sale and styling of apparel.[24]

The so-called "trickle-down theory" suggests that most fashion designs from these cities are copied by all levels of manufacturers and sold in all types of retail stores. Some sell expensive copies of the original designs; others translate these

---

[24]Dwight E. Robinson, "The Importance of Fashions in Taste to Business History: An Introductory Essay," *Business History Review,* Spring/Summer, 1963, pp. 29, 30.

fashions into the popular-priced dresses. An interesting aspect of all this is that the original designer dresses are a small part of the total fashion output and, as in the case of Dior, are practically subsidized by the foreign textile industries in order to stimulate dress production. On the other hand, they seem to be an important ingredient in influencing demand. Other observers downgrade the "trickle-down theory" as an important factor. For example, it was noted that the chemise, developed in the early 1950's, was a financial failure.[25] This view holds that basically consumers' tastes prevail and tend to influence the styling of clothes. Certainly, this view is less subject to question in the styling of men's clothing. In either case, some stores are thought to be highly fashion-conscious and therefore the place to shop for those interested in the latest "look." The many fashion specialty stores on Fifth Avenue in New York represent just such a market.

Many observers, though not rejecting the "trickle-down theory," have noted that fashions actually go through a three-stage cycle: distinctiveness, emulation, and economic emulation.[26] The distinctive stage in the fashion cycle represents the point at which an apparel product represents a new style and is available only in choice retail outlets at a high price. Many distinctive-stage products emanate from the fashion capitals of the world. In the second stage other manufacturers copy and emulate the distinctive fashion styles. At this stage, manufacturers copy the styles that hold the highest promise even though they are priced considerably above the mass-appeal market. Gradually, if the style at stage two shows promise of gaining the interest of the mass market, it then moves into the third stage where emphasis is put on quantity products at a relatively low cost.

From the viewpoint of management, the sale of high-fashion merchandise at stages one and two represents greater risks, reflected in the fact that some firms are geared to take a much higher rate of reduction on fashion merchandise than on the sale of staple or lower-priced merchandise. For example, in a recent report by the National Retail Merchants' Association it was reported that markdowns in a fashion dress department averaged 20 per cent in large stores, or considerably above the 5.8 per cent average for the store.

Seasonality as a Factor

When To Buy — Seasonality and Weather   The choice of when to buy is in many cases governed not only by economic conditions but also by the time of year. Food retailing offers excellent examples of wide seasonal variations in consumer demand for products. The fluctuation in demand affects not only the amount purchased but the price paid for the items purchased. In the food field, demand for some food products may fluctuate widely over the year and remain relatively stable for others. Figures 8-6 to 8-9 give us some indication of the variation in purchases of food products in Atlanta, Georgia. In particular, as we might expect, ice cream purchases vary widely over the year. Other wide variations occur in the sale of fresh fruits and eggs. Stability of demand is most apparent in the purchases of whole milk.

---

[25] See Stanley C. Hollander, "A Note on Fashion Leadership," *Business History Review,* Winter, 1963, p. 448.

[26] E. Jerome McCarthy, *Basic Marketing,* rev. ed. (Homewood, Ill.: Richard D. Irwin, Inc., 1964), p. 401.

Index of Seasonal Variations: Weekly per Capita Purchases and Expenditures of Eggs, Atlanta Consumer Panel, by Quarters, 1958-1962   FIGURE 8-6

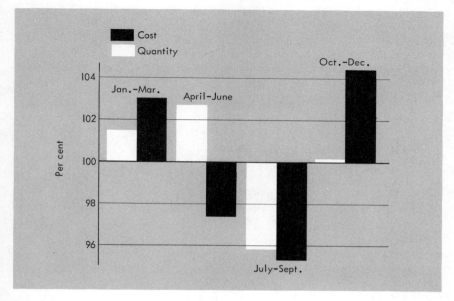

Adapted from K. E. Ford and N. M. Penny, "Seasonal Variation in Food Purchases and Costs," Georgia Experiment Station, University of Georgia College of Agriculture, Bulletin N. S. 114, May, 1964.

There are other types of purchases besides food where demand varies throughout the year. Buyers have to consider these variations when making their estimates.

Weather

The weather has a pronounced effect on daily, short-term demand. Poor weather conditions affect the ability of the consumer to get to the store and influence the type of merchandise sold. Long periods of hot weather will greatly increase the sale of air conditioners and fans. Weather obviously affects the sale of apparel merchandise.

The ability of the firm to isolate the effects attributable to weather can be of great value in the forecasting of sales. One example is that of a bakery chain which attempts to predict sales on the basis of weather.[27] This chain is interested not only in the total effect of weather on sales but also in its influence on the different store locations. For example, will bad weather be more likely to cause a decrease in the sales of downtown or suburban stores? The bakery firm's studies seem to indicate that suburban stores are more likely to lose the sales when inclement weather prevails.

---

[27]A. T. Steele, "Weather's Effect on the Sales of a Department Store," *Journal of Marketing,* Vol. XV, No. 4 (April, 1956), p. 446.

FIGURE 8-7   Index of Seasonal Variation: Weekly per Capita Purchases and Expenditures of Ice Cream, Atlanta Consumer Panel, by Quarters, 1958-1962

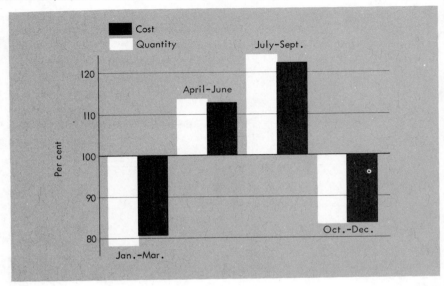

Adapted from Ford and Penny, *op. cit.*

FIGURE 8-8   Index of Seasonal Variation: Weekly per Capita Purchases and Expenditures of Fresh Fruits, Atlanta Consumer Panel, by Quarters, 1958-1962

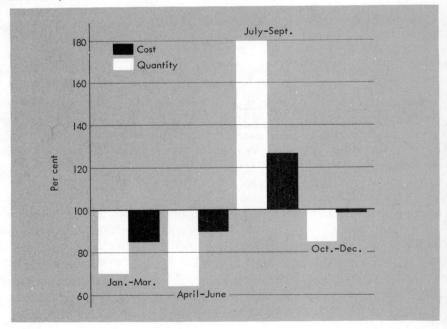

Adapted from Ford and Penny, *op. cit.*

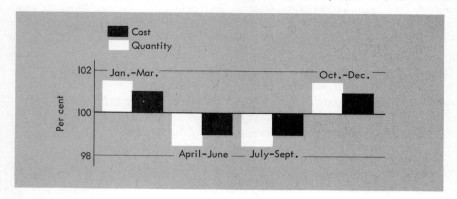

Adapted from Ford and Penny, *op. cit.*

Weather also has a longer-range dimension in decision making. Weather conditions that prevail over a month can influence strongly the usual demand for a product. An excellent illustration of this is offered by Fabian Linden who suggests that a long spell of warm weather extending into the fall season would call for an adjustment of as much as 25 per cent in fall forecasting plans in a women's coat department.[28] This study seems to indicate conclusively that weather does greatly affect the sale of certain types of merchandise.

SUMMARY

Inventories in the J. C. Penney Company comprise 50 per cent of the total assets of this gigantic firm. For this reason, management is extremely concerned with the proper performance of the buying function.

In organizing the buying department in a store, the small retail firm simply does all of its buying through the owner. Larger firms use either a centralized or a decentralized organizational arrangement. In the food chain centralized buying includes the use of the buying committee that makes all final decisions on new products.

A firm has two ways of obtaining goods for its customers. The first and more obvious is from manufacturers or their representatives. The other means is buying by specification, when the retailer asks the manufacturer to change a product offered by a vendor. Specification buying is used to obtain private brands, developed by a retailer and sold only in his stores.

In evaluating new product lines to be carried, management usually considers potential competition, profits, and the reaction of customers to the new line in the present store. The growth of non-food products in supermarkets clearly indicates that the need to evaluate new lines is a continuing process in retailing today.

---

[28]Fabian Linden, *The Business of Department Stores,* Technical Paper No. 7, National Industrial Conference Board, 1959, p. 28.

Increasing the width of the store's assortment refers to adding a new line (e.g., shoe polish in a shoe store); increasing the depth refers to adding variations of the present lines (e.g., adding color or size). Decisions on increasing depth or width depend on the location of the store and the willingness of people to travel and the extra sales (or profit) the buyer feels he will net by additions.

In selecting which product to buy, the retailer considers many things. Among the top factors will be the profitability, the exclusiveness, and the usefulness of the product. His decision will also be affected by the types of goods he is selling, namely, shopping, convenience, or specialty goods. The availability of imported goods and fashions further complicate the retailer's selection of merchandise. When to buy is strongly influenced by seasonability and the weather.

QUESTIONS

1. List 3 types of shopping goods for which demand fluctuates considerably during the year.

2. List 3 types of convenience goods for which demand fluctuates considerably during the year.

3. Describe the organization problems of the following types of retail organizations:

    a. large traditional department store with branches in the same area.

    b. large traditional department store with branches in New York and California

    c. (F.W. Woolworth) variety store

    d. small independent variety store

4. Evaluate the following products as candidates for specification buying by a large retail store:

    a. television sets

    b. dinette table

    c. children's dresses

    d. candy bars

5. In selling to a food firm that uses the committee buying technique, what problem do you envision a manufacturer's salesman will have to cope with?

6. How has "scrambled merchandising" affected the retail buying organizations?

7. Evaluate a new food product on the basis of Table 8-4.

8. How does top management aid in the determination of what goods a store buyer should sell?

9. Classify the following as either *shopping, specialty,* or *convenience* goods:

    a. automobiles

    b. candy bars

    c. women's dresses

    d. men's wear

    e. women's hats

    f. nails

10. How does your classification in Question 9 affect retail strategy for each of these products?

11. Why are appliance sales affected by the business cycle? Relate this peculiarity to the problem of the individual retailer.

12. Identify and discuss the impact of weather on 3 types of retail outlets.

13. How will rising consumer income affect the buying organization in the typical apparel specialty store?

14. John Cameron, a buyer of cosmetics for a large department store, is considering buying a line of sun-glasses for his department. What factors should he consider in making this decision?

15. If the buying committee of a food chain were considering the following products what considerations might be given the most weight?

    a. razor blades

    b. canned fruit

    c. canned soup

Securing Merchandise

9

OBJECTIVES YOU SHOULD MEET

1. *List* functions ordinarily performed by wholesalers.
2. *Distinguish* between the two types of buying representatives.
3. *Restate* in your own words how buying representatives differ from wholesalers.
4. *Name* several major types of wholesalers.
5. *Explain* how cooperatives aid small retail firms.
6. *Cite* the factors that influence the retailer's ability to secure favorable terms from a manufacturer.

Those familiar with a small family retail business think of the local wholesaler as the supplier of merchandise. However, the wholesaler's role as a supplier of merchandise is limited today, and many retailers, particularly large ones, now deal directly with the manufacturer of goods. In doing this they assume some of the functions of the wholesaler, since middlemen perform functions that are needed. The functions performed by the wholesaler are discussed elsewhere. However, when we speak of dealing directly with the manufacturer we do not always mean actually calling up a manufacturer and ordering goods. Though this may be the case, in many other instances the retail firm may be represented by a buying specialist (sometimes retailer owned) in certain markets that will represent the firm's interest. In addition, since firms are not limited only to goods available in this country, it may be represented by international buying specialists.

Buying Representatives

Buying representatives do not usually act directly to supply the retail firm with merchandise. The good representative acts mainly as a guide or an aid to the organization, supplying valuable market information concerning the availability of merchandise. More recently, a number of former buying organizations in the general merchandise field have established separate wholesaling corporations — corporations which actually perform the wholesaler's function, in order to qualify for additional discounts.

The buying representatives are usually located in central markets (such as New York City for apparel buying firms) and are a great service to smaller specialty stores. Large firms (particularly the large general merchandise chains) normally maintain their own staff offices in important markets.

Buying representatives are divided into *independent offices* and *store-owned offices.* The former, as the name implies, are independent and actively solicit stores as paying clients. The fees of the independent offices range from 1.2 per cent of sales volume for the smallest stores to less than 0.03 per cent of the sales volume for the largest stores.[1]

The store-owned buying office is owned outright by a group of stores. The two major offices of this type are the Associated Merchandising Corporation and Frederick Atkins, Inc. The latter represents over 50 retail department-store and specialty-store companies, with a sales volume of over $2 billion annually. Atkins, as part of their services to the members, maintains representatives in London, Hong Kong, Korea, Tokyo, Frankfurt, and other parts of the world. In New York the firm maintains a staff of over 50 buyers.

Aside from alerting the member stores to the availability of merchandise, Atkins provides research, electronic data processing, and statistical reports to all firms. They also organize meetings and services for specialized areas in the store. For instance, they may hold a national meeting of all sales promotion managers of the member stores.

Atkins provides desk space and phone service for all store buyers who are in New York on business trips. As a matter of routine the office also places special orders, handles adjustments, and checks on the status of orders placed by the stores. In addition, Atkins helps coordinate the publishing of Christmas and other seasonal catalogs that are mailed to customers of the stores. Last, Atkins helps the stores develop and promote private brands available only in their stores.

In order to service the stores, Atkins staffs several divisions within the firm, namely, merchandising, management information, EDP, finance, and an international department, which handles imported merchandise. Atkins also maintains a wholesale company (AWC) that handles merchandise for its stores. The latter firm has grown because of the availability of discounts on certain classes of goods sold through a wholesaler. In order to qualify for these discounts and to stay within the legal bounds of the Robinson-Patman Act, it also sells its merchandise to stores that are not members of the Atkins Company. All the member stores of Frederick Atkins, Inc., own stock and receive dividends when the operation accumulates a surplus.

Regardless of the organizational arrangement or the reliance on buying offices, firms either buy from wholesalers or manufacturers. As noted above, when they buy directly from manufacturers, the functions of the wholesaler must still be performed, whether it be by the manufacturer or the retailer. The section below will discuss the functions performed by the wholesaler.

[1]John W. Wingate and Joseph S. Friedlander, *The Management of Retail Buying,* (Englewood Cliffs, N.J.: Prentice-Hall, Inc., 1963), p. 65.

✗ Wholesale buying for our purposes is defined as *all buying from institutions other than the manufacturer.* This may include brokers (who may or may not take title to the merchandise), wholesalers, rack jobbers, agricultural cooperatives, and other assorted middlemen. In all cases, they perform needed functions for the retailer.

✗ One of the major functions performed by wholesalers is to carry large assortments of merchandise and thereby to be able to supply a retailer relatively quickly. If a wholesaler performs this function well, he can service both large and small retail establishments. For example, a wholesaler handling drugs and cosmetics can be of great service to a large department store. This comes about because of the numerous items that must be stocked and the inability of a large store to adequately predict its needs for each of these items. In addition, some of these items cannot be economically ordered in small quantities. In the same manner, wholesalers can serve the needs of the local drug store operator who has the same problem on a smaller scale. In addition, the drug wholesaler may maintain an exceptionally speedy service for prescription drugs.

Wholesalers need not handle only the needs of local customers. Many are national in scope. The operations of the Stem Distribution Company in Cleveland are perhaps typical of this type.[2] This firm supplies about 600 discounters and hardgoods stores. Its products include tools, paints and home improvement articles, plumbing and electrical supplies, sporting goods, automotive supplies, lawn and garden equipment, and supplies and miscellaneous products including pet and school products.

Presently the firm maintains a 165,000 square-foot warehouse and ships all orders from Cleveland. A sales force is maintained to take orders and refill depleted stocks in these stores.

The firm operates on about a 10 per cent markup on cost, restricting its buying to branded lines of products, in fact to only a relatively few branded lines. For instance, 62 per cent of its volume for tools comes from dealing with 21 manufacturers. Just 12 manufacturers of paint and home-improvement products account for about one half of the firm's volume. Approximately 5 per cent of the firm's volume is handled through the warehouse. Much of the volume is drop-shipped from manufacturers.

✗ Aside from supplying the retailer with a fast reorder source, the firm also pretickets items and is experimenting with supplying promotional brochures for retailers to mail to their customers.

✗ The wholesaler, however, performs other functions. In some cases, the wholesaler can offer the retailer more liberal credit terms than he can secure from the manufacturer. This means, in effect, that the retailer would require less available cash than if he bought directly from the manufacturer. For by buying in quantities more closely attuned to his day-by-day needs, his outstanding bills are usually much smaller. Possibly an example will clarify this point. If a retailer plans to sell twenty-four units of an item per month, he can secure this merchandise from either the manufacturer or the wholesaler. He knows that if he buys from the manufacturer he may have to place an order for forty-eight of these items, since the

---

[2]"One-Stop Hardgoods Depot for Discounters," *The Discount Merchandiser,* August, 1972, pp. 37-50.

manufacturer takes two to three weeks to process and deliver an order. In addition, the forty-eight could well represent the manufacturer's minimum shipping order. Once the goods are shipped, the retailer has an accounts payable for the forty-eight items. On the other hand, dealing directly with the wholesaler, the retailer need only purchase a week's supply (six items). His accounts payable is now for only six items. We might quickly add at this point that though it would seem that the retailer would therefore prefer a wholesaler, in actual fact the retailer generally prefers to deal with the manufacturer simply because he may have an opportunity to obtain a discount price similar to that paid by the wholesaler, and hence obtain a higher markup. However, in making this choice of channels, the retailer must balance the benefits outlined above.

Other functions can also be performed by the wholesaler. For example, the wholesaler may assume the role of a market adviser to a retailer. This would be particularly true of the food broker (discussed below). Retailers are also well aware that the wholesaler salesman offers an endless source of new product information and can keep them aware of the actions of their competitors.

In addition, the wholesaler, by using salesmen, relieves the retailer of the time and effort needed to go into the market and search out merchandise. In effect, the market comes to the store.

Some observers emphasize the function of the delivery service and the regrouping of carload lots (or large assortments) to smaller shipments as other important functions performed by the wholesaler.

Examples of Wholesalers

All of the above functions are rarely performed by one type of wholesaler. Some may perform only one of these functions, others several. The different roles played by wholesalers can best be understood by describing the services performed by full-service wholesalers, food brokers, rack jobbers, and merchandise marts.

I Merchant Wholesalers

Table 9-1 lists the most numerous type of wholesaler — the merchant wholesaler. The merchant wholesaler performs most of the functions discussed above. In addition, he characteristically takes title to the goods. The full-service wholesaler is by far the largest and, as the title implies, provides full services to his customers.

II Food Brokers[3]

Serving the food field, one finds over two thousand food brokers, who employ over 15,000 salesmen. The food broker is an integral part of the food distribution field. He acts on behalf of the seller of food products, and his compensation is in the form of a brokerage fee paid by this same source.

During the 1930's the broker could act on behalf of the buyer. However, a decision rendered in the Great Atlantic and Pacific Tea Company case branded this

---

[3]See publications of the National Food Brokers Association, "Selling Non-Foods in the Supermarket," "How Does the Food Broker Serve You."

TABLE 9-1   Sales of Merchant Wholesalers, 1965-1970

	(in millions)		*Percentage Change*
	1970	*1965*	*1965-1970*
Merchant wholesalers, total	246,643	187,141	+32%
Dry goods apparel	10,391	8,766	+19%
Groceries and related products	50,430	44,131	+14
Electrical goods	15,809	12,518	+26
Hardware, plumbing, heating, etc.	10,634	8,366	+27
Beer, wine, distilled alcoholic beverages	12,862	9,380	+37
Furniture, home furnishings	5,343	3,803	+40

Source: *Statistical Abstract,* 1971, p. 738.

function as being discriminatory. The Court suggested that brokerage fees in this particular case represented price discrimination, favoring the large buyer.

Brokers in the food business act today as representatives of the manufacturer in a local area, or in some cases, in a region. Briefly, the food broker (or his representatives) visits food stores, helps the store manager with displays, offers promotional advice, and, of course, takes orders for the manufacturer's products. As the manufacturer's agent in a marketing area, he may call on wholesalers and a chain headquarters. His customers include candy and tobacco wholesalers, bakery and dairy supply wholesalers, variety and department stores. In recent years he has gained entrance to the non-foods area and may represent manufacturers of cleaning supplies, health and beauty aids, paper products, pet supplies, and apparel.

In the sale of food products he may represent canners, packers, and manufacturers. He differs from wholesalers in that he does not take title to the goods he sells. In a sense he is the manufacturer's sales force in a local area. He usually represents one producer.

The advantage to the manufacturer is obvious. Food brokers represent his products and bring their knowledge of local grocery retailing to bear on the sale of his products. By definition food brokers are not involved in reshipment of the merchandise by the manufacturer. They perform not only a selling but also a sales promotion function, while the manufacturer pays for this function. In some cases the food brokers carry many lines of products and therefore do not devote as much attention to a particular manufacturer's product as does his own trained sales force.

Rack Jobbers

With the advent of "scrambled merchandising" such as the addition of non-foods into the food chains or the sale of non-drug items in drug stores (phonograph records), a new wholesaler emerged during the fifties. He is called the rack jobber. This middleman helps the retailer merchandise products that are unfamiliar to him. In effect, the rack jobber may set up a display, keep the display stocked adequately, and completely merchandise the section set aside by the retailer. His reward may simply be a percentage of the total sales or profits from the operation.

156

Typically, a non-food section of a supermarket, such as a hardware department, may be completely merchandised by a rack jobber.

Rack jobbers are no longer small businesses as they were in their early days after World War II. Several service well over 5,000 stores. One of the largest, APL Corporation, is reported to have a volume of nearly $100 million.

Rack jobbers in recent years have also started to branch out beyond supermarkets. Many now service discount stores, drug and variety stores, and in some instances even department stores.[4]

Merchandise Marts

A growing source of merchandise, located in major cities throughout the U.S., are the so-called merchandise marts. These marts serve as showrooms for major manufacturers and their representatives. The largest mart in the country is found in Chicago, containing hundreds of offices for firms handling goods ranging from furniture to apparel.

The second largest mart is found in Atlanta. Occupying the largest office building in the South, it houses hundreds of representatives of major manufacturers. In effect this center acts as the showroom and marketplace for retailers throughout the South, particularly the Southeast. In addition to serving as a showroom, the center stages trade shows for various industries. These serve to call attention to the merchandise promoted in this building.

Essentially, the merchandise mart serves as an area showroom and display office for manufacturers.

Cooperative Wholesaling

The growth of large retailing chains and the development of shopping centers has put heavy pressure on independent merchants to make innovations in their organization. The retailer, in order to compete successfully, has two major choices: (1) to expand his business by opening up additional units or to relocate and expand the size of his store; (2) to join other retailers in order to consolidate functions.

Though many small independents have expanded their operations, many others are not in a financial position to take this necessary step. The second choice is a popular means of overcoming the independents' inherent weaknesses. The retail firm can join cooperatives that are either retailer-owned or wholesaler-owned, or the newest form of cooperatives, the *franchise*.

1) In the *retailer-owned cooperative* the retailers band together to organize a wholesale firm. The members of the cooperative, in effect, own the wholesaler and share in the profits or losses. This form of cooperative differs from the *wholesaler-owned cooperative* chain (which again represents a group of retailers that band together) in which a voluntary group is formed on the initiative of the wholesaler. The wholesaler however is not owned by the retailers and the retailers' cooperation is voluntary. Both of these types of organization are important, especially in the drug, food, and variety fields. Many of these firms are national in

[4]Philip Corwin, "Racking Up Profits," Jan. 29, 1968, pp. 5 and 14.

scope, though they can be formed on a regional, or even local basis. Voluntary groups on the national scale are Butler Brothers, Walgreen Company, and Western Auto Supply.[5]

The size and importance of voluntary and cooperative wholesalers is considerable. Table 9-2 lists some of the largest in the grocery field. These firms serviced 13,258 stores in 1968. In 1971 it was reported that voluntary wholesalers serviced an average of 329 stores versus 284 for retail cooperatives.[6]

The voluntary and cooperative groups operate on a basis similar to that of other grocery wholesalers. For example, in Table 9-3 one sees that their average margin (difference between cost of merchandise and selling price) was about equal to the average for all wholesalers. Compared to unaffiliated (that is, independent) wholesalers, their margins are lower. There are several reasons for the relatively low margins, the first being that the co-ops do not have to spend much money on sales and marketing costs because they have a guaranteed market in their member stores. Second, by having this market they can usually make economical purchases that have a guaranteed reception.

Many voluntary wholesalers not only supply services to member stores but also maintain retail store operations of their own. Consolidated Foods and Red Owl Stores are two large combination wholesalers and retailers in this group. The general trend is for voluntary wholesalers to expand into their own retail operations, which increases their purchasing power and thereby spreads their overhead costs among more products.

Some retailer-owned cooperatives have also managed to take advantage of concentrated purchasing by organizing buying groups. For example, the Chicago-based National Retailer-Owned Grocers, Inc. (NROG), is owned by 85 retailer-owned cooperatives. This organization controls trademarks (e.g., Energy, Shurfine, Tastewell) and 30 food product lines sold only in member stores. Over 20,000 stores are members of NROG.

Cooperative groups are not made up solely of independent stores. Much of their membership is derived from chains. Though recent statistics are not available, it is reported that in 1958 thirteen per cent of all food chains belonged to cooperatives.

In addition to buying activities, many cooperatives supply member retailers with promotional aids. For example, it is not uncommon for members of a food cooperative to sponsor newspaper ads featuring special price offers on a weekly basis. The co-op may also produce circulars featuring price promotions in any given week among the member stores.

Though this type of distribution has managed to thrive both nationally and on the local level, there are numerous problems. The chief problem is the lack of cooperation on the part of member stores. To develop successful promotion requires cooperation on the part of all retailers. Many are slow and negligent in cooperating in these efforts. Second, it is difficult to plan these efforts democratically and hence a central group puts itself into a position of making all decisions. Much bickering and criticism follow many of these cooperative decisions.

The advantages are equally obvious. The stores through central purchasing are

---

[5]William P. Hall, "Franchising — New Scope for an Old Technique," *Harvard Business Review,* January/February, 1964, p. 63.

[6]*Progressive Grocer,* April, 1972, p. 91.

TABLE 9-2 Sales Changes Among Leading Voluntary and Cooperative Wholesalers 1958-1968

	Wholesale Sales (millions)			No. Stores Served			Estimated Sales of Stores Served (millions)		
	'58	'68	% Change	'58	'68	% Change	'58	'68	% Change
Affiliated Food Stores (Okla.)	$ 15.8	$ 48.0	+203.8	219	421	+ 92.2	$ 37.0	$ 120.0	+224.3
Associated Food Stores (Utah)	32.9	200.0	+507.9	355	941	+165.1	90.0	500.0	+455.6
Associated Grocers (Fla.)	15.7	73.0	+365.0	211	605	+186.7	30.0	185.0	+516.7
Associated Grocers (St. Louis)	46.4	134.3	+189.4	660	788	+ 19.4	92.0	300.0	+226.1
Associated Wh. Grocers (Kansas City)	26.0	175.0	+573.1	440	730	+ 65.9	100.0	425.0	+325.0
Certified Grocers (Calif.)	292.6	471.0	+ 61.0	1,466	1,827	+ 24.6	1,330.0	2,000.0	+ 50.4
Certified Grocers (Ill.)	115.8	270.0	+133.2	700	700	—	250.0	650.0	+160.0
Fleming Company	125.8	630.0	+400.8	546	1,850	+238.8	221.0	1,300.0	+488.2
Godfrey Company	46.6	98.6	+111.6	135	96	− 28.9	62.0	120.0	+ 93.5
Malone & Hyde	53.0	341.0	+543.4	565	1,710	+102.7	100.0	700.0	+600.0
Oshawa Wh. Ltd.	37.4	163.0	+335.8	182	238	+ 30.8	112.4	127.4	+ 13.8
Scot Lad	46.5	345.8	+643.7	210	520	+147.6	140.0	650.0	+364.3
Scrivner-Boogaart, Inc.	17.3	100.0	+478.0	125	180	+ 44.0	34.0	200.0	+488.2
Spartan Stores	60.1	185.0	+207.8	437	470	+ 7.6	175.0	350.0	+100.0
Super Valu	165.2	739.8	+347.8	601	1,622	+169.9	293.4	1,100.0	+274.9
United Grocers (S.F.)	32.2	75.3	+133.9	398	310	− 22.1	80.0	151.0	+ 88.8
Wakefern Food Stores	45.0	580.0	+1,188.9	75	250	+233.3	200.0	2,000.0	+900.0
Wetterau Company	51.9	197.0	+279.6	NA	415*	—	NA	350.0*	
Totals	$1,226.2	$4,826.8	+293.6	7,325	13,258	+ 81.0	$3,346.4	$10,878.4	+225.1

*not included in totals
Source: *Progressive Grocer*, April, 1969, p. 85.

TABLE 9-3   Margins in Grocery Wholesaling

| | *Average Margin on Total Sales* | | | |
	1964	*1966*	*1967*	*1968*
All wholesalers	5.5%	5.6%	5.7%	5.8%
Voluntary	5.4	5.4	5.5	5.7
Cooperative	5.3	5.3	5.5	5.6
Unaffiliated	7.0	7.0	7.1	7.3

Source: Adapted from *Progressive Grocer, op. cit.*, p. 81.

able to obtain substantial discounts. There are also savings in advertising and promotional programs. Many small firms also consider the management know-how of the wholesaler a particularly worthwhile advantage.

Many of the problems emanate from the fact that independent stores are managed by people who cherish their personal independence. Nevertheless, the cooperative form of central purchasing does manage to bolster the independent retail firm.

Franchising

One area of retailing that has been growing in recent years is franchising.[7] In a sense the franchise operator is a member of a form of cooperative because of his relationship with the wholesaler or manufacturer of the product.

 By definition a franchise is a license to sell a firm's goods or services in a given area under a contractual arrangement. These franchises number in the thousands.[8] Among the better-known franchises are Macdonald's, Midas, Howard Johnson, Dairy Queen, Hertz, and Dunkin' Donuts.

The relationship between the franchisee and the owner of the franchise is similar to that among firms in a cooperative group. Though contractual arrangements may vary greatly, the relationship is that of complete cooperation among the members to guarantee that a member's customer buying the product or the service in one state will find it to be a product similar in quality to that carried in another state by another member.

In reference to the franchise arrangements some firms charge the franchise a fee for their services; others a fee based on gross sales; other sell the franchise holder all of the products he uses in his business. The concept is the same, however. All franchisers provide a complete management and training program. They also offer expert advice in selecting sites and if necessary constructing a store.

The franchisee in most cases is obligated to purchase many of the ingredients for his products or the services offered by the franchise owner. For instance, restaurant operators are usually obligated to buy the firm's meat and many other products used in their meals. In most cases the franchisee is obliged to deal with the owner on the basis of a legal contract that spells out the rights of each of the parties.

---

[7] For a complete study of the franchising industry see "Special Issue on Franchising," *Journal of Retailing* (Winter 1968-1969).

[8] Robert Rosenberg's *Profits From Franchising* (New York: McGraw-Hill Book Company, 1969), contains 63 pages listing the thousands of franchises presently operating.

In recent years franchise operations have increased markedly. There are many reasons. First is the general prosperity within the economy that has enabled individuals to accumulate the necessary capital to invest in a business. Second is the recognition that buying advantages accrue to small retailers joined together in order to concentrate their purchasing power. Last, there is a group recognition among business promoters that systematizing a retail operation can produce profitable stores.

Retailers are constantly striving for advantages over their competition. One of the means of achieving these advantages is to buy merchandise for less. The ability to buy merchandise for less need not be merely in the form of lower prices. It can, for example, be in the form of additional cooperative advertising, extension of credit terms, additives to the present product, or a number of other different ways. In most cases, however, the buyer is given an advantage over his competition. In an earlier chapter, we discussed the role of federal law in controlling the retailer. Nevertheless, even with our laws, advantages do accrue to bigness. In effect, there remains an area of buying where only large buyers qualify for certain discounts.

In this section we will discuss the benefits which may accrue to bigness. However, this is not to say that there are advantages only to large firms. We do recognize the fact that some smaller firms have distinct advantages over larger firms, some of which will be discussed later in the chapter.

Factors
Influencing
Favorable
Terms
in Securing
Merchandise

Economies of Scale

Large firms have many advantages over their smaller rivals. The advantages in the manufacturing field are well known to all students of business. The advantage that a General Motors, for example, has over a small automobile company are not only obvious but have accounted no doubt for the demise of many of the smaller firms.

Advantages that accrue to retailers because of bigness are less obvious. Nevertheless, they exist, and management is well aware of their possibilities.

ⅅ Buying Power Advantages

The large retail firm possesses its greatest advantages in obtaining lower prices over smaller firms in many markets. Its ability to do this is governed by (1) the interpretation of the Robinson-Patman Act; and (2) the nature of competition in the markets where they purchase merchandise.

The Robinson-Patman Act makes it unlawful to discriminate in such a way between purchasers of the same or similar quantities of merchandise as to injure competition. As is known, the wording of the law is subject to court interpretation, and many of these interpretations serve as guidelines to business. In effect, the law does allow the manufacturer to charge different prices to different retailers. However, variations in the prices charged must result from either differences in actual cost or necessary steps to meet competition.

As a result of interpretations of the law, it has been established that a firm offering discounts for quantity purchases must make these discounts available to all levels of buyers. For example, the court ruled against the Morton Salt Company simply because only five large chains qualified for its discount schedule. In effect, the ruling suggests that a firm offering quantity discounts must do so only on a sliding-scale basis.

There are numerous other cases that support the government position that discounts must be offered equally to all buyers. As a result of these decisions, many manufacturers are placed in the position of tending to de-emphasize price discounts as a strategy and emphasize so-called nonprice elements in the manufacturing mix.[9] The reader should not, however, think that discounts are unknown in the retailing field. As a matter of fact, they are widely available. It depends, however, on the field in which the merchandise is secured and the competitive structure of that industry. By the competitive structure of the industry we mean (1) the importance of a manufacturer's product and his ability to differentiate it from other products; and (2) the number of manufacturers producing a product.

Product Differentiation

Manufacturers spend a great deal of their marketing effort trying to obtain an advantage for their product. In the economists' language, they are trying to differentiate their goods. The purpose of this effort is to help the firm achieve a high level of consistent demand for the product. Most of this effort on the part of the manufacturer may be aimed at the consumer or the retailer. In some cases, by fostering a strong advertising campaign the manufacturer may convince the consumer that his product is superior to that of his competitors. In doing this, the manufacturer forces the retailer to carry the product at all times. Products such as Colgate toothpaste, Ivory Soap, and Chanel No. 5 fall into this grouping. One would certainly agree that a drugstore would not have a complete stock without Colgate's toothpaste prominently displayed on its shelf.

On the other hand, consumers hardly distinguish between brands of sweaters, nor are they brand conscious in their choice of shoes. The manufacturer may then differentiate his product in other ways. For instance, the manufacturer's product may be priced below competitive products. It may carry services not offered by others (2-year warranty on a television set). In any case, some manufacturers have developed products with features that make them more desirable to consumers. Many of the features make these products highly desired by retailers.

Situations such as this afford manufacturers a competitive edge and may preclude their offering price inducements to large purchasers. As a general rule, firms *with a largely differentiated product are less likely* to offer price inducements. On the other hand, firms that are unable to convince either the consumer or the retailer of the superiority of their product over another are more likely to engage in price cutting or the offering of nonprice inducements. In many of the apparel fields this is particularly true. A recent FTC investigation of advertising allowances in the apparel field supports this conclusion.

---

[9]E. Jerome McCarthy, *Basic Marketing, A Managerial Approach* (Homewood, Ill.: Richard D. Irwin Company, 1960), p. 658.

Product differentiation is a major factor in determining the degree of price shading by manufacturing firms. However, it is not the only factor. Competition and its relationship to the number of firms in the industry is another important consideration.

Referring again to the apparel field, one finds that its major size characteristic is the large number of firms that make up this industry. For example, in the *Census of Manufacturers* it was reported that there were over 10,000 manufacturers of dresses in the country. Very few can be considered large. In this situation bargaining strength usually lies with the large retailers. By carefully planning his orders and maximizing their impact, the retailer can obtain price concessions. His ability to do the same in a field of high concentration is much more limited.

As will be shown in a later chapter, most of the cooperative advertising dollars accrue to large retailers. Though manufacturing firms, under the Robinson-Patman Act must offer cooperative advertising on a promotional basis to all buyers, in reality only the large buyers can actually accumulate enough cooperative dollars to run advertising. To illustrate, a drug firm offering a 5 per cent advertising allowance to retailers would find the druggist earning a $5 allowance on $100 in orders. The department store at the same time would most likely qualify for $250 based on purchases of approximately $5,000. Though advertising allowances were the same proportionally, realistically only the department store's allowance would be a reasonable contribution to a display ad in a newspaper.

Countervailing Forces

✗ Though the size of the organization (or "bigness") does influence buying terms, it is nevertheless true that small retail firms do possess certain means of countervailing "bigness." It must be remembered that retailing is a relatively low-concentration field as compared, for example, with the automobile industry, aluminum producers, or a host of other large industries — the major reasons being that retailers require a low capital investment and hence entry is made easy. As a result, with capital investment in merchandise the well-controlled smaller firms can maintain an efficient organization. By being smaller, the firm's owners and management are closer to the consumer and hence in many cases are more aware of consumer needs. In addition, by being small they can be more flexible.

In performing the buying function, the smaller firm possesses other advantages that can at least neutralize some of the large firms' purchasing powers. For example, large department stores must carry wide assortments of merchandise for their customers. A customer may expect to see four or more brands of white shirts of the same style, for example. A smaller retail firm such as an apparel discount store or a small men's wear specialty store may carry only two brands of shirts. As volume increases in these two stores their buying power is now concentrated on only two shirt manufacturers. Thus, they may have as much purchasing power with their two suppliers as the larger firm has with four or more. As the smaller firms add outlets, their limited assortments act to their advantage in that centralized buying is easier to maintain and operate with limited assortments. Though this aspect will be discussed in a later section, it is well recognized that the department stores have difficulties in maintaining centralized buying because of organizational problems and the wide assortments that need to be carried.

Trade or Functional Discounts

In spite of the legal restrictions on discounts, manufacturers do offer them to either retail buyers or wholesalers. Aside from the quantity discounts allowed large purchasers, the manufacturers must have established the so-called functional discounts for buyers of his products. *Functional discounts are discounts allowed institutions for performing selling services for the manufacturer.* For example, a manufacturer of candy can choose to sell directly to retailers, or through distributors. If he sells to distributors it is assumed that the distributor will perform the functions required by retailers. By selling to a distributor in a given territory the manufacturer need not employ salesmen, can expect to make shipments usually to one central office or warehouse, and needs to make only one billing to the distributor. Indeed, he rarely has to worry about the credit rating of the distributor. These are direct savings that may accrue to the manufacturer. In recognition of these savings the manufacturer may sell to the wholesaler at a retailer's price minus a trade (or functional) discount — the discount being the manufacturer's estimate of the savings the wholesaler offers him plus a profit for the wholesaler.

On the other hand, the manufacturer may choose to sell directly to a retailer, particularly a large retailer. The question arises as to whether or not he should offer the retailer the same price that he offers the wholesaler. If he does, we again must assume that the retailer performs the same functions as the wholesaler. This judgment has become an area of governmental conflict. Those questioning the manufacturers' decision to offer a wholesaler's discount to large retail buyers point out that the large retailer in many cases shifts some of the above-mentioned functions to the manufacturer. For example, the large retailer may ask the manufacturer to send relatively small shipments to each of their numerous outlets. In addition, the critics note that by allowing large retailers to buy at prices similar to the wholesalers the small retailers who are the major customers of wholesalers are immediately at a price disadvantage. This conflict has reached the House of Representatives where legislation has been considered for a number of years that would force the manufacturer to sell to wholesalers at a price below that offered to direct-buying retailers.

As the law is now interpreted, manufacturers are free to offer trade discounts, as long as they are offered to *all* buyers in each category. However, the question revolves around who qualifies in each category. That is, does a large retailer that warehouses large quantities of merchandise qualify for a wholesalers' discount? The answer to this question at this stage is yes; the large retailer can qualify for a wholesalers' discount.

This interpretation is presently in the so-called "gray area" of legality. As noted earlier, Congress has been disturbed by this viewpoint. In actual fact the Great Atlantic and Pacific Tea Company case was decided against the firm on the basis that huge savings that accrued to sellers still did not qualify the firm for a brokers' discount. Yet firms that could sell to any buyer chose to sell at a lower price to

A & P simply on the basis that the A & P purchasing power assured the producer of savings.

Our previously mentioned rack jobber offers us an excellent example of the workings of a trade discount system. The manufacturer carrying a line of (retail) houseware products might sell the product directly to retailers such as food chains, houseware stores, variety stores, and department stores for 60 cents. Over the years he has noted that rack jobbers have been entering the food field and selling and developing his product. Obviously, if he sells through rack jobbers he cannot hope to maintain the same discount system, because they perform additional services. For instance, they buy in quantities (probably greater than the supermarket), as they may concentrate on selling housewares. Therefore, he may set up an additional trade discount by offering the jobber the item at 55 cents. The jobber in turn may charge the food chain 65 cents — or 5 cents more than the price at which the chain can purchase the product directly. The chain, of course, will ordinarily go along with this arrangement since the jobber performs numerous services such as setting up displays, maintaining retail inventories, and a host of other promotional activities related to the sale of housewares.

SUMMARY

Though retailers buy merchandise from a manufacturer or a wholesaler, they require other services. Buying representatives provide services to retailers. Two types are identified, independent offices and store-owned offices. The former solicits independent stores as members; the latter is owned outright by its members. These firms provide merchandise information, hold seminars and meetings, and supply technical information and dozens of other services. Wholesalers in order to exist perform functions, including maintaining large assortments of merchandise, offering liberal credit terms and market advice, and providing delivery and salesmen to call on retailers.

Types of wholesalers include merchant wholesalers, food brokers, and rack jobbers. Merchandise marts located in several sections of the country provide a type of wholesale display headquarters for manufacturers.

Small firms have developed retailer-owned and voluntary cooperatives to help protect themselves from large chains. Franchises are a form of cooperative arrangement.

Large firms have advantages over smaller rivals. The ability to get the lowest price depends on the size of the retailer versus the ability of the manufacturer to differentiate his product among consumers and the number of manufacturers producing a product. The more differentiated the product, the less power the retailer has to gain a price advantage over a rival. The larger the number of manufacturers, the less likely it is that one manufacturer can resist the pressure of a large retailer. By concentrating its purchases on only a few vendors the small retailer can offset to some extent the buying power of a large store that buys from a large number of vendors.

Aside from quantity discounts, manufacturers do offer functional discounts to retailers and wholesalers for performing services for the manufacturer.

1. Under what conditions would a canned food manufacturer use a food broker?

2. What tendencies in consumer patronage motives have catapulted the rack jobber to his present position in supermarket retailing?

3. Relate product differentiation to quantity discounts offered to retailer.

4. Relate the number of firms in an industry to the ability of a retailer to obtain discounts.

5. How do trade discounts differ from quantity discounts? Under what conditions could trade discounts be illegal?

6. Retailer A is a medium-sized grocery store with sales of over $300,000 last year. Recently a chain supermarket moved into the area and is selling merchandise at what seems to be lower prices than Retailer A. Management blames this differential on the chain's ability to buy its products at lower prices. How can Retailer A reduce this price differential.

7. A wholesaler charges Retailer A 35 cents for a particular drug item. This item can be purchased directly from the manufacturer for 30 cents.

    a. Under what conditions should Retailer A purchase the item from a wholesaler?

    b. Under what conditions should Retailer A purchase the item from the manufacturer?

8. Why is it necessary for a large retail firm to join a buying organization?

10. Distinguish between "buying representatives" and "wholesalers."

11. In what ways can a buyer of apparel obtain legal price advantages for his firm?

12. What is a merchandise mart? What functions do they perform for:

    a. the manufacturer

    b. the retailer

13. In what ways are franchise operators similar to voluntary cooperatives? In what way are they dissimilar?

Services

10

OBJECTIVES YOU SHOULD MEET

1. *State* why most retailers prefer to engage in service competition rather than price competition.
2. *Identify* some services offered by food stores.
3. *State* the major reasons retail firms offer services.
4. *Identify* some of the major services offered by large stores.

Aside from the products he sells, the retailer offers the consumer various services. Though services will be discussed later in this chapter in terms of their impact on demand, we have listed in Table 10-1 most of the services usually offered by retailers.

Careful study of this table will show that not all services offered by the retailer require special handling or effort on his part. Some services, such as shopping hours, may be completely out of the hands of the retailer. The policy of the shopping center promoter may control the hours a store will be open, or the local downtown association may be the primary force in the setting of shopping hours. Nor can retailers do much about improving the convenience of the present location they offer the consumer. Nevertheless, retailers can change most of the services they offer and can greatly influence the quality of these services. The firm's ability to do this may often be the deciding factor in the survival of its business.

Most retailers *do not offer* all the services enumerated in this impressive list. During the postwar period, many firms, particularly discount houses, deliberately made it their policy to offer the consumers as few services as possible. Though these discount houses did attempt to eliminate services, it is interesting to note that

TABLE 10-1   Customer Services Offered by Discount Houses, Department Stores, and Specialty Retailers

CANNOT
REALLY
Improve

{ Convenience of store location
{ Shopping hours

Layout and appearance
Number and extent of lines carried
Selection of lines carried
Pricing: Merchandise marked
                Lowest value
                Flexibility
Window display
Interior display
Advertising
Salesmanship
Testing before buying
C.O.D. delivery
Special orders
"Will-call" or "lay-away"
Mail orders
Information and telephone orders
Trade-ins
Gift certificates
Open charge accounts
Installment credit
Accepting checks
Cashing checks
Wrapping
Delivery
Installation
Adjustments
Returns
Credit and allowances
Servicing (repair)
Special estimates
Testing services
Engraving
Refills
Advice on using merchandise

Source:. Adapted from Claire M. Gross, "Services Offered by Discount Houses in Metropolitan New York," *Journal of Retailing,* Spring, 1956, p. 3.

where they did offer services they put great emphasis upon them. For example, the apparel discount firm emphasized three services in particular: convenience of (highway) location, free parking (not listed in Table 10-1), and liberal return policies. Though we may not think of the last item as an important service, efficiency and ease of returns can be a major attraction to a customer — particularly a customer who is dubious about the products offered in the store.

Services offered by food stores are listed in Table 10-2. Over half of the food stores are open on Sundays; over one third offer money orders, and 22 per cent maintain a service delicatessen. Four of the eight listed services seem to involve a sort of elaboration of the firms' basic business, which is food.

Percentage of Food Stores Offering Services **TABLE 10-2**

Open Sundays	52%
Money orders	37
Service delicatessen	22
Film processing	12
On-premises bakery	9
Catering	7
Restaurant (snack bar)	5
Prescription service	1

Source: Adapted from *Progressive Grocer,* April, 1972, p. 80.

The ability of store management to become strongly service-oriented can in most cases mean the difference between success or failure in meeting the needs of customers. Though it is not the purpose of this chapter to describe in detail each service and its influence on the consumer, we shall discuss a number of important services and the audiences to which they are directed. First, it is necessary to be aware of the use of services as a tool of management.

Services as an Influence on Demand

Services are nonprice devices used to help the retailer differentiate his offerings in order to achieve higher sales and thereby maintain a certain segment of the market. We must distinguish at this point between price and nonprice competition and in particular why the latter is favored by most segments of retailing. Price competition is an attempt to alter the amount demanded by reducing prices. In some cases this may be done surreptitiously; however, eventually price cutting becomes known to competitors. Nonprice competition is an attempt to change demand without changing prices. Offering the customer services is, of course, the most widely used means of accomplishing this.

Why do retail firms prefer to compete on the basis of nonprice competition rather than price? The answer lies in the ability of the retail competitor to retaliate. To match a competitor's price discounts is relatively easy though admittedly dangerous. For example, if a food chain should start selling milk at prices either equal to or slightly below cost, competing chains would simply adjust their prices in accordance with this competition. Specifically, if a large chain reduced the price of a quart of milk to 25 cents, competing chains would be forced to meet this price. On the other hand, if Firm A offers customers free gift wrapping on all purchases made, retaliation on the part of the competitor is more difficult. Though all may offer the same service, the quality of service may differ considerably among competing stores. Given the imperfection of the worker this is easy to understand.

Many of us have found, for example, that the speed of deliveries varies considerably from one store to another. Hence, the reliance on nonprice competition.

Denies (Non price Pevice)

1) Delivery

✳ Delivery of merchandise directly to the customer's place of residence is a major service offered by many stores. The attractiveness of this service is enhanced by the fact that it can be used in conjunction with other store services such as telephone selling. Its major drawback is that the costs may be spread over all products sold by the store and hence (theoretically) the cash-and-carry customer also pays for this service without receiving its benefits. The importance of this observation can be attested to by the actions of department stores following World War II. These firms have consistently offered the consumer free delivery of all merchandise purchased. However, in their attempts to meet the competition of discount houses in the sale of small and large appliances, the department stores were forced to advertise low-priced merchandise without delivery service. Consumers who wanted this service had to pay an additional charge.

Though more will be said subsequently about the costs of services, Table 10-3 shows the cost of delivery services in a selected number of retail stores: it ranges from a low of 1.2 per cent to a high of 9.8 per cent of the total expenses of the

TABLE 10-3   Store Delivery Compared to Total Operating Expenses

	Delivery Expenses As A Per Cent Of Net Sales	Total Operating Expenses	Delivery As A Per Cent Of Total Operating Expenses
Furniture stores[1]	3.23%	39.8%	8.1%
Florists[2]	3.55	36.4	9.8
Department stores[3]	0.9	32.0	2.8
Specialty stores[4]	0.8	35.7	2.2
Liquor stores	0.4	15.3	2.6
Lumber and building materials dealers	1.6	19.8	8.1
Pharmacies[5]	0.4	32.2	1.2

[1] Sales volume over $1,000,000
[2] Sales volume $25,000 to $50,000
[3] Source: National Retail Merchants' Association, Sales over $50,000,000
[4] Source: National Retail Merchants' Association, Sales over $ 5,000,000
[5] Sales over $400,000
Source: *Expenses in Retail Businesses,* The National Cash Register Company

stores. Since World War II this cost has increased greatly. The reasons for this are many. First, with the rapid unionization of truck drivers, labor costs have become a major cost item. Second, the movement to the suburbs has forced the widening of areas of "free" delivery. And in the more sparsely settled suburbs fewer deliveries can be made in a given amount of time than in the cities.

One of the services offered customers in the postwar years has been an increase in the hours the store is open. This increase has been particularly marked in the suburban areas where many firms remain open late every night of the week. The purpose of adding shopping hours is to increase customer convenience, and it often constitutes a direct response to competition.

The economics of extended shopping hours has great appeal to management. Stores in general have high fixed costs, and additional sales volume tends to spread the fixed costs over more units. Though this theory sounds logical, management must still carefully examine any extension of store hours and first derive answers to the following questions:

1. Are the costs incurred by keeping open additional hours covered by an increase in profitable volume?

2. Are the additional sales all extra sales or would they still be obtained by maintaining the *status quo?*

The tendency in recent years has been to extend the hours of shopping. This extension has gone in two related directions, namely Sunday openings and extension of shopping hours.

The growth of Sunday openings in the past ten years has been dynamic. As noted previously in Table 10-2, over 50 percent of food stores are open on Sunday. The major change in Sunday openings, however, has been forged by the general merchandise and specialty stores. Major retailers such as Sears and J. C. Penney opened stores on Sunday where competitors were following that practice.

In addition, several department stores joined the competition and opened on Sunday, particularly during busy seasons such as Christmas. For instance, J. L. Hudson, Detroit's largest downtown department store, scheduled Sunday openings during the 1972 Christmas season.[1]

In recent years the supermarket chains spearheaded a move to extend store hours. Pathmark, Jewels, and Arlain's chain moved to open some or all supermarkets 24 hours a day.

It was Pathmark's view that the around-the-clock openings would not add much to the cost of the total operation for several reasons. First, the firm's stores are so large that they require nighttime delivery of stock, meaning that the stores were active at night in any case. Thus, the firm required only a small addition to the staff at these hours. Certain other expenses such as rent remain the same.[2] Second, the firm felt that the longer hours would attract additional shoppers and tend to relieve congestion at the regular shopping hours. Whether the 24-hour store becomes a national trend remains to be seen. The continuation of the energy crisis could severely limit store hours.

Regardless of the answers to the above questions, however, management may still extend the shopping hours if a major competitor remains open. The pressure to add to shopping hours arises from the fact that many American households contain a working wife who does not have time to shop during the day. In addition, the

---

[1] *Women's Wear Daily,* September 25, 1972, p. 30.

[2] *Time,* August 14, 1972, p. 60.

very nature of suburban living requires the use of the family car, which is not available in many households during the day. Both of these circumstances produce pressure for night openings in suburban stores.

 Credit

 The use of credit is probably one of the most important services a retailer can offer, and is probably the one most closely related to sales. This is understandable if one acknowledges that credit reinforces purchasing power.

The importance of store credit can be seen in its growth since 1950. In 1950 credit outstanding as a ratio of disposable personal income was 10.4%. By 1970 (a recession year) it was 18.5% or approximately 80% higher.

How important is credit as a service in stores? One survey reported that credit sales in the typical department and specialty store averaged about 55 per cent of total sales. Thus, six out of ten dollars spent in these stores were credit sales.[3]

On the other hand, there are many retail firms that do not offer the consumer credit. The most obvious are the chain food stores where credit has contributed little to their growth. The development of the discount house has also been made without the use of credit, though there has been a tendency in these firms to help the customers obtain loans from financial institutions.

Nevertheless, credit is a major factor in many retail organizations. And the credit manager's decision to accept charge account customers has a definite impact on a firm's sales volume. A firm with an easy credit policy may therefore increase its sales volume substantially, although this policy carries with it the danger that bad debt losses may exceed the firm's profits. On the average, however, losses from bad debts approximate .5 per cent of sales.

[A] Forms of
Credit

The two basic types of credit usually available to the shopper are:

1. Store Charge Accounts: a customer credit plan that can be used only in the store's outlets. Such accounts usually require payment within 30 days after the purchase. Many plans include an *installment payment* or an interest-charge payment on all remaining balances. In most cases the customer is issued a charge card.

2. Bank Credit Cards: a credit plan sponsored by a bank. In some instances the credit card can be used in retail outlets. Some bank cards are used only locally, others throughout the world.

Store Charge Accounts

The store charge account is most commonly used in department and general merchandise stores.

In firms selling appliances, television sets, and other durable goods the installment account takes precedence over the 30-day charge account. W. T. Grant, the billion-dollar general merchandise chain has expanded its stores' goods mix from apparel to appliances, home furnishings, and sporting goods. To accomplish this the

---

[3] *Financial and Operating Results of Department and Specialty Stores in 1970,* National Retail Merchants Association, 1971.

firm has expanded its credit operation, which presently accounts for 25 per cent of the firm's sales. It expects their share to increase to 35 per cent on the basis of increasing the selling space of this merchandise to 50 percent and offering installment credit to the customers.[4]

Installment credit is the mainstay of many small retailers. For instance in a study of retailers in low-income areas of Washington, D. C., the Federal Trade Commission found that in 93 per cent of such sales installment credit was used. Retailers selling in all areas of the district used installment credit for 27 per cent of their retail sales.[5]

৩) Bank Credit Cards

The use of bank credit cards has increased substantially in the past 5 years. Most cards are used to charge airline tickets, pay restaurant bills, and pay for a variety of purchases in small stores. Large stores, particularly department and chain stores, have been reluctant to honor bank credit cards.

The reasons that stores prefer their own charge-account systems revolve around at least four major considerations:[6]

1. The possible loss of management control and customer loyalty. The store's view is that the consumer tends to patronize the store because of the availability of a store charge account.

2. Cost of the bank discount fee. The banks charge stores a fee on each sale charged to the bank credit card. Thus, on a $100 sale the retailer receives from $95 to $98 net.

3. Lack of consumer demand. Though there are millions of users of bank credit cards, the large stores feel that the bank card user also maintains a department store credit account. Thus, the user of a bank credit card is not an additional customer for the store.

4. Monthly statements issued by the store provide a tool for promotional literature, and the list of credit customers provides a forum for direct mail advertising.[7]

Conversely, bank credit-card firms suggest that the discount that the stores pay is substantially less than the cost of maintaining an in-store credit department.

Ultimately, the final decision will be made by consumers. At this point the bank credit user seems to be ignored by most major stores.[8] However, even at this stage many large firms have started to accept these cards, including now Zayres, Tiffany, S. H. Kress, and Roos-Atkins. The acceptance of bank credit cards is reported also to be under serious consideration by Gimbels.[9]

Aside from losses from bad debts the cost of credit can be substantial in the retail firm. For instance the 30-day charge account offered in department stores involves

Cost of Credit

---

[4]*Forbes,* May 1, 1972, p. 42.

[5]*Economic Report on Installment Credit and Retail Sales Practices of District of Columbia Retailers,* Federal Trade Commission, March, 1968, p. IX.

[6]*Women's Wear Daily,* August 9, 1972, p. 8.

[7]*Women's Wear Daily,* August 2, 1968, p. 28.

[8]Michael J. Etzel and James H. Donnelly, Jr., "Consumer Perception of Alternative Retail Credit Plans," *Journal of Retailing,* Summer, 1972, p. 73.

[9]*Women's Wear Daily,* August 9, 1972, p. 8.

the cost of maintaining a credit department. In addition the maintenance of such a department involves large sums of money necessary to finance hundreds of accounts.

To offset such costs many stores offer customers revolving accounts that automatically add an interest charge when the customer does not pay within the 30-day period. Here one finds that the cost of credit may be balanced against the income. The monthly charge is usually 1-1/2 per cent or 18 per cent annually $(12 \times 1\text{-}1/2\%)$.

A recent study by J. C. Penney seems to indicate that the 18 per cent does not offset the total cost of credit. In 1969 J. C. Penney collected $79 million in interest charges on customer receivables. It cost the firm $44 million in bank interest charges to finance these accounts. Bad debts totalled $16 million, and the firm claimed to have spent $42 million to administer customer credit through its regional credit offices. Thus the total cost of credit at J. C. Penney exceeded income by $23 million.[10] Yet this does not tell the whole story, in that a retailer offering credit may not be able to maintain a higher markup than a competitor not offering credit.

In the study previously mentioned of retailers in low-income areas of the District of Columbia, the Federal Trade Commission (FTC) concluded that easy installment-credit practice

1. takes the form of higher product prices.
2. markups on comparable products are two or three times higher than those charged by retailers servicing all areas of the city.[11]

Though the FTC noted that some of the higher cost could be attributed to bad-debt expense, much of the added expense is due to expenses associated with the collection and processing of installment contracts plus marketing costs, usually associated with salaries and commissions.[12]

Cost of Services to Management

The cost of services weighs heavily on management's attitude toward their value and ability to shift the demand curve.

Management's problem, stated simply, is to measure this cost and balance it against the return to the firm.

Cost Measurement

All services cost the firm money. Some expenditures may be more subtle than others. For example, a liberal return policy may increase costs in two ways: (1) it may require a large staff of employees to process the returned merchandise and return it to stock; (2) higher markdowns may result because of damaged merchandise and returns made late in the season. A proper calculation for management's use in decision making cannot be made until we can balance these costs against the additional sales volume they produce. Services in effect move the

---

[10] K.S. Axelson, "Penney's Credit Costs," *Stores,* May, 1971, p. 40.
[11] *Economic Report, op. cit.,* p. XIII.
[12] *Idem.*

demand curve to the right in the same manner as the firm's investment in advertising.

The cost of services offered to the customer depends on the continuity of the costs. Some services require a large initial investment, while others vary according to the level of sales and continue throughout the year. Offering the consumer decorative surroundings requires a heavy original investment on the part of the firm but is unrelated to the level of sales. Conversely, the cost of free delivery service is related directly to the level of sales and is a continuous cost.

If services were proportional in cost to all sales, management would find it easier to determine the true cost of a service. Unfortunately, the costs of services are not proportional to sales, and the impact on the firm's sales volume is not easily measured. For example, not all customers avail themselves of charge accounts or other credit services within the store. Others prefer to shop in person rather than by phone; still others have most merchandise delivered. Many customers are greatly concerned about the caliber of sales help in the store; others prefer self-service. Hence, management is always in the dark as to the exact impact of each of these services on sales, since not all consumers use them or are equally exposed to all services. One last factor that management must take into consideration in measuring the cost of services is competition. Obviously, though the cost of a service may far exceed the return from sales, management might still be forced to initiate or continue a service if it is offered by its competition.

Services are not offered only by large firms. The consumer often expects the local small grocer, for example, to offer free delivery and credit and to take orders over the phone. The same may be expected of the local independent drugstore.

Management is well aware that customers do need and prefer services in many of the stores they shop in. In addition, management is well aware that in many cases a reduction of services will immediately reduce sales volume. In general, consumers expect services from certain types of stores, and management must meet these expectations.

Cost of Services

In Table 10-4 are listed some major cost items that can be attributed to the firm's effort to service the customer in the large department store. These expenses range from a low of 0.33 per cent of sales to a high of 8.16 per cent. Obviously the cost of services varies considerably, and a management decision to either improve or discontinue a service may well be based on its ranking in this expense list or the factors discussed above.

All of these factors are taken into consideration in making a decision of this nature. Let us examine, for example, a recent decision by a major Philadelphia department store to charge customers for returning merchandise through the firm's delivery service. This decision required that the firm add a customer service charge when goods were returned because of a customer whim rather than an error on the part of the store. According to management this decision was relatively easy to make. By simply studying customer returns through the delivery service, they established the fact that a large number of returns were being made by the same individuals. It was management's belief that these individuals were chronic "returners" and that a service charge would fall heavily on them and reduce this

TABLE 10-4   Selected Expense Items Related to Servicing a Department Store Customer (Stores with annual sales exceeding $50 million)

C ost as Demand

	Percentage Of Total Sales
Depreciation[1]	1.26%
Credit and collection	1.40
Direct selling	8.16
Customer services[2]	0.33
Wrapping	0.59
Delivery	0.92
Total	12.66%

[1] Service in the sense that the more elaborate the decor, the higher the cost of the plant.
[2] Includes such items as mail and telephone selling, parcel checkroom, elevator operation, and the like.
Source: *FOR, Financial and Operating Results of Department and Specialty Stores in 1970,* New York: National Retail Merchants Association.

costly problem. At the same time management felt that the reduction would not hamper the firm's service image to a majority of their customers. In addition, management was well aware of the fact that the other Philadelphia department stores were joining them in this plan.

On the basis of these simple facts this decision would seem to have been an easy one, for management had most of the facts needed. However, this was a relatively minor decision. Suppose management were considering the complete discontinuance of delivery service because of its high cost. How would management make that decision? And, more important, could management obtain the needed information to make the decision. In order to assemble the facts, management would probably work within the confines of our theoretical framework outlined earlier. That is, management would estimate its effect on total store demand and balance this against the reduction in costs. This estimate would also include management's evaluation of the damage that would be done to the firm's image (assuming the projected image includes services) and its long-run effects. From the practical point of view management might well examine its merchandise mix and make a more detailed study of the particular departments that were most affected by the dropping of delivery services, i.e., furniture, appliances, carpeting, etc. Management might also determine whether if this service were dropped customers could be offered reductions in prices or some other concession that would help the store maintain a competitive position.

SUMMARY

Retailers sell not only goods but also services. Retailers prefer to engage in service competition rather than price cutting simply because it is more difficult to retaliate to better service than to a price cut.

Though retailers offer dozens of services, one of the most important seems to be delivery, which ranges from a high of just under ten per cent of total expenses to a low of 1.2 per cent for various types of outlets.

Extending the shopping hours seems to be another form of service that is becoming of greater interest to shoppers. In recent years there has developed greater acceptance of Sunday openings and longer hours in all major retail outlets. The pressure for extended shopping time comes from the increase in working women and the movement to the suburbs that requires an automobile, which is more likely to be available at nonworking hours and during nonworking days.

Credit is offered in two forms, ordinarily, store charge accounts and bank credit cards. The latter are being resisted by the large retail firms, which find them costly and feel that they lose control over their customers. Against the use of bank-sponsored credit cards the stores must weigh the cost of maintaining their own credit departments. This cost can be reduced by the interest income that accrues from customers who do not pay their accounts in 30 days and thus incur an extra interest charge.

It is estimated in department stores that the cost of offering all services approximates 12.66 per cent.

QUESTIONS

1. What customer services are the most important in the:
   a. department store
   b. discount store
   c. men's wear store
   d. variety store
2. In Table 10-4 why is depreciation listed as a service?
3. Department store A would like to discontinue its credit service. What factors must it take into consideration?
4. Distinguish between services and price cuts as a promotional tool of management.
5. What future changes in our economy could result in an increase in store hours? A decrease?
6. What service would seem to be the most expendable in the department store?
7. What services listed in Table 10-4 could be offered by the corner grocery store?
8. Under what conditions would adding services increase prices in a store?
9. Under what conditions would adding services decrease prices in a store?
10. Store A, a furniture store, finds that its delivery expenses represent 10 per cent of its total operating expenses. This is 1.3 per cent higher than the average store (see Table 10-3). The merchandise manager believes this expense is not higher than one would expect from a store of this type. Why?
11. The controller of Store A believes that delivery expenses are much higher than they should be. Offer reasons that he might present for their being higher.
12. Why are department stores generally opposed to the acceptance of bank credit cards? Offer counter-arguments to their view.
13. It has been stated that stores that offer credit discriminate against the customer who pays cash. Do you agree?
14. What is the cost of service in a department store? Is this the total cost?

Retail
Pricing

11

1. *Differentiate* between pricing in a retail firm and in a manufacturing firm.
2. *Distinguish* between the store pricing policies of pricing *under* and *above* the market.
3. *Identify* the major internal and external considerations a firm must weigh in setting retail prices.
4. *Define* fixed and variable costs and the break-even point.
5. *Define* markup, gross margin, and retail reductions.
6. *Relate* markup on retail and markup on cost.

 On any given day a shopper can find the *same item* selling at different prices in different stores. This phenomenon has always existed in retailing and will continue. The reason is obvious. From the economist's point of view retailers are able to set different prices for the same product because of the existence of monopolistic competition. By monopolistic competition we mean that each seller's offerings differ to some extent from those of his competitors. In the case of retailing, however, this difference must be looked at not from the point of view of the individual item being sold but from the overall view of the store itself. For consumers do not judge an individual item in a store; instead they judge the total store — meaning the products it sells and the services it offers.

As can be seen from our previous discussion the consumer's view of the stores in a particular line may vary considerably according to a number of factors other than prices, such as location, services, amenities, and so forth. The retailer is well aware of this. He knows that a large segment of his customers has for various reasons chosen to patronize his store instead of his competitors, and that he can continue to appeal to it if he maintains his present policies. Therefore, in many cases he does not have to meet the price competition of his competitors at all times. On the other hand, he knows that he must price somewhat within reason; his price differential must not tempt his customers to shop elsewhere.

Thus, prices in the retail field are not set by the marketplace. Though more will be said about this later in the chapter, it is proper to note here that the retailer and his internal organization have the power to set prices as they see fit. Though this may seem obvious, it should be remembered that if we were talking about agricultural marketing, there would be many areas where these considerations would not apply, simply because prices in many agricultural markets are set by outside market forces. In a sense, therefore, prices in retailing are *administered,* that is, they are set by administrative action of the firm. This does not necessarily mean that administrative prices are always higher than they should be. It simply means that the firm has a choice or alternative in setting prices. How this choice is made and the factors that enter into it are the subject matter of this chapter.

Major differences exist between manufacturers and retailers, but they can best be seen in the area of pricing. In the case of the manufacturer, an overall price policy can be set for each of his products. In addition, an executive can be assigned the title of product manager, a job that entails maintaining the policy for each product or small group of products. In addition, the firm can apply minimum policy standards to each product (though it need not). For example, one major oil company applies a minimum percentage return on investment to all of its new products. This serves as a guide for choosing new products for testing. The retailer is not so fortunate, mainly because of the multitude of products he handles. Thus, most retail firms cannot insist on a minimum percentage return on each product sold, simply because of the nature of retailing. For example, some products are sold at less than average markup in a food store. Insisting that each individual product be sold at the goal markup of the firm could cause catastrophic consequences.

Another major difference between the retailer and manufacturer is their geographical outlook toward pricing. The manufacturer in setting a product price considers its implications nationally. A shirt manufacturer must take into consideration transportation charges from his plant to the far-flung markets of the United States. Thus, if a price of $4.00 is set on a nationally advertised shirt, the transportation for the total market must average out in the selling price to the retailer — particularly if the shirt is to be promoted nationally and the price emphasized in a national advertising campaign. The retailer is more concerned with a local market and hence pricing at a local level. In a sense, the retailer must be more flexible in his pricing and is more likely to adjust his prices over the year than the manufacturer.

The retail price-making organization also differs dramatically from that of the manufacturer. Manufacturing prices are usually set by top management. For example, the top management of General Motors involves itself in all price making during each model year. In addition, all needed price adjustments are handled in the same way. The retail price-making organization operates very differently. Though top management may set the average margin goals of the organization, the lower-level price makers, such as the buyers, set the retail prices in the store. In

**Manufacturer-
Retailer
Differences**

addition, they are responsible for making needed price adjustments. Though a buyer in a retail store may receive some guidance from the middle executive level, such as the merchandise manager, the very magnitude of the job requires the buyer to make most of these decisions.

There is another difference that is becoming increasingly important. It has to do with what the manufacturer and retailer consider to be the product they are pricing. The manufacturer is pricing a product only and in its price he includes the cost of the product, the cost of promoting it, and the margins necessary to interest the middleman in selling the product for him. The retailer takes into consideration many of the same things the manufacturer does with one basic difference: The retailer in most instances considers the services he offers as a price factor. What we are saying is that the retailer places great emphasis on services — a factor, incidentally, that is separate from the product but an integral part of it in the mind of the consumer.

Pricing
Goals
and Policies

Probably no organization is as aware of the importance of pricing as the retail firm. Yet retail firms use pricing policies in many different ways. Some firms establish pricing policies that are openly aggressive; to others, pricing is a more passive activity. In all firms it requires careful study.

In this section price as a competitive weapon will be discussed in depth. Along with price as a weapon we will discuss price policy in terms of the goals of the retail firm.

Price as a Competitive Weapon

Price by its very nature is a competitive weapon in the sense that retailers must price merchandise that they sell. The manner in which the firm prices its merchandise indicates to competition and consumers the emphasis on this competitive weapon. If, for example, a firm tends to de-emphasize price — that is, sets prices on the basis of its traditional competitors — then its emphasis must shift to other facets of its effort to attract customers. Thus, the traditional department store, in lieu of offering prices below its most vigorous competition, may emphasize its services, use advertising extensively, and offer the customer large assortments of goods. The neighborhood grocery store may also emphasize services, in the form of free delivery, credit, or check cashing, in contrast to his competitor, the chain supermarket, with its emphasis on price advertising.

Prices in retail stores, as we noted above, are usually set by the lower-level echelon, i.e., buyers or store managers, or in the case of the small firm, the owner himself. As with all firms, however, top management offers the lower-level price-makers guidelines which represent the goals of the firm. Some of these are exact and indicate to the price-maker that a certain return on investment is expected; others are of a more general nature and offer the price-maker a guideline to meet competitive prices at all times. In all cases, management does set certain policies for price-makers to follow.

A & P for many years has practiced a form of price leadership that can be characterized as pricing under the market. As noted in an earlier chapter A & P has become more aggressive in this role. The firm developed the A-Mart discount stores as a first step, but more recently it has shifted gears by concentrating its efforts in the development of the WEO stores. The pricing differentials that exist between the traditional A & P store and its two discounting counterparts can be seen in Table 11-1. One should note that $18.72 worth of merchandise purchased in the traditional A & P store cost $16.31 or approximately 13% less in the WEO stores.

Comparative Prices of 3 Types of A & P Stores   TABLE 11-1

	Traditional A & P	*A-Mart*	*WEO*
Milk (1 qt.)	31	31	29
Butter (1 lb.)	89	87	71
Bread (22 ozs.)	30	30	25
Beans (Cambell's)	19	17	14
Tuna (7 oz.)	39	39	37
Peas (16-17 oz.)	25	20	19
Rice (Carolina, 1 lb.)	25	23	22
Corn Flakes (Kellogg, 8 oz.)	23	21	21
Peas (green split, 1 lb.)	15	15	13
Chicken (2 lbs.)	58	58	50
Franks (all meat, 1 lb.)	69	69	65
Total price for 38 selected items	$18.72	$17.84	$16.31

Source: Adapted from the *New York Times,* September 22, 1971.

Other firms have also followed this policy at times, to their advantage. For instance, the post-World War II discount firms (e.g., E. J. Korvette, Polk Brothers) have followed this same aggressive pricing policy. In the early stages of the development of the discount industry, these firms attempted to sell well-recognized brand name products at a discount price.

Among traditional stores, this policy can also be used to advantage. The R. H. Macy Company has maintained a policy of pricing 6 per cent below competition when not prevented from doing so by the fair trade policies of manufacturers. How closely Macy's adheres to this policy has been questioned by its competitors, but there is little doubt that the consumer finds it attractive.

Price Follower

In retailing usually one or two firms at the most are fighting to become the price leaders. This is particularly true in the large metropolitan markets. For instance, among food supermarkets in any given area usually one supermarket tries to maintain a price leadership image among consumers; among the traditional department stores in this same area the same battle may be going on. In the small town, price competition among stores is limited simply because there are fewer retail outlets. Traditionally, in the small town, price competition usually emanates from the large chain or discount firm that is considered by the local merchants to be an outsider.

Taken as a group, most retail firms can be classified as followers. That is, they watch their competitors closely and within reason will attempt to set their prices in direct competition. In a sense, therefore, the retail firm is pricing with the market. However, it cannot set its prices exactly with the market, for the obvious reason that it would have to constantly keep abreast of all price changes made by its nearest competitors. In some cases this would require maintaining a huge shopping staff — a task that is beyond the financial means of most retail firms.

On the other hand, it is not much of a problem for the retail firm to keep track of a retailer's advertised products. All he has to do in this case is to follow the local newspaper ads. Though meeting advertised prices may seem to be a simple matter, in actual fact it is difficult for the retailer to do this for two reasons:

1. *The firm must have an adequate assortment of the advertised item in stock.* This is not always possible, particularly in stores where the assortment of merchandise is rather limited. Thus, a retailer seeing a competitor's ad for a Brand A electric razor may not carry this item in stock. And even if he does carry it, he would probably only have a few on hand. His feeling may well be that it is hopeless to attempt to compete against an advertised item, for which many weeks of buying and planning may have preceded the ad.[1]

2. *The exact item may be unavailable.* Even if a retail firm attempts to match an advertised price of a competitor at a later date, it may find that the item is simply not available. For example, an end-of-season bathing suit sale offers a firm little opportunity to compete, if it does not have a great number of bathing suits in stock. In most cases the firm wanting to compete will find that bathing suits are simply not available at this late date from manufacturers.

 In effect, therefore, retail firms find that meeting day-to-day prices set by their competitors is extremely difficult, if not impossible. As a general practice, retail firms do not meet the short-run prices of their competitors. On the other hand, in the long run a retail firm must meet price changes by its competitors. The long run, however, is a matter of overall departmental price changes. Or, in some cases, retail firms must show concern for changes in certain large groups of merchandise. For instance, if the ABC food supermarket reduces all prices on its non-food items, its competition (particularly nearby) will probably set prices at the same level. This does not mean that a shopper on a given day will find the price of buffered aspirin exactly the same in each store, but it does mean that the overall markup in each store will place each price within a competitive pricing range.

As noted above, most stores are followers. As indicative of this, one study shows that where it is in the same territory as the Great Atlantic and Pacific Tea Company, the Kroger food chain tends to follow the leader in pricing. In fact, there is little evidence that Kroger puts pressure on the local grocery price structure in areas where it operates. In practice, Kroger isolates itself from the severest form of

---

[1]For an account of this problem in the apparel discount firms, see David J. Rachman, "A Study of the Environmental Forces and Internal Organizational Factors Affecting Price Making in Apparel Discount Firms in Boston" (Unpublished Doctoral Thesis, New York University, Graduate School of Business, 1965), p. 174.

price competition by carrying national brands that are not available to many of its competitors.[2] As will be noted later, A & P carries mainly private brand merchandise.

Some firms go so far as to state their pricing policy (in this case, that of the price follower) in their store operating manual. The following are excerpts from a manual published by Safeway Stores:

> We will at all times be competitive with those grocery stores that are properly regarded as major or effective competitors. . . .
>
> We will not initiate or be the first to make sales below cost or at unreasonably low prices, except when necessary to avoid or minimize loss due to spoilage or threatened spoilage of perishable products; to move or liquidate surplus supplies of seasonal products that have or are about to become obsolete; to dispose of imperfect or damaged products; or to close out products to be discontinued.
>
> We will not resort to loss leader prices or a low price structure or locality price discriminations or engage in any other activity for any unlawful purpose, such as destroying competition or eliminating a competitor.[3]

Pricing Above a Market

As noted in an earlier chapter, retailing is a strongly competitive business. Therefore, it is unlikely that many firms can price above a market. That is, few firms can command a higher price for the same goods if they offer the same services as their competitors. The key words are *offer the same services*. If a firm can differentiate its services, it can, at least theoretically, command a higher price than competitors. For example, a firm that delivers a product to a customer's home will probably be able to command a higher price than the firm that does not.

There are many ways in which a firm can price its offerings above the market. For example, as was noted in an earlier chapter, it can carry products that most stores do not have. The Fifth Avenue specialty shops are examples of firms that search the world for products that are not readily available to their competitors. Because of this they can command a higher price for their products. For example, an exclusively designed sweater sold by Saks Fifth Avenue should command a higher price than a sweater of similar material sold in a less exclusive department store. Similarly, if a store offers liberal credit terms, it can be assumed that prices will reflect this service. Location is also a service offered by retail stores for which the consumer may be willing to pay a premium. The most obvious example of this is the pricing policy of the corner grocery store versus the chain supermarket. The consumer is well aware of the fact that she may be paying a premium for a quart of milk; however, in many cases it is not worth the effort for her to travel a great distance to obtain a lower price on a quart of milk. Thus, the corner grocery in direct competition with other corner grocers and with the chain supermarkets prices above the market but survives by offering the consumer convenience or other services.

---

[2]A. D. H. Kaplan *et al., Pricing in Big Business* (Washington, D.C.: The Brookings Institution, 1958), p. 206.

[3]Jules Backman, *Pricing: Policies and Practices,* National Industrial Conference Board, New York, 1961, p. 101.

Even where firms offer similar merchandise and similar services, prices are not necessarily the same. Some writers refer to this as price discrimination. Under ordinary competition one would expect firms with similar offerings to have similar prices, yet, as any shopper can tell you, they don't. Examination of Table 11-2 affirms this observation. As can be seen in this comparison of mainly branded products, prices vary within the same city and surely from city to city.

The reasons for price differentials (or price discrimination) are obvious. Some of the reasons noted above, such as the inability of the firm to police all prices, are surely applicable. In addition, however, is the belief by retailers that consumers are not aware of all prices; hence retailers tend to mix their pricing procedures where it will cause the least harm. For example, in the case of food products that are not bought often (such as salt) the retailer rightly feels that a substantial markup on such an item will be apt to go unnoticed. On the other hand, products purchased every day such as milk, bread, butter, etc., must be priced competitively. In addition, most retailers are aware of the fact that their pricing need not be exact: there is pricing within zones. That is, if one retailer prices a television set at $100, a competitor can still be competitive if his price is 10 per cent higher because not all consumers are going to shop around for lower prices and not all consumers are interested in the lowest price.

Price discrimination continues to exist in many forms. For example, the local gasoline station may give discounts to trucks, to members of local automobile clubs, or simply to local businessmen. Drug stores have been known to give members of organized groups, such as unions, special discounts. The clergy qualify for discounts in many department stores.

Pricing Goals

Aside from general overall pricing policy of the firm as outlined above, the large retail organization may insist that the firm attain certain specific goals through its pricing policies. These may be spelled out in one of two ways: (1) the establishment of a particular rate of return; (2) the maintenance or increase of the present share of the market.

1) *Return on investment.* Though the individual pricing of products is intuitive and policies can be general, such as meeting competition, a retail firm can have as an overall goal a profit in terms of return on investment. Sears, Roebuck, it has been reported, stipulates earnings of 10 to 15 per cent after taxes.[4]

In the case of the large retail chain, such a policy can be implemented by applying these standards to the individual store. The store managers who exceed this target are awarded additional compensation. This system only applies in firms where the store management has a great deal of leeway in setting prices and choosing merchandise.

2) *Share of the market.* A legitimate pricing goal of a retail firm may be to maintain or increase its share of the market, either local or national. The Great Atlantic and Pacific Tea Company is an example of a firm that at one period in its

---

[4] A. D. H. Kaplan *et al., Pricing in Big Business* (Washington, D.C.: The Brookings Institution, 1958), p. 188.

TABLE 11-2 Food Store Shelf Prices of Selected Items in Ten Cities

Item	Amount and Size	Chicago National Food	Chicago Jewel Food	Cleveland Pick N Pay	Cleveland Rego's Stop-N-Shop	Denver Miller's	Denver Safeway	Houston Belden's Food Giant	Houston Wein-garten's	Los Angeles Safeway	Los Angeles Vons
Homogenized milk	1qt.	$ .29	$ .29	$ .23	$ .25	$ .27	$ .28	$ .31	$ .32	$ .25	$ .25
Campbells' tomato soup	2 cans, regular	.25	.24	.22	.22	.34•	.20	.22	.20	.22	.23
Tide	1 lb. 4 oz.	.39	.33	.33	.28	.35	.35	.34	.35	.33	.76¶
White bread, least expensive brand	1 lb. loaf	.25	.19	.26	.22	.27	.27	.25	.23	.19	.29
Ground round steak	1 lb.	.99	.77	.79	.99	.89	.89	.79	.95	.79	.65
Kellogg's corn flakes	12-oz. box	.27•	.27	.32	.32	.30	.29	.31	.35	.29	.29
Triscuits	1 box	.43	.43	.34	.43	.43	.39	.39	.43	.43	.43
Bird's Eye frozen corn	2-10-oz. packages	.50	.39*	.45	.34	.48	.40	.37	.43	.43	.47
Dole pineapple slices, canned	1-8½-oz., 4-slice can	.22	.18*	.20	.26	.18*	.20	.19	.29*	.20	.20
Blue Bonnet margarine	1 lb.	.35	.31	.33	.31	.33	.33	.27	.31	.42	.39*
Maxwell House coffee, regular grind	1 lb.	.79	.79	.79	.75	.78	.78	.73	.69	.69	.69
Service charge or tip		—	—	—	—	—	—	.10	.10	—	—
Tax		.11‡	.17	.01	.00‡	.13	.13	.01	.01	.01	.03
Total		$4.84	$4.36	$4.27	$4.37	$4.75	$4.51	$4.28	$4.66	$4.25	$4.68

TABLE 11-2 (Cont.)

Item	Amount and Size	Milwaukee Farwell Food-Land	Kohl's	Minneapolis National Food	Red Owl Stores	New York Grand Union	A & P	Norwalk, Conn. First National	Daitch Shop-Well	Pleasantville, N.Y. Grand Union	A & P
Homogenized milk	1 qt.	$ .30	$ .29	$ .24	$ .25	$ .28	$ .30	$ .28	$ .28	$ .28	$ .28
Campbell's tomato soup	2 cans, regular	.26	.24	.22	.20	.24	.25	.25	.24	.24	.24
Tide	1 lb. 4 oz.	.36	.35	.34	.34	.33	.33	.35	.32	.33	.33
White bread, least expensive brand	1 lb. loaf	.26	.26	.21	.21	.30	.23	.22	.20	.23	.20
Ground round steak	1 lb.	.99	.99	.89	.79	.89	.89	.79	.99	.99	1.09
Kellogg's corn flakes	12-oz. box	.29	.29	.31	.37*	.26	.29	.30	.36	.26	.26
Triscuits	1 box	.43	.43	.43	.43	.43	.43	.43	.41	.43	.43*
Bird's Eye frozen corn	2-10-oz. packages	.50	.50	.49	.46	.43	.35*	.66*	.58	.43	.35*
Dole pineapple slices, canned	1-8½-oz., 4-slice can	.23	.23	.21	.21	.20	.20	.19	.20	.20	.18*
Blue Bonnet margarine	1 lb.	.53†	.55†	.43†	.55†	.32	.35	.49	.49	.45	.33
Maxwell House coffee, regular grind	1 lb.	.79	.79	.79	.79	.81	.81	.81	.79	.75	.81
Service charge or tip		—	—	—	—	—	—	—	—	—	—
Tax		—	—	—	—	.02	.02	.01	.01	.01	.01
Total		$4.94	$4.92	$4.56	$4.60	$4.51	$4.43	$4.80	$4.87	$4.60	$4.51

‡Undercharged   *Substitute brand   ¶Only large size available   †Includes tax   *Overcharged

Source: "Meaning Behind Consumer Strikes," *Printers' Ink*, December 23, 1966 (Vol. 293, No. 12) pp. 10-11.

186

development had a market share concept as a company goal. As early as 1941, the firm set as its target 20 per cent of the grocery business in each of its divisional areas of the country.[5]

It must be remembered that the goal of maintaining a market share may be in direct conflict with a rate of return goal (as outlined above). Many times in order to maintain a share of the market, the retail firm must price its products at unprofitable levels. Theoretically, therefore, in an area where A & P encountered extremely sharp competition, pursuing a market share goal required price adjustments that made many stores unprofitable over long periods of time. Implementation of this policy automatically made A & P the price leader in almost any area it entered.

Sears, on the other hand, has no fixed policy related to market share. It does, however, keep a careful record of its share of the market. For instance, being national in scope it can compare its sales of vacuum cleaners with the yearly national published totals. If this volume averages around 8 to 10 per cent of the national market, the company considers it has done an adequate job.[6] Nevertheless, share of the market does not seem to be its major goal.

The local retail firm (large or small) usually does not consider market share to be a major objective. Possibly the main reason for this attitude is the inability of the firm to get meaningful data on its share of the local market. Some of these problems are discussed in Chapter 20. Aside from basic research problems, the retailer is faced with the difficulty of adequate definition. For example, what comprises the market for men's shoes in City "A"? Should the definition of the market include all shoes? Should it include all styles of shoes? Should teen-age boys' shoes be included? The problems of definition and collection have always seemed to be insurmountable to retailers interested in some measurement of their share of the market.

Pricing Organization

Price making in the retail firm is generally decentralized, meaning that prices are not set by top management. This is not so in the manufacturing firm. Management in most industrial firms is vitally concerned with the price of its products. Much time is spent on determining these prices, with the thought of gaining some advantage over competition. As has been noted previously, the retailer is handicapped in price determination because of the unavailability of data and the huge number of products being offered. Price changes by General Motors in a model year may be of sufficient interest to the *New York Times* to run a front-page story; however, a price change in a department of Macy's would hardly attract the attention of anybody except a nearby Macy rival.

Except for the small owner-operator, prices in the retail store are made at either the store management level or the buyer level. In the case of chain stores prices are generally made in the central buying office. However, these prices are often only suggested prices, and the manager of the store may adjust the prices as he sees fit. In chain food stores the findings of one study seem to show that both the buyers and the operations people set the prices.[7] As a matter of fact, responsibility for

---

[5]*Ibid.*, p. 182.

[6]*Ibid.*, p. 198.

[7]McKinsey-General Foods Study, *The Economics of Food Distributors* (General Foods, White Plains, N.Y., 1963), p. 16.

pricing was so diffuse that many Company decisions on over-all strategy and markup levels seemed to be ignored.

When it comes to price setting, A & P store managers are given little discretion. Though pricing is decentralized to the extent that major regional divisions are responsible for price setting, store managers are offered little latitude and must follow the regional pricing guidelines. Sears, however, follows the opposite course. As a matter of policy, central prices are considered to be guidelines for store managers, but managers are free to adjust prices to the local conditions.[8] Though the Sears policy may seem risky for management, it has proven to be successful. The main reason for its workability is the fact that the Sears' store manager is responsible for the final profits of the store. In addition, he shares in these profits. Thus, any foolhardy pricing policy on his part would eventually affect his profit-sharing income.

Prices in department stores are set by the buyer. However, these prices are set within the guidelines spelled out by top management. In addition, the firm may use national averages for department stores as a basis for establishing these guidelines: we will have more to say about this later in the chapter. For example, a department store may set an average markup goal of 40 per cent for its cosmetic department — arrived at by referring to the annual published report of the National Retail Merchants Association.[9]

Though most retail firms decentralize price making, the newness of the organization may have some effect on its responsiveness to the consumer. Thus, in the older organizations, as noted above, management tends to price merchandise in the same manner as it did fifteen or twenty years ago. On the other hand, a study of the newest major form of retail outlet, the apparel discount store, seems to indicate that new firms respond more promptly to consumers than do their competitors. In general, it was found that the buyer has more freedom, is unencumbered by controls and paperwork, and seems to have shorter lines of communication with top management.[10] It might be assumed that a study of these same firms ten years from now would show their pricing apparatus to be as inefficient and unresponsive as are many of the major traditional retail firms today.

Price Determination

Prices are determined by many things: the retailer must take into account both internal and external considerations. Professor Bliss has called this behavior of the retailer "looking out" and "looking in." Figure 11-1 illustrates this concept. Note particularly the many aspects of the firm's environment that affect setting prices, each of which will be discussed below.

Internal Pricing Considerations

Internal pricing considerations are probably the most important ones for the retailer in determining the level of prices. Among these considerations are pricing goals, organizational structure (both discussed in the preceding section), costs, and the type of merchandise offered.

[8] Kaplan, *op. cit.,* p. 197.

[9] *Departmental Merchandising and Operating Results of Department and Specialty Stores,* published annually.

[10] Rachman, op. cit., p. 161

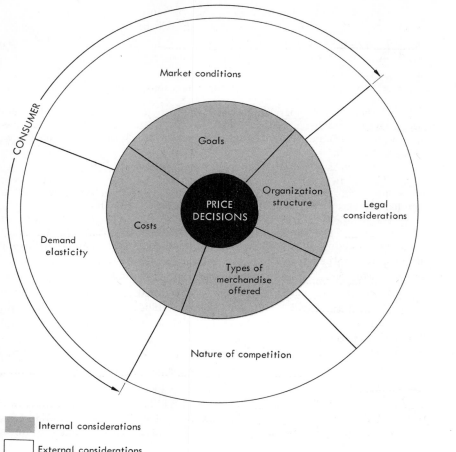

Adapted from Donald V. Harper, *Price Policy and Procedure* (New York: Harcourt, Brace and World, Inc., 1966), p. 293.

i) Cost[11]

Many people have the impression that costs determine prices; that is, once a retailer or manufacturer determines his costs of doing business he can simply add a markup to the merchandise he sells and arrive at a price. If this were all the retailer had to do, there would be little need for this chapter — or for that matter, for any knowledge of retailing. Costs constitute one, but by no means the only, factor in price determination.

It is also important to distinguish among costs. The retailer is concerned with three types: cost of merchandise, variable costs, and fixed costs.

---

[11] Though some authors distinguish between "expenses" and "costs," in this book the terms are used interchangeably.

A) **Merchandise Costs**

A retail merchant must, of course, take account of the prices he pays for his merchandise in settling his own price. In Chapter 16 it will be seen that merchandise costs remain relatively stable from firm to firm. In actuality, merchandise costs fluctuate much less from firm to firm than costs related to running a retail firm.

Merchandise costs serve two functions in relationship to pricing merchandise:

1. The costs of merchandise act as a general determinant of the level of prices, i.e., if a retailer purchased men's ties at $1 each, his retail price level would be somewhere around $2. If he paid more, let us say $3, the price of his ties would be about $5 each.

2. The costs of merchandise act as a base below which most firms will not set prices. Though in our later discussion of loss leaders it will be seen that some firms occasionally set prices below merchandise cost, this is unusual. The cost of the merchandise is generally the starting point in computing the retail price.

That cost of merchandise is not a major determining factor in setting retail prices is substantiated by Figure 11-2. This chart contains two major indices of price movements for a bedroom set: the consumer price index, which indicates the prices which retailers are charging the consumer, and the wholesale price index, which indicates the prices retailers are paying for the bedroom set and manufacturers are paying for the plywood.[12] This chart seems to indicate clearly that the consumer price did not move either with the cost of the raw material (plywood) or with the finished wholesale cost price. Thus, in 1955 when prices of the finished product started to move upward, retail prices seemed to be dropping. Here again there is strong evidence that demand at the retail level is probably more of a determinant of price than cost.

On the other hand, where price changes are reflected promptly there is a closer relationship between wholesale and retail prices. For example, changes in prices of produce sold in food stores, particularly perishables, are closely related to wholesale price movements.

B) **Fixed Expenses**

Expenses in retailing are generally fixed; that is, the costs are only obliquely related to the sales volume of the retail firm. In effect, fixed costs occur whether the retail firm is opened or closed; they include rent, most salaries, light, and heat. Table 11-3 shows three important fixed expenses in a number of retail firms. As can be seen from the table, the ratio of fixed costs to total expenses is fairly high. Fixed costs in most of the firms exceed 40 per cent of all expenses.

c) **Variable Expenses**

Variable costs are those that vary with the volume of sales. Though the division of costs into fixed and variable is convenient for analytical purposes, it can be misleading. For example, sales help (particularly management and stock clerks) is

---

[12] The bedroom set consists of a bed, a dresser, and a chest.

Price Movements of a Bedroom Suite Traced from the Raw-material Stage to the   FIGURE 11-2
Retail Level

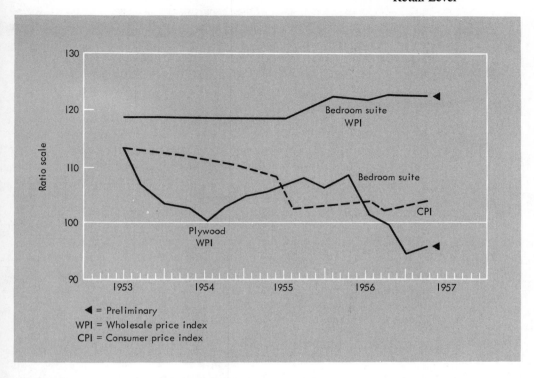

Adapted from "Do Retail Prices Follow Wholesale Prices?," *The Conference Board Business Record,* National Industrial Conference Board, Vol. XIV, No. 6 (June, 1957), p. 275.

Operating Statistics of a Selected Number of Retail Stores, Proprietorships   TABLE 11-3

Line of Business	Total Expenses	Salaries and Wages	Rent	Depreciation, Amortization Depletion
Apparel stores, women[1]	23.09%	8.58%	4.80%	0.70%
Book stores	30.60	17.00	4.10	0.80
Florist	36.42	11.91	2.55	2.25
Gift and novelty shops[1]	26.74	9.79	5.60	1.50
Hardware stores	26.80	9.90	2.40	0.50
Liquor stores	15.39	5.86	2.12	0.84
Pharmacies[2]	32.20	14.60	2.50	1.00
Variety[1]	26.84	11.17	5.05	0.85

[1] Volume $25,000 to $50,000.
[2] Volume over $400,000.
Source: Expenses in Retail Business, N.C.R., n.d.

usually classified as a fixed cost, yet some of this can vary with sales volume. For example, if a firm experiences a huge increase in sales volume, it may be forced to hire more sales clerks and possibly another departmental manager.

So too with advertising costs. Though they are usually considered to vary with sales, a case can be made for putting some of this cost into the fixed category. For example, some retail firms spend monies on institutional advertising, which by definition is long range in its impact and rarely tied in with immediate sales.

Short- and Long-Run Costs

Though costs have been classified in this section as fixed or variable, one must be careful to distinguish between the long and the short run. In the short run most retailing costs are fixed. For example, over the next three-month period the retail firm has already placed its orders for merchandise and is prepared to stock it as it is received. In terms of operating the business this same firm has scheduled a great deal of its advertising, and has committed itself in many other areas: it has more or less determined the size of its sales force; it is committed to the maintenance of its personnel staff; it may have long-term contracts regarding its delivery operation; and it usually has an established rental agreement in its present location. Essentially, therefore, the retailer in the short run looks at his costs as being what the economists call "sunk" — meaning that the firm is committed to most of its costs. Thus a 5 per cent decrease or increase in sales would probably result in only a small change in the set pattern of expenditures.

In further support of this view is the observation that the retail firm is underutilized; that is, in relation to its sales volume on any given day and the size of the plant and staff the firm maintains. Though the retailer adjusts the size of his work force over the year he still must maintain a staff that is based on the size of the plant rather than on any given day's business. For example, a service retail firm such as a department store must maintain a sales person in a silverware department all year around (plus a relief sales person) even though sales of silverware may be seasonal. This is necessary to prevent pilferage of merchandise and to offer a customer information, even though the inquiries may be infrequent. These are continuing expenses.

On the other hand, a sharp increase in sales over any long period would result in an adjustment of the firm's expense structure. For example, if the same firm lifted its sales volume by 20 per cent over a five-month period the store would be forced to increase its operating expenses. Over the short run in terms of day-to-day pricing decisions, however, the retail firm considers most expenses to be fixed.

Allocation of Costs

As noted later in this study, the retailer has been unsuccessful in his attempts to develop cost accounting systems that can be easily used in allocating costs to each unit sold. The reasons have been outlined in detail. On the other hand, cost information is still useful to the firm since overall planning requires that management have some indication as to the sales volume needed in order to run a profitable operation.

One of the useful guides used by management is the break-even chart. In the construction of this chart management must have data usually accumulated from the previous year. The data must include a breakdown of store costs, including separate tabulations for variable and fixed expenses, and information concerning the cost of merchandise. The cost of merchandise refers to the cost of merchandise sold which in turn, when subtracted from sales, gives management an estimate of gross margin. Stated another way, gross margin is simply the difference between the selling price and the cost of merchandise. This gross margin is a key figure in management estimates of profits since all expenses of operating the firm and profits are derived from its gross margin.

Perhaps more emphasis should be given to the understanding of gross margins in the retail firm. It must be remembered that the retail firm does not manufacture goods. Its contribution to the distribution system is in the form of value added to products that already exist. That is, the retail firm adds services and a marketplace for the goods it sells, and thus commands a price. The difference between what the retail firm pays for the product and what it manages to collect from the consumer is the gross margin.

Once the firm is able to determine its fixed cost of doing business and make estimates of its variable costs, it is simply a matter of mathematical calculation to determine the *break-even point*. By definition, this point is the minimum sales volume required to avoid an operating loss.[13] Again the assumptions are that fixed, variable, and merchandise costs (gross margin) will remain the same.

Figure 11-3 is an example of how a break-even chart can be calculated. In this chart one can see that fixed expenses are estimated to remain at $140,000 regardless of the sales volume. Knowing this, two ratios must be then determined from the previous year's experience, namely, the *variable costs* and the *expected gross margin*. In this same example variable costs are estimated to be 16 per cent of sales, and gross margin is expected to approximate 36 per cent. According to this estimate, variable expenses will remain at 16 per cent of sales regardless of the volume produced. Thus, if sales volume reaches $1 million annually, variable costs should run to $160,000. Conversely, if sales volume should reach only $500,000, variable costs would be $80,000. Therefore, while variable expenses increase in actual amount, percentage-wise they remain the same. Fixed costs, however, act in an opposite manner. At either of the above mentioned volumes, fixed costs remain the same in total (i.e., $140,000) but decline as a percentage of sales from 28 per cent to 14 per cent. Thus a doubling of sales volume reduces fixed costs as a percentage of sales by one half!

Further calculation shows that if gross margin is 36 per cent and variable expenses remain at 16 per cent, then if one can find the point at which fixed expenses equal the remaining 20 per cent of sales, this will be the exact break-even point. By dividing .20 into fixed expenses of $140,000 one arrives at the break-even volume of $700,000. It is at this point (see Figure 11-3) that the firm neither makes a profit nor shows an operating loss.

Once management is aware of these facts it can then determine how to increase volume above this point. Here is the point where the firm's pricing policy comes

[13] John W. Wingate and Elmer O. Schaller, *Techniques of Retail Merchandising,* 2nd edition (Englewood Cliffs, N.J.: Prentice-Hall, Inc., 1956), p. 72.

FIGURE 11-3   Break-even Point

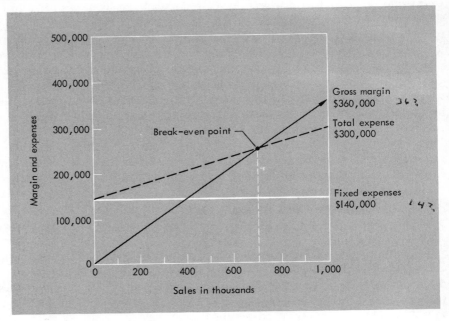

Adapted from Wingate, *op. cit.,* p. 73.

into effect. Though more will be said a little later about demand elasticity, it is sufficient at this stage to note that any manipulation in price within the retail firm will affect total sales volume. This sales volume increase or decrease must also ultimately affect the gross margin. For example, if this same firm reduces its prices by 10 per cent, gross margin will decrease proportionately. Management, therefore, must be assured of a much larger increase in sales volume before it would take such drastic action.

As can be seen by the above calculations, the break-even volume estimates can play an important role in price determination for the over-all firm. In particular, a top-level calculation of this sort will affect the various pricing guidelines used throughout the store.

Cost Allocation

In spite of the problems of applying costs to each unit of merchandise, retail firms have made some attempt to allocate individual costs to merchandise. The focus has been not on the individual unit but on types of merchandise. A system was discussed and developed by merchants in the early 1950's under the name of Merchandise Management Accounting. In essence, this system attempts to identify variable costs that are incurred by selling different types of merchandise. It was the hope of the developers of this system that the buyer of merchandise would have cost guidelines that would enable him to make buying and particularly pricing judgments in a more meaningful way.

194

For example, in one attempt it was noted that carrying apparel merchandise incurs different costs than carrying cosmetics. Typically, it was found that the sale of apparel involved heavy receiving and marking costs, alterations, and a particularly low delivery cost. On the other hand, a cosmetic product would rate low on all of these items.[14]

Though this system would seem on the surface to afford a departmentalized store an excellent guideline for pricing, as of now few stores are using it. Some firms have reported that the collection procedure is too costly in terms of the results. Others have felt that the data collected show little significant difference from judgment decisions that could be made at any time. More significant, however, is the belief that prices are governed by demand, a factor that is left out of MMA procedures.[15]

Merchandise Offered

As noted earlier, the retailer must take into consideration the type of merchandise being offered in terms of establishing prices. In later sections it will be shown that certain merchandise is unresponsive to price cuts. Conversely, an increase in markup does not seem to greatly affect the sale of other merchandise, for example, certain types of clothing, particularly if the margin is reasonable.

As a matter of policy, most firms attempt to increase their margins as much as possible, particularly if they can maintain the same volume. To accomplish this, firms in recent years have been paying much closer attention to the development of fighting brands, popularly called *private brands*. These brands are usually developed by the retail firm and cannot be purchased elsewhere. This fact represents one of the major advantages of selling private brands. However, just as important is the fact that the retailer is able to sell the private brand product at a higher markup and at a lower retail price (in most cases) than a manufacturer-owned, nationally branded product.

Some insight into this observation can be obtained from Table 11-4, which is a cost comparison between private brand items sold by Sears, Roebuck and its competitors. In effect, it shows that Sears savings (reflected in the retail price) are found in the cost of national distribution. That is, a manufacturer selling directly to Sears need not incur any cost of distribution such as advertising, sales costs, and other promotional costs. Other savings accrue to Sears by following the path of vertical integration or becoming a stockholder in one of the firms supplying Sears. The result of this private brand operation is to feature retail prices ranging from 15 to 30 per cent below competitive lines.[16] In recent years, owing to the growth of discount houses, this price differential has declined considerably. It has been estimated, however, that over 90 per cent of Sears' volume is done in private brands.

On a lesser scale one finds department stores such as Macy's developing a large consumer following for their private brands in drugs, cosmetics, apparel, and

---

[14] For a more detailed analysis of this system see the Special Issue on Merchandise Management Accounting, *Journal of Retailing*, Spring, 1958.

[15] A possible attempt to overcome this deficiency has been outlined by Gordon B. Cross, "A Scientific Approach to Retail Pricing," *Journal of Retailing*, Vol. XXXV, No. 3 (Fall, 1959), p. 118.

[16] Kaplan, *op. cit.*, p. 195.

TABLE 11-4 Factory Production Costs, Distributions Costs, and Retail Selling Price, Selected Products, Sears, Roebuck and Company

Cost Item	Water Heater		Refrigerator		Men's Shoes		House Paint		Dress Shirts	
	Com-petitors	Sears	Com-petitors	Sears	Com-petitors	Sears	Com-petitors	Sears	Com-petitors	Sears
Raw material	$ 30.52	$ 30.92	$77.02	$ 77.12	$ 3.45	$3.36	$1.72	$1.90	$1.02	$1.15
Direct labor	3.20	3.17	15.91	15.93	.96	.99	.08	.08	.33	.37
Factory overhead	12.60	12.51	36.82	38.67	.74	.45	.29	.29	.25	.20
Administrative expense	3.27	2.10	2.55	2.55	.32	.20	.26	.06	.02	.03
Factory cost	49.59	48.17	132.30	134.27	5.47	5.00	2.14	2.32	1.63	1.75
Factory margin	16.41	12.73	33.53	31.70	.54	.44	.41	.38	.06	.07
"Manufacturing Cost"	66.00	60.90	165.83	165.97	6.01	5.44	2.55	2.70	1.69	1.82
National distri-bution cost	6.11	—	10.73	—	1.09	—	.52	—	.54	—
Jobbing margin	21.85	—	29.42	—	—	—	.53	—	—	—
Retail markup	43.70	44.05	103.77	103.98	3.85	2.51	1.79	1.59	1.42	1.16
Selling price	137.66	104.95	309.75	269.95	10.95	7.95	5.39	4.29	3.65	2.98

Source: Kaplan, *op. cit.*, p. 194.

TABLE 11-4 (cont.)

Cost Item	Silverplate		Garden Hose		Shot Gun		Girdle	
	Competitors	Sears	Competitors	Sears	Competitors	Sears	Competitors	Sears
Raw material	$10.70	$11.70	$1.32	$1.51	$ 4.85	$ 5.20	$ 2.39	$2.16
Direct labor	6.36	6.57	.51	.46	10.33	7.29	.65	.59
Factory overhead	7.63	7.98	.86	.71	23.52	18.64	.78	.70
Administrative expense	.86	.75	.10	.06	1.30	1.18	.23	.21
Factory cost	25.55	27.00	2.79	2.74	40.00	32.31	4.05	3.66
Factory margin	3.20	2.25	.66	.35	9.33	8.14	.41	.37
"Manufacturing Cost"	28.75	29.25	3.45	3.09	49.33	40.45	4.46	4.08
National Distribution cost	3.20	–	.35	–	3.25	–	.59	–
Jobbing margin	10.65	–	.90	–	11.12	–	–	–
Retail markup	28.40	26.75	2.05	1.89	21.25	24.50	4.95	3.95
Selling price	71.00	56.00	6.75	4.98	84.95	64.95	10.00	7.98

Source: Kaplan, *op. cit.*, p. 194.

appliances. A & P with its Bokar coffee and Ann Page food products has gone in heavily for private brands. Again, in practically all private brand merchandising price is established below the competing nationally branded product.

In addition, the retail firms' margins almost always exceed the margin offered by the manufacturers of national brands. One interesting exception to the latter observation is found in New York State where private brand liquor, though sold at a price below the national brands, carried a margin of almost half the national liquor. This peculiar situation is brought about by the fact that most of the price of liquor is made up of state and federal tax; hence, little can be passed on to the retailer in the form of cost savings. This demonstrates, however, the significance of private brands to the retailer, since most distillers consider the sale of private brands to be a major competitive factor in New York State.

External Price Considerations

External considerations are also very important in setting prices in the retail firm. The retailer is always mindful of competition, demand elasticity, market conditions and their relationship to the consumer and legal consideration. Legal considerations were covered in Chapter 4, and information on the consumer market in Chapter 5. In the following sections, demand elasticity and competition and their impact on pricing will be discussed.

ı) Demand

The relationship of consumer demand for retail products to pricing is complex. Demand for retail products is on two levels. The first refers to the total demand for products and services within the store's trading area. This demand has little to do with retail management in that the firm cannot increase or decrease this amount to any great extent. This level is also concerned with the demand for the products of a store in this area. Upon management's interpretation of the demand for the products of this store, the overall firm price strategy is formed. Our analysis of consumer demand in Chapter 5 dealt with area demand as will Chapter 17.

The second level refers to the demand for groups of products and individual products in the store. Pricing decisions of this nature can be made at the top levels, but the burden of setting these prices rests with the lower-level price-setting echelons. In the chain it may be the chain buyer, with some leeway resting in the hands of the store manager. In the department store the pricing of types of goods probably rests with the buyer, who works within the confines of policies set by management. In the small independent store most decisions of this nature are made by the owner.

The first level decisions are made mainly on the basis of intuition,[17] in the sense that although they are based on some previous experience there is little opportunity for management to be scientific or exact. Though decisions on the second level are also made mainly on an intuitive basis, there exists some evidence that can shed light in making the proper decision. In addition, in second level pricing the retailer

---

[17]Though his definition of the pricing levels within the retail store differs somewhat from the interpretation in this section, this level delineation has been suggested by Douglas J. Dalrymple, "Estimating Price Elasticity," *Journal of Retailing,* Vol. 42, No. 4 (Winter 1966–1967), p. 1.

does have an opportunity to experiment by changing prices on his products and testing the results or at least judging them in terms of sales volume.

In many respects retailing offers an excellent opportunity for study of the effect of price changes on demand within product groups. There are several reasons for this:

1. Prices are an important sales factor; they are featured in the firm's promotion efforts and customers shop among stores.

2. Prices are unusually flexible in terms of the firm's total effort; seasonal patterns and style changes make careful price administration indispensable in the profitable management of large retail inventories.

3. Though there is substantial competition among retail stores, there exists some leeway in setting prices.

4. There exists keen competition between substitute products, which represents an ideal arrangement for the conducting of controlled experiments.[18]

In effect therefore, the retailer in setting prices on groups of products must either intuitively or experimentally determine the price elasticity of his products. Price elasticity refers to the increase or decrease in sales experienced by the retailer when he raises or lowers the price of a product, i.e., the amount of merchandise sold tends to increase as price decreases and vice versa. These changes are usually measured in terms of one per cent. Thus, an elasticity of 3.0 indicates that a decrease in price of one per cent would result in a three-fold increase in sales volume. Such a product is highly elastic, that is, price changes have a strong impact on sales. Conversely, an elasticity of .5 would indicate that the product is relatively inelastic, that is, price changes have a weak impact on sales.

A product or a group of products can experience one of the following with a decrease in price:

1. A more than proportionate increase in sales volume (elastic demand).

2. A less than proportionate increase in sales volume (inelastic demand).

3. An increase in sales volume in exact proportion to the price cut (parity demand).

Thus, it would seem that all price changes made for groups of products (such as men's furnishings) must be made with some knowledge concerning the elasticity of demand. For example, if a price cut of 10 per cent would only increase sales volume by 5 per cent, obviously a firm would not continue making decisions of this nature. The reader should be cautioned, however, about the above simplification on several counts.

First, although the price cut may not bring the needed increase in sales in the department, it may bring many more shoppers to the store who will buy other merchandise in sufficient quantity to more than fill this gap. This is what is referred to as cross-elasticity of demand, i.e., the impact of a price change on a competing firm's sales volume.[19]

[18] Joel Dean, *Managerial Economics* (Englewood Cliffs, N.J.: Prentice-Hall, Inc., 1956), p. 187.

[19] In a more restricted sense, cross-elasticity also refers to the impact of the sale of product A within a store on product B, for example, the impact of a price cut on a private brand when a national brand reduces its price. For further elaboration on this point see Ralph Cassady, Jr., *Competition and Price Making in Food Retailing* (New York: The Ronald Press Company, 1962, p. 34.

Second, the retailer's policy is much more complex in terms of the arithmetic shown above, particularly in the retail firm. It may be recalled that the retailer does not change the product in any way; he simply adds services and provides a marketplace. For this he is entitled to a profit secured by adding a markup to merchandise he offers for sale. Thus, the retailer is markup conscious. That is, he is *not* concerned with sales as such, but with the difference between the selling price and the price he pays for his merchandise. Hence, any discussion of elasticity of demand must take into consideration not only the change in sales volume, but the reduction in markup incurred by retailers. As an example, consider the retailer who is selling an item for $1 and who plans a price reduction of 10 per cent (or a price of 90 cents). If the retailer originally paid 80 cents for this item, the reduction in margin may amount not to 10 per cent, but to a whopping 50 per cent! Therefore, in order for a retailer to maintain his same gross margin dollars, a product reduced in price by 10 per cent would have to increase sales by 50 per cent.

Elasticity and Merchandise

Table 11-5 shows some interesting data collected over a 24-month period concerning elasticity of demand for products within departments of a major department store. In examining this table several things should be noted.

First, correlation coefficients range from .875 to -.694. This indicates that among the positive correlations high markups were associated with high-sale months. Conversely, negative coefficients indicate that high markups were associated with low-sale months.

TABLE 11-5   Correlation Coefficients Between Initial Markup and Sales, By Departments, 24 Monthly Observations

Department	Correlation Between Initial Markup and Sales R	Department	Correlation Between Initial Markup and Sales R
Men's furnishings	.875*	Men's clothing	.043
Women's sportswear	.555*	Cosmetics	.014
Moderately priced dresses	.467*	Sporting goods	.011
Gifts	.357	Foundations	-.078
Women's accessories	.334	Women's sports shoes	-.120
College shop	.266	Infants	-.231
Junior sportswear	.221	Silver	-.233
Stationery	.109	Housewares	-.310
Hosiery	.096	Women's shoes	-.435*
Lingerie	.069	Toys	-.694*
Better dresses	.048		

*Correlation coefficient significantly different from zero ($P < .05$).
Source: Douglas J. Dalrymple, "Estimating Price Elasticity," *Journal of Retailing* (Winter 1966-1967), p. 3.

Second, five departments show significant relationships statistically.[20] Among the top three departments (Men's Furnishings, etc.) it could be assumed by management that price elasticity was low and consumers were either unconcerned with prices or that they were not aware of price changes.[21] The low negative correlation for the Toy and Women's Shoe departments indicates that elasticity is very high and consumers are sensitive to changes in prices.

ﺝ Competition

Though demand and costs weigh heavily in setting prices in the retail store, competition is an important consideration. As a rule, where competition is lacking the retailer is prone to charge higher prices. Take the development within the past five years of the Grand Bahama Island, 75 miles off the coast of Florida. The island government closely controls the number of businesses through the issuance of licenses to qualified individuals or corporations. The restriction of licenses to food supermarkets has created a monopoly position. As a result, food prices have been estimated to be two or three times higher than in the same supermarkets in Florida.

In most areas of the country, however, retailers face competition from similar outlets. It is a rare firm that has a monopoly within its trading area. On the other hand, firms are aware that they do not exist in perfectly competitive markets either. In essence, the retail firm does set prices and need not concern itself with meeting the exact prices of its competitors. The economist would refer to this as an indication that retail competitive markets are imperfect; they fall somewhere in between monopoly and perfect competition.

Perhaps this point should be elaborated on since it has an important effect on pricing. A good starting point is the definition of perfect competition. Perfect competition exists where:

1. There can only be one price prevailing in a market at a given time.
2. No producer by his own efforts can alter the market price for a product; a decision to offer this product is made on the basis of the cost conditions.
3. The product offered by all producers must be substitutable and consumers must be indifferent as to where they purchase them.[22]

Perfect competition is a theoretical concept that represents a starting point in our thinking about competition. Few perfectly competitive markets exist today. If forced to point out a perfectly competitive market, one might suggest certain areas of the agricultural market where the price the farmer receives for his product (such as wheat) is set by the market place independently of the amount of wheat the individual farmer produces. There is little the farmer can do to alter the fact that on any given day he will receive only the going market rate. The buyers of his product consider that all bushels of wheat are the same and one bushel easily substitutable for another.

Even in agricultural marketing, however, farmers or the organizations representing farmers are continually striving to differentiate their product. For instance, the

---

[20] Dalrymple, *op. cit.,* p. 3.
[21] Dalrymple, *idem.*
[22] Henry Smith, *Retail Distribution* (London: Oxford University Press, 1937), p. 118.

farmer may join a cooperative that attempts to attach a brand name or some identifying mark to its product, the purpose being to develop a consumer preference for the product and eventually command a premium price in the marketplace. Calavo avocadoes are an example of an attempt on the part of farm co-ops to attach such an identification to a product that formerly went to market completely unidentified.

Retailers, as we have seen, are constantly trying to differentiate their offerings. Their purpose is no different from that of the farm co-ops — that is, a direct attempt to command a higher price for their product by differentiating their offerings. This explains the retailers' interest in monopolistic locations (such as a site in a restricted shopping center), exclusive merchandise, distinctive services, and an elaborate decor. These aspects of the retailers' operations are referred to as nonprice offerings. Their purpose is to take the consumers' mind off price, and in the case of exclusive merchandise, to restrict the consumers' ability to make price comparisons.

Identifying competition. Not all retail stores are in direct competition. As noted in an earlier chapter, there are many varieties of retail firms. Management must at some point identify those stores that seem to compete for the same segment of the retail market. This is not always easy to figure out. In addition to stores nearby carrying similar products, his estimation of competition may include firms not located in the immediate vicinity. For instance, a large downtown department store, in determining its competition, would probably include all other major department stores in the city as direct competitors. The problem arises when the individual department manager must determine his competitors. This may vary considerably from the view of top management and is dependent on the type of merchandise being sold.

Consider the view of the buyer of men's clothing and the cosmetic buyer. The buyer of men's clothing would most assuredly be interested in the competition of other department stores, since in his view the shopper would expend the effort to cross town to save money or at least purchase a suit that meets his value requirements. In addition, this same buyer is faced with the competition of numerous men's clothing specialty stores: large independents, national chains (such as Robert Hall), and local chains. Thus, his pricing must take into account the competition of a large variety of stores.

The cosmetic buyer would probably have an entirely different estimate of his competition. Though his products can be found in the same competing department store, he may think that users of cosmetics will expend little energy in order to obtain better value. Thus, his view of competition may well be restricted to nearby stores within a short walking distance and he would be interested mainly in cosmetic prices featured by the local drugstore or specialty cosmetic stores.

Judgment

Though various considerations in setting prices have been outlined in this section, in actuality the firm is unable to measure in an exact way many of these factors.

The manufacturer can construct a demand curve for many of his products, but to do this in the retail firm is impractical, as it is for cost measurements. As a practical matter, therefore, the retailer makes judgments about the prices to attach to his merchandise based on experiments he has conducted in the past and on his years of experience. In most cases his judgment is inexact and later adjustments in prices have to be made (see section on markdowns below). Nevertheless, whether the retailer does so formally or not, he does give consideration to all of the above-mentioned factors in setting prices.

Aside from computing a price for each product or line of products the retailer is always faced with problems that defy exact computation. For example, he must consider whether the price he sets relates to the needs of the consumer. This calls for a consideration of such pricing techniques as price lining, and psychological, loss-leader, and bait pricing.

Special
Pricing
Techniques
of Retailers

i) Price Lining and Price Points

Setting prices on the basis of demand, cost, or other competitive factors alone can cause customer confusion. For example, using these factors as guidelines, men's ties in a store could be priced at $1.00, $1.19, and $1.25. The pricing of ties in this manner would raise a number of problems in the mind of the consumer and eventually in the mind of the salesman.

The first would be the consumer's question as to the difference in values offered. He would certainly want to know why the highest-priced tie is worth 6 cents more than the next highest. The probable answer would be that there is little basic difference in these price lines. Thus, most general merchandise retailers tend to offer specific price lines whereby meaningful differences can be presented to the consumer. This makes it easier to develop sales training information in that sales clerks do not have to have knowledge about a large number of price lines.

There are a number of other advantages to the retailer. Probably the most important is that the buyer can go out in the marketplace and find merchandise that specifically fits into his price lines. Through this process he can clearly reject other merchandise that would not fit into his range of price lines. It is of interest to note that many manufacturers have adjusted to this standard price line by producing goods that fit specifically into the retailer's pricing format. In a sense the retailer has set guidelines for manufacturers which help them with their decision making in producing a product.

Consider, for example, the manufacturer who sells a $1.00 retail line of products to the variety chains. In all cases he must charge the retailer a maximum price of 60 cents to enable him to maintain his usual markup. If the manufacturer was considering a new product with additional features to fit into the same line, he might be forced to increase his costs of production and hence sell at the next highest price, which could be $1.50 retail. However, the manufacturer may be reluctant to move into this new price line since he may find that his sales volume will be affected. Hence, his decision may be either not to produce the new product or to add the new feature at the expense of some other feature in the product. In any case, his decision is controlled to an extent by the retailer's price line policy.

Price lines do have disadvantages, however. In particular they may be difficult to maintain during times of rising costs. They may also leave large gaps in quality that the consumer wants. It must be remembered that price lines are points where the retailer feels demand is greatest. In many cases the retailer may find that his estimation was wrong.[23] One of the greatest dangers, however, stems from the retailer's competition. A retailer must be careful that his competitor does not have lower price lines. More important, many traditional retailers found during the postwar period that in many lines of branded hard goods it was not possible to maintain price lines as products were sold at many different prices. In addition, many different apparel discounters were using traditional price lines as a basis for giving bargains to the consumer. This was particularly true where branded merchandise was unavailable to the discounter. For example, in the boys' wear field, shirts are sold by traditional outlets in two major price lines of $1.99 and $2.99. Discounters would simply set prices of boys' shirts below these two lines. By doing this they were signifying to the consumer that their product was similar but selling for less in each of these price-line groupings. For example, a discounter by offering a shirt for $1.79 would in effect be telling the consumer that this product has a list price of $1.99.

Not all retail firms use price lines. Food retailers do not practice price lining in its purest form.[24] However, the food retailer attempts to meet the needs of his customers by offering products at different price levels. It is not uncommon for a retailer to stock one product at three different price levels. For example, a chain supermarket may carry tuna fish at a price of 35 cents, 39 cents, and 53 cents. The lowest priced item is the firm's private brand, the second highest a well-known, nationally advertised brand, and the highest a well-known "gourmet" line of tuna. Instead of aiming at specific income markets, the retailer may stock his food items according to grades, with the lowest price attached to the lowest-grade item.

Psychological Pricing

At some point retailers must place an exact price on the merchandise being sold. In some cases the merchandise may be set within a price line; in others it may have to be pre-retailed. Pre-retailed means that the retailer places a retail price on the purchase order for the product before it is received.

In setting an exact price on a product the retailer has an option in many cases of reducing or increasing his prices by a few cents. Many firms have established a standard policy of using prices ending in zero, nines, and fives. For example, some firms selling toys may use prices such as 99 cents; others 95 cents; and still others may round out the price to the nearest dollar. The latter practice is least often followed. The firm may choose to sell a product at 95 cents or 99 cents rather than a dollar for several reasons. The first is the belief that more consumers will buy the product at these lower prices: the fact that 99 cents is not quite a dollar or that $3.99 is much less psychologically than $4.00.

Second, and related to the first, the belief that odd prices denote a bargain to many consumers. Thus, price endings of 99 cents or 95 cents seem to imply greater

---

[23]Harper, *op. cit.,* p. 246.
[24]Cassady, *op cit.,* p. 126.

value to consumers than rounded figures. Does the consumer's view coincide with the view of the merchant regarding these price endings? From a theoretical point of view there is some question. Few sales transactions today are completed without adding a federal excise tax or sales tax to the price. For example, in a City where the sales tax is 5 per cent, a $3.99 price becomes $4.19; 99 cents becomes $1.04. Thus, the psychological price becomes meaningless. One's interpretation of this depends on how customers view a product. Do they make judgments on the price offered or on the final transaction price? If the former, then psychological pricing might be meaningful.

What have tests shown? One of the few studies conducted on the impact of psychological pricing on mail order sales showed that it was not possible to come to any firm conclusion either way.[25] Yet psychological pricing persists. Table 11-6 shows that almost 60 per cent of the advertised prices of chain food stores end in "9" digits.

3) Loss Leaders

A retail firm must always maintain the interest of the customer in bargains. But because of its huge assortment, particularly in the case of a food supermarket, for example, the firm must restrict bargains to only a limited number of items in the store. This is less true of the general merchandise store. To develop a bargain image in the mind of the consumer, the retailer reduces prices drastically on a few items in the hope of obtaining the consumer's patronage and selling to her from his regularly priced stock. Food stores offer the customer loss leaders on almost a weekly basis. Department stores are more apt to offer "special buys," that is, items that have been purchased at a reduced price and marked up at the average rate.

The size of the reduction depends on company policy. A & P, for example, does not price its leader items at a loss. Until 1950, 3 per cent was the minimum markup on a product for most stores.[26] Other firms may actually offer leader items at cost or below. Before Thanksgiving it is not unusual for food chains to price turkeys below cost.

The choice of the item to be offered as a loss leader is usually based on three criteria:

1. The product should be favorably known to the consumer; in addition, it should be of a recognizable standard of quality.

2. The product should be purchased repeatedly so that the consumer recognizes the importance of saving money in its purchase.

3. The product should be of relatively low price so that the consumer will be discouraged from simply buying the one item and storing it for future use.[27]

The above criteria are important in determining loss leader items. However, one should note that where an item is priced slightly above cost, it can become quite profitable provided the markup covers the basic variable cost of the firm. An illustration of this can be seen in Figure 11-4. Here the dollar sales per week seem

---

[25] Eli Ginsberg, "Customary Prices," *American Economic Review,* Vol. XXVI, No. 2 (1936), p. 296.

[26] Kaplan, *op. cit.,* p. 183.

[27] Cassady, *op. cit.,* pp. 169–170.

TABLE 11-6   Per Cent of Advertised Prices Ending in Each Digit[a]

Market	Leading Chain	No. Of Prices	1	2	3	4	5	6	7	8	9	0
New York	A & P	172	1	2	10	1	17	0	6	1	60	2
Newark	Shop-Rite	275	1	1	5	3	22	1	7	1	55	4
Chicago	Jewel Tea	82	0	0	5	6	21	2	1	5	55	5
Los Angeles	Safeway	132	1	1	5	6	12	0	6	2	59	8
Philadelphia	Acme	149	3	3	11	1	17	0	7	5	52	1
Detroit	A & P	145	1	2	8	3	10	0	6	4	63	3
Boston	First National	78	0	0	5	4	19	0	8	6	50	8
San Francisco	Safeway	115	0	0	4	9	7	2	6	1	68	3
Pittsburgh	A & P	78	1	4	5	5	12	0	0	1	68	4
St. Louis	Kroger	97	2	3	10	2	7	2	3	4	58	9
Washington, D.C.	Safeway	93	9	5	8	2	17	1	2	0	55	1
Cleveland	Pick-N-Pay	110	5	2	13	9	8	2	7	5	43	6
Baltimore	A & P	188	2	2	10	4	17	1	6	2	52	4
Mpls.-St. Paul	Red Owl	54	9	0	6	2	15	2	6	4	50	6
Buffalo	Loblaw	89	6	1	0	3	8	0	8	1	70	3
Houston	Weingarten	112	6	0	7	4	21	0	12	1	49	0
Milwaukee	Kohl	82	2	0	6	6	17	2	7	5	46	9
Seattle	Safeway	78	0	0	0	3	22	0	3	5	57	10
Dallas	Buddies	120	1	1	6	4	18	2	13	4	45	6
Cincinnati	Kroger	85	1	0	5	0	12	1	8	5	64	4
Kansas City	Safeway	71	0	1	1	1	8	0	3	0	79	7
San Diego	Safeway	111	1	1	7	4	17	2	5	4	59	0
Atlanta	Colonial	81	0	0	6	2	15	0	7	7	59	4
	Total	2,597	2	1	7	4	15	1	6	3	57	4

[a]Retail grocery advertisements of June 2, 3, and 4, 1965, for each of the leading chains in the top 23 "A" Metropolitan Areas.

Source: Dik Warren Twedt, "Does the '9 Fixation' in Retail Pricing Really Promote Sales?," *Journal of Marketing,* Vol. 29, No. 4 (October, 1965), p. 55.

to be closely related to the size of the maintained margin. For example, items with a margin exceeding 25 per cent sell at the rate of $2 per week. Conversely, cigarettes with a 6 per cent margin contribute about $13 a week per sales.

In essence, the retailer's attempt to maximize profits requires that he sell some items below or slightly above cost to interest consumers in his store. The merchandising strategy of his firm requires, however, that he price his merchandise in such a manner as to maximize his sales.

Bait Pricing

Similar to loss leader pricing is bait pricing, the major difference being that firms which use bait pricing usually have no intention of selling the product that they advertise at an attractively low price.

FIGURE 11-4 Weekly Dollar Sales Related to Margins of Selected Food Items

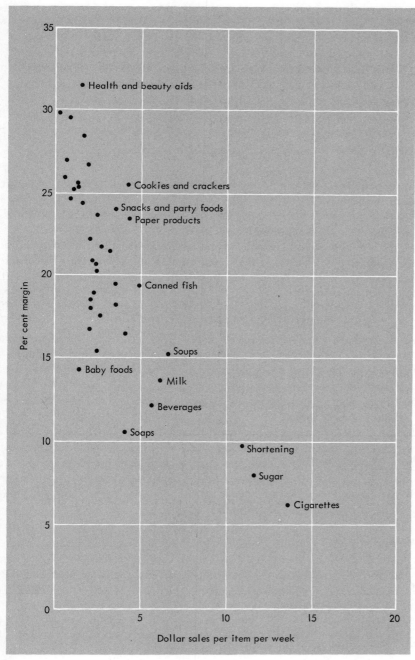

Adapted from W. G. McClelland, *Studies in Retailing* (Oxford: Basil Blackwell, 1963), p. 98.

Few major firms use bait pricing as a strategy. However, in many small retail firms or specialized chains bait pricing is almost a way of life. Typically, an appliance retail firm will advertise a well-known, branded television set at an extremely low price (e.g., $50). The customer intent on buying this product will find the salesmen also intent on switching the customer's interest to another brand or type of television set. Failing this, the salesman can announce that the advertised item is not in stock or can simply take the order for the item. The latter step is merely a stall to get the customer out of the store since the firm has no intention of delivering the television set.

Obviously bait advertising is an unethical practice and firms that persist in this type of behavior usually run afoul of the local business groups and in many cases the legal authorities.

The Mathematics of Retail Pricing

✳ At some point the retailer has to compute a price. In making these computations he must consider the following: markup, gross margin, markdowns, shortages, and employee discounts. In the following sections each of these factors will be discussed and will then be related to formulas used in pricing.

Aside from the obvious reasons for not using an average markup to price all goods, there are others such as the arguments implied in our earlier discussion of Merchandise Management Accounting. In the application of this method to setting prices it was observed that each general group of merchandise incurs different costs in terms of promotion, servicing, and general handling. In addition, the selling effort required can very considerably from item to item.

As an example, consider the sale of men's clothing as against the sale of a lamp. In the sale of men's clothing artful selling is a major criterion. In addition, the alteration department represents an important service. In many firms the presence of an alteration room automatically means that the firm must have space for measuring suits and a delivery system so that customers do not have to come back for the suit at a later date.

Selling lamps involves other problems. Though most of the above services do not apply, the lamp department must have a delivery service. In addition, the cost of delivery of lamps is much higher than apparel because of the breakage factor and the bulky nature of both the lamps and the shades. Applying the same markup to both men's suits and lamps would seem, therefore, to involve assumptions concerning costs that would not be based on fact.

Markup

Markup in the retail store is defined as the differences between the selling price and the cost of merchandise in the retail store.[28] It is usually expressed as a percentage of the retail price. Thus, goods costing 60 cents and selling for $1.00 have a markup of 40 per cent. Markup is used by the retailer as a valuable planning guide. In addition, it is widely used to limit the alternatives of the suppliers.[29] For

---

[28] Cost includes the price of the merchandise less trade discounts, less cash discounts, and plus inward freight where freight is not included in the invoice price.

[29] See Roger Dickinson, "Markup in Department Store Management," *Journal of Marketing,* Vol. 31 (January, 1963), pp. 30–34.

example, in our previous discussion we noted that many suppliers produce products for certain price lines offered by the store. Thus, in the boys' wear field they manufacture shirts to sell in the stores at $1.99. Since most traditional retailers prefer to sell at an average markup of approximately 40 per cent, the prices that can be charged by the manufacturer dealing with these markets is somewhat limited by the markup constraints. As a matter of fact, the only option available to the manufacturer caught in this bind is to develop a new production technique that lowers cost, find a substitute material (such as a synthetic fiber replacing wool), or simply reduce the quality of his product.

One is aware in retailing that there exists no one markup that suffices for all types of retailing stores. In Table 11-7 one sees a tabulation of the selling price of an item costing 50 cents to the retailer. Note that the final selling price varies considerably among the different types of retail stores. The range of the final selling price for the item costing 50 cents varies from a low of 69 cents to a high of $1.11.

Selling Price of Items Costing 50 cents in Various Retail Outlets   TABLE 11-7

Outlet	Markup*	Price of Item
Florist	55%	$1.11
Jewelry	46	.93
Gift	40	.83
Variety	39	.82
Bookstores	36	.78
Department	34	.76
Liquor Stores	27	.69
Supermarket	22	.64

*Gross margin or gross profit.

The variation among these stores is interesting in that it also reflects the types of products sold. Thus the florist with the highest markup ordinarily carries products that are perishable and purchased only occasionally by the ordinary consumer. The lowest markup is found in the grocery store, which carries products purchased weekly. These products characteristically have a high turnover, a situation that tends to prevail in low-markup outlets.

In a sense the volume of business that can be derived at a given markup plus the types of goods carried determine the markup. The florist's product involves great risks of perishability; the products sold in a liquor store involve a minimum risk and high turnover, thus the lower markup. Department stores with their high-risk apparel items counterbalanced by lower-risk durable goods fall somewhere in between.

Though it may seem that applying a markup to the cost of merchandise would represent a relatively simple way of arriving at a price, the mathematics of it is more complex than this. The difficulty stems from the definition and understanding of markup.

A retailer is concerned with two aspects of markup. His first interest is the *initial markup* of his product. This markup must include not only adequate allowance for his costs and profits but must make an allowance for what are called retail reductions. *Retail reductions* refer to the deterioration of the initial price of the product due to markdowns, shortages and discounts to employees. Thus when an item is sold at an initial markup of 40 per cent its average price may reflect a maintained markup (or gross margin) of much less. This is due to the fact that some of the merchandise in stock may be marked down (see below), some may be stolen, and other parts of the stock may simply be reduced in price as an accommodation to employees and other shoppers (such as clergy) who are often offered a special discount. Hence, in setting prices the retailer must make an estimate of these reductions so that his gross margin will reflect these expected occurrences.

The mathematics of this are quite simple. If a firm, for example, wanted to maintain a gross margin of 35 per cent it would make an estimate of retail reductions. In this case an estimate of retail reductions of 5 per cent would involve the following calculation, using the formula:[30]

$$\text{Initial markup} = \frac{\text{Gross Margin} + \text{Retail reductions}}{100\% + \text{Retail reductions}}$$

$$\frac{35\% + 5\%}{100\% + 5\%} = 38.09\%$$

Application of the above formula indicates to the retailer that in order to end up with a gross margin (or maintained markup) of 35 per cent the department must apply an initial markup of 38.09 per cent. Though the above formula may satisfy the planning needs of the department the buyer is usually faced with everyday problems that involve the known cost of the merchandise and the unknown retail price which must be computed. For example, one might ask: What price should be placed on ten items having a total cost of $7.20 to provide an initial markup of the above 40 per cent? The following formula is usually applied:

$$\text{Retail Price} = \frac{\text{Cost}}{100\% - \text{Markup}} \times 100$$

$$= \frac{\$7.20}{60\%} \times 100 = \$12.00$$

Thus each item should retail at $1.20.

In engaging in yearly planning the firm may wish to convert its planned estimates into an estimated initial markup. For example, a firm may make the following estimate:

Planned Expenses	$ 30,000
Planned Profit	5,000
Planned Reductions	6,000
Planned Sales	100,000

What is the required markup necessary to reach this goal?

---

[30] This section draws on illustrations found in Delbert J. Duncan and Charles F. Phillips, *Retailing, Principles and Methods,* 5th ed. (Homewood, Ill.: Richard D. Irwin, Inc., 1963), pp. 338– 449. For more detailed information on retail reductions see footnote 3 in Chapter 16 of this book.

$$\text{Initial Planned Markup } \% = \frac{\text{Planned Expenses} + \text{Planned Profit} + \text{Planned Reductions}}{\text{Planned Sales} + \text{Planned Reductions}}$$

$$= \frac{\$30,000 + \$5,000 + \$6,000}{\$100,000 + \$6,000} = \frac{41,000}{106,000} = 38.7\%$$

The initial markup necessary to meet the goal is 38.7%.

Markup On Individual Items

Buyers have to calculate the retail selling price of individual items. Though the calculation is relatively simple, the retailer must bear in mind that all prices are expressed as a percentage of the retail price.

For instance, suppose a buyer purchased an item for 80 cents and wishes to mark up his merchandise 40 per cent, in order to cover his estimate of planned profits, expenses, and reductions. What price shall he set on the merchandise?

As markup is based on the retail price, the retailer's calculation is based on the following formula:

$$\text{Retail Price} = \frac{\text{Cost of merchandise}}{100\% - \text{Desired markup percentage}} \times 100$$

$$\text{Retail Price} = \frac{.80}{100 - 40} = \frac{.80}{.60} \times 100 = \$1.33$$

Some retailers prefer to convert the markup on retail to a markup on the cost of the merchandise. To accomplish this, they must make the calculations on the basis of an additional step, as follows:

$$\text{Markup on cost} = \frac{\text{Markup on retail}}{100 - \text{Markup on retail}} \times 100$$

$$= \frac{40}{100 - 40} \times 100 = 66.6 \text{ per cent}$$

$$66.6\% \text{ of } 80 \text{ cents} = 53.3 \text{ cents} + 80 \text{ cents} = \$1.33$$

The same answer as above.

To reduce the cumbersome calculations required, the retailer using the cost method can use a conversion table as illustrated in Table 11-8. Thus, in solving the above problem, a 40% markup on retail can be converted to 66 2/3 per cent. Applying this percentage to the 80-cents cost, (80 × 66 2/3 per cent = 53.3 cents + 80 cents = $1.33) eases the computation.

Store Markup Policy

Once a retailer has settled upon the important criteria, he is then in a position to determine the average markup that should be applied to all goods sold in his store. As a matter of procedure, management may set markup goals for the department and insist that the buyer or department or store manager adhere to this average markup. However, this does not necessarily mean that the retailer must apply this markup to all merchandise. Our previous discussions concerning demand elasticity, competition and the maximization of sales should indicate that applying one markup to all merchandise would be a poor business policy.

TABLE 11-8 Markup Conversion Table

Margin Per Cent of Selling Price	Markup Per Cent of Cost	Margin Per Cent of Selling Price	Markup Per Cent of Cost	Margin Per Cent of Selling Price	Markup Per Cent of Cost
4.8	5.0	18.0	22.0	32.0	47.1
5.0	5.3	18.5	22.7	33.3	50.0
6.0	6.4	19.0	23.5	34.0	51.5
7.0	7.5	20.0	25.0	35.0	53.9
8.0	8.7	21.0	26.6	35.5	55.0
9.0	10.0	22.0	28.2	36.0	56.3
10.0	11.1	22.5	29.0	37.0	58.8
10.7	12.0	23.0	29.9	37.5	60.0
11.0	12.4	23.1	30.0	38.0	61.3
11.1	12.5	24.0	31.6	39.0	64.0
12.0	13.6	25.0	33.3	39.5	65.5
12.5	14.3	26.0	35.0	40.0	66.7
13.0	15.0	27.0	37.0	41.0	70.0
14.0	16.3	27.3	37.5	42.0	72.4
15.0	17.7	28.0	39.0	42.8	75.0
16.0	19.1	28.5	40.0	44.4	80.0
16.7	20.0	29.0	40.9	46.1	85.0
17.0	20.5	30.0	42.9	47.5	90.0
17.5	21.2	31.0	45.0	48.7	95.0
				50.0	100.0

Source: *NCR, op. cit.*

Markdowns

In setting prices, all retailers find that adjustments need to be made. Though a retailer attempts to establish a profitable markup on his merchandise he invariably finds that markdowns are necessary. In Table 15-1 (Chapter 15) one sees the extent of markdowns in some departments of a department and specialty store. Note that these markdowns range from a low of 4.7 per cent to a high of 13.8 per cent.

Since most price setting is based on judgment, errors in pricing are bound to occur in a retail firm. As a matter of fact, most large retailers actually budget planned markdowns during each planning period. Though in most cases markdowns are for the purpose of adjusting price errors, sometimes they are not. For instance, many firms take markdowns in order to increase sales. In effect, they are a merchandising device.[31] In many cases they are considered to be an integral part of the firm's merchandising strategy.[32] The use of markdowns as an integral part of the firm's merchandising program can be a questionable practice. One method of using a markdown as a merchandising device is to deliberately overprice an item, later reducing it to normal markup levels.[33] This practice, widely indulged in by general

---

[31] Wingate and Schaller, *op. cit.*
[32] Oswald Knauth, "Considerations in the Setting of Retail Prices," *Journal of Marketing,* Vol. XIV, No. 1 (July, 1949), p. 5.
[33] Knauth, *op. cit.,* p. 6.

merchandise stores, often attracts large numbers of customers with the result that other slower-selling items are exposed to large in-store traffic.

Markdowns are also taken in cases where the continuity of the goods offered has become incomplete. For example, in a men's shirt department after a period of time the retailer may find he is left with extreme sizes such as 14's and 17's, or a chinaware department may find that full sets are broken because of damage, pilferage, or in some cases selective buying. In both of these cases the merchant is obliged to drastically reduce the price if he wishes to avoid using valuable space for broken inventories.

A good case can be made for the belief among merchants that in selling certain types of merchandise markdowns are an integral part of the merchandising. For example, they point out that in the sale of fashion merchandise a new style can command a premium price at the beginning of the season. There exists a segment of the market that can be considered innovators, i.e., they pride themselves on being first in their community to wear the latest fashion. A high original markup is in keeping with the demand of this limited but profitable group. As the season progresses the firm may take its first markdown which will bring the fashion item into line with the prevailing average markup in the apparel department. Toward the end of the season it may further reduce its prices to move the remaining items that have by now lost their continuity (that is, all sizes are not available) and in some cases have lost their appeal to consumers.

Additional Markup Mathematics

The difference between the price a buyer pays for an item and the price he sells it for is called the markup. This markup must be sufficient to cover the expenses and profits of the store. Thus, one of the important tasks of a buyer is to estimate the markup necessary to cover the expenses and operating profits of the firm. To accomplish this properly he must be aware of the relationship of the retail price, the markup, and the cost of the product. The relationship may be expressed as follows:

Cost + Markup = Retail

Thus an item costing the firm $6 and retailed at $10 has a markup of $4.

Markup Percentage of Retail

As noted elsewhere most major firms calculate percentages on the retail price. Thus in the above example the $4 markup represents 40 per cent of the retail price ($4 ÷ $10). The cost price in this case is 60 per cent of the retail price.

As so often happens, however, the buyer does not have all the information necessary to make such a simple calculation. For example, suppose a buyer finds a dress in the market that he feels he can sell for $18. He knows for instance that he must maintain a 40% markup on this item. His problem then becomes one of determining how much he can pay for the dress. Using the above formula he arrives at the following calculation:

Cost + Markup = Retail
60% +   40%   = 100%
     As 100% = $18, the cost he can afford is 60% of $18 or $10.80

Thus, the buyer can pay $10.80 for the dress and yet sell it for $18, maintaining his required 40% markup.

Suppose in the above problem the buyer knew the *cost price* and his *markup* requirements but needed to calculate the retail price. How would he accomplish this?

Cost + Markup = Retail
$10.80 + 40% = 100%

To complete the equation one should note that the $10.80 represents 60 per cent of the total retail price, as the needed markup is 40%. Thus:

60% of Retail = $10.80
1% of Retail = $ .18 ($10.80 ÷ .60)
100% of Retail = $18.00 (100 × .18)

Thus, with the cost price known and the markup requirements given the buyer can determine the retail price.

You should be able to solve these problems:

1. A buyer finds a chair in a furniture factory that he believes he can sell in quantity at a retail price of $50. He requires a markup of 42%. How much should he pay for the chair?

2. A buyer of housewares is offered a typewriter by a manufacturer for $72. The buyer must get a 40% markup. At what price should he sell the product?

3. Goods costing $24 a dozen are sold at $3 each. What is the percentage markup on retail?

4. A buyer plans to buy $1,000 worth of merchandise in the coming month. He also plans to mark up half the merchandise by 37% and the other half by 40%. What will be the total retail value of his merchandise?

5. If a buyer maintains a $50 markup on all appliances sold in his department and his average markup over the year is 20% of the retail price, what is the average cost of the appliances he sells?

Markup Percentage of Cost

Though as noted above large firms usually calculate markup on the retail price, many small firms and wholesalers use a markup on cost to calculate the selling price.

To calculate the markup on cost the same formula is applied, with one exception. In this case the cost price is always 100% and the retail price is more than that. Thus, in the problem where the item costs $1 and the markup is 50 per cent of cost the formula is as follows:

Cost + Markup = Retail
(100%)$1 + 50% = 150%
Thus: Retail is 150% of cost or $1.50.

In some instances it may be necessary to convert from markup on cost to markup on retail, which can be done easily by referring to a table such as Table 11-8.

Where the markup on retail is known and the buyer wishes to calculate the comparable markup on cost (without using the table) the following method is employed.

Assuming the markup on retail is 40%, he can make the calculations in the following manner:

Let $1 = Retail Price
Markup = 40% of $1.00 = $.40
Cost = $.60 ($1.00 − $.40)

$$\text{Markup on cost} = \frac{\$.40}{\$.60} = 66\ 2/3\%$$

Thus, a markup on retail of 40% is comparable to a 66 2/3% markup on cost. You should be able to solve these problems:

1. A firm marks up its merchandise 20% of cost. What is the selling price of an item costing $20?
2. What is the cost of an item selling for $30 where the firm markup is 20% of cost?
3. A store obtains a markup of 78 cents per tie on a line for which the markup on cost is 70 per cent. Find the cost and retail price of the tie.
4. A markup in a retail florist is 50 per cent of the retail price. Calculate the markup on cost.
5. A markup of 35 per cent of cost is equivalent to what percentage on retail?

Aside from the markup estimates the merchant must make for individual purchases of merchandise, the store owner or buyer must plan the over-all markup for his total operation.

Planning Initial Markup

His problem derives from the fact that all markup estimates must take into consideration the fact that his initial markup may not be maintained because of markdowns, shortages, and discounts to employees. The latter are usually referred to as retail reductions. Thus should a merchant make a sales estimate of $100,000, he must allow for retail reductions. Should he determine that retail reductions will approximate $10,000, than he must include that fact in his initial markup.

In essence the merchant's initial markup must include estimates of his expenses, retail reductions, and also profits.

Assuming forecast sales of $100,000, expenses of $35,000, profits of $10,000, and retail reductions of $10,000, the following formula would apply:

$$\text{Initial markup percentage} = \frac{\text{Expenses} + \text{Profits} + \text{Retail Reductions}}{\text{Sales} + \text{Reductions}}$$

$$\frac{35\% + 10\% + 10\%}{100\% + 10\%} = \frac{55\%}{110\%} \text{ or } \frac{\$35,000 + \$10,000 + \$10,000}{\$100,000 + \$10,000} = \frac{\$55,000}{\$110,000} = 50\%$$

Thus, to cover the given expenses, profits, and retail reductions, the buyer must mark up the merchandise in his department 50% of the retail price.

You should be able to solve these problems:
1. The expenses in a department are 28%, the profits 5%, and the reductions 7%. Determine the initial markup necessary to cover these estimates.
2. A suit department plans to sell $10,000 worth of suits in the coming month. What should the initial markup be if expenses are estimated to be $2,000, retail reductions $500, and profits $500?
3. Expenses in a department run about 25 per cent of sales. Retail reductions are

estimated to be 5%. What percentage markup will assure that the department will break even?

4. Expenses in a department are 41 per cent; profits 3 per cent, and the initial markup 47 per cent. Find the retail reductions.

5. A department issues the following statement:

Expenses	$25,000
Profits	4,000
Markdowns	3,000
Shortages	1,000
Employee Discounts	1,000

Find the initial markup.

Markdowns Percentages

If a dress is originally priced at $100 but reduced to $80 what is the percentage markdown? There are two answers to this question. It can best be seen if we summarize the problem in the following way:

$100 original retail price
$ 20 markdown
$ 80 final sales price

$$\text{Markdown percentage} = \frac{\$\ 20}{\$\ 80} = 25\%$$

$$\text{Markdown percentage} = \frac{\$\ 20}{\$100} = 20\%$$

As noted in Chapter 18 the retailer as a general rule relates all expenses and most markup data directly to sales. Thus, in the case of markdowns he would use the first formula above and record a markdown percentage of 25% as $80 was the final selling price.

On the other hand if he plans to advertise the dresses to the public he will probably communicate the fact that the markdown on these dresses is 20%, a reduction based on the original selling price. You should be able to solve these problems:

1. A buyer wishes to mark down the merchandise in his toy department by 10 per cent during the next month. After he completes the month's sale what percentage markdown on the final selling prices will be recorded?

2. The records of the Brown shoestore showed that for the month of July sales were $32,300 and markdowns on merchandise amounted to $3,085. Compute the markdown percentage.

3. If goods in a department are reduced 33 1/3 per cent in price and sold, what is the markdown percentage?

4. If goods in a department are reduced 40 per cent in price and sold, what is the markdown percentage?

5. How much should a department manager reduce the present value of $1,000 worth of merchandise in order to have a markdown percentage of 7% of the final selling price?

SUMMARY

Retailers set prices on hundreds of items. In large firms the lower echelons in the organization are usually responsible for making individual price decisions. However, these decisions are made within the framework of the over-all policies and goals set by top management. Major policies include pricing *under* the market, pricing *above* the market, and price follower. Most stores fall into the latter category. Goals include return on investment and maintenance of a share of the market.

Prices are established by both internal and external considerations. Internal considerations include the firm's pricing goals, the organizational structure, costs (merchandise, fixed and variable), and the type of merchandise offered. One of the tools for relating sales volume to the total expense structure of the firm is the break-even point. By definition the break-even point is the minimum sales required to avoid an operating loss. External price considerations include demand elasticity, market conditions related to the consumer, and legal considerations. The retailer is concerned with the price elasticity of products sold in his store. Price elasticity refers to the increase or decrease in sales experienced by the retailer when he raises or lowers the price of a product.

Aside from setting price based on an exact computation, retailers also use special techniques such as price lining and price points, psychological pricing, loss leaders and bait pricing. In making a mathematical calculation as to the exact price to be set a retailer establishes a markup on the retail price. In setting the markup he must consider potential retail reductions and the eventual grown margin or maintained markup. Several formulas are available to make these calculations.

QUESTIONS

1. Name three ways in which legislation can affect pricing.

2. "A" states that the actions of a discount competitor on his block have not had any effect on the level of prices in his store. Assuming "A" is correct, how would this be possible if we assume that the discounter carries the same type of products that "A" does?

3. How is it possible for a food supermarket to "price above the market"?

4. How does the pricing organization within the retail firm differ from that of the manufacturer? From the point of view of pricing effectiveness, how does the retail firm compare with the manufacturer?

5. Explain what is meant by "looking out" and "looking in" in pricemaking in the retail store.

6. What costs concern the retailer in pricing merchandise? What role do variable and fixed costs play?

7. List five major (non-food) stores in your area and rank them in terms of their emphasis on pricing as a competitive weapon. Rank the same stores according to servicing. Are the lists roughly reversed; that is, does the store ranked highest in pricing rank lowest on the service list? Explain.

8. Discuss the advantages of having a decentralized pricing organization in a chain of food supermarkets. Do the same reasons apply to the J. C. Penney Company? Explain.

9. What impact does private brand merchandising have on a firm's pricing strategy?

10. Relate:

a. Gross margin and initial markup

b. Stock shortages and initial markup

c. Employee discounts and gross margins

d. Retail reductions and gross margin

e. Cost of merchandise and initial markup

11. Differentiate between bait and loss leader pricing. What types of products are used in loss leader pricing in general merchandise and food stores?

12. Relate the products shown in Figure 11-4 to your understanding of elasticity of demand.

13. Relate price lines at the retail level to the marketing strategy of the manufacturers.

14. List eight possible causes of markdowns in a retail store.

15. An item costs the retailer 90 cents. The retailer wishes to achieve a 40 per cent markup on retail.

a. Demonstrate the price calculation based on a retail markup.

b. Demonstrate the price calculation based on cost by using Table 11-8.

INTRODUCTION TO
THE COMMUNICATION MIX

The over-all purpose of this section is to acquaint the reader with one of the controllable facets of the retail firm — the communication mix. This term will be defined more explicitly in Chapter 12; it refers in general to the firm's advertising, free publicity, and personal selling.

In the next two chapters we will define the mix and identify its management, compare its function in retailing with that in manufacturing, and study its makeup. In the main, we will examine the mix from the point of view of management, emphasizing some of the economic overview and its measurable impact on the consumer. In addition, we will discuss the organizational structure used to allocate and direct funds in order to maximize the efficiency of this function.

The reader will note a heavy concentration on newspaper advertising. Retailers are among the largest users of newspaper space and tend to spend most of their advertising on this medium. The important topic of retail selling will be discussed in a separate chapter.

The Communication Mix

12

OBJECTIVES YOU SHOULD MEET

1. *Relate* in your own words a definition of the communication mix.
2. *Describe* the major purpose of retail advertising.
3. *Distinguish* between national and local advertising rates.
4. *Show* how cooperative advertising is used to benefit both retailers and manufacturers.
5. *Describe* the three major budgeting techniques used in budgeting advertising expenditures.

In the sections that follow we will consider the promotional activities of the firm. However, before getting into the many aspects of the sales promotion effort of the firm we should distinguish the use of the term "sales promotion" in manufacturing from that in retailing and the relationship of this activity to the communication mix.

The manufacturer is well aware of what makes up his sales promotion activities. Were he questioned about it, he would probably list the following:

1. The preparation and issuing of catalogs and brochures by direct mail.
2. Developing shows and exhibition.
3. Developing dealer contests.
4. Preparing visual aids for distributors.
5. Issuing product information bulletins for middlemen.

If asked to define sales promotion, he would probably state that sales promotion in the *manufacturing* firm refers to activities that supplement the firm's regular advertising and selling programs. If he were asked to elaborate on the goals or

221

objectives of the sales promotion effort, he would probably explain that the sales promotion effort of his firm gives vigor to its organization. In some fields manufacturers might point out that the sales promotion activities at the retail level are the major means by which a firm can move its merchandise. Certainly the cosmetic industry maintains a happy balance between its sales promotion activities at the retail and wholesale levels and its national advertising campaign. In fields such as apparel, the sales promotion activities of the firm often take precedence over all other efforts.

The term "sales promotion" in the *retail firm* is used in a different sense and refers to different activities. An adequate definition of retail sales promotion would be: ". . . all methods of stimulating customer purchasing, including personal selling, advertising, and publicity."[1] By implication, all activities that contribute in any way toward the promotion of sales are included.

The use of the term "publicity" by retailers in speaking of their sales promotion effort is not consistent, however. The broad view considers publicity as consisting of advertising, display, and all nonpaid news. By definition this view excludes personal selling. The narrow view defines publicity as only nonpaid favorable advertising of the firm. This type of publicity usually appears in newspapers or magazines and frequently takes the form of publicizing store fashion news or store services offered to consumers. The broad view of publicity is the more widely accepted definition.

The communication mix referred to in this section is similar to the retailer's definition of sales promotion, i.e., it includes publicity (broad view) and personal selling. It differs only in its outlook; that is, it classifies all attempts by the retailer to communicate his sales message to the customer as representing the communicative aspects of his job. Hence, in this chapter, the emphasis will be on the performance of the advertising functions, particular by newspaper advertising. The second chapter will consider display, direct mail, television or radio advertising, and the use of trading stamps. Personal selling (the only direct contact with the customer) will also be covered in Chapter 14.

Developing a Communication Strategy

The developing of a communication strategy in a retail firm is limited by the media a firm may use and by the limitations of these various media.

In addition, and taking into consideration the difficulties of measuring the effectiveness of the firm's communication strategy, one must also consider the limits placed upon the firm by its own resources. These resources, in the case of the large firm, are supplemented by the manufacturer in numerous ways, the most effective of which is through cooperative advertising. This aspect of the communication mix will also be covered in this chapter.

Assuming the availability of media and resources, the firm strategy for reaching markets at a profit is developed by management in response to the following questions:

1. What type of a store are we developing?
2. What segment of the market are we trying to reach?
3. How best can we reach this market?

---

[1]"Marketing Definitions," compiled by the Committee on Definitions of the American Marketing Association, 1960.

The type of store being presented to the public represents a basic decision on the part of management. Price appeal may be used for one type of audience; high-fashion appeal for another. Between these two extremes there are many gradations. There are other kinds of strategy based on the types of merchandise sold. A general merchandise store may emphasize hard goods rather than apparel. Others may emphasize only apparel and ignore for the most part the furniture or home furnishings department. In other cases we find firms emphasizing the width of their assortments. Along with or aside from the merchandise offered and the various fashion and price appeals, the firm may choose to emphasize the service aspect of its business — delivery or customer services, such as gift wrapping, credit, catalog selling, are commonly offered in stores in most of the large cities.

The firm's communication strategy does not remain the same at all times; strategy and store emphasis do change. Yesterday's low-price appeals may be today's high-price institutional advertising. Such changes are usually gradual, however, and require careful coordination with the merchandising programs throughout the store.

) **Reaching the Market**

The media used and the degree of usage vary according to the type of market aimed at. Retail firms rely heavily on newspaper advertising and on a rather narrow range of newspapers. The limited value of television, radio, and direct mail also has a bearing on this problem.

Nevertheless, stores do distinguish between newspapers. For example, in New York City few prestige-type specialty stores would fail to advertise in the *New York Times*. On the other hand, the reader of the *Times* is rarely exposed to the ads of a highly promotional retail apparel firm. Both types of firms have made a basic decision concerning the value of a particular newspaper for their type of customer. Such a decision is usually made on the basis of experience with advertising results and in some cases (where institutional advertising is resorted to) on the basis of a firm's evaluation of the social class of the consumers reading the paper. It may also depend simply on the location of the audience to be reached rather than the social class. The choice of a suburban newspaper, for example, in a large metropolitan area may be governed by the location of the audience rather than by the social class of the readers.

Theoretical Concepts

The communication effort of the firm has one obvious purpose — to bring in additional business at a given level of prices. In economic terminology, the purpose of the promotional expense is to shift the demand curve to the right. This theoretical concept is illustrated in Figure 12-1.

In theoretical terms one distinguishes between the impact of promotional expenses on the demand curve of the firm and the obvious cost aspects of this function. Promotional expenses are *costs* that are incurred *to gain additional sales*.

FIGURE 12-1   Demand Following Sales Promotion Activities

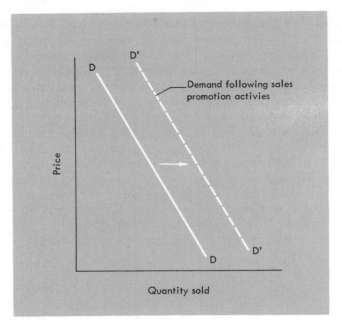

What we are saying, in other words, is that promotional expenses cause sales. Conversely, they are not related to the cost of merchandise or store expenses and can only be tabulated as a ratio after the fact.

On the other hand, the cost of merchandise is directly related to the firm's business and can be functionalized. Possibly an example can clarify these observations.

If a retail food firm has for sale one thousand boxes of candy for $1.00, its merchandise costs (or cost of goods sold) can be calculated accurately. If we assume a 40 per cent markup on retail, these costs approximate $.60 per box. Knowing this can we now predict these costs if the firm sells an additional 100 boxes of candy? The answer is obvious. In the same vein, can one predict the cost of advertising (as a ratio of the additional sales) if one runs a $500 newspaper ad? The answer again is obvious — one *can't* predict its impact and more importantly it is not a direct function of the number of boxes of candy one sells. Possibly the ad will bring in 5,000 candy purchasers. On the other hand, it may not sell any candy. In any case, its impact is on the *demand for merchandise* and is not related to the cost of the merchandise.

Retail
Advertising

Economists have often disputed the social value of advertising in the United States. The usual argument against advertising is that it interferes with the economic allocation of productive resources. This is partially true in time of full employment, since money could be spent in production of more goods instead of shifting business from one firm to another. But, in times of less than full employment, advertising creates jobs and seems to be less undesirable. Many

224

economists have a more favorable view of advertising. Their position seems to be that advertising communicates basic information concerning products and prices that would ordinarily be unavailable to consumers. This argument is strongest for the introduction of new products and services; it is weakest when one considers most of the advertising viewed on television.

Retailing and Manufacturing Advertising

The endless debate that surrounds advertising usually does not take into account retail advertising. Most comments and articles are concerned with terms such as "Madison Avenue," "subliminal advertising," and other terms that originate with national advertising. Few critics of advertising single out retail advertising. To understand why, consider the advertising of a consumer goods manufacturer and a retail department store.

The manufacturer's advertising programs are concerned almost entirely with the product itself: its features and possibly (when advantageous) its price. In some cases, the firm may emphasize the company name in its advertising but more often only the product name. Major media, such as television, radio, newspapers, and other forms of publicity, are employed.

The retailer's approach is different. He is not selling the product alone, since in most cases the exact product can be purchased in a number of stores in his trading area. His advertising is for the purpose of increasing consumer patronage. The retailer hopes by advertising to increase the sales not only of the product advertised but also the sale of other products in the store. The choice of the product to be advertised, for example, could be a man's shirt with the thought of selling male customers a complete outfit — or simply, to bring the male customer into the men's department of the store.

In addition, the retail advertising message differs from that of the manufacturer. As a rule, retailers do not extol the features of a product. The retailer, in most cases, assumes that the consumer is well acquainted with these features through the advertising efforts of the manufacturer. In stores where price is emphasized the advertisement may simply list the product name and a price. In other stores, it may be one of several items in a small part of the total display ad. In any case, the goals of each type of advertising do differ, and though they are sometimes brought together by cooperative advertising (discussed later in the chapter), it is many times an unhappy "marriage." For, in basic strategy, they do differ.

One last word on the social aspects of advertising. One of the major reasons those opposed to advertising have not concerned themselves with the attack on retail advertising is that it does play an informative role. That is, it does often inform the consumer of the availability of a product at a low price. In addition, the consumer is informed of the services that accrue to him if he purchases this product.

Complaints about retailer advertising do exist, however. Some were covered in the chapter on legislation. These complaints usually have to do with false price advertising, or mislabeling of merchandise, and seem to be the concern of the local Better Business Bureau or, in some cases, the Federal Trade Commission. One of the major conflicts of this type that has arisen during the postwar period is the posting of so-called "regular prices" in ads, along with the so-called "discount price." A typical illustration of this is the following: "A Westinghouse toaster regularly $19.95 — our price, $12.95"; or, "Boys' jackets — sold regularly at $14.95 — today, only $9.95." The major complaint of the regulating authorities centers around the use of the term "regular." It has been proven that many products said to have been "sold at regular prices" were never offered at these prices. The list price may also be misleading. As a matter of fact, in many industries manufacturers actually cooperate with retailers and print up misleading regular price labels, which have little relationship to the value of the product. The product may be an irregular or a so-called "second." In the case of appliances, it may be a discontinued style, or a product that has been out of style for two or three years.

Retailers Organizational Approach

Unlike large manufacturers, the large retail firm rarely uses the services of an advertising agency. Most advertising in the retail firm is handled within the advertising department of the firm. This department usually consists of an advertising director, copywriters, and art and production workers.

Advertising agencies handling a manufacturer's advertising receive a commission (usually 15%) from the media through which the advertising is placed. Thus, an advertising agency placing $1 million in advertising with a television network would receive a commission of $150,000 from the network.

This fee structure is not available to retailers, as (as will be noted later) the retailer receives local rates from most media that are not commissionable negating the advantage of using an agency.[2]

Other reasons encourage retailers to develop their own advertising. One is the time factor. Retail advertising must be prepared in a relatively short period of time, because of the daily competitive nature of retailing and the fact that merchandise can not be purchased months in advance. Advertising agencies handling products of manufacturers usually take months to prepare campaigns and develop commercials for the various media.[3]

Second, because the firm has hundreds of products, a close daily study of the firm's customers and their buying habits is required.

In addition the advertising department has to deal closely with all levels of management — the merchandise managers, the credit department, and all other departments within the store — a task best handled on the premises.

Advertising
Cycle —
Long Run

Expenditures for advertising in the United States are summarized in Table 12-1. Note particularly the expenditures on local newspaper advertising. Most of the expenditures in this category are made by retail firms. Newspaper advertising has more than doubled since the early postwar period, and local newspaper advertising during the same period has tripled. Local advertising by retailers, however, seems to be much more sensitive to business declines.[4] This tendency results from the

[2]Maurice I. Mandell, *Advertising* (Englewood Cliffs, N.J.: Prentice-Hall, Inc., 1968), p. 122.
[3]*Idem.*
[4]David M. Blank, "Cyclical Behavior of National Advertising," *Journal of Business,* Vol. XXXV, No. 1 (January, 1962), p. 15.

Year	1950	1960	1970
Total	$5,710	$11,932	$19,715
MEDIUM			
Business papers	$ 251	$ 609	$ 714
Direct mail	803	1,830	2,736
Magazines	515	941	1,321
Newspapers	2,076	3,703	5,850
National	533	836	1,040
Local	1,542	2,867	4,810
Outdoor	143	203	237
Radio	605	692	1,278
Television	171	1,590	3,660

Source: Statistical Abstract of the United States, 1962,
p. 851 and 1971, p. 746.

techniques used to budget advertising expenditures. The use of a ratio of advertising expenditures to planned sales is a technique that accounts for the ability of the retail firm to respond to the vagaries of the business cycle. Conversely, national advertising is not as responsive since plans and commitments are made well in advance.

The reader may wonder why advertising expenditures are usually cut during a downtrend. It might seem — and it has actually been proposed — that a firm should increase its advertising allotments when struck by a business decline. Nevertheless, the business firm usually doesn't react this way.

In retail advertising there are also fairly well-established patterns of movement within the short run. This might be expected since budgeting of advertising is made on the basis of short-run forecasts. The major budgeting technique, the ratio of advertising expenditures to planned sales, will be discussed in a later section.

Advertising Cycle — Short Run

In addition to being large users of newspaper advertising, department stores spend time, effort, and money on a strong publicity and display program. Table 12-2 shows a distribution of sales promotion expenditure over the year. Note that these promotional expenditures peak in November and December and that they bear a close relationship to sales. One interesting side to this analysis is the variance of newspaper costs and sales. The highest variance occurs in December (11.3%–17.3%). In other months the reverse occurs. By actual count, nine months feature newspaper space costs above the expected share of total sales. Though not an exact measurement, this table indicates that the elasticity of demand varies considerably but reaches its peak toward the end of the year.

Product Advertising

Product advertising expenditures do vary considerably over the year. In general they are allied with retail sales. The average can be deceiving and many appropriations vary greatly throughout the year. The data in Figure 12-2, derived

TABLE 12-2   Distribution of Sales and Promotion Expenditures by Month for Department Stores

Month	Percentage of Total Year's Expense			
	Newspaper Space Costs	Display Expenses	Total Sales Promotion Expenses	Total Net Sales (Owned Depts.)
February	6.5	7.7	6.6	5.5
March	8.5	8.9	8.4	6.8
April	8.6	7.3	8.3	7.9
May	8.5	7.1	7.9	7.7
June	7.5	7.1	7.3	7.4
July	6.4	7.3	6.8	6.6
August	8.2	8.0	8.1	7.4
September	8.7	8.5	8.9	8.5
October	9.6	9.3	9.5	8.9
November	9.6	11.3	10.1	9.6
December	11.0	9.9	11.0	17.7
January	6.9	7.6	7.1	6.0
	100.0%	100.0%	100.0%	100.0%

Source: *Departmental Merchandising and Operating Results,* National Merchants Association, 1965.

FIGURE 12-2   Monthly Share of Annual Advertising Expenditures for Selected Products Five Year Average — 1960-1964

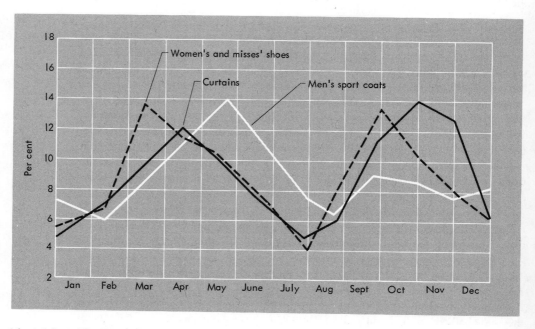

Adapted from *The Neustadt Red Book of Seasonal Patterns, 1965* (New York: George Neustadt, Inc., 1966).

from actual department-store advertising records in nine major cities, demonstrate wide fluctuations for the three products selected — women's shoes, curtains, and men's sport coats. Although most retail advertising dollars are spent in December, these figures show that advertising expenditures for women's shoes peak in March and September; curtains in October; and men's sport coats in May!

Advertising represents an important outlay in a retail firm. Next to payroll expenses, advertising and rent are usually the firm's largest expenditures. In Table 12-3, we see that advertising ranges from 7.8 per cent to 9.7 per cent of total expenses in the department store. Small wonder the firm is concerned with its advertising program. However, there is another way of measuring the advertising expenditures of the firm, as in Table 12-4 where advertising expenses are shown as a per cent of sales. Note particularly the range in ratios from 0.9 per cent to 2.7 per cent (1968), where the difference between the lowest and highest is about 300 per cent.

The Significance of Advertising Expenditures

Advertising Expenses in Department Stores Related to Expenses   **TABLE 12-3**

Sales Volume	As a Percentage of Sales Advertising Expenses	Total Expenses as a Percent of Sales	Advertising Expenses as a Percentage of Total Expenses
Annual Sales Volume of:			
$ 1- 2 million	2.54	34.65	8.4
$ 2- 5 million	2.86	32.06	8.9
$ 5-10 million	2.84	33.47	8.5
$10-20 million	2.91	30.07	9.7
$20-50 million	2.77	33.46	8.3
Over $50 million	2.48	31.99	7.8

Source: FOR, *op. cit.,* p. XXI.

Retail Advertising Expenditures as a Per Cent of Corporate Sales   **TABLE 12-4**

	1948	1958	1968
Total retail	1.5	1.4	1.5
Food	0.9	0.5	1.2
General merchandise	2.5	2.2	2.7
Apparel and accessories	2.4	2.5	1.9
Furniture and house furnishings	3.3	3.0	3.2
Automobile dealers and filling stations	0.9	0.9	0.9

Source: *Economic Almanac,* National Industrial Conference Board, 1962 and 1964, and Internal Revenue Service, *Statistics of Income,* 1968.

Another significant fact is revealed by examining the ratio of advertising expenditures to sales volume. Referring again to Table 12-3, it can be seen that in general as department-store sales volume increases, the ratio of advertising expense decreases. This phenomenon is due to a number of factors, most of which revolve around the economies of scale of large retailing firms. In particular, the application of a newspaper ad by a department store to its branch stores as well and the cooperative advertising program that favors large retailers account for the declining cost of advertising as volume increases.

The Importance of Newspaper Advertising

How important is newspaper advertising in the retail field? What impact does it have on the consumer? Even if we assume that one can measure the effectiveness of newspaper advertising, the answer is that its impact varies considerably. This variation may be due to uncontrollable factors such as the number of newspapers in the city, the amount of advertising linage carried by the newspaper, and the family income level of the readership.

A study of the readership and buying influence of grocery store advertising found its impact to be considerable — probably higher than management suspected. Among all readers surveyed, 50 to 75 per cent frequently read food store advertising. About one third of all those surveyed reported that they were influenced in their shopping by these same ads.[5] Direct mail or handbill promotions were also found to be important. This finding about food store advertising is of interest in two respects. First, it demonstrates that the largest proportion of consumer expenditures, namely, food (which totals about one quarter of all expenditures) is influenced by retail advertising. Because of the nature of the retail food business the impact of this advertising is not seasonal but occurs throughout the year. However, food store advertising does appear most frequently toward the end of the week. The tendencies of firms to pay employees on Friday and the Saturday shopping of consumers have strongly influenced this strategy.

Second, the impact of food advertising on the consumer is important in another respect, in that it favors the larger retail firm. It is a well-known fact that the large food stores receive the largest share of cooperative advertising. Though the amount of cooperative advertising available to large stores is important in bettering or at least maintaining their market position, there are *other* scale advantages which accrue to food chain stores. By simply concentrating stores in an area and coordinating advertising promotions, the chains can spread the cost of one advertisement over a number of stores — assuming, of course, that a newspaper covers the total market.

Newspaper
Retail Rate
Structure

Retail firms spend most of their promotional monies in the local newspapers. There exists, therefore, a strong alliance between the local newspaper and the local retail advertisers. The amount of free publicity major stores get is noted in other sections, and is an indicator of this relationship.

The growth of other media has not affected the revenue accruing to newspapers from retail advertising. Though large amounts of money have been spent on television advertising by manufacturers, most retail advertising on television is institutional. In addition, only a limited number of products can be shown in the allotted commercial period. On the other hand, retail newspaper advertising puts greater stress on multi-product presentation, with a decided emphasis on prices.

[5]Ralph H. Oakes, "Readership of Food-Store Advertising," *Journal of Marketing,* Vol. XVI, No. 1 (July, 1951), pp. 66–68.

Studies have also shown that retail ads increase consumer readership. Newspapers are well aware of the fact that the more retail ads they have the better their chance of increasing circulation.[6] Therefore, local advertising is not only an important source of revenue to the newspapers but also serves to increase the circulation.

It is notable that two types of ads appear in the daily newspaper, the above-mentioned local ad and the so-called "national" ad, which is usually paid for by the distributor or manufacturer of a nationally distributed product. As a rule these ads are not so closely read by the consumer as are retailing ads. On the other hand, national ads are placed mainly in the largest newspapers in the city. This represents a vicious cycle in that newspapers are not able to attract many national ads without first having the necessary circulation. The necessary circulation accrues to the newspaper that can develop a consistent representation of retail advertising — a major attraction of a newspaper. Because of this situation, most newspapers charge advertisers what are called local and national rates. The local rate is, as the name suggests, the rate for local retail advertisers and is considerably below the national rate, the theory being that the more local advertising a newspaper can develop, the more opportunity it has to increase its circulation and thus increase its national advertising and its national rates. Documenting this fact is a study showing that national ads accrue to a great extent to large-circulation newspapers. In other words, the gains in national advertising tend to be greatest among the largest newspapers. As a result, the rate differential is greatest in the large city newspapers.[7]

Why is this so? And how large is this differential? It is so because the lower the retailing rates, the greater the retail demand for space, which should increase the newspaper circulation. It follows, therefore, that the larger the circulation, the more likely it is that the newspaper will obtain national advertising. Hence, the differential. Though there are no exact figures on the differential, it has been estimated that the local rate is approximately 65 per cent of the national rate.[8] Certain types of retail firms, however, because of their quantity discount, pay even less. Again it has been estimated that department stores and grocery chains average closer to 50 per cent of the national charge.

The importance and attractiveness of this differential is obvious. If, for example, a manufacturer has one dollar to spend on advertising, it will go twice as far if he can channel it through a grocery chain. On the other hand, the grocery chain is well alerted to this differential and will probably not charge the manufacturer at the 50 per cent discount rate, but usually at a figure above this. They may charge the manufacturer 75 per cent of the national rate, taking into account their processing cost. Yet even a 75 per cent rate represents a bargain to the manufacturer.

Level of Rates

Though newspapers are concerned with the attitudes and preferences of retailers, they rarely try to obtain additional advertising through rate reductions. Most

---

[6]James M. Fergusson, *The Advertising Rate Structure of the Daily Newspaper Industry* (Englewood Cliffs, N.J.: Prentice-Hall, Inc., 1963), p. 29.

[7]*Ibid.*, p. 53.

[8]Edward C. Crimmins, "The Case for Cooperative Advertising," *Media/Scope*, August, 1963.

studies of the rate structure of newspapers seem to conclude that newspaper rates are rigid. That is, they rarely go down during recessions, and probably increase in line with rising costs of producing the paper.[9]

The rigidity in rates seems to stem mainly from the tendency toward "one newspaper" cities. In addition, where competition does exist, it has been found that newspapers are still reluctant to cut prices. They prefer to compete by offering advertisers special services — services that in most cases a retail firm would be expected to pay for. Some offer free layout of copy services, research studies, and other merchandising services. Newspaper executives believe that a cut in rates would simply mean less revenue, since retailers and national advertisers would not increase their advertising linage proportionally.

Source of Funds

Retailers usually have two sources of advertising funds. The major, and most obvious, source is their own organization. Their allocation of these monies and the budgeting of this function will be discussed in detail in the last part of this chapter. The other major source of funds is the vendor (manufacturer). These funds usually accrue to large retailers and have legislative implications. They have always been under close scrutiny by the government and can be described as being in the "gray" area of business activities. Let us examine cooperative advertising first.

Cooperative Advertising

Cooperative advertising is a method whereby a manufacturer and a retailer (and, in some cases, a group of retailers) share in the cost of consumer advertising. This usually takes the form of newspaper advertising, but is sometimes used for other areas of promotion, such as display, radio, television, and sales personnel. Two types of cooperative arrangements have been noted in the postwar period: the so-called horizontal and vertical arrangements. The former is simply an arrangement whereby two or more retailers join in sponsoring a media ad in a local area. Programs of this nature constitute only a very small segment of the total cooperative effort spent.

The vertical cooperative agreement, however, supplies an important part of the advertising funds. Most of these funds are funnelled by the manufacturer to the larger retail operations. This does not mean that a manufacturer can offer advertising allowances only to his larger accounts. The Robinson-Patman Act specifically outlaws arrangements of this type. Also, it forces the manufacturer, through its "proportionally equal" provisions, to offer similar allowances to smaller retailers. In practice, however, the smaller retailer rarely qualifies for allowances, since his "proportionally equal" allowances are usually too small to pay for any significant advertising program.

Size of Cooperative Advertising Expenditures

Estimates of the size of cooperative advertising funds range from about one billion to two billion dollars annually. The Newspaper Advertising Bureau, Inc.

---

[9]For example, see Royal H. Ray, "Competition in the Newspaper Industry," *Journal of Marketing,* Vol. XV, No. 4 (April, 1951), p. 456. Also Charles V. Kinter, "Rigidity in Advertising Rates in Depression and Boom Years," *Journalism Quarterly,* XXIV (June, 1947).

estimates that in 1973 28.5 per cent of the newspapers total revenue was derived from this source.

How important is cooperative advertising to the retail store? In a study of department stores in Pennsylvania, it was noted that this form of advertising allowance can be substantial. It was estimated that 10 per cent of total retailer advertising funds were derived from cooperative deals.[10] The range was from about 7 per cent of total advertising for stores with a volume of under $1 million annually to an average of 13 per cent for stores with sales over $3 million annually. In general, the author concluded, the larger the store, the higher the proportion of advertising allowances accruing to it.

The details of these arrangements were also revealing. For example, in the smaller stores, on the average, a little over ten departments received advertising allowances. However, stores with sales volume exceeding $3 million annually received cooperative allowances for as many as twenty-six departments. Cooperative advertising allowances by department are seen in Table 12-5. They reveal that the millinery departments received 100 per cent advertising allowances. The next highest were the appliance departments with 62 per cent.

Advertising allowances, however, are not limited to department stores. Drug stores, food chains, and many other retailers are offered cooperative deals.

Cooperative Strategy

The major purpose of a cooperative advertising program is to help the dealer to sell merchandise. The ad, of course, is to act as a stimulant to the consumer. The manufacturer feels that his products need advertising exposure particularly if he is launching a new product. The dealer, on the other hand, increases his sales at a cost well below his usual expenditure. Of course, this does not always happen since the ad (many times made up by the manufacturer) may not be as effective as the retailer's ordinary advertising effort. Nevertheless, it usually does help to solve the retailer's never-ending problem of acquiring promotional dollars.

The amount of cooperative advertising offered by the manufacturer varies considerably. As noted above, millinery is often on a 100 per cent cooperative basis. The contributions by shoe manufacturers are much less. The decision as to how much and who gets the allowance from the manufacturer is usually covered by two major considerations: (1) what the law allows; and (2) the manufacturer's control over the outlet for his product and the type of product he sells.

The laws mentioned previously are quite clear on this point: an allowance of any size can be given, provided that it is proportionally distributed to retailers of all sizes.

The proportion of the ad costs the manufacturer pays is a direct function of the control over the outlets to which he is selling. For example, manufacturers of grocery products have little control over the number of outlets to which they sell. Since food products are in the nature of convenience goods, maximum exposure is necessary. In addition, the food manufacturer is usually faced with competing products, which are sold alongside his own products. Therefore, the grocery

---

[10] Rolland L. Hicks, *The Cooperative Advertising Practices of 44 Pennsylvania Department Stores,* Pennsylvania State University, 1956.

TABLE 12-5 Lines of Merchandise for Which Cooperative Advertising was Used and the Percentage Paid by Co-op Funds for 44 Pennsylvania Department Stores[1]

Number	Line of Merchandise	Percentage of Department Advertising Paid by Co-op	Low and High Per Cent Paid by Co-op Advertising
21	Major appliances	62	31–100
22	Small appliances	47	5–90
16	Housewares	39	1–65
18	Radio, phonograph, TV	50	30–75
5	Records and instruments	30	10–50
11	Furniture and bedding	36	5–75
18	Mattresses and springs	38	5–75
3	Lamps and shades	27	5–50
9	Rugs and carpets	29	5–75
6	Other floor coverings	56	50–75
9	Draperies and curtains	22	5–5
7	China and glassware	26	1–5
3	Gift shop	31	10–50
8	Toys and games	36	2–85
2	Luggage	27½	5–50
4	Small leather goods	32½	10–50
2	Candy	55	10–100
6	Silverware and jewelry	54	2–100
3	Clocks and watches	23	10–50
9	Costume jewelry	36	10–75
8	Women's coats and suits	24½	2–50
16	Women's dresses	30	2–50
32	Underwear, slips, robes	41	5–50
34	Corsets and brassieres	52	5–100
8	House dresses, aprons, etc	15	3–33
35	Hosiery	52	5–80
19	Women's shoes	37	5–100
12	Blouses, skirts, sportswear	27	3.7–50
5	Millinery	100	100
5	Girl's wear	37	10–50
12	Infants' wear	31	3–50
9	Men's clothing	24	1–50
8	Children's shoes	36	5–100
9	Men's furnishings and hats	34	5.7–50
7	Boys' wear	28	1.3–50
3	Men's shoes	7	2–10
10	Piece goods and domestics	25	2–75
14	Notions	40	10–50
3	Books and stationery	27	15–50
4	Soaps and cleaners	50	50

Number	Line of Merchandise	Percentage of Department Advertising Paid by Co-op	Low and High Per Cent Paid by Co-op Advertising
22	Drugs and toiletries	52	50–75

[1] 44 stores checked at least 1 type of merchandise.
Source: *Advertising Allowances,* Hearings before the Select Committee on Small Business, United States Senate, Eighty-Eighth Congress, First Session, on Competitive and Antitrust Aspects of Joint Advertising Programs by Retailers, and the Nature and Purpose of Advertising Allowances Given to Retailers By Manufacturers and Wholesalers, United States Government Printing Office, Washington, D.C., 1964.

manufacturer is more than willing to pay the full cost of cooperative advertising. Food retailers, of course, are alert to this situation, encourage it, and are likely to stock a product whenever a cooperative ad is offered. As a result of this cooperation in the food industry, cooperative advertising is not only a strategic weapon for gaining consumer acceptance, but just as important, it gains outlets for the products.

On the other hand, automotive dealers will usually pay more than half of the cost of a manufacturer's sponsored advertising. In this case, the automobile manufacturer controls the franchise and can pressure the retailer to cooperate. The large capital investment required to maintain a car dealership usually signifies a need for sales volume, and hence a mutual interest is usually maintained in reference to promotional activities.

When we contrast the capital investment and need for volume in the automobile dealership with the problems faced by the sellers of soaps, detergents, etc., in the numerous grocery outlets, it is easy to understand the various strategies needed in order to meet the pressures of the marketplace.

Other Cooperative Allowances

Though most cooperative advertising expenditures are given for newspaper display ads, it is important to recognize that not all cooperative monies are spent in this way. Many of the ways in which retailers can obtain allowances from manufacturers are listed below.[11] Many of these payments, in effect, help to increase the sales volume or the net profit of the retail firm.

1. Cooperative advertising allowances.
2. Payments for interior displays including floor fixtures, self-extenders, dump displays, "A" locations, extra facings, aisle displays, overhead banners, general promotional cooperation, and the like.
3. Payments for window display space, plus installation costs.
4. Push money for salespeople.
5. Contests for buyers, salespeople, and so on.

[11] Hearing before the Antitrust Subcommittee (Subcommittee Number 5) of the Committee on the Judiciary, House of Representatives, Eighty-Seventh Congress, First Session, August 30, 1961 (Serial No. 19), *Functional Discounts.*

6. Allowances for a variety of warehousing functions.
7. Payments for seasonal inventories.
8. Demonstrators.
9. Label allowances.
10. Coupon-handling allowances.
11. Free goods.
12. Guaranteed sales.
13. Local research work done through retailer.
14. Delivery costs to individual stores of large retailers.
15. Payments for mailing to store lists.
16. Liberal return privileges.
17. Contributions to favorite charities of store personnel.
18. Contributions of infinite variety to special store anniversaries and to store openings. (The great hoopla at the opening of giant new stores is largely financed by manufacturers, brokers, sales agents, and wholesalers).
19. Payments for use of special fixtures owned by the store.
20. Payments for store improvements, including painting.
21. An infinite variety of promotional and merchandising allowances.
22. Payment of part of salary of retail salespeople.
23. Trade deals of innumerable types.
24. Time spent in actual selling on retail floor by manufacturers' salesmen.
25. Inventory adjustments of many types.
26. Transportation allowances.

How They Budget — Large Retail Firms

Though the reader may agree with all that has been said previously concerning theory, the reality of the situation is such that retailers are not able to estimate the promotion-sales relationship with any finality. Nevertheless, the basic decision as to how much to spend for advertising is made concurrently with the sales and budget estimates for a six-month period.[12] These techniques may be divided into the following:

1. The top-to-bottom approach
2. The bottom-up approach
3. All you can afford[13]

These techniques may be supplemented during the year by reactions to competitors or unusual reactions to environmental conditions. In this section the large retail firm is discussed. The smaller firm will be covered in the following section.

Before considering the actual management practices concerning the budgeting of sales promotion outlays, perhaps it is best to demonstrate first the theoretical concept (touched on earlier in this chapter) regarding the determination of the point where it does not pay the firm to spend beyond its budget. Figure 12-3

---

[12]Again, we are speaking of newspaper advertising, though other forms of sales promotion are made in roughly the same manner.

[13]For a variation of these techniques applied to manufacturing firms, see Joel Dean, "How Much to Spend on Advertising," *Harvard Business Review,* Vol. XXIX, No. 1 (January, 1951), p. 68.

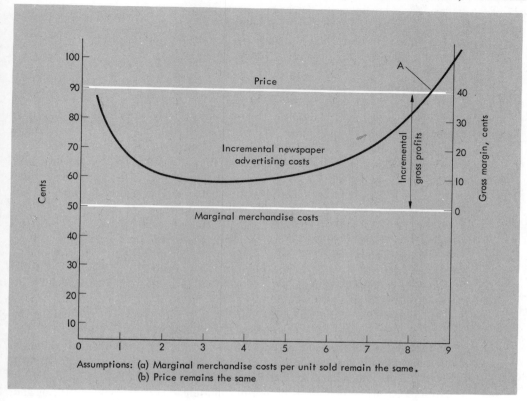

Assumptions: (a) Marginal merchandise costs per unit sold remain the same.
(b) Price remains the same

Adapted from Joel Dean, *op. cit.,* p. 66.

demonstrates this concept. This simplified version shows that each additional unit sold returns to the firm 40 cents in gross margin. Management, therefore, by increasing promotional opportunities, can increase sales, and hence gross margin will keep accruing to the firm. The firm naturally can do this until the cost curve touches the price paid by the consumer. When we examine the advertising incremental cost curve, we can see how it drops sharply in the beginning and rises to meet the price line (or 40-cent incremental point) at the end. This line logically shows that the initial advertising attempts usually bring in a flurry of sales, by making a strong impression on consumers who are "leaning" toward the store before reading the advertising. However, as the advertising outlay is increased the media used must attempt to convert less likely prospects. Finally, the last advertising outlay reaches the point (A) where it costs more than 40 cents to add one unit to the firm's sales volume. Outlays, of course, should not be made beyond the point where it requires more than 40 cents in advertising cost to bring in 40 cents gross margin. Conversely, it does pay management to promote up to point (A). since each additional expense increases volume, and increases the total gross margin.

The problem of management, therefore, is quite clear: advertise until you reach the point where it doesn't pay to advertise. Unfortunately, the point is not easily

237

determined. Nevertheless, understanding the theoretical aspects of advertising outlays should help us to determine the weakness and the value of the various methods now employed to determine point (A) on the chart.

The following pages take up some of the methods employed by the firm to determine the total sales promotion outlay.

Top-to-Bottom

The top-to-bottom technique is the one most widely used in retail stores. In essence, management determines the firm's sales goals for the year, or for the period under study, and proceeds to estimate advertising expenditure on the basis of a certain ratio of sales. Much of this reasoning is based on past experience, and the drive to maintain similar ratios as measured against published national averages is very strong. This approach appeals to the better established retail firms — those that rarely have a wide sales fluctuation from year to year.

Once the total budget has been established (for example, as 2 per cent of planned sales) it is a simple matter to divide this expenditure among the various parts of the organization. The chain would divide the advertising allotment among its stores (sometimes through the intermediary of regional management) and the department store with its branches. The next step is the internal allocation of funds to departments or store divisions.

Management favors this technique as it allows for the control of expenditures in relation to sales. In addition, adjustments can be made by simply raising or lowering the ratio. Use of this method leaves much to be desired. Possibly its major failing is that it completely ignores the ideal theoretical model outlined above. Indeed, it appears to operate almost in direct opposition to this technique. The result of top-to-bottom technique is not to measure additional increments of advertising and its impact on sales, but simply to arbitrarily assign advertising costs as a function of planned sales or, more accurately, the previous year's sales.

Bottom-to-Top

Bottom-to-top planning comes closer to the theoretical model outlined above. The planned advertising expenditures start within a merchandise group which is responsible for sales. By being closer to the consumer, this type of planning is probably better in theory than the top-to-bottom technique.

The main characteristic of advertising estimates made in this manner is that the planning is done on a departmental basis and is broken down usually into day-to-day or weekly estimates. Planning takes the form of actually outlining the number of pages of advertising to be contracted for in the period under study. From this detailed planning a total advertising budget eventually emerges.

This method is not widely used, simply because the decentralized projections are likely to exceed the preferred management estimates.

All You Can Afford

The methods just described, and particularly the first, are the most widely used techniques for determining the total amount to be spent on advertising. It is probably safe to say that the typical traditional retail firm seems to be comfortable with these techniques. The regularity of retail demand with few wide-swinging fluctuations in promotional activities seems to account for their continued use. On the other hand, retail innovators are not faced with a stable demand from year to year and are usually forced to use other techniques. Moreover, even among traditional firms, competitive pressures or the sudden availability of manufacturers' closeouts force retailers to make what we call "non-historical adjustments" of sales, which are in turn accompanied by increases in advertising. This means estimates that are not based on last year's experience but are made solely because of a need on the part of management to increase the firm's penetration of the market.

The recent growth of discounting lends support to this field. The very fact that these firms during the 1950's managed to increase sales at a rate well above national norms precludes any attempt to apply the standard criteria for changing or estimating promotional expenditures. These firms are forced to plan advertising according to what they assume they can afford, without the past as a guide.

The traditional firm, faced with an unusually heavy competitive situation, has also had a number of promotional problems. The opening of a new store or the expansion of present facilities by a competitor are occurrences that can force a retailer to increase his advertising budget. The start of a price war is an event that comes under this heading. Any one of these occurrences may force management to forget the past and rely on a much more subjective estimate of future advertising expenses.

Advertising is not restricted to large stores. Table 12-6 shows that in one study of Ohio retailers about 75 per cent of all medium-sized and small retailers spent money on advertising. No doubt the funds they spend are small in comparison with large firms; nevertheless, they do allot a considerable amount of their time to advertising and planning. The planning period, as we might expect, is not the same for all types of outlets. The apparel store, for example, is apt to plan over shorter periods of time, while stores selling durable merchandise plan over somewhat longer periods.

How they
Budget –
Smaller
Stores

Determining Size of Budgets

In determining how much to spend, the small- or medium-sized store follows expected patterns. The most popular technique by far is some form of the percentage-of-sales method.[14] Most rely on past sales information and a projection of future sales. However, setting an arbitrary amount for advertising was the technique used in one out of five cases. Some retailers believe that within arbitrary limits they can design a merchandise and advertising program that will attain the needed sales volume.

SUMMARY

The communication mix of the retailer includes advertising, display, all nonpaid news, and personal selling. This chapter discusses only newspaper advertising, the retailer's most widely used means of communicating to the public.

[14]Dorsey Forrest, "Advertising Practices of Ohio Retailers," Bureau of Business Research, The Ohio State University Research Monograph Number 55, Columbus, Ohio, 1949, p. 39.

TABLE 12-6 Percentage Distribution of Small and Medium-size Retailers who Advertise and who Make an Advance Advertising Plan or Budget, By Kind of Business, Ohio

Kind of Business	Percentage Distribution (Total Advertisers = 100)			(Total Returns = 100)		
	Planners	Non-Planners	No Answer As To Plan	Total Advertisers	Number of Non-Advertisers	Total Number
Drug	55	29	16	73	27	100
Furniture	58	39	3	93	7	100
Grocery	39	38	24	61	39	100
Hardware	65	23	13	91	9	100
Jewelry	57	29	14	100	0	100
Lumber	87	13	0	92	8	100
Men's-boy's clothing	53	47	0	79	21	100
Shoe	71	21	7	93	7	100
Women's ready-to-wear	78	11	11	90	10	100
Other	46	49	5	72	28	100
Total	53	35	12	75	25	100

Source: Dorsey Forrest, "Advertising Practices of Ohio Retailers," Bureau of Business Research, The Ohio State University Research Monograph Number 55, Columbus, Ohio, 1949, p. 10.

Assuming the availability of media and resources, the firm's strategy for reaching consumers is governed by:

1. The type of store being presented to the public.
2. The type of market the firm is trying to reach.
3. The media available to reach that market.

The communication effort has one purpose — to move the demand curve to the right and thus increase sales. The retailer, though he sells products and features them in his advertising, is more concerned with increasing store patronage rather than selling an advertised product.

Local (retail) advertising in newspapers has increased at a faster rate than national advertising. All advertising and display expenditures peak during the month of December. However, the advertising expenditure for individual products may peak during other months. For instance women's shoes peak in March & December, curtains in October, and men's sport coats in May. Store advertising expenses represent about 10 percent of all expenses, in spite of the fact that retailers qualify for a local rate from newspapers and thus pay less per line than national advertisers.

Retailers have two sources of advertising funds, namely, their own resources and cooperative advertising received from manufacturers, where the cost of an ad is usually shared with the retailer.

In budgeting advertising funds within the firm, retailers use one of three techniques: the top-to-bottom approach, the bottom-up approach, and the all you can afford approach.

QUESTIONS

1. Distinguish between the following:
a. sales promotion in the manufacturing firm
b. sales promotion in the retail firm

2. Define publicity and relate it to Question 1.

3. It has been observed that advertising expenditures in most firms decline during a recession. Some observers suggest that business should increase its expenditures during this period. Do you agree? Support your arguments.

4. How does the strategy of the advertising program of the retailer differ from that of the manufacturer?

5. Table 12-5 lists cooperative advertising percentages in typical department stores. Why the variance among these departments?

6. Evaluate advertising expenditures in the retail firm
a. by the size of the firm
b. by the type of firm
c. in relation to the total expenses of the firm

7. From an economist's point of view, what is the over-all purpose of sales promotion?

8. Discuss several ways that manufacturers of appliances can offer cooperative allowances separate from advertising. Discuss how management can make a meaningful choice in its selection of the type of allowance to be offered.

9. Discuss the importance and relationship of newspaper circulation and national and local advertising rates.

10. In what basic ways do the three techniques of budgeting advertising expenditures vary?

11. Pointed out in this chapter was the fact that retailers prefer newspaper advertising as their major promotional media. Can you foresee the development of other media by retailers? If so, in what types, and what factors are relevant to any changes that you may foresee?

12. What type of media aside from newspaper advertising would lend itself to the sale of these products at the retail level?
a. automobiles
b. major appliances
c. perfume
d. fashion apparel
e. fur storage services

13. Sales expenses in a store selling housewares for the past year are 5 per cent; advertising, 3 per cent. If management were forced to reduce one or the other expense, can you visualize how different managements would approach this problem?

14. Is it difficult to budget the costs of sales promotion?

15. Offer several reasons why a department store does not use an advertising agency.

16. Under what conditions would a retailer use an advertising agency?

Communicating
with the
Customer
13

OBJECTIVES YOU SHOULD MEET

1. *Account* for the growth of television advertising among retail firms.
2. *Describe* the role of radio in the retailer's mix.
3. *Explain* the importance of the statement "space is money."
4. *Define* free publicity.
5. *Explain* the recent decline of trading stamps.

 Retail management has other ways besides newspaper advertising to communicate with its audience and hence increase sales. Among these techniques are television and radio advertising, display, free publicity, special purpose publicity, direct mail promotion, trading stamps (particularly in food stores), and direct selling. The use of these techniques varies from firm to firm.

Television and Radio

Until recently the retailer's use of television has been limited, the general attitude being that the time periods available to retailers are too limited, too much planning is required to produce a show and a commercial, and television simply costs too much.[1]

In recent years, however, the retailer's attitude toward television has changed considerably. Retailers have generally been broadening their media mix; however, the growth in their use of television has been particularly dramatic. Whereas in 1965 retail television commercials numbered 30,000, by 1970 the number had increased to 60,000.[2]

---

[1] Irving Settle, "Why Retailers Bypass Television," *Journal of Retaining,* Vol. XXXI, No. 4 (Winter, 1955-56), pp. 181-182.

[2] *Grey Matter,* Grey Advertising, Inc., December, 1971.

Behind the change has been an over-all adjustment in the media mix by several large retailers. Sears, for instance, in the first six months of 1971 spent $14.3 million on television advertising, up 22 per cent from a similar period the year before. Woolworth and A & P chalked up increases of 45 per cent and 75 per cent respectively, during the same period.[3]

The growth of television advertising among retail firms is attributable to many factors. An important consideration is the belief that television can reach large audiences more easily. With the movement of much of the population to the suburbs, stores find that they must advertise in several newspapers to reach their customers. They find that by advertising on television their ability to reach an audience is enhanced.

Retail firms have also found that television advertising can develop an image for the firm better than the newspapers can. Most newspaper retail advertising is based on price, and the firm trying to develop a store personality has found that a focus on price may distort its profile. On television, through the use of live actors in fanciful skits, the firm can develop its message and the visual message can be more lasting. In addition, color television shows products more realistically than black-and-white newsprint.

Though the increase in television advertising has been dramatic, most retail firms are reluctant to participate. The major reasons seem to be that television commercials are costly, and their production requires an advertising agency. The Grey Agency produces commercials for both Macy's and J.L. Hudson (Detroit). Stores consider not only the initial cost of a television commercial high, but also the fact that such a brief message cannot call attention to the total firm. A typical newspaper ad may feature five or six products in one ad, whereas a television commercial cannot do justice to such a variety. In addition, because TV commercials must be prepared weeks in advance, they cannot be as timely as newspaper ads.

The importance of the high cost of producing a commercial combined with the cost of air time in affecting the firm's strategy can be seen in Table 13-1; the bulk of retail commercials seem to be aired during the daytime when costs are at their lowest. Only 13 per cent of retail commercials are run during prime time.

To overcome this high cost, many department stores have set up their own commercial studios in their stores. Many commercials that took several weeks to produce are now made on inexpensive tapes. One report noted that Famous Barr paid only $50,000 for 60 tape commercials.[4]

On the other hand, the television commercial has helped large national chains to promote a product line in direct competition with a manufacturer's product. The advertising of Sears appliances and tires seems to be in direct competition with many nationally advertised brands.

Table 13-2 shows what types of products are advertised on television by retailers. Appliances lead the list for Sears, whereas apparel and home furnishings predominate in the typical department-store spot commercial. In a recent year in New York Sears spent over half the firm's TV dollars for appliance adver-

[3]*Grey Matter, op cit.,* and "A & P Doubled TV Ads," *Women's Wear Daily,* March 15, 1971, p. 1.
[4]*Business Week,* November 23, 1968, p. 63.

TABLE 13-1 Summary of Time Periods Used by 50 Leading Department Stores*
(as Monitored by Broadcast Advertisers Reports, Inc., One Week per Month
January through June, 1971)

Time Period	#Spots	Percentage
6 A.M. to 5 P.M. (daytime)	3,021	51.3%
5 P.M. to 7:30 P.M. (early fringe)	1,064	18.2
7:30 P.M. to 11 P.M. (prime time)	777	13.2
11:00 P.M. to sign off (late night)	1,014	17.3
Total	5,876	100.0%

*This time breakdown for 50 top department stores includes total spots placed by Macy's, Gimbels, Jordan Marsh, May Co., and others, which operate stores and use TV in more cities than the 27 markets where their key stores are located. Spots placed by manufacturers for stores not included.
Source: Station Representatives Association, Inc., 230 Park Avenue, New York, n. d.

tising. One should also note the number of general and institutional ads that promote the store personality in both cases.

The use of radio and its comparison to television and newspaper varies little by type of retailer. A recent study by the National Retail Merchants Association seems to indicate that discount stores spent 44 per cent of their promotional dollars on newspaper advertising and 8.6 per cent on radio and television. Similarly, the same study reported that department stores spent 52.5 per cent of the total sales promotion and publicity budget on newspapers and 5.3 per cent on television and radio.[5] In both cases the amounts spent on newspaper advertising are substantially more than on radio or television.

Yet the use of radio is widespread among retailers. In a recent study of 31 stores in seven large cities, the findings indicate that 28 stores used radio as a supplement to the much larger newspaper expenditures.[6]

Radio advertising traditionally has been used to publicize the services of retail firms and sales by major stores. Upholstering, furniture rebuilding, and rug cleaning are services that lend themselves effectively to the radio message. In addition, the announcement of the start of an all-week sale or a one-day event such as a warehouse clearance or a rug sale on radio is known to be an effective means of increasing the impact of the firm's newspaper advertising.

The Robert Hall clothing commercials on radio support the notion that good retail advertising can be used to develop a store's institutional image — in this case, for low-price merchandise. For the most part, however, radio is used like television, to support a firm's regular advertising program. Rarely is it self-sustaining.

---

[5] R. Paul Zucker "A Little Something Extra from the Media," *Merchandise Week,* November 29, 1971, p. 12.
[6] *Advertising Age,* June 28, 1972, p. 20.

All TV Spots Placed by 50 Top Department Stores and by Sears, by Classification   **TABLE 13-2**
(as Monitored One Week per Month by Broadcast Advertisers Reports, Inc., Jan.-June 1971)

Classification	50 Dept. Stores 27 Markets	Sears* Same 27 Mkts., Same Cities
Appliances	215	1,357
Auto center	106	572
Beauty aids	183	201
Building materials	6	134
Custom services (slipcovers, etc.)	170	626
Garden center	35	60
Health aid	20	90
Hobby crafts	2	40
Home furnishings	945	340
Office supplies	0	53
Optical dept.	4	956
Plumbing & heating	0	1
Sewing center	130	144
Sport center	14	40
Tool center	0	2
Variety**	1,826	597
Apparel (general)	1,298	207
(Men's)	0	230
(Women's)	0	522
(Childrens)	0	240
Total Spots	4,954	6,412

*Sears monitored same week as department stores in each city.
**Variety spots are to be considered general or institutional commercials.
Source: Station Representatives Association, *op. cit.*

A manufacturer once said that in stores "space is money." By that he meant that **Store Space**
as more space is assigned to his product, he will sell more.[7] His reason is simply that **Strategy**
many customers entering a retail store make a substantial number of unplanned purchases; they will often accept a substitute product if they cannot find the product they planned to buy.

Table 13-3 illustrates this view, showing that almost half of all consumers entering a supermarket make unplanned purchases. In addition, close to 20 per cent will either accept a brand substitute or purchase a product that was generically planned as a purchase, rather than specifically planned. Though purchase in drugstores or liquor stores may be more specifically planned, in both cases the number of shoppers uncommitted to a brand is substantial.

---

[7]For a measurement of this effect on the sales of products see Ronald E. Frank and William F. Massy, "Shelf Position and Space Effects on Sales," *Journal of Marketing Research* (February, 1970), p. 59. Also see Peter J. McClure and E. James West, "Sales Effects of a New Counter Display," *Journal of Advertising Research* (Jan., 1969), p. 29.

Comparison of Studies of Buying Decisions in Various Types of Retail Outlets   TABLE 13-3

Type of Retail Outlet	Specifically Planned (%)	Intentions-Outcomes Categories		
		Generally Planned (%)	Brand Substitution (%)	Unplanned (%)
Drugstores	56.0	15.0	7.0	22.0
Package liquor stores	62.5	19.5	9.8	8.2
Supermarkets	31.1	17.2	1.8	49.9

Source: James F. Engel et al., *Consumer Behavior* (New York: Holt, Rinehart and Winston, Inc., 1968) p. 487.

The importance of display space can also be seen by the actions of manufacturers in their competition for display and shelf space in all stores. Recently it was reported that R. J. Reynolds Tobacco Company has been paying several retail food chains $14 a month per store for the opportunity of stacking Winston, Salem, and Camel cigarettes in most supermarkets. The cost of such a practice can be considerable, considering that a chain with 2,000 stores would receive $336,000 from the firm.[8] Reynolds is the leading firm in the industry. Liggett and Myers discontinued this practice a few years ago, and most of their products occupy the bottom shelf.[9]

Retailers also use space to their advantage, again accenting the importance of store space. For example, the typical retail chain uses five to ten times as much shelf space to display the firm's private-brand soda as it devotes to the competitors' products. In a typical major supermarket chain, the best-selling brands such as Coca Cola, Pepsi, and 7-Up are relegated to smaller spaces than the private brands sodas (such as A & P's Yukon).

This strategy accomplishes several goals, the most important being to encourage the sale of the private-brand soda, which has a higher markup than the national brands. In addition, the sale of these products encourages the consumer to shop in the chain again, as the private brands can be purchased only there. This strategy is followed in many areas of the store in offering private brands for sale.

 The most important part to remember however is that space, position, and sales are closely related, that is, the more space a product is given and the better the position, the more likely higher sales are to result.

Display   The display of merchandise has a cost element attached to it. This cost element is potentially high in stores that rely on self-service mass displays. Food supermarkets are a case in point. The lifeblood of a food store is its available space. Manufacturers of food products are generally well aware of this fact, and their "salesmen" are experts in the art of displaying merchandise, taking advantage of the space allotted, and, in some cases, wheedling more space from the management. "Space is money" is an old axiom in retailing and is well demonstrated in the food supermarket.

[8]*Advertising Age,* Feb. 21, 1972, p. 3.
[9]*Idem.*

Though display space is important in the retailing field, the tendency for all types of outlets is to have less and less available. The main reason for this is the tremendous increase in the number of products and lines carried. For example, the average supermarket handles about 7,900 items today, whereas in 1950 the estimate was about 2,200 items. Since there has not been a proportionate increase in the size of the average store, the assumption must be that space is becoming even scarcer.

Costs

Costs of space also seem to be prohibitive in the typical retail store. To measure costs of space we must determine the capital expenditures for the building, land and fixtures, the investment in merchandise, and the cost of maintaining the space in tiptop shape throughout the year. One author estimates the capital investment for each foot of counter space in a food supermarket at over $400. The maintenance, he notes, averages about $125 a year for each square foot of counter space.[10]

Display costs (both investment and annual maintenance costs) in other outlets are probably much higher, since the food supermarket is of less elaborate design than, for example, the department store. In addition, food supermarkets are able to use most of the total space of the store for selling and display, whereas traditional stores use much less.

The problems in making judgments concerning space costs are great. The most obvious problem involves the attempt to allot fixed costs (such as rent) to a given space in a store. This type of allocation requires arbitrary accounting decisions. Another problem in making judgments concerning space costs involves the fact that the space allotted to a classification of goods rarely remains the same all year round. This is especially true in a grocery store where new products and product sizes are continually being added to the firm's offerings. Nevertheless, allocation of costs has been attempted, with some interesting results. One recent major study of grocery industry reported the following findings concerning a variety of grocery products and their relationship to shelf space:

1. Coffee, canned fruit and vinegar take up almost the same shelf space in the stores studied. Yet, coffee returns more than ten times the direct product profit per cubic foot when compared to canned fruit, and thirty-five times when compared to vinegar.

2. Cereal returns almost $3 per cubic foot to the grocery store when confined to only eight cubic feet. Similarly, flour confined to only six cubic feet actually loses money.[11]

Whether the firm is a food supermarket or a downtown department store, it is incumbent upon management to maximize the sales productivity of each foot of selling space.

---

[10] Edgar A. Pessemier, "The Management of Grocery Inventories in Supermarkets," *Economic and Business Studies,* Bulletin No. 32 (Pullman, Wash.: Washington State University, 1960), p. 2, fn.

[11] McKinsey-General Foods Study, *The Economics of Food Distributors,* General Foods Corporation, October, 1963, p. 36.

Display as a major communicative tool in the retail firm is probably no different in its impact on the demand curve than advertising, price reductions, credit, or a whole host of devices used by store management. Measuring the impact of display on the sale of the product presents innumerable problems, for it is difficult to isolate the other factors that also affect the sale of merchandise. For example, it is possible that in any measurement of grocery displays the impact of a display may be a direct function of the store traffic. That is, on an extremely busy day even a poor display will draw a large number of customers, and on a poor traffic day, a display that is aesthetically appealing and attuned to the consumers' needs may fail to attract customers. Allowance must be made, therefore, for these external variables. Some of the attempts to measure the effectiveness of display and its impact on the sales of merchandise will be covered in Chapter 19.

The use of display as a communicative strategy, however, varies significantly among stores. For example, a store specializing in women's fashions may rely almost totally on both window and in-store displays to project its image to the public. On any given day crowds on Fifth Avenue may be seen gazing for long periods of time at the fashions displayed in the windows of this type of store, while little attention is paid to most of the other store windows.

Window display can be used in many ways:

1. As a means of projecting a fashion or quality image. This is achieved by changing windows according to a regular schedule and filling them with merchandise that is considered to be "the latest."

2. As a means of projecting a value or price image. Here the store's best buys are prominently displayed in the window with the price tickets clearly visible.

3. As a means of supporting other sales promotion activities of the firm. Thus, by inspecting the window, a shopper is made aware of the products that were offered for sale in the latest newspaper advertising or through other media.

4. As a means of showing the shopper the types of merchandise being sold in the store. Typically, these windows may display hundreds of products being offered throughout the store.

The use of windows as a strong communicative aid to the store has declined considerably in recent years. This has come about because of the decline in importance of downtown stores and the growth of the suburbs. The suburban stores do not usually have windows because the shopper does not find it necessary to window-shop. Most of the large suburban stores have "see-through" entrances, where the shopper can simply see the display of merchandise being sold in a department.

People shopping in suburban centers usually drive up to a store and enter directly, which reduces the opportunity to interest them in window displays away from the main entrance.

In the downtown areas the situation is much different in that most customers come into the area by means of public transportation and walk from store to store. Therefore window displays make more sense in these areas.

Public relations is defined as obtaining favorable publicity without spending money. The phrase "without spending money" may, however, be misleading, especially as applied to the large retailer. Free publicity usually takes three forms: Free Publicity

1. Favorable comments appearing in the local press covering the firm's community activities.

2. Favorable comments appearing in the press covering a firm's merchandising promotions.

3. Favorable comments in the local press covering the firm's role in the business community or national economy.

The purpose of free publicity is basically the same as for newspaper advertising. All roads lead to the same goal, namely, the presentation of the firm's name in its most favorable context.

Though we speak of free publicity, actually the larger firms expend considerable money and effort to maintain a constant flow of publicity in the local press. The local press is favorably inclined to offer this publicity to certain general merchandise firms if they supply a great deal of the newspaper's income. Because of the size of newspaper advertising expenditures by some retail firms, a great deal of favorable newspaper publicity can accrue to the same firms. Many sections of the newspaper are devoted to this. For example, the women's fashion page, the financial news sections, and the general news columns all contribute to this endeavor. Even the comments of the local gourmet may be closely allied with the advertising expenditures of the large local restaurants.

The most cherished section of free publicity in the local press is usually the fashion pages. This is so because in most departments, especially chains, the female shopper is in the majority. Therefore, the presentation of a store as having the latest fashions direct from European fashion centers becomes an important source of free publicity.

What are the criteria of newspapers in originating stories that appear on the fashion pages? Are the stories based on the fashion news originated by each store or is the criterion the more businesslike one of advertising expenditure by the store in the local paper? It seems to be the latter if we are to judge by a study by Steven A. Shaw,[12] who notes that there is a direct relationship between the size of the firm's advertising expenditures in the paper and the amount of "free" publicity.

Though the major public relations impact may appear as free publicity in the newspapers, there are also special public relations areas within the store's control that usually involve a cost. Contests, lectures, concerts, parades (for example, the Macy's and J. L. Hudson Thanksgiving Day parades), demonstrations, fashion shows, and many other efforts not related directly to a store's merchandise are examples of special purpose publicity.[13] Special-Purpose Publicity

[12] "Store Press Publicists and Their Work on the Women's Pages," *Journal of Retailing,* Vol. XXXII, No. 4 (Winter 1956-1957), p. 168.

[13] For detailed breakdowns of this division, see Charles M. Edwards, Jr. and Russel A. Brown, *Retail Advertising and Sales Promotion* (Englewood Cliffs, N.J.: Prentice-Hall, Inc., 1959), p. 493.

Special-purpose publicity efforts have been increasing in the past few years, particularly in the suburbs. Many retail department stores have set aside community rooms to serve the contiguous population. These rooms are used as meeting rooms by many of the local organizations such as the League of Women Voters, Scouts, etc. In addition, the stores hold lectures and classes directed toward children and adult cultural activities. Art, theater classes, book discussion groups, and music lessons are not uncommon offerings. The particular appeal of these classes to middle-class suburbanites is obvious. Most suburbanites are partaking of the recent surge of interest in "culture." In addition, many of these activities are oriented toward social situations that one commonly encounters in the suburbs. In this classification are bridge lessons, teen-age charm classes, cooking, and party-hostess type classes.

However, many of these special exhibits do cost the store money and sometimes require a specific allocation of store space. Nevertheless, they constitute an important aspect of the firm's total effort to reach the public.

Direct Mail Advertising

Though newspaper advertising is the most widely used means of reaching the public, it does have several distinct disadvantages. One of its most outstanding failures can be seen in its wasted circulation: the newspaper may circulate in areas where the store does not have outlets and/or the newspaper has readers who would never consider buying at this particular outlet even if it were located nearby.

In order to overcome this problem, retail firms supplement many of their promotional activities by trying to reach consumers who are more likely to become their patrons. One of the ways stores accomplish this is through direct mail advertising. Direct mail promotion in the retail firm can take many forms. The most widely used is to send mass mailings to the firm's charge-account customers during special sales periods. So-called manufacturer mailers may be enclosed in each charge-account bill in order to obtain additional sales volume for the firm. In almost all cases the retail firm directs its mail efforts toward known customers or former customers of the firm. Many of the major mail order catalog firms are so concerned with promoting their delivery to high-potential customers that they send the catalog only by request or to those who have purchased a minimum amount of merchandise from the catalog within a stipulated recent time period.

Measuring Direct Mail

Measuring direct mail results seems relatively simple. One must consider the price of the merchandise plus the total cost of the mailing. If, for example, a firm sends out 100,000 pieces of mail at a total cost of $6,000, a 1 per cent return on a $50 item results in a sales cost of 12 per cent, or an order cost of $6.[14] The same return on a $25 item would double the sales cost. It would be tautological reasoning, however, to assume from the above analysis that management should promote only high-priced items! To understand why a store need not necessarily promote higher-priced merchandise we must go back to our previous discussion

[14]Edward N. Mayer, Jr., "Direct Mail Advertising," *Harvard Business Review,* Vol. XXIX, No. 4 (July 9, 1951), p. 37.

concerning the impact of advertising on total demand. Lowering the price of the product has no effect on the total cost of the direct mailing. It does, however, greatly enhance the sales of the product. Therefore, the lower sales price may increase the volume substantially.

Sears, Roebuck, Montgomery Ward, and other large firms have developed substantial volume through the use of direct mail catalogs. Estimates are that approximately 20 per cent of Sears' total retail business is done through mail catalogs. The typical Sears (annual) catalog contains over 1,600 pages with well over 20,000 items.

Firms using catalogs of this type are faced with two pressing problems: (1) the selection of items to be included in the catalog; (2) the determination of the proper inventory of the items selected.[15] The prediction of what will sell is always a major problem for retailers. It is doubly so in the making of a catalog which has to be used over a long period of time. This, of course, precludes any changes or adjustments in the original merchandise offered for sale.

During the fifties and sixties trading stamps became a major promotional aid, particularly in food chains. In recent years the number of food stores offering trading stamps has declined considerably. One study indicates that at its peak in 1963 approximately 65 per cent of all supermarkets were offering the consumer stamps. More recently a similar study seems to indicate that only 25 per cent are now offering stamps. During this same period the percentage of families saving trading stamps has declined from 84% to 64%.

This decline is due to several causes, the first being that the price inflation that developed in the late sixties has put pressure on the food stores to maintain prices and thus reduce costs. One way for the stores to reduce costs in the short run is to cut out stamps.

The second reason for the decline in stamp usage is the growth of discount food retailers during this same period. The typical discount food store in conjunction with lower prices has avoided offering the consumer frills in the form of stamps and other services. The resultant price competition has forced traditional stores also to reduce their frills, and stamps have suddenly become expendable.

Most recently the use of trading stamps has declined in gasoline stations a major customer of the stamp firms. The decline is due mainly to the energy crisis which reduces the need for the individual station to compete for customers.

Nevertheless, stamps are still offered by a large number of retail stores. Their purpose is still to increase the sales and profits of the retailer. Like advertising, stamps must pay off.

The Nature of Stamps

Though trading stamps and advertising may produce a similar consumer reaction, the effect on sales varies. For instance, the impact of trading stamps on sales is store-wide, whereas advertising may increase sales volume in only a certain number

[15]Seymour Banks, "The Prediction of Dress Purchases for a Mail Order House," *Journal of Business,* Vol. XXIII, No. 1 (January, 1950), p. 48.

of departments. Advertising can be directed to certain large categories of merchandise, but trading stamps after their initial impact cannot.[16] More important, however, all retail firms have access to the same advertising medium, but they do not have equal access to the same trading stamps. Therefore, one must evaluate stamps as a promotional device, taking into consideration: (1) the sales and profit impact of trading stamps on the consumer, and (2) the impact of trading stamp A on the consumer.

Retail management must always be aware of the relationship and differences between advertising and trading stamps as promotional tools. More specifically, let us ask whether management should treat advertising and its possible impact on sales volume in the same manner as it treats trading stamps? Or does it matter whether a 10 per cent increase in volume is achieved as a direct result of advertising or by using trading stamps? Recalling our earlier discussion of the impact of advertising on the demand curve, one finds that the final results vary considerably if the same increase in sales volume is achieved by trading stamps or by newspaper advertising. The reason is obvious. In the food store, the consumer receives a trading stamp for each dollar purchased. Essentially, for each dollar increase in sales, the cost of trading stamps increases in a direct ratio. Newspaper advertising, however, does not operate in this manner. Its cost per dollar of sales increase may be higher or lower than trading stamps. On the other hand, they have the common attribute of affecting the demand curve. However, the cost of trading stamps is a function of the sales volume, whereas newspaper advertising is not. Management must, of course, bear this in mind when contemplating tactical maneuvers in this direction.

Stamps have been particularly successful in the sale of convenience goods. As noted above, their major success has been in the sale of food products. In addition, they have been widely used by all types of small retailers, from gasoline stations to the corner drugstore. More recently, the stamp companies have been experimenting by offering stamps to users of car rental services, and even funeral parlors. In one case, Sunday churchgoers have been attracted by trading-stamp giveaways. Trading stamps have been notably unsuccessful in department stores. Small stores join stamp plans in large numbers as they can thereby associate themselves with a large retailer. Usually small stores find that stamps create an impact that could not be created by monies expended on a newspaper advertising campaign.

The success of stamps in convenience goods stores is attributable to the fact that stamp plans are successful only when the customers can collect them quickly and in quantity. Hence, they become a regular supplement to their buying patterns.

Impact on Consumer and Competitors

In order to be effective, stamps must produce additional sales. Otherwise, the firm is obligated to raise prices in order to completely assume the cost of the plan (an unlikely event). The cost of a stamp plan, assuming prices and volume remain the same, may go as high as 2 cents for each dollar of sales for the large stores, and 3 cents for the smaller stores. One expert suggests that a retail firm must increase its

---

[16] We are, of course, ignoring the well-known tactic of offering double or triple stamps on certain products. However, this technique is usually restricted to a small group of items and rarely covers a department.

sales volume by 12 per cent in order to make a profit; others suggest a range of 10 to 20 per cent.[17] Whatever the precise figure, it is obvious that sales must increase substantially.

The next pertinent question is, Where is the increase in sales volume to come from? If from competitors, it can be assumed that there would be an immediate reaction. Competitors might indulge in price cuts or take on a competing stamp. If the former practice is followed, it may also be assumed that the consumer will be made aware of the lower prices in the non-trading-stamp stores. The multiplicity of products, and the availability of various grades, sizes and other qualitative factors, make any judgment as to relative value very difficult for the consumer.[18]

If a firm, as a defense reaction, takes on a competitive stamp, the problem simply becomes one of the influence of stamp plan A versus the influence of stamp plan B in the major marketing area. If a stand-off ensues, that is, if the competing major stores are unable to capture additional consumers, food prices will probably increase. Does this happen in actual practice, or does a consumer switch patronage to stamp plan A or its competitor because of preferences? Again, the answer is not clear — nor should it be. There is evidence that large firms can increase patronage by starting a stamp plan. For example, one study reported a 9 per cent increase in store patronage in one large chain when stamps were first introduced. Shifts of this type, however, are short-run at best, and it is more appropriate to determine the long-run patronage. However, no evidence is available to make a proper evaluation of these tendencies. One is forced to assume, therefore, that based on postwar tendencies, many firms have been able to increase sales (and prices, if necessary) enough to cover the cost of trading stamps.

Impact on Retail Profits and Prices

How do stamps affect store profits? Our knowledge of the retail field at this stage should lead us to the obvious answer, that the ability of stamps to produce profits in turn depends entirely on the retailer's ability to manipulate the total communication, physical distribution, and goods and services mix. Evidence for this is available in retailing literature. One study of failures of retail firms from 1947 to 1956, for example, showed that retail failures in cities with trading stamps were approximately the same as in cities without trading stamp activities.[19] This study supports the belief that there is no correlation between profits and trading stamps. As we suspected, factors other than stamps are more important to the retailer's success or failure. One study of a retail firm established in Indianapolis showed that the small retailer found that profits were neither increased nor undermined by the

---

[17]Delbert J. Duncan and Charles F. Phillips, *Retailing, Principles and Methods,* 6th ed. (Homewood, Ill.: Richard D. Irwin, Inc., 1963), p. 544.

[18]For insight into this question, see Bob R. Holden, *The Structure of a Retail Market and The Market Behavior of Retail Units* (Englewood Cliffs, N.J.: Prentice-Hall, Inc., 1960), p. 68. In this book, Holden noted that it took him 300 hours to tabulate price differences in eight food stores. Even these tabulations were subject to question, since he was forced to make a number of important compromises in order to establish the proper price levels.

[19]Charles Franklin Phillips, "Trading Stamps and Retail Failures," *Journal of Marketing,* Vol. XXII, No. 3 (January, 1958), pp. 304-305.

use of trading stamps. The author of this study states: "Apparently, stamps alone will not correct the basically weak competitive position."[20]

The question of whether stamps increase prices recently became a national issue. In recent years many of the supermarkets have been deluged with pricing protests and boycotts by well-organized women's groups concerned with the increasing costs of food. These protests have taken place in many cities. In two cities which drew national attention, Denver, Colorado, and Levittown, Pennsylvania, the boycotts of stores received considerable local support. Supermarkets that gave stamps were blamed for much of this price inflation.[21] Though the boycotts extended through the year 1966, *Progressive Grocer,* a leading trade magazine, was able to announce that the boycotts had ended in January, 1967.[22] However, as a result, many of the boycotted supermarkets took the opportunity to drop trading stamps, a device considered by the public to cause higher prices.

Major firms which took this action reported varying success. Stop And Shop, a large food chain located in New England, dropped stamps and reported a 15 per cent sales gain during the same period.[23] Many other independent and local chains followed suit, for varied reasons. Many found it to be an opportune moment to cast off a promotional device that in management's view was not as effective as had been hoped. By combining the abandonment of stamps with sharp price cuts retailers thought they could offset the protests of stamp-saving customers, who constituted the majority of the shoppers.

Whether the price cuts are permanent or only temporary remains to be seen. It is probably safe to say that the price cuts instituted when stamps were dropped have been reinstated to a large extent. A study seems to confirm this observation.[24]

Other Promotional Devices

In spite of the price protests and the drop-off in the use of trading stamps, the food chains have found some interest among customers in games and contests. In addition, the gasoline stations, being stamp users, have also engaged in contests as a means of attracting — or in some cases simply retaining — the consumer.

In the food field the chains have developed games such as "TV Bingo," "Super Poker," "Three-of-a-Kind," and "Let's go to the Races." The latter is a particularly successful promotion used in over a dozen top chains. The sponsor of this game hands out horse-racing entry cards at participating supermarkets. Once a week or at any designated period of time, the sponsor shows filmed races on a local TV channel for a half-hour. These races are filmed reruns of races run over the past few years. Those holding the winning entry cards can win up to $1,000.[25]

One observer has suggested that to be successful a game must meet the following requirements:

---

[20]Taylor W. Meloan and Burt C. McCammon, "Use of Trading Stamps by the Small Retailer," *Journal of Marketing,* Vol. XXIII, No. 2 (October, 1958), p. 177.

[21]A situation no doubt brought about to a great extent by the Vietnam conflict.

[22]*Progressive Grocer,* January, 1967, p. 167.

[23]*Progressive Grocer,* May, 1967, p. 6.

[24]F. E. Brown, "Price Movements Following the Discontinuance of Trading Stamps," *Journal of Retailing,* Vol. 43 No. 3 (Fall, 1967), p. 4.

[25]Progressive Grocer, October, 1966, pp. 280-284.

1. It must be simple to understand and enter.
2. It must be *fun*. One contest had 1,500 winners a month.
3. It must contain an element of suspense.
4. It must offer a minimum of frustration.
5. It must have continuity.
6. It must be low in cost to the supermarket. Whereas stamps may cost 20 per cent of sales, a game may cost up to 10 per cent maximum.
7. It must be equally appealing to both sexes.[26]

However, even here the stores have witnessed a general decline in the use of games and such devices as promotional tools. The same reasons offered for the decline of stamps seems to apply.[27]

SUMMARY

Aside from newspaper advertising, retail stores have other means of communicating with the consumer. In this chapter several techniques are discussed, namely, television, radio, display, free publicity, special-purpose publicity, direct mail promotion, and trading stamps.

Television has become of greater importance to retailers in recent years. Its advantage is its ability to reach large audiences and to project a store image. Its distinct disadvantages are cost and its lack of timeliness, at least in comparison to newspaper advertising.

Though stores do not spend much of their funds on radio, they do use it as a supplement to newspaper advertising. It is also used to advertise a firm's special services, such as rug-cleaning, upholstering, and the like.

The effective use of store space is an important part of a retailer's strategy. The importance of space can be seen from the fact that unplanned purchases represent a substantial proportion of purchases, and many manufacturers actively compete for space in many outlets. Stores promoting private brands use space as a means of increasing the sales of their own brand.

In establishing the proper allocation of space one must bear in mind that space is a scarce commodity. For instance in 1950 the average supermarket handled 2,200 items, whereas today it handles about 7,900 items. Cost of maintenance and capital investment in a supermarket runs about $525 for each square foot of center space. Supermarkets spend a minimal amount, and these costs are much higher for other types of stores.

Window displays can be used to project a fashion or quality image, show a value or price image, support other sales promotion activities in the firm, and show the shopper the products sold throughout the store. With the movement toward the suburbs windows are becoming less useful, as branch stores ordinarily do not feature windows because of different traffic patterns.

---

[26]*Ibid.*, pp. 283-284.

[27]For a discussion of the problems the oil companies faced in dealing with games see Eugene D. Jaffe and Joseph A. Wegrzynovicz, "Can You Sell Gasoline with Games?" *Business Horizons* (October, 1969), p. 43.

Free publicity is a major sought-after source of promotion. It includes favorable comments in the press concerning the firm's activities, whether they be merchandising, community, or business efforts. Though a public relations staff usually places stories of this type, no cost is involved in such publicity. On the other hand, special-purpose publicity does involve cost. This form of publicity refers to contests, concerts, parades, fashion shows and all other efforts to develop a favorable community image.

Direct mail advertising is used widely by large retailers. Though it does not replace newspaper advertising, it supplements it and, more important, can be directed to previous customers of the store, thereby avoiding wasted circulation. Direct mail advertising is mainly directed to names on charge-account lists; it varies in form from mailing catalogs to inserting manufacturer "mailers" in the monthly customer charge-account bill.

Though trading-stamp use is decidedly lessened, stamps still represent an important retail promotional tool. Trading stamps like any other promotional tool must be evaluated on the basis of the sales and profit impact on the consumer. This impact must be related to a particular trading stamp, which may vary in different areas of the country. Trading stamps have been particularly potent in the sales of consumer goods.

Another promotional device used by retailers is supermarket games, but their use has declined severely. Price inflation has increased the need to reduce costs, which in turn has meant dropping all kinds of promotional devices, and the growth of food discounting has again forced traditional firms to reduce costs with the same effect.

QUESTIONS

1. Why has television usage grown among large retailers?
2. What problems are associated with using television as an advertising medium?
3. Does the continued use of trading stamps force a food firm to raise prices?
4. Distinguish between television and radio as a means of communicating with a firm's retail audience.
5. Discuss some limitations of selling merchandise by catalog. Compare these limitations to the alternative of using newspaper advertising.
6. Why do some stores consider the term "free publicity" a misnomer?
7. What types of free publicity should a major store look for in your city?
8. Develop a special-purpose publicity program for a sporting goods store.
9. Do the same as in Question 8 for a high-fashion apparel specialty store.
10. In Table 13-3 it is stated that specially planned purchases by the consumer are highest in liquor stores and lowest in supermarkets. Explain.
11. How does a firm use space as a supplement to a merchandising strategy?
12. Why has the use of window displays declined in suburban areas?
13. Why has the use of trading stamps declined in recent years?

Retail Selling

14

OBJECTIVES YOU SHOULD MEET

1. *Distinguish* between self-service and self-selection.
2. *Discuss* some of the major barriers to maintaining an efficient sales force.
3. *Explain* why many retail firms maintain retail sales people.
4. *Distinguish* among the four major methods of compensating retail sales people.
5. *Cite* the types of products that lend themselves to telephone selling.

One of the clearest impressions a customer gets from a store comes from dealing with the firm's sales personnel. This can be a negative or a positive impression.

Firms strive to give the consumer a strong positive impression through the salespeople, but it is obvious to even the most casual shopper that consumers get many negative impressions when shopping, and from this point of view the management of the store has failed.

The problem of developing an efficient sales force that creates a favorable image is perhaps one of the most challenging tasks facing management. It involves overcoming obstacles such as low wages, low status, and organizational problems. In addition one must consider the great demands on the salesperson such as the seasonality of the business and the tremendous number of new products that are always moving onto the retailer's shelves.

In facing up to these problems the retailer has little choice. One of his very few alternatives seems to be to sell his merchandise on a self-service or self-selection basis. Even this can be done only in the sale of a limited number of product categories.

The retail sales worker is one of the lowest paid workers in the national labor force. As a result, retail selling (particularly in large stores) is often conducted by inexperienced and unskilled personnel. This has led to a debate in retailing circles as to the value of retail selling. Some observers bluntly state that the fewer the barriers between the customer and the merchandise, the better for the store. Others, however, point out that many firms which have developed selling to a high level benefit from its results; they conclude therefore that proper selling is an important asset to a store. Both views are extreme and there is probably some truth in each statement. There are instances where eliminating the sales force resulted in more profitable business and, conversely, where adding skill to the sales force increased sales.

Determining the Amount of Selling

On the surface, making a management decision as to the role of selling in the firm is simple. From experience, however, we have found that the elements which determine the right decisions are difficult to isolate and more difficult to measure. Nevertheless, management can make only three choices.

1. It can maintain a completely self-service store. By definition, this means a store devoid of personal selling.
2. It can maintain a fully staffed store.
3. It can maintain a combination of the above, that is, a self-selection store or a store where some departments are fully staffed and others are operated on a self-service basis.

Self-selection, in this case, is defined as the procedure whereby the customer selects the merchandise by himself. It differs from *self-service* in that the sales person locates, wraps, and performs some of the processing functions needed to complete the transaction. The supermarket food store is an example of self-service in operation. Self-selection takes place in many variety stores, where the customer may select the item and then hand it to a salesperson, who proceeds to collect the money and wrap the merchandise. In some cases, the salesperson may actually have to locate the exact item for the customer.

Choosing the proper sales arrangement for a retail store depends on various factors, some of which will be discussed below. However, the reader should bear in mind that there are many varieties of sales arrangements that work for the same types of goods. For example, the sales organization of the drug department varies considerably in the corner drugstore, the department store, and the discount house. The last one may use self-service; the others may prefer self-selection.

Maintaining Self-Service

The trend toward self-service operations during the postwar period suggests that substantial demand exists for this type of arrangement. In a sense, it signifies that consumers are willing to serve themselves and perform many of the functions of the salesperson. A self-service arrangement that has been around since the 1930's is the supermarket. In no other retail operation has acceptance of self-service been as widespread as in the food field. The shopper in a modern supermarket strolls through the store choosing items (some on her shopping list — others not) at her leisure. When she completes her purchasing, she takes the merchandise to a checkout counter where the purchases are tabulated and put into bags. At this point she pays for the merchandise and in some cases may choose to have the packages delivered to her home or car or may simply carry the complete order home herself. Variations of this technique are almost always found, even within the supermarket. For example, the supermarket may contain a bakery department or appetizer counter where sales are made by experienced salespeople.

Many other types of retail firms rely on self-service arrangements. The "hard goods" and "apparel" discount houses which have appeared largely during the postwar period have accepted these methods. Even the gasoline station has been affected, with the introduction of the self-service gasoline pump and the automatic vending of products.

Self-Service Factors

To make a proper decision about developing a completely self-service operation, consideration must be given to the consumers' possible reaction to the goods *within the store*. The last phrase "within the store" refers to the size of the store and the ability to present merchandise adequately. These two factors are, of course, almost a prerequisite to a self-service operation. A narrow store, in most cases, will not afford management an opportunity to adequately display or stock merchandise in the open. Probably management would choose to display a small selection of each item for sale and carry adequate depth on each item in stock areas behind counters, on wall shelves, or in a stockroom. The small "momma and papa" independent grocery is an example of this arrangement. In many cases, this outlet is forced to wait on customers simply because space does not allow the operators the liberty of maintaining a wide-aisle, large-fixture self-service outlet.

However, given the adequate space, the retailer must then determine the consumer reaction to selling goods in this manner. He defines the consumer reaction by determining whether the consumer favors this type of arrangement and whether goods can be sold more effectively in this way. For example, relatively few firms have been able to sell high-priced men's clothing on a self-service basis. The consensus seems to be that the male shopper for this type of item prefers to consult a salesman and looks to the salesman for advice as to general fit, color, and the workmanship of the garment. Conversely, shirts, ties, and underwear are examples of men's furnishings that are sold in great quantity on a self-service basis in outlets such as chain and discount stores.

The Retail Selling Function

Retail sales promotion techniques can bring a customer into a store (in the case of telephone or mail order advertising this of course does not apply). However, it usually takes a certain amount of selling to complete the transaction. Just how much varies with the type of store, the merchandise being sold, and many other variables that will be discussed in this section.

Though one should recognize the trend toward automation, self-service, and self-selection in servicing the customers, selling is still being performed in the majority of retail stores. In the next section, the role of retail selling will be carefully examined by judging its efficiency and observing some of its problems. In addition, retail selling will be viewed from the point of view of management decision making. What elements go into the decision to maintain or do away with a retail sales force? How do we determine the size of the sales force? What are the consumer attitudes toward retail selling? These are some of the questions that retail management needs to think about and answer in order to function properly. Bear in mind, however, that retail selling is something more than an attitude; it is a communication function. It cannot operate in a vacuum; it must be integrated into the whole communication mix. Though we treat it in these chapters as being apart from the whole, it is vital to remember its relationship rather than its distinctions.

Nature of the Consumer

The importance of developing efficiency in selling can best be understood if we realize that a large percentage of consumers shop around. Studies show that for every 100 transactions completed in one store there were 23 more completed only after the consumer shopped in more than two stores. In terms of dollars, for every $100 spent in shopping in the first store only, an additional $47 (or about 50 per cent more) was spent in shopping in two or more stores.[1] Other data have also appeared in recent years supporting the view that a large segment of the shoppers do shop around. Thus, management has been rightfully concerned with its sales force and particularly with the problems associated with it.

Where and Why Sales Are Lost

By the very nature of the goods sold, it is obvious that some consumers will shop around more for some articles and less for others. Table 14-1, derived from the

TABLE 14-1 **Transactions Completed After Customer Shopped at Least Two Stores for Every 100 Completed in the First Store, by Type of Merchandise**

Items	Number	Dollars
Housewares and hardware	18	$28
Boy's wear	26	30
Miscellaneous merchandise	15	32
Domestics	24	32
Infants' items	28	34
Men's wear	22	35
Girls' wear	29	37
Women's wear	27	45
Home furnishings and major appliances	43	91

Source: Harrie F. Lewis, *op. cit.,* p.57.

[1] Harrie F. Lewis, "Lost Sales Opportunities in Retailing," *Harvard Business Review,* Vol. XXVII, No. 1 (January 1949), p. 55.

above-mentioned studies, shows the differences in shopping around for goods. Note that the greatest increase in shopping around occurs in items that are relatively high priced or that involve fashion and styling. This table ties in with our previous discussions concerning self-service and self-selection. The data would help the retailer make a decision as to what products in his store are most likely to need the aid of sales people and what types lend themselves to self-selection.

It is pertinent to examine briefly the types of products sold in the "apparel discount" store. Table 14-2 lists the products sold on a self-service basis in these stores. Note again that certain categories of merchandise are missing or are ranked low in their acceptance by consumers. For example, women's shoes are not sold to a great extent by these stores nor are better dresses or women's coats. These categories continue to require the aid of salespeople.

Categories of Merchandise Purchased Regularly at Discount Houses by Over 10 Per Cent of Discount Shoppers TABLE 14-2

	Percentage
Toys and games	40.8
Notions	29.4
Men's sport shirts	29.0
Men's underwear	28.3
Auto accessories	27.1
Men's work clothes	26.2
Garden supplies and equipment	26.0
Children's clothes and accessories	25.3
Draperies and curtains	24.8
Housewares (including small appliances)	24.3
Women's underwear, slips, and nightgowns	23.8
Records, sheet music, and instruments	23.3
Cameras and film	23.0
Women's hosiery	22.5
Men's slacks	22.4
Cosmetics	22.3
Drugs	22.1
Boys' underwear	22.0
Men's dress shirts	21.2
Women's blouses, skirts, and sportswear	21.2
Radios, phonographs, televisions	20.8
Infant's wear	20.2
Stationery	20.0
Sporting goods	19.8
Lamps and shades	19.2
Boy's sport shirts	18.6
Boy's slacks	18.6
Women's corsets and brassieres	18.4
Women's handbags and small leather goods	17.8
Books and magazines	17.5

TABLE 14-2 (Cont.)

	Percentage
Major household appliances	17.0
Women's aprons and housedresses	16.8
Women's handkerchiefs	16.8
Women's gloves	16.8
Men's suburban outerwear	16.8
Men's ties	16.8
Women's dresses	15.7
Candy	15.2
Men's accessories (wallets, belts, cufflinks)	15.0
Boy's accessories	14.3
Boy's dress shirts	14.1
Millinery	14.1
China and glassware	13.9
Women's neckwear and scarfs	13.7
Boys' ties	13.4
Linens and towels	12.5
Subteen clothes and accessories	12.5
Boy's coats and outerwear	12.2
Laces, trimmings, ribbons	12.1
Costume jewelry	12.0
Women's coats and suits	11.7
Teen clothes and accessories	11.6
Women's shoes	10.9
Domestics — muslins and sheeting	10.8
Silverware, clocks, watches	10.0

Source: David J. Rachman and Linda J. Kemp, "Profile of the Boston Discount House Customer," *Journal of Retailing,* Vol. 39, No. 2 (Summer, 1963), p. 8.

Barriers to Retail Selling

The barriers to creating an effective retail sales force are many. Perhaps the most difficult to overcome is the low wages offered salespeople. A wage comparison is shown in Table 14-3. Here one sees that retail workers have the lowest earnings among six major industries. The earnings differential ranges to $1.41 per hour. Even when compared to service industries, the range differential is considerable. Thus, the selection of retail-selling employees is limited to the unskilled and those among the lowest wage levels in our society.

In spite of the low wages, the cost of retail selling can be considerable. For instance, in Table 14-4 one sees that the selling cost as a percentage of sales ranges from a low of 5 per cent to a high of 9.8 per cent. Measured as a percentage of the stores total expenses, selling expense among gift stores is responsible for over one third of the store's expenses. Among the larger department stores, selling expense

Average Hourly Earnings of Employees in Selected Industries TABLE 14-3

Industry	Average Hourly Earnings
Transportation and public utilities	$3.85
Wholesale trade	3.44
Manufacturing	3.36
Finance, insurance, and real estate	3.07
Services	2.84
Retail trade	2.44

Source: Department of Labor, Bureau of Labor Statistics.

Comparison of Selling Costs and Total Expenses of Retail Firms TABLE 14-4

	Selling Costs as a Percentage of Sales	Total Expense as a Percentage of Sales	Selling Costs as a Percentage of Total Expense
Department and specialty store	7.73%	31.76%	24.3%
Furniture store	7.21	36.41	19.8
Gift and novelty shops	9.79	26.74	36.6
Jewelry stores	9.8	38.5	25.5
Appliance and radio-TV dealers	5.0	28.3	17.7
Mens wear stores	9.7	35.1	27.6

Sources: 1. National Retail Merchants Association
2. National Home Furnishings Association
3. Accounting Corporation of America (wages excluding proprietor's wages)
4. Retail Jewelers of America, Inc. (sales volume over $500,000)
5. National Appliance and Radio-TV Dealers Association (sales volume over $500,000)
6. Menswear Retailers of America

accounts for almost one quarter of the total expenses of the store. These statistics seem to indicate that salespeople represent a costly service.

Of course the high cost of selling can be offset by increasing the sales of the individual salesperson. Should the department store be able to double the sales volume of each salesperson, its sales ratio would be cut in half.

This principle is illustrated by Figure 14-1. One can determine that if a salesperson is receiving a salary of $90 per week (1) and our firm has a goal of maintaining a 15 per cent salary to sales ratio, (2) this salesperson must sell $600 worth of merchandise (3) during this period. If he fails to achieve this sales goal and sells only $500 (4), the salesperson warrants a $75 salary (6).

As if low wage levels are not enough, one might consider that society has relegated the salesclerk job to a low rung in terms of social class. In a study of the prestige ratings of 90 occupational groups, a retail clerk ranked 70th.[2] The

---

[2] Robert W. Hodge, Paul M. Siegel and Peter H. Rossi, "Occupational Prestige in the United States 1925-1963," in Reinhard Bendix and Seymour Martin Lipset, eds., *Class, Status, and Power,* 2nd ed. (New York: The Free Press, 1966), pp. 324-325.

Source: *Expenses in Retail Business* (Dayton, Ohio: National Cash Register Company, n.d.), p. 46.

FIGURE 14-1 How Much a Salesperson Should Sell

SALARY
SALES

(6) (1)

SALARY COST

$72.50	$75.00	$77.50	$80.00	$82.50	$85.00	$87.50	$90.00	$92.50	$95.00	$97.50	$100.00
48.3	50.0	51.7	53.3	55.0	56.7	58.3	60.0	61.7	63.3	65.0	66.7
45.3	46.9	48.4	50.0	51.6	53.1	54.7	56.3	57.8	59.4	60.9	62.5
42.6	44.1	45.6	47.1	48.5	50.0	51.5	52.9	54.4	55.9	57.4	58.8
40.3	41.7	43.0	44.4	45.8	47.2	48.6	50.0	51.4	52.8	54.2	55.6
38.1	39.5	40.8	42.1	43.4	44.7	46.1	47.4	48.7	50.0	51.3	52.6
36.2	37.5	38.7	40.0	41.3	42.5	43.8	45.0	46.3	47.5	48.8	50.0
34.5	35.7	36.9	38.1	39.3	40.5	41.7	42.9	44.0	45.2	46.4	47.6
32.9	34.1	35.2	36.4	37.5	38.6	39.8	40.9	42.0	43.2	44.3	45.5
31.5	32.6	33.7	34.8	35.9	37.0	38.0	39.1	40.2	41.3	42.4	43.5
30.2	31.2	32.3	33.3	34.4	35.4	36.5	37.5	38.5	39.6	40.6	41.7
29.0	30.0	31.0	32.0	33.0	34.0	35.0	36.0	37.0	38.0	39.0	40.0
27.9	28.8	29.8	30.8	31.7	32.7	33.7	34.6	35.6	36.5	37.5	38.5
26.8	27.8	28.7	29.6	30.6	31.5	32.4	33.3	34.3	35.2	36.1	37.0
25.9	26.8	27.7	28.6	29.5	30.4	31.3	32.1	33.0	33.9	34.8	35.7
25.0	25.9	26.7	27.6	28.4	29.3	30.2	31.0	31.9	32.8	33.6	34.5
24.2	25.0	25.8	26.7	27.5	28.3	29.2	30.0	30.8	31.7	32.5	33.4
22.3	23.1	23.8	24.6	25.4	26.2	26.9	27.7	28.5	29.2	30.0	30.8
20.7	21.4	22.1	22.9	23.6	24.3	25.0	25.7	26.4	27.1	27.9	28.6
19.3	20.0	20.7	21.3	22.0	22.7	23.3	24.0	24.7	25.3	26.0	26.7
18.1	18.8	19.4	20.0	20.6	21.3	21.9	22.5	23.1	23.8	24.4	25.0
17.0	17.6	18.2	18.8	19.4	20.0	20.6	21.2	21.8	22.4	22.9	23.5
16.1	16.7	17.2	17.8	18.3	18.9	19.4	20.0	20.6	21.1	21.7	22.2
15.3	15.8	16.3	16.8	17.4	17.9	18.4	18.9	19.5	20.0	20.5	21.1
14.5	15.0	15.5	16.0	16.5	17.0	17.5	18.0	18.5	19.0	19.5	20.0
13.8	14.3	14.8	15.2	15.7	16.2	16.7	17.1	17.6	18.1	18.6	19.0
13.2	13.6	14.1	14.5	15.0	15.5	16.4	16.8	17.3	17.7	18.2	18.7
12.6	13.0	13.5	13.9	14.3	14.8	15.2	15.7	16.1	16.5	17.0	17.4
12.1	12.5	12.9	13.3	13.8	14.2	14.6	15.0	15.4	15.8	16.3	16.7
11.6	12.0	12.4	12.8	13.2	13.6	14.0	14.4	14.8	15.2	15.6	16.0
11.1	11.5	11.9	12.3	12.7	13.1	13.5	13.9	14.2	14.6	15.0	15.4
10.7	11.1	11.5	11.8	12.2	12.6	13.0	13.3	13.7	14.1	14.4	14.8
10.4	10.7	11.1	11.4	11.8	12.1	12.5	12.9	13.2	13.6	13.9	14.3
10.0	10.3	10.7	11.0	11.4	11.7	12.1	12.4	12.8	13.1	13.4	13.7
9.7	10.0	10.3	10.7	11.0	11.3	11.7	12.0	12.3	12.7	13.0	13.3
9.3	9.7	10.0	10.3	10.6	11.0	11.3	11.6	11.9	12.3	12.6	12.9
9.1	9.4	9.7	10.0	10.3	10.6	10.9	11.3	11.6	11.9	12.2	12.5
8.8	9.1			10.6	10.9	11.2	11.5				

PERCENTAGES

WEEKLY SALARIES

$160.00	$165.00	$170.00	$175.00	$180.00	$185.00	$190.00	$195.00	$200.00	$205.00	$210.00	$215.00	$220.00	$225.00	$230.00	AMOUNT OF WEEKLY SALES
106.7	110.0	113.3	116.7	120.0	123.3	126.6	130.0	133.3	136.6	140.0	143.3	146.6	150.0	153.3	$ 150
100.0	103.1	106.3	109.4	112.5	115.6	118.8	121.8	125.5	128.1	131.2	134.3	137.5	140.6	143.7	160
94.1	97.1	100.0	102.9	105.9	108.9	111.7	114.7	117.6	120.5	123.5	126.4	129.4	132.3	135.2	170
88.9	91.7	94.4	97.2	100.0	102.7	105.5	108.3	111.1	113.8	116.6	119.4	122.2	125.0	127.7	180
84.2	86.8	89.5	92.1	94.7	97.4	100.0	102.6	105.2	107.8	110.5	113.1	115.7	118.4	121.0	190
80.0	82.5	85.0	87.5	90.0	92.5	95.0	97.5	100.0	102.5	105.0	107.5	110.0	112.5	115.0	200
76.2	78.6	81.0	83.3	85.7	88.1	90.4	92.8	95.2	97.6	100.0	102.3	104.7	107.1	109.5	210
72.7	75.0	77.3	79.5	81.8	84.1	86.3	88.6	90.9	93.1	95.4	97.7	100.0	102.2	104.5	220
69.6	71.7	73.9	76.1	78.3	80.4	82.6	84.7	86.9	89.1	91.3	93.4	95.6	97.8	100.0	230
66.7	68.8	70.8	72.9	75.0	77.1	79.1	81.2	83.3	85.4	87.5	89.5	91.6	93.7	95.8	240
64.0	66.0	68.0	70.0	72.0	74.0	76.0	78.0	80.0	82.0	84.0	86.0	88.0	90.0	92.0	250
61.5	63.5	65.4	67.3	69.2	71.1	73.1	75.0	76.9	78.8	80.7	82.7	84.6	86.5	88.4	260
59.3	61.1	63.0	64.8	66.7	68.5	70.3	72.2	74.0	75.7	77.7	79.6	81.4	83.3	85.1	270
57.1	58.9	60.7	62.5	64.3	66.0	67.8	69.6	71.4	73.2	75.0	76.7	78.5	80.3	82.1	280
55.2	56.9	58.6	60.3	62.1	63.8	65.5	67.2	68.9	70.6	72.4	74.1	75.8	77.5	79.3	290
53.3	55.0	56.7	58.3	60.0	61.6	63.3	65.0	66.6	68.3	70.0	71.6	73.3	75.0	76.6	300
49.2	50.8	52.3	53.8	55.4	56.9	58.4	60.0	61.5	63.0	64.6	66.1	67.6	69.2	70.7	325
45.7	47.1	48.6	50.0	51.4	52.9	54.2	55.7	57.1	58.5	60.0	61.4	62.8	64.2	65.7	350
42.7	44.0	45.3	46.7	48.0	49.3	50.6	52.0	53.3	54.6	56.0	57.3	58.6	60.0	61.3	375
40.0	41.3	43.0	43.8	45.0	46.2	47.5	48.7	50.0	51.2	52.5	53.7	55.0	56.2	57.5	400
37.6	38.8	40.0	41.2	42.4	43.5	44.7	45.8	47.0	48.2	49.4	50.5	51.7	52.9	54.1	425
35.6	36.7	37.8	38.9	40.0	41.1	42.2	43.3	44.4	45.5	46.6	47.7	48.8	49.9	51.0	450
33.7	34.7	35.8	36.8	37.9	38.9	40.0	41.0	42.1	43.1	44.2	45.2	46.3	47.3	48.4	475
32.0	33.0	34.0	35.0	36.0	37.0	38.0	39.0	40.0	41.0	42.0	43.0	44.0	45.0	46.0	500
30.5	31.4	32.4	33.3	34.3	35.2	36.1	37.1	38.1	39.0	40.0	40.9	41.9	42.8	43.8	525
29.1	30.0	30.9	31.8	32.7	33.6	34.5	35.4	36.3	37.2	38.1	39.0	40.0	40.9	41.8	550
27.8	28.7	29.0	30.4	31.3	32.1	33.0	33.9	34.7	35.6	36.5	37.3	38.2	39.1	40.0	575
26.7	27.5	28.3	29.2	30.0	30.8	31.6	32.5	33.3	34.1	35.0	35.8	36.6	37.5	38.3	600
25.6	26.4	27.2	28.0	28.8	29.6	30.4	31.2	32.0	32.8	33.6	34.4	35.2	36.0	36.8	625
24.6	25.4	26.2	26.9	27.7	28.4	29.2	30.0	30.7	31.5	32.3	33.0	33.8	34.6	35.3	650
23.7	24.4	25.2	25.9	26.7	27.4	28.1	28.8	29.6	30.3	31.1	31.8	32.5	33.3	34.0	675
22.9	23.6	24.3	25.0	25.7	26.4	27.1	27.8	28.5	29.2	30.0	30.7	31.4	32.1	32.8	700
22.1	22.8	23.4	24.1	24.8	25.5	26.2	26.8	27.5	28.2	28.9	29.6	30.3	31.0	31.7	725
21.3	22.0	22.7	23.3	24.0	24.6	25.3	26.0	26.6	27.3	28.0	28.6	29.3	30.0	30.6	750
20.6	21.3	21.9	22.6	23.2	23.8	24.5	25.1	25.8	26.4	27.1	27.7	28.3	29.0	29.6	775
20.0	20.6	21.3	21.9	22.5	23.1	23.7	24.3	25.0	25.6	26.2	26.8	27.5			800

(4) (3)

importance of this finding is that even if wages were increased somehow, the talented worker would probably still not enter retail selling because of its low ranking on the social-class scale. It is interesting to note in this same table that the outside salesmen rank 57th.

Another barrier to creating a quality retail sales force is the fluctuating demand in retail stores, which is obvious during various seasons of the year. The large department store faces the awesome task of hiring hundreds of salespeople during the Christmas buying season, and the children's store faces the same problem during the back-to-school season in early fall. The hiring of a large temporary staff causes the retailer to lower his standards of quality in order to meet the demand of the customer for this relatively short period of time.

The fluctuating demand within the day and the week also causes severe staffing problems in the retail store. The typical suburban department or specialty store is faced with doing the bulk of its business during the evening hours, and before noon most such stores are not busy. Conversely, the downtown store is more likely to be extremely busy at the lunch hour and around the 6 o'clock dinner hour, these being the hours the office worker has available for shopping.

The fluctuation of sales in retail stores during the typical week also varies. Department stores usually find that Saturday is a particularly busy day. In supermarkets, sales tend to concentrate toward the end of the week because people ordinarily get paid at that time. To further complicate the problem many stores are now open on Sundays, which forces the firms to hire larger staffs. Fluctuating demand and increased selling days tend to complicate management's problem of properly staffing the store.

Other barriers also exist. The large number of products carried by the typical store makes it difficult for the salesclerk to know enough to meet all the customer's needs. A typical salesperson in a department store may have a thousand or more products in her department, making it almost impossible for the individual to become knowledgeable about all the products in the department. The constant flow of new products tends to reduce limited knowledge to an even more superficial level.

Positive Aspects of Retail Selling

1) Although establishing a quality retail sales force in a store poses problems, accomplishing this goal can make a firm successful. The importance of this thought should not be underestimated.

For example, it is true that many goods offered in stores can be sold only through retail salespeople. Men's high-priced suits, jewelry, and cosmetics are just a few of these items. Few retailers, for instance, have been able to sell men's higher-priced suits on a self-service basis. Most stores featuring such merchandise have found that only low-priced suits can be sold in this manner. Many cosmetic firms have had similar experiences. Some of the top cosmetic firms tend to get retailers to hire trained cosmeticians to sell their products. Some, such as Revlon, go as far as to pay part of their salaries.

2) Another positive aspect of retail selling is that if the retail firms can establish a high level of quality selling, it has a competitive edge that is hard to duplicate. Though a firm can match a competitor's price cuts or advertising programs, it is much more difficult to train a sales force to offer quality service. Establishing a quality sales force usually takes years of work. In some cases a competitive store may be so large that its ability to accomplish this may be practically nonexistent.

3) An efficient retail sales force is also useful in reducing shoplifting by customers. In recent years the amount of stock pilferage has become enormous. Much is blamed on the salesclerk who leaves counters unattended or ignores the potential shoplifter.

Last, the attempt to improve the quality of the salespeople has been helped by the movement to the suburbs. Here, the retailer finds a greater reservoir of potential sales personnel, mostly because the stores provide one of the few areas of employment in the suburbs. In addition, the people living in the suburbs have attained higher educational levels and thus function better in the retail selling position.

Though in most cases compensation in the retail field is paid for by the store, there are deviations from this. In particular, numerous plans have been devised

Sources of Wages

whereby the manufacturer pays the employees' salaries. These plans fall into two different categories: compensation based on sales and special inducement plans.

Special compensation plans are usually found in departments that have earned consumer brand acceptance. For example, many of the major cosmetic companies pay a proportion of the salaries of retail sales employees. As a matter of policy, many of these firms actually recruit, hire, and train these employees. As a reward to the companies for compensating their employees, the stores in turn assign them to the counters featuring the companies' products. These salespeople in many cases also perform the functions of taking inventory and actually recording merchandise. Compensation plans in this kind of arrangement are usually based on volume of sales generated by line of product.

Less elaborate and less costly are the plans whereby manufacturers at various times offer retail sales personnel special monetary inducements to sell their merchandise. In some cases, these inducements are in the form of a flat dollar rate for selling the product. This form of compensation is usually found in the home furnishing departments of stores. Contests are also often used as an incentive. Free vacations and merchandise are among other major incentives.

The purpose of all of this is to persuade the retail sales employee to sell the manufacturer's product. There are two failings to these programs. One is that they are usually not continuous, so that if the manufacturer drops the program his sales may decline more than might ordinarily be expected. One author suggests another problem connected with this program: the retailer loses control of his merchandising program.[3] In essence, he notes that by offering special inducements the manufacturer may be violating the retailer's planned program by selling less profitable merchandise. Nevertheless, the manufacturer in some cases finds this technique a useful device for selling merchandise without much extended effort on his part.

Store Compensation

Retailers use four major methods of compensating salespeople:

1. Straight salary
2. Salary plus commission
3. Straight commission
4. Variations such as quotas and special inducements

Straight salary and salary plus commission are among the most widely used methods of compensation in retailing. Straight salary simply means that a salesperson receives a wage by the hour or on a weekly basis (the latter based on an agreed-upon work schedule). Typically, a retail worker may receive a salary of $90 per week. This method, of course, suffers from the obvious disadvantage of not offering the worker an incentive to sell more. In other words, average weekly sales of $1,000 are not compensated for if the department average is only $800. On the other hand, some firms will take the higher average into consideration when adjusting salaries paid in the next period.

---

[3]See T. Dart Ellsworth, "Do Stores Favor Manufacturer-Paid Spiffs," *Journal of Retailing,* Vol. XXX, No. 3 (Fall, 1954), p. 138.

To overcome the straight salary disadvantage, many of the larger stores conceived a salary program with a commission incentive. For example, one large New York department store offers all salespeople an additional 1 per cent commission on all sales. It is believed that this commission motivates a salesperson to increase sales and offer consumers suggestions in further purchasing, and generally strikes a balance between a straight salary and straight commission plan.

The straight commission plan (or full incentive plan) tries to overcome the failings of both the straight salary and salary plus commission plans. The latter plan, it has been thought, does not offer the salesperson enough of an incentive. The commission plan, however, pays the salesperson only what he earns (though in most cases the salesperson is allowed to draw in advance against a special account). This plan, it is hoped, induces salespeople to attempt to sell as much as possible and hence earn a higher salary. From management's point of view, its major advantage is that it sets wages in advance. For example, a salesman may be paid a 5 per cent commission; knowing this management can plan sales costs at this level. In reality, however, this plan cannot function in this manner in many retail firms. Typically, in the large firm we find departments that do not quite generate enough business for a salesperson to make an adequate salary. A hobby shop or patterns department, for example, may not do enough business to cover a commission: if a department does less than $50,000 worth of business a year it can hardly support salaries for the two salespeople needed to cover the department. As a result, in many of the large stores there is usually a dual policy in effect; that is, some departments pay straight commission, others a straight salary, and others a combination of both.

To digress briefly, the reader may wonder why a large store should have departments that cannot afford to pay a living wage to personnel. The answer is simple and stems from the overall objectives of the firm discussed earlier. Many stores, particularly large department or variety chains, have developed the policy of carrying all kinds of merchandise. Some of these departments are profitable; others are not. In either case, however, they must be carried to fulfill the firm's policy. It is, of course, the belief and goal of management that in carrying out this policy the firm will make an overall profit.

Variations

Though the above plans predominate, variations do exist. For example, some firms have developed plans that establish quotas for each salesperson. Salespeople exceeding their quotas are offered additional compensation usually in the form of commission over and above their quota. Profit-sharing plans have also appeared in recent years; some are company-wide and include executives and managerial employees.

The complexities of the retail firm produce many problems for management. Outstanding among them is the organization and control of the sales force. Again, the sales force in the manufacturing firm is more easily directed since the single manufacturer sells relatively few products (in comparison with the retailer), and rarely deals directly with the ultimate consumer.

Organizational Problems

The retail salesman, on the other hand, deals only with the public, is involved with the sale of numerous products, and usually has only limited knowledge about these products. Organizing and controlling this function within the large store can be very complex. The smaller store (the owner-management type) avoids many of these problems because of its direct control relationship with the salespeople. The lack of direct control and the delegation of power within the large retail organization have resulted in further complicating this situation. Where buying is conducted on the departmental level, the problem is compounded since both the buying and selling are conducted basically within the confines of one store. As a result, two groups have an interest in the selling techniques of the department, namely, the sales supervisor and the buyer.

Figure 14-2 demonstrates this organizational problem. Careful examination of this chart (typical of a department store) outlines this conflict. The main store pattern, in particular, shows the dual loyalty of salespeople — to both the buying and store service groups. Obviously, a dichotomy of this nature presents basic management conflicts. For example, and most important, which view prevails? The answer, or so it seems to observers, is that there is a basic conflict of interest between the service store management group and the merchandising division. The merchandising group has been characterized as being sales-volume oriented; the former group-expense oriented.

There have been many attempts to resolve this conflict. Recently firms have attempted to eliminate the merchandising organization from this dual allegiance. Macy's in New York has turned the supervision of salespeople over completely to the service department of the store.

Relationships

The fact that the personal goals of many salespeople differ from those of the firm represents a problem in itself. A number of studies have pointed out the extent of this conflict. Resolving this problem, however, is not simple. One study of the salesperson in action showed that group pressures within the selling group had, to a great extent, limited the sales volume of each individual in the department. For example, a study of a children's department in a department store showed that each employee's daily sales volume tended to remain within a range of all other employees. One factor cited by the author as causing this tendency for the sales staff to sell around an average was the group pressures exerted by a number of the senior salesclerks. Though many of the pressures were subtle, they existed nonetheless, and seemed to take precedence over the directions (and goals) of the firm management. The few salesclerks who exceeded the group norms by selling well above the average (incidentally by following the directions of management) were socially ostracized and characterized as "grabbers" by their fellow workers.[4]

Thus, firms trying to solve the problem of improving their sales productivity must not only contend with the organizational problems but must face up to the psychological relationships among the selling group members.

---

[4]See George F. F. Lombard, *Behavior in a Selling Group* (Boston: Harvard University, 1955), p. 90.

Typical Plan of Organization presently in Use by a Representative Company under a Basic Main Store System   **FIGURE 14-2**

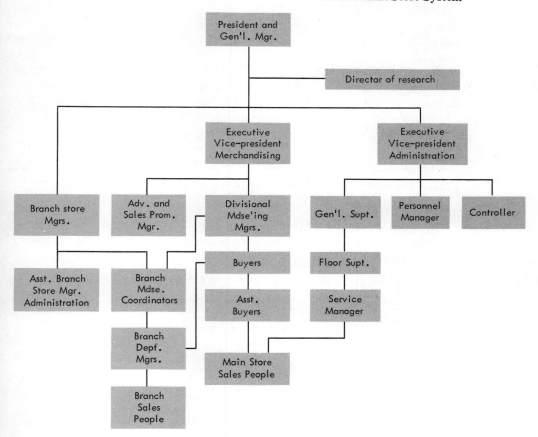

Adapted from *Survey of organization of Multiunit Department and Specialty Stores,* National Retail Merchants Association, 1961, p. 14.

Not all selling in a store involves a one-to-one relationship with a customer. Most notable is telephone selling in the store.

Telephone selling in stores comes about in one of two ways. The most usual is that the store offers the opportunity to purchase advertised products over the phone. In some cases the customer call may be in response to a direct mail piece such as a catalog. Most telephone selling, however, occurs in response to an advertisement placed by the retailer. Telephone response from customers offers the retailer an additional avenue of sales volume.

The other means is direct phone solicitation by the retailer. Sears, Roebuck follows this policy by regularly calling customers who have made a recent purchase through their mail-order catalog.

However, not all telephone selling is looked upon as a total plus by management. For instance, the acceptance of phone sales on advertised items defeats the purpose

Telephone Selling

269

of most advertising, in that the customer is not persuaded to enter the store, where he is likely to buy more.

Additionally, the profits on telephone selling may be lower, as an advertised item is usually a lower-profit item and involves a delivery cost. As was noted in one study, the rate of returns of merchandise from phone sales is higher, for obvious reasons.[5]

The costs of telephone selling may be even higher when the firm sets up an in-store telephone bureau manned by telephone operators. In the above study over three quarters of the firms indicated that they used such a system.

Product Sold

Not all products can be easily sold through telephone selling. Usually, high-priced merchandise and fashioned goods are difficult to sell in this manner. One assumes that most customers would rather see fashion merchandise before making a purchase.

On the other hand, the list of products that are best sellers over the telephone are extensive. Table 14-5 lists some of the best sellers according to a study made by a phone company.

TABLE 14-5   Top-Ranked Selected Items Consumers Would Buy by Phone if Available

Bed linens
Children's underwear
House dresses
Kitchen needs
Men's socks
Men's underwear
Sewing needs
Stationery
Toys and games
Women's hose
Women's underwear

Source: *Stores,* August, 1968, p. 23.

In examining the list one can conclude that the best-selling items in telephone selling are:

1. usually staples.
2. generally low-priced.

SUMMARY

The problems of maintaining a sales force in a store can be avoided by maintaining a self-service store in which the customer waits on himself, as in the

[5]Stores, August, 1968, p. 23.

supermarket. A compromise can be reached by providing for self-selection with a salesperson available if needed. Determination of which type of service to offer is usually based on the customer's willingness to accept a certain type of service for a particular kind of merchandise.

There are many barriers to maintaining a sales force within a store. Some of the more important are the low wages and low status of retail selling, fluctuating demand in the store, and the thousands of products that a salesperson must be familiar with.

In spite of low wages, the selling costs of stores are still high. In the large department stores selling costs account for one quarter of all expenses, and in the smaller gift store they account for about one third of all store expenses.

On the more positive side, there is no substitute for retail selling in the sale of many products. If a firm can establish a quality sales force it is very difficult for a competitor to establish a similar sales force in response. An efficient sales force can also reduce the amount of customer pilferage. The quality of salespeople has improved in the suburbs, where retailing provides one of the major sources of employment.

Retailers use four major methods of compensating salespeople, namely, straight salary, salary plus commission, straight commission, and variations such as quotas and special inducements, which include bonuses and profit-sharing.

Organizational problems within the store also exist. One particular problem is the dual loyalty within the large departmentalized store, if the salesperson reports to both the service supervisor and the buyer. The second problem revolves around the conflicts between the goals of the store and its management versus the goals of a person within a store selling group. Here the salesperson is concerned with group pressures.

Not all retail selling involves a one-to-one relationship with a customer. One of the more useful techniques is telephone selling, allowing the customer to purchase a product from an advertisement or in response to a catalog mailing. Some retailers actively seek business through direct phone solicitation.

Because all phone sales involve delivery and special handling many retailers find that this type of selling can be costly. Not all types of merchandise can be sold by telephone; as a general rule, staples and low-priced items are most likely to be sold in this manner.

QUESTIONS

1. How can group pressures influence sales productivity in a selling department? How can these same group pressures be used to attain the goals of management?

2. Discuss two organizational problems faced by the departmentalized store and their influence on its ability to communicate with the customer.

3. Distinguish between self-selection and self-service selling.

4. Why is retail selling a low-status position? What counter-arguments could you offer to this status ranking?

5. Offer three important reasons why a retailer needs to create an efficient sales staff.

6. Is telephone selling more or less expensive than in-store selling? Why?

7. According to Figure 14-1, how much should a person earning $97.50 a week sell if a 13 per cent salary-to-sales ratio is to be maintained? Should he sell only $575, what should his salary be?

8. During the Christmas season a large store may sell about 25 per cent of its total annual volume. Discuss some of the more difficult problems that this season places on those involved in the management of the sales force?

9. It has been stated that unions have made few inroads in retailing in spite of the low wages offered. Explain some of the practical problems a union may have in organizing retail stores.

10. List five types of goods that can be easily sold on a self-service basis. Do these items possess similar characteristics?

11. In essence, does the small retailer have the same sales problems as the large retailer?

12. Discuss the disadvantages of using a straight commission system in a retail selling department.

13. Compare the problems of selling in a retail store and selling for a manufacturer.

INTRODUCTION TO
THE PHYSICAL DISTRIBUTION MIX

The typical retail firm has most of its investment in the store structure itself and the goods it carries. The firm's ability to choose the location of its stores wisely and control the size of its inventories is a major aspect of its management effort. This effort, referred to as the *Physical Distribution Mix,* along with the *Communication and Goods and Services* mixes constitutes the total management effort of the firm.

Physical Distribution Mix

15

OBJECTIVES YOU SHOULD MEET

1. *Give* a general definition of the term physical distribution mix.
2. *Indicate* why the retailer is so concerned with the size of his inventories.
3. *Define* and *identify:* Consumer risk and internal risk.

One of the never-ending tasks of management is to control the flow of merchandise to the outlets where consumers are exposed to them. Any discussion of the total physical distribution effort of the retail firm requires a knowledge of store locations and store inventories and their control.

Store location is concerned with the channels of physical distribution. In effect, the interest of management in this area is where to locate stores and how to supply them with the needed merchandise. This aspect of the physical distribution mix will be discussed in Chapter 17.

Our immediate concern in the next two chapters is with the firm's inventories. This chapter provides the reader with a background in understanding the overall problems of retail inventories. The next chapter discusses the various techniques management uses for *controlling* the store inventories.

What are the costs involved in maintaining an inventory? What are some of the risks? Why do retail inventories fluctuate? These are some of the questions that will be answered in this chapter.

The performance of the physical distribution function by the manufacturer has always been clearly delineated in marketing literature. Though physical distribution may not always be treated as a separate function, books on marketing always give

Distribution
Functions

consideration to the best control techniques and the implementation problems involved in the performance of this function. In one analysis of the food processing and manufacturing industry the following physical distribution functions were listed:[1]

1. Transportation
2. Materials Handling
3. Production Planning
4. Warehousing
5. Inventory Control

The performance and control of the physical distribution function by the larger retailer differs little from manufacturing operations except in the complexity of the problem. Possibly the major area of difference is in the number of products handled. The retailer, of course, is faced with the control of many more products than the manufacturer. As a result he can give little attention to the unit and must concentrate more on the overall product classification. The manufacturer can concentrate on promoting his individual products and can deliberately set out to develop a product image for each type of goods he sells. Nevertheless, many of the above-mentioned functions performed by manufacturers are similar to those of the retailer.

Transportation and materials handling are problems faced by both retailers and manufacturers. Transportation in the retail firm is involved in delivering goods to warehouses, between stores in multi-unit operations, and to customers. Materials handling, though different in function in the manufacturing firm, is still quite similar to the function of receiving and marking in the large retail firm. Production planning in the manufacturing firm is closely akin to the merchandise planning and final choice of actual products offered in the retail store. Though a great deal of the manufacturer's production is produced for "order," most consumer products are produced in anticipation of consumer needs. It is this latter type of production planning that is similar to a retailer's merchandise planning. It may be recalled that the "production planning" function of the retail firm was considered in an earlier chapter. Warehousing and its relationship to the control of inventories are also of prime interest to the retailer. Though this subject will not be treated separately in this text, some inventory control techniques and problems raised by retail warehousing are mentioned in the next few chapters.

The Distribution Cycle

Though the maufacturer and retailer perform similar physical distribution functions, the manufacturers' and distributors' (wholesalers') problems of physical distribution are to some extent affected by what is happening at the retail level. Though we will discuss the problem of controlling inventories later on, it is

---

[1] AMA Management Report No. 49, *Management of the Physical Distribution Function,* p. 8. © 1960, American Management Association Inc. The "administration" function for obvious reasons is not listed.

pertinent to examine the relationship of retail sales and inventories to the suppliers of these inventories, namely the distributors and manufacturers.

What happens at the retail level is always of concern to a manufacturer or distributor. Wide retail fluctuations can greatly affect a manufacturing firm's production processes or a wholesaler's inventories. In many manufacturing industries where the manufacturer has a direct relationship with the retailer (as in the apparel field) what happens at the retail level has a direct and immediate effect on the manufacturer's position. In other cases (as in the sale of phonograph records) there is not this immediate reaction since wholesalers stock up on the product in large quantities. Though there is always some lag between the channels of distribution, all firms are affected to some extent by consumers' reactions at the retail level. This lead and lag relationship is illustrated in Figure 15-1.[2] The top section shows a typical retail sales curve (for a product) over a 24-month period. Retail sales, represented by the dotted line, ranged from a high of +10 per cent to a low of -10 per cent. On the other hand factory output, indicated by the solid line, experienced a wide range of from +62 per cent to -100 per cent.

Since a product must first be produced before it can be sold, there is a time lag between production and retail sales. Hence, output of goods cannot fluctuate in the same manner as retail sales. Nevertheless, production is a direct function of retail sales. In this illustration it can be assumed that a retailer delivers a product three days after he sells it, and within a week he orders a replacement from the distributor. In some cases the lag may be even greater, depending on the store reordering policy. Conceivably the reordering could be done every two weeks. In addition, the firm may find that a tightness in cash flow or an unwillingness on the part of retail management to increase vendor commitments at this time may also influence the ordering time period. In any case the distributor receives his order and receives the merchandise from the manufacturer two weeks later. Comparison of the first and second curves of Figure 15-1 illustrates this occurrence. Note in the first curve that retail sales increased by 10 per cent; at the same time in the second curve we see a retail inventory decline of 7 per cent. However, this situation is quickly remedied as we can see by the increasing inventory line which reverts to about the original level. Conversely, a 10 per cent decrease in retail sales brings about a 22 per cent increase in store inventory — a temporary condition shortly rectified. Note how the retail sales curve and the inventory curve seem to go temporarily in opposite directions.

The third and fourth curves illustrate the impact of retail sales on inventories at both the distributor and factory level. The time lag between retail sales and order placement with both distributors and the factory causes these wide swings. In essence, while retail sales are increasing by 10 per cent and retail inventories are depleted by 7 per cent on account of ordering lags, distributors' inventories decline by 11 per cent and factory inventories by 42 per cent. Conversely, a sales loss at the retail level results in a temporary increase in inventories at the factory and distribution levels; this period, however, is followed by a sharp drop in these same inventories.

This rather simple illustration points out the complexities of the physical distribution function. From the manufacturer's point of view, an ability to

---

[2] This section draws heavily on the findings presented in AMA Management Report, *op. cit.*

FIGURE 15-1   Relationship of Sales and Inventories at Retail, Distributor, and Factory Levels

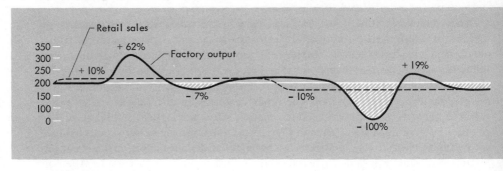

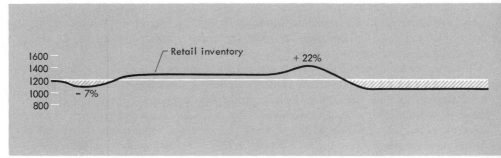

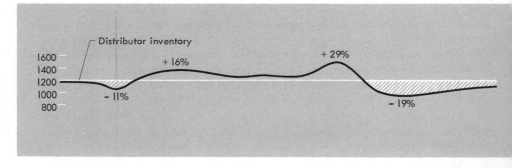

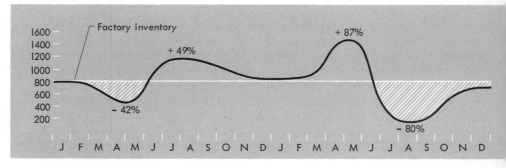

Source: AMA Management Report, op. cit.

anticipate the retailer's needs, through better communication, can reduce the problems he faces, particularly a widely fluctuating inventory and production schedule. The same situation applies, of course, to the distributor.

Though retail inventories seem to be subject to less fluctuation than do distributor and factory inventories, they are particularly delicate in that these fluctuations can involve a lost sale. That is, if the product is not available, the consumer may simply not return to make the purchase, or may purchase the product elsewhere — a situation the retailer strives to avoid.

Having shown the impact of retail inventory fluctuations on all the distribution channels, we still need to determine why fluctuations occur at the retail level. Inventory fluctuations on the whole are strongly influenced by business conditions. The management of a retail firm, which has little control over business conditions, must constantly adjust controls and decisions to this reality. Therefore, a study of inventory fluctuations must encompass not only the changes brought about by economic conditions but also the impact of actions by those immediately involved in the buying and selling of goods.

Possibly the most obvious example of fluctuating inventories over a short period of time took place just prior to the start of the Korean War in 1950. At the beginning of the war, business firms stocked up on raw materials, and consumers engaged in a great deal of scare buying. As a consequence retail sales soared. At the same time the cost of living index rose more rapidly than in the preceding years.[3] As abruptly as this inflation and panic buying began, it halted, and by mid-1953 the economy went into a major decline. This decline, precipitated by the scare buying, lasted approximately one year during which time inventories at both the retail and manufacturing level were cut back severely. This movement, because it represented a wide swing, enabled us to observe closely the reaction of retailers to any changes in their business fortunes. As a corollary to this swing, one retailing expert outlined the three main motives that influence a department store buyer to overbuy during such a crisis. He found them to be, in their order of importance:

1. *Fear of shortage.* This is triggered by the manufacturer who notifies the buyer that the company is receiving orders beyond its capacity to produce. The buyer naturally is concerned that his competition will place orders and improve their positions. The buyer, by appealing to management, gains their support in order to overbuy and ignore previous plans.

2. *Expectations of price increase.* Again, the buyer, well aware of the supply and demand forces of the free market, senses the possibility of price rises. In many instances he commits himself for greater quantities than he would normally. By doing this he can expect to attain a higher gross margin than he ordinarily achieves.

3. *Expectations of increased sales.* Anticipation of a buying scare by the public of course raises the sales sights of the buyer. Stock controls maintained by the store automatically allow him to purchase more merchandise, if the sales expectations become a reality.[4]

All good things eventually come to an end and, of course the "Korean

---

[3]George Katona, *The Powerful Consumer* (New York: McGraw-Hill Book Company, Inc., 1960), pp. 36-39.

[4]Myron Silbert, "Retailing and Economic Stability," *Explorations in Retailing,* Stanley Hollander (East Lansing, Mich.: Michigan State University Press, 1959) pp. 28-29.

Prosperity" did just that. Here our expert suggests three main causes for the rapid cutback in stocks following this splurge:

1. *A downturn in the trend of sales.* An actual downturn may take place before or well after the cutback in buying has started. However, the sales increases (adjusted for seasonality) over the previous months may show indications of slowing down even before buying cuts are undertaken.

2. *Inventories increasing more rapidly than sales.* As a result of the sales drop, inventories are slow to decline and are in many cases larger than needed because of previous buying commitments.

3. *Expectation of a downturn in business and employment.* When this condition prevails, the buyer usually overreacts.[5] If he finds the economic outlook to be somewhat precarious, he may react with a 20 per cent rather than a more rational 10 per cent cutback in buying.

Inventories and Their Size

Probably the major concern of retailers has to do with the size and assortments of their inventories. An adequate assortment and variety of inventories is a prime requisite for a sound retail business. A retailer must offer the consumers the merchandise they want, and in the form they want it, if he is to maintain a profitable enterprise. However, even if this evaluation of consumer needs is made correctly, the job of maintaining the proper inventory levels is a major undertaking. Consider for example our observation in the chapter on research that the typical department store may carry as many as 213,000 items on any given day. The sheer complexity of this task makes retailing a precarious business.

The enormity of the task of controlling the sale of these 213,000 items is further complicated by the fact that many of these products are sold in different sizes, colors, and perhaps in different materials. The number of sizes and colors can create enormous complications. Figure 15-2 lists the 168 different body sizes that can be carried in a men's suit line. Though it is doubtful that a store would carry all these sizes for one number, the list demonstrates the complexity of the retailer's job in maintaining an in-stock inventory position.

Manufacturers are also concerned with the task of controlling the size of their inventories, and we should not underestimate their problems either. General Motors, for example, maintains parts and raw material inventories valued in the millions. However, it must be remembered that much of the automobile manufacturer's inventory is destined for a particular automobile that has been planned years in advance. The division planning production makes its sales estimates and begins placing its orders for tires, generators, engine blocks, braking systems, etc., well in advance of the production year. This in turn acts as a guide to the steel industry, rubber industry and other allied industries to start estimating their needs. During the production year errors in estimates are adjusted upward or downward as the case may be.

Retailers, however, are not so fortunate. Since they carry many lines of products, they are not in a position to make forecasts for each product line. In addition, they buy the merchandise before they can estimate consumer demand, and their evaluation of demand is subject to a great deal of error.

[5]*Ibid.,* p. 30.

FIGURE 15-2

32 Extra Short	33 Short	33 Extra Short	34 Short	34 Extra Short	35 Short	35 Extra Short	35 Regular	36 Short	36 Extra Short	36 Regular	36 Long	37 Short	37 Extra Short
37 Extra Portly Short	37 Portly Short	37 Extra Long	37 Regular	37 Long	38 Short	38 Extra Short	38 Extra Portly Short	38 Portly Short	38 Extra Long	38 Portly Regular	38 Short Stout	38 Regular Stout	38 Regular
38 Long	39 Short	39 Extra Short	39 Extra Portly Short	39 Portly Short	39 Extra Long	39 Portly Regular	39 Short Stout	39 Regular Stout	39 Regular	39 Long	40 Short	40 Extra Short	40 Extra Portly Short
40 Portly Short	40 Extra Long	40 Portly Regular	40 Short Stout	40 Regular Stout	40 Long Stout	40 Regular	40 Long	41 Short	41 Extra Short	41 Extra Portly Short	41 Portly Short	41 Extra Long	41 Portly Regular
41 Short Stout	41 Regular Stout	41 Long Stout	41 Regular	41 Long	41 Portly Long	42 Short	42 Extra Short	42 Extra Portly Short	42 Portly Short	42 Extra Long	42 Portly Regular	42 Short Stout	42 Regular Stout
42 Long Stout	42 Regular	42 Portly Long	42 Long	43 Short	43 Extra Short	43 Extra Portly Short	43 Portly Short	43 Extra Long	43 Portly Regular	43 Short Stout	43 Regular Stout	43 Long Stout	43 Regular
43 Portly Long	43 Long	44 Short	44 Extra Short	44 Extra Portly Short	44 Portly Short	44 Extra Long	44 Portly Regular	44 Short Stout	44 Regular Stout	44 Long Stout	44 Regular	44 Portly Long	44 Long
46 Short	46 Extra Short	46 Extra Portly Short	46 Portly Short	46 Extra Long	46 Portly Regular	46 Short Stout	46 Regular Stout	46 Long Stout	46 Regular	46 Portly Long	46 Long	48 Extra Portly Short	48 Portly Short
48 Extra Long	48 Portly Regular	48 Short Stout	48 Regular Stout	48 Long Stout	48 Regular	48 Portly Long	48 Long	50 Extra Portly Short	50 Portly Short	50 Extra Long	50 Portly Regular	50 Short Stout	50 Regular Stout
50 Long Stout	50 Regular	50 Portly Long	50 Long	52 Portly Short	52 Extra Long	52 Portly Regular	52 Short Stout	52 Regular Stout	52 Long Stout	52 Regular	52 Portly Long	52 Long	54 Portly Short
54 Extra Long	54 Portly Regular	54 Short Stout	54 Regular Stout	54 Long Stout	54 Regular	54 Portly Long	54 Long	56 Portly Short	56 Extra Long	56 Portly Regular	56 Short Stout	56 Regular Stout	56 Long Stout
56 Regular	56 Portly Long	56 Long	58 Extra Long	58 Portly Regular	58 Regular Stout	58 Long Stout	58 Regular	58 Portly Long	58 Long	60 Portly Short	60 Long Stout	60 Regular Stout	60 Portly Long

Source: Barney's Men's Store, New York.

Figure 15-3 shows another major consideration on the part of management. You will note that the retailer has from 60 to 80 per cent of his sales dollar tied up in the cost of goods. The latter end of the scale is occupied by the food chain, and the former by the variety store and drugstores. Manufacturers, on the other hand, find that most of their final selling price reflects labor costs and capital investment rather than the cost of the goods. This is logical since manufacturers usually add something to the product by altering the raw materials they start with. The tire manufacturer, for example, begins with raw rubber or synthetics and processes this

281

FIGURE 15-3 Cost of Goods Sold and Gross Margins of Selected Retail Firms

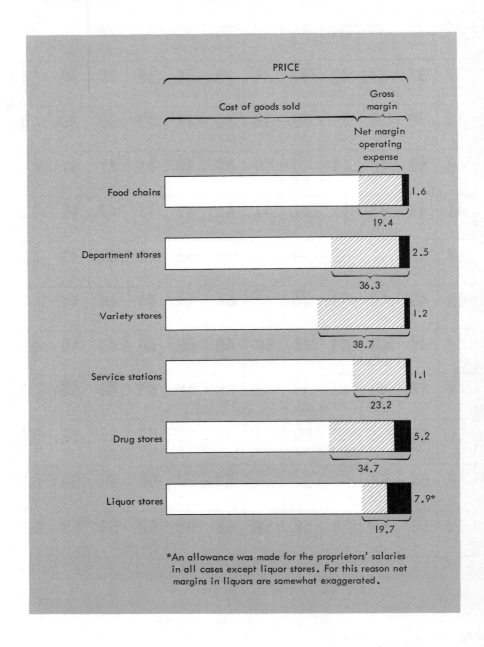

Source: Leonard W. Weiss, Economics of Industry (New York: John Wiley and Sons, 1961), p. 395.

material, turning out a product which has a high labor and capital investment content. In oil production, the same condition prevails. The oil itself is relatively low priced in comparison to the transportation and labor content involved. Retailers purchase these finished products and sell them to the consumers; only rarely do they alter the products they receive.

The manufacturer producing a product with a high labor content can change his labor cost (and eventually the cost of his product) by simply laying off workers or adjusting his working force in any one of many ways. In the retail firm, however, inventories represent a relatively fixed cost for the retailer. As shown in Figure 15-3 the retailer (excluding the very small one), regardless of his business, has little opportunity to reduce the cost of his goods, or at least to change it significantly. The slight decrease shown in Figure 15-4 in the cost of goods sold may be due to the retailer's ability to obtain quantity discounts or to reduce his freight cost by larger lot buying. Nevertheless, there is only a comparatively minor cost saving in the purchasing of this merchandise. In essence, the retailer finds that his cost of merchandise remains relatively stable.

**Relationship of Increasing Sales Volume and the Cost of   FIGURE 15-4
Goods Sold**

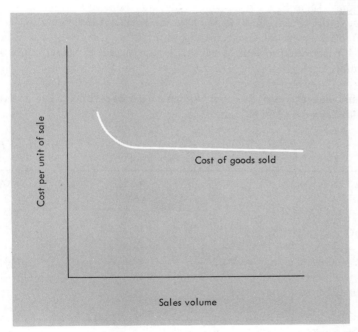

Inventory Costs

As a large percentage of the retailer's dollar is tied up in merchandise, this would seem to be reason enough for a retailer to concentrate a good deal of his energy on the control of merchandise. However, there are many other reasons as well. As an astute retailer is aware, there are many risks and costs attached to the inventory problem. These costs may be divided into the "consumer risk" and the "internal risk."

Consumer risk. One major error that occurs when a retailer does not control his inventories properly (which we have probably all detected in our shopping) is that the retailer may not carry enough stock and thereby risks losing a sale. In theory the retailer may not only be losing a sale but in the long run he may lose most of his customers simply because the buying public may tire of not finding what they want. This policy could lead eventually to the complete loss of the firm's business.

The "consumer risk" aspect entails considerable risk if we regard the consumer as choosing stores on the basis of balancing costs. As previously noted, the consumer may balance (1) the probability of finding a set of items in a store versus (2) the costs incurred in making the purchase. Obviously, the lower the probability of finding the wanted item, the less likely the consumer will be to shop in the store. In essence, this theory suggests that the retailer who is not in stock most of the time is faced with a possibility of losing not only a sale but also a customer.

Internal risk. The policy of carrying more inventory than is needed involves the risks of markdowns. Markdowns are simply another way of saying that a retailer is forced to reduce the selling price of his merchandise in order to move the merchandise off the shelves. Markdowns can be a heavy price to pay for overstocking. Table 15-1 demonstrates this fact. Sometimes even markdowns may fail to move the merchandise. In the case of seasonal merchandise, the chances are slim that markdowns can move merchandise during the out-of-season period. We can well imagine the problem of selling Christmas cards in January or bathing suits in September.

TABLE 15-1   **Markon and Markdowns of Selected Women's Wear Departments in Department Stores with Sales over $50 Million**

Department	Markon Per Cent	Markdown Per Cent (At Retail)
Dressy & tailored coats	43.5%	14.0%
All dresses	46.6	16.3
Hosiery	44.8	2.9
Footwear	49.1	14.5
Gloves	49.9	8.1
Handbags and small leather goods	49.9	6.4
Lingerie, sleepwear and robes	45.3	6.4
Aprons, housedresses and uniforms	45.6	12.0
Suits	46.0	25.4

Source: *Merchandising and Operating Results of 1971,* Financial Executives Division, National Retail Merchants Association, 1972.

Markdowns are not the only costs involved in inventory control. Other costs, however, are not as easy to measure, nor is management as aware of their existence. We are referring in particular to *ordering* or *carrying costs.*[6]

---

[6]Joseph Buchanon and Ernest Koenigsburg, *Scientific Inventory Management* (Englewood Cliffs, N.J.: Prentice-Hall, Inc., 1963), pp. 2-3.

Ordering Costs are defined as the cost attached to placing of orders of any size with vendors. It is a known fact that it costs a store about as much in terms of time and paper work to buy one button as it does to buy a refrigerator. In each instance an order is written and sent to the vendor; as a result a procedure is started which includes the receiving of the merchandise and the eventual payment of the bill. This all costs money, and if a firm places ten times the number of orders it has to, the cost (though it may not increase proportionately) will be much higher than necessary. Incidentally, ordering costs are usually highest in stores that carry inadequate stocks and hence are always calling vendors for fill-in merchandise.

Carrying Costs involve two costs – the cost of storing the merchandise and the cost of foregoing opportunities for better use of the store's money.[7] If, for example, a firm carries an inventory valued at $200,000 when an inventory of half the value would suffice, the cost of space and financing costs would be much greater. Since the firm pays rent (or amortizes the cost of the property), the space costs money, and in this instance more money than would ordinarily be the case. In addition to the space costs, the money tied up in extra inventory could probably be put to better use. It may in some cases be used to reduce the firm's indebtedness, or simply to collect interest in a bank. In either instance, it costs the firm more money than is needed to do the same job.

The total costs of performing the inventory management function in stores are usually not available nor is it possible to make these tabulations. For example, to make a proper tabulation you would have to determine what the markdown ratios would be if you did not have well-organized control; tabulations as to the loss of business under the same condition would also have to be made. Nevertheless, attempts have been made to measure some of the actual expenses involved in maintaining a proper inventory management control. Table 15-2 shows a recent tabulation of the related expenses in large department stores attributable to the management of the firm's inventory.

Inventory Expenses of Department Stores with Sales Volume of Over $50 Million   TABLE 15-2

Expense Item	Percentage of Net Sales
Maintenance of reserve stock	.49
Receiving and marking	.86
Merchandising management and control	1.38
Stock shortages	2.37
Imputed interest	2.50
Total inventory expenses	7.60

Source: *Financial and Operating Results of Department and Specialty Stores of 1970,* National Retail Merchants Association and Estimates.

The first three tabulations are payroll-related expenses (i.e., wages, employee discounts, benefits, and so on) for stores with a sales volume of over $50 million.

---

[7]For a more detailed analysis of holding costs see Donald E. Edwards, "Is Your Sales Dollar Being Consumed By Inventory Holding Costs?" *Journal of Retailing* (Fall, 1969), p. 55.

The last two items, stock shortages and imputed interest, are more directly related to the size of the inventory. Imputed interest is similar to our earlier discussion concerning opportunity costs for the uses of money. In effect, by charging interest to the business based on the values of certain assets, the firm is recognizing that management has alternatives to investing its capital in a business. Therefore, if management had not elected to invest its money in assets, it could have received interest on the funds from savings banks, institutional bonds, and the like. This principle recognizes that, in order to invest in a firm, somebody has to forego another investment opportunity.

The relationship of imputed interest to inventories is easily understandable. Imputed interest charges will be lower if inventories are managed efficiently and are carried at manageable levels, with a minimum of overstocking. Inventory shortages are also closely related to the problem of controlling the firm's inventory. The larger the size of the inventory, the greater the chance of an inventory shortage.

Table 15-2 shows that expenses amounting to 7.6 per cent of net sales are incurred by large department stores as a cost of managing the inventory. Though this tabulation does not include all of the costs mentioned in the above analysis, it does highlight the fact that management of a firm's inventory accounts for a high percentage of the firm's total expense.

SUMMARY

Physical distribution, as the term is used in manufacturing, includes the functions of transportation, material handling, production planning, warehousing, and inventory control. The physical distribution functions as performed by the retailer are the same, except that the retailers handle more products. Production planning in the manufacturing firm is akin to the merchandise planning of the retailers.

As a product must be produced before it can be sold, there is a time lag between production and retail sales. Hence the inventories held by distributors and manufacturers vary considerably. Aside from inventory fluctuations the retailer has other important considerations in attempting to control inventories. Perhaps the most important is that he may handle as many as 213,000 different items in his store, which may be carried in different sizes, colors, and materials. Most of the retailer's sales dollar represents the cost of goods. The cost of goods in various types of stores may range from 60 cents per dollar of sales to as much as 80 cents.

There are many costs and risks attached to the proper management of the firm's inventory, which may be divided into the "consumer" and the "internal" risks. The consumer risk includes the important risk that if the retailer does not carry an item, he may lose a sale and even more importantly a customer. The internal risk involves the risks of increasing costs and expenses of inventory handling. Among the major items are markdowns and what are usually referred to as ordering and carrying costs. The latter involves two costs, the cost of storing merchandise and the cost of foregoing opportunities for better use of the store's money. Inventory costs that can be documented approximate 6 per cent of sales in a large department store. However, markdowns and the cost of losing sales add to this estimate.

QUESTIONS

1. Why are inventories of continuing interest to retail management?

2. In this chapter three causes for overbuying are offered. Give some examples of this occurrence in recent years in specific product groups.

3. Table 15-1 lists markdowns in a dress department as averaging 16.3 per cent. Offer reasons why they are seemingly high as compared to other departments in the store, such as the cosmetic department.

4. Why do retail inventories fluctuate less than manufacturing inventories?

5. Retailer A maintains an inventory of $200,000 a year. Retailer B, doing approximately the same sales volume, maintains an inventory of $150,000. What additional costs does Retailer A incur by carrying a larger inventory? Does he derive any benefits from his larger inventory?

6. Why does the cost of goods remain relatively fixed for both small and large retail firms?

7. Compare the physical distribution functions as performed by the retailer and manufacturer. In what way are they dissimilar?

8. Give examples of products sold at retail where the inventory would fluctuate considerably during the year. Offer examples of products where the inventory would remain relatively stable.

9. Discuss the risks a retailer takes when he carries an inventory that is considerably below his needs.

10. How can a retailer avoid carrying the 168 sizes of men's suits for a single line of suits?

Planning
and Controlling
Inventories
16

OBJECTIVES YOU SHOULD MEET

1. *Describe* two ways sales forecasts are made.
2. *Identify* several important economic indicators used in making sales forecasts.
3. *Indicate* how the planned stock is developed for a forthcoming period.
4. *List* the three formal techniques used by retailers in establishing a merchandise plan.
5. *Define* the term "balancing stocks."
6. *Relate* stock turnover, stock sales ratios, markdowns, shortages, and employee discounts to balancing stocks.
7. *Outline* four major techniques for controlling stocks.
8. *Explain* the role of lead time, safety stocks, and economic order quantity in determining order size.

The planning and control of the firm's inventories is a major function that must be performed by retail management. However, before a plan can be developed and the means of controlling the planned merchandise devised, a sales estimate must first be made. This chapter delves into all of these aspects.

The final chapter in this section will discuss the choice of a location for selling this merchandise.

Estimating Retail Sales   The first step in developing any inventory plan for a retail firm is to make a sales estimate for the period under consideration. Sales estimates, which are used in short-term planning, are also of considerable value in long-range planning — particularly in considering new areas for retail outlets or the expansion of present facilities. In this section we are interested only in the short-term forecasts that are made periodically for use in merchandise planning.

Developing of sales estimates in retail stores is handled on two levels: the top-level executive groups and the *lower departmental* or *store* levels. At each level the means and particularly the outlook differ.

Making sales estimates for a retail firm is not a very precise task and is often frustrating. Nevertheless, as will be seen in the following discussions, if management is to control its inventory position and profits it must start with a merchandising plan based on an estimate of sales. In developing a forecast a firm can avail itself of either of two approaches: the "personal judgment" of a reliable executive (or committee) or a formalized forecast formulated after the collection of data.

Top Level
Sales
Estimates

Personal Judgment

The personal judgment technique means roughly what it implies. Some executive is appointed to forecast sales for the period under study and does just that based on his personal observations. This judgment need not rule out knowledge altogether. As a matter of fact, he may have an assistant (or committee) to advise him of economic trends. However, use of this technique implies that the executive does not make a strong effort to analyze all of the data that are available. In other words the executive in charge of this forecast relies on his experience, intuition, and possibly a few indicators that he considers reliable. This is not to imply that the technique does not work, for it does in many cases. However, a more thorough job of forecasting can be done, and reliance on one or two indicators year after year may be misleading.

For example, let us suppose that in making a forecast of jewelry store sales, a controller of a chain of such stores considers the following indicators for the coming year:

1. Personal disposable income: estimated change from previous year +3 per cent.
2. Marriage rate: estimated change from previous year +3 per cent.

In addition to these two indicators he relies on his judgment of business trends. Based on examination of these two available figures he is optimistic about the firm's changes and predicts a 4 per cent increase in the firm's business.

Analyzing this technique, we find that it is basically simple and relies largely on the controller's personal judgment. For one recent year, however, his prediction could have been wrong by a considerable amount because of the impact of the government's first attempt at cutting taxes to fight a threatened business recession. Had the controller maintained a more detailed interest in this problem he would have read the views, and in some cases personally solicited the views, of an economist on the impact of this tax cut, particularly on the sale of jewelry. The point is that a firm which does not take account of the maze of circumstances that can affect its sales forecast is taking a risk.

Formalized Forecasting

Formalizing a firm's sales forecasts requires the formulation of two steps by management. The first is the determination of what economic factors are good indicators of the firm's potential business. This can be tricky and often requires years of observation. Second, the firm must determine how to measure these factors and in particular what impact each may have on its forecast.

It is recognized that certain economic factors are closely related to the retail business. Figures 16-1 and 16-2 show the close correlation between retail sales and both business investment and personal income. In addition to these two factors, it is well recognized that *disposable* personal income and retail sales are also related. Though it is obvious how personal and disposable income are related to retail sales, the relationship to business investment is more subtle. Investment, according to this theory, is the key to income. A decline in business investment can result in

FIGURE 16-1   **Expenditures for New Plant and Equipment and Retail Sales Y $49.88 (billion) X 4.36 (billion)**

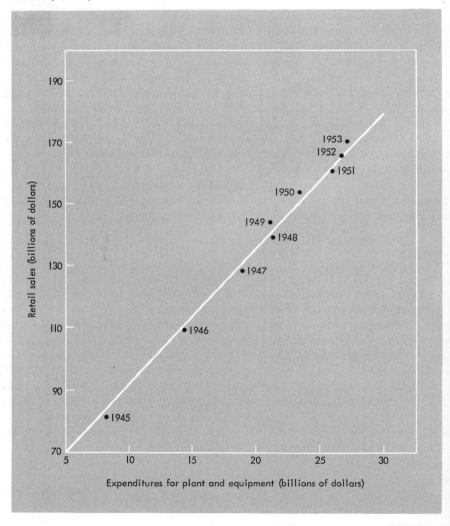

numerous studies that are available — for example, the Sales Management Buying Power Guide. The types of statistics needed vary considerably. Table 16-1 shows a typical data collection sheet used for developing a sales forecast by a local department store.

Business Conditions March 19 **TABLE 16-1**

		Non-Farm Employ-ment (in 1000)	Manu-facturing Employ-ment (in 1000)	Registered Unemploy-ment % Change from Year Ago	Housing Starts	Production Workers in Mfg.	
						Average Hours	Weekly Earnings
New York City	TY*						
	LY**						
Nassau-Suffolk Counties	TY						
	LY						
Westchester County	TY						
	LY						

*TY = This Year, **LY = Last Year
Source: A Major New York Department Store

The lower management levels are rarely concerned with the more formalized techniques of forecasting. However, they do use certain guidelines in developing sales estimates and in many cases rely on the estimates made by top management. By the lower echelon we are referring to the buyer, divisional merchandise manager, or in some cases the store manager. They not only must develop a reasonable sales estimate for the coming year, but must transfer this total dollar estimate into individual units of merchandise.

**Lower-Level
Sales
Estimates**

As will be shown in a later section, merchandise plans flow either from top to bottom or bottom to top. Firms following the former pattern are likely to rely on the more formalized techniques of sales planning. The fact that many firms using this technique are national chains that are affected by national business conditions accounts for their interest in more formalized techniques. Firms with only a local scope are usually less interested in developing forecasts based on the national economic outlook. Nevertheless, regardless of the size of the firm or the scope of their retailing activities, at some point in the forecast the firm must consider local conditions and the buyer must consider his department's future.

As a matter of practice the departmental forecast by the buyer is usually based on what is currently happening in his department or what has happened within the past six months. These facts weigh heavily on his forecast. For example, if in the past six months the buyer has been able to increase sales by 10 per cent he will no doubt feel optimistic about the next six months. Although reliance on this type of forecast may be dangerous, many firms, as pointed out above, make overall economic forecasts. In most cases, the buyer must use these forecasts as his guideline and develop a merchandise plan accordingly.

Though the lower levels will no doubt be impressed by the national economic forecast for the year ahead, they are likely to place greater reliance on happenings within their own departments. This is not to deny that the firm's departmental managers will take into account optimistic forecasts affected by a change in governmental fiscal policy. However, the realities of the situation are such that changes within a department can be as critical a factor in influencing sales as general economic conditions.

 Some of the factors that could influence the department's outlook for sales in the coming year would be one, or a combination, of the following:

1. Planned increases in the advertising budget for the coming year.

2. Increase or decrease in the total assortment of merchandise.

3. Increase in the total departmental space brought about by store expansion, additional branches, or simply shifts in the present store alignment.

4. Miscellaneous factors, such as increase in store services, change in selling techniques (more or less reliance on self-selection).

5. Increase in competition for the merchandise lines in this particular department.

The advertising budget is always subject to change and reevaluation in the retail firm. Though it is strongly influenced by the firm's resources, outside influences can also have an effect. For example, a change in a vendor's advertising allowance policy can certainly affect the amount a department will spend on advertising. As shown in a previous chapter, advertising plays a major role in the retailing mix, and a disproportionate increase in its use could affect any sales forecast.

Changes in competitive conditions from year to year have a direct impact on the departmental sales forecast. For example, an increase in departmental size by a nearby competitor or the addition of a discount house can have an adverse effect on sales. On the other hand, competition can in some cases have the opposite impact on sales. For example, the expansion of a shopping center from twenty to thirty-five stores, with the accompanying increase in merchandise offered and the greater availability of funds for shopping center promotion, can increase the center's total drawing power by attracting consumers from a greater distance. This is particularly relevant for the small retailer with limited resources.

Lastly, the departmental forecast can be greatly altered by an increase or decrease in store services. The addition of credit services in the jewelry department of a discount firm can certainly have a salutary effect. Adding sales help in a department that was previously self-service is another example of this type of consideration.

All of these factors can affect the sales forecast to a degree. The manager's interpretation of their impact on his next year's sales certainly will influence the forecast as much as the top-level overall forecasts for the store and for retail business in the area.

 To summarize, the firm should first make an initial forecast of business conditions nationally, and second, project sales locally. At this point we should emphasize that the more economic statistics studied the more accurate the forecast. Third, the firm must promulgate this information to the individual units or departments for their use in making their own plans. Lower echelon groups rarely achieve the level of sophistication developed by the top management levels.

One last point: though it is important in forecasting retail sales that management develop correlations between the firm's sales and certain economic statistics, it must be emphasized that a good forecast depends on the skills of the forecaster and his evaluation of these correlations. Therefore, though we noted that personal judgment is a weak method of making forecasts, a great deal of reliance must still be placed on subjective evaluations by the forecaster. That is why it is important to put forecasting in the hands of a skilled and thoroughly informed individual.

Planning the Amount of Inventory

After completing its *sales estimate* the firm proceeds to the next step, which is to develop a *planned stock* for the forthcoming period. Here again overall store planning is usually conducted at the top level, and the more detailed plans are developed by the buyer's divisional merchandise manager or, in some cases, store heads. More will be said about this later.

The key to the store inventory is the *merchandise plan*. The plan includes the previously discussed *sales estimates* and the *stock requirement estimates*. In order to develop such a plan, management must set up guides (usually stock turnover statistics), basic minimal stock levels (represented by model stocks of basic assortments), and controls.

In the following section we will cover the *merchandise plan,* the *turnover criteria, stock-sales ratios,* the *development of basic assortments,* and lastly the *controls.*

Merchandise Plan

The merchandise plan in the retail firm is important for two major reasons. First, it represents *the goals of management* stated in dollars for the forthcoming period. Though plans vary from firm to firm, usually sales and inventory goals are expressed in this way for the next planned period. In addition, a firm may decide to include projections of retail reductions[3] for the period covered. Second, it is more important from the management point of view to consider that the merchandise plan, however developed, represents *management's view of its market.* In other terms, and mainly in connection with the outlook of this text, the development of the merchandise plan is basically management's interpretation of the probability of success of the firm's mix, i.e., the physical distribution, communication, and goods and services offered the customer. In another sense it represents management's view of how the consumer will react to the strategic moves the firm is planning to make in the forthcoming period. It would not be idle fantasy to consider the merchandise budget as the center of management's thinking since planning of this nature is basic to a firm's opinion of its ability to make inroads into its market. Once a firm completes its merchandising plan it is in a position to complete other plans (or budgets) such as expense and advertising.

As the merchandise budget represents the firm's interpretation of its marketing mix, it is important that we consider all of the factors that go into developing a merchandise budget. In addition, it is important to understand the organizational arrangements and techniques used by retailers in arriving at a final merchandise budget.

---

[3]Retail reductions are the sum of markdowns, merchandise shortages, and discounts to employees or customers. In effect, this sum represents the difference between the original planned retail price of the merchandise and actual selling price.

Before we consider the major factors involved in developing a merchandise plan, it is pertinent to discuss the general organizational approaches to merchandise planning used by retail firms. Two types of planning approaches seem to be distinguishable; the *informal* and the *formal* planning techniques. The former need not be discussed, as its approach is purely one of guessing. The latter, however, is divided into "bottom-to-top," "top-to-bottom," or "all-level" planning.

Large retail firms must always engage in planning for the future. As a large retail firm usually contains numerous departments and has a decentralized management, a plan is particularly important in order to demonstrate to management where each aspect of its business stands and particularly where the firm is heading. A merchandise plan, therefore, requires the cooperation of all levels of management. Hence a number of theories governing the channels of planning have developed that vary from firm to firm.

Bottom-to-Top Planning

Both the chain and the departmentalized firm follow the type of planning routine shown in Figure 16-3. In effect, this technique follows the management philosophy that the best place for a plan to begin is with those who by the nature of their job are closest to the consumer and therefore in a position to detect consumer trends. Thus firms using this technique tend to rely on the lowest management echelons to initiate plans. Typically this burden may fall on store buyers or, in some major chains, on the firm's main office buyer. After developing a plan the buyer may pass his plan on to the next level of management which (as can be seen in Figure 16-3) may be a departmental manager or merchandise manager. After review and discussion the plan will probably be passed along to one of the top officers of the firm.

At this point the firm's philosophy of management plays a major role. If management believes that the executives closest to the consumer are in the most advantageous position to judge the future sales and demand for the department's products, then they at this point will suggest only minor changes. On the other hand, if management feels that the department managers' or buyers' position is limited in scope and is not the last word in forecasting, they will be apt to make more substantial changes in the proposed budgets. Both philosophies have merit.

The former view that the buyers and department managers are in the best possible position to determine the proper goals for their areas of control is widely held in retailing. However, in many chain organizations the company executives take great liberties in adjusting the individual plan. In any case, under these conditions all planning starts at the lower levels and progresses upward.

Top-to-Bottom Planning

The reverse procedure of planning is used in many retail chains (see Figure 16-4). In particular this technique is found in chains where most of the buying and financing operations are centralized. In actual fact this procedure does not start

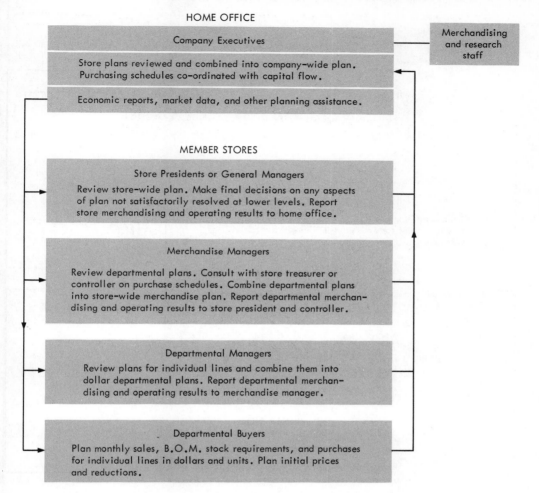

HOME OFFICE

Company Executives

Merchandising and research staff

Store plans reviewed and combined into company-wide plan. Purchasing schedules co-ordinated with capital flow.

Economic reports, market data, and other planning assistance.

MEMBER STORES

Store Presidents or General Managers

Review store-wide plan. Make final decisions on any aspects of plan not satisfactorily resolved at lower levels. Report store merchandising and operating results to home office.

Merchandise Managers

Review departmental plans. Consult with store treasurer or controller on purchase schedules. Combine departmental plans into store-wide merchandise plan. Report departmental merchandising and operating results to store president and controller.

Departmental Managers

Review plans for individual lines and combine them into dollar departmental plans. Report departmental merchandising and operating results to merchandise manager.

Departmental Buyers

Plan monthly sales, B.O.M. stock requirements, and purchases for individual lines in dollars and units. Plan initial prices and reductions.

Source: Richard M. Hill, "Merchandise Planning Organization in Department Store Chains," *Journal of Retailing,* Vol. XXV, No. 2 (Summer, 1959), 76.

precisely at the top, that is, at the presidential level; it is more likely to start at a major merchandising level.

Possibly the major difference between this type of planning and the previously mentioned bottom-to-top planning is the role of the store management personnel. In the former method, the store management group plays a major role in the development of the final plan. In a number of firms they may actually have the final word in the development of the plan. In top to bottom planning, the role of the store executives is to implement the plan and in particular to keep the main office informed of their progress in doing so. Here again, the philosophy of management is paramount. Does the firm centralize or decentralize decision making? If the firm is in the habit of centralizing its decisions it will probably use the top-to-bottom planning procedure.

FIGURE 16-4 Top-to-bottom Planning Organization General Pattern

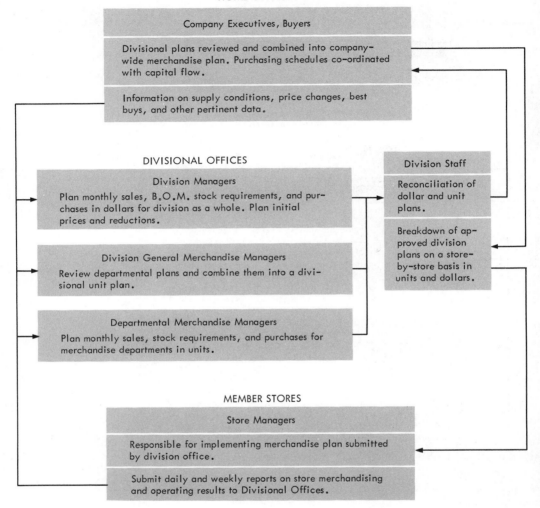

HOME OFFICE

Company Executives, Buyers

Divisional plans reviewed and combined into company-wide merchandise plan. Purchasing schedules co-ordinated with capital flow.

Information on supply conditions, price changes, best buys, and other pertinent data.

DIVISIONAL OFFICES

Division Managers

Plan monthly sales, B.O.M. stock requirements, and purchases in dollars for division as a whole. Plan initial prices and reductions.

Division General Merchandise Managers

Review departmental plans and combine them into a divisional unit plan.

Departmental Merchandise Managers

Plan monthly sales, stock requirements, and purchases for merchandise departments in units.

Division Staff

Reconciliation of dollar and unit plans.

Breakdown of approved division plans on a store-by-store basis in units and dollars.

MEMBER STORES

Store Managers

Responsible for implementing merchandise plan submitted by division office.

Submit daily and weekly reports on store merchandising and operating results to Divisional Offices.

Source: Hill, *op. cit.*, p. 77.

All-Level Planning

Figure 16-5 depicts another type of organization for management planning. This type can be considered as a sort of compromise between the two plans discussed above. Management assumes that benefits are to be derived from both plans and salvages the best features of both. In essence, firms using the all-level planning method still rely on the stores to develop merchandise plans and submit them to the main executives of the firm. However, before they develop these budgets they are given a master plan by the top echelon which must serve as their guide. From here on the planning is strictly a communication and adjustment problem. The key motivating force is the "togetherness" of the planning.

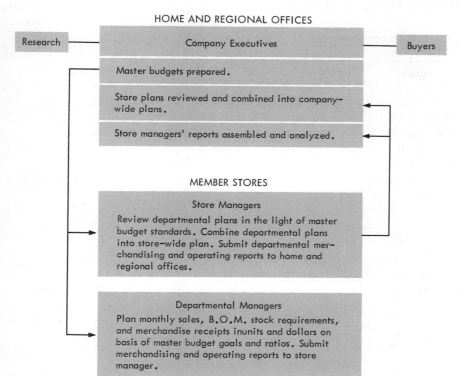

HOME AND REGIONAL OFFICES

Research — Company Executives — Buyers

Master budgets prepared.

Store plans reviewed and combined into company-wide plans.

Store managers' reports assembled and analyzed.

MEMBER STORES

Store Managers

Review departmental plans in the light of master budget standards. Combine departmental plans into store-wide plan. Submit departmental merchandising and operating reports to home and regional offices.

Departmental Managers

Plan monthly sales, B.O.M. stock requirements, and merchandise receipts in units and dollars on basis of master budget goals and ratios. Submit merchandising and operating reports to store manager.

Source: Hill, *op. cit.*, p. 78.

The fundamental goal of the firm, which is to maintain the stocks the customer needs and to meet the inventory goals set by management, is referred to as *balancing stocks*. Stores rarely achieve a perfect balance between their sales and their stocks. The term "balancing" may remind some readers of the economist's use of the term "tendency toward equilibrium," a sort of perfect state that is rarely achieved. However, it is the stated objective of management to get as close to that equilibrium point as possible. To do this, management must engage in planning as described above. In larger stores these plans may encompass hundreds of hours of work on all levels. In the smaller store, the manager may simply jot down a few figures in order to plan his purchasing over the next few months. Nevertheless, at some time the firm decides to develop a plan that when used properly will tell them where they have been and where they are going.

At the top level, merchandise plans are usually in total dollar figures. That is, a firm plans sales for the following six months of $500,000 and average inventories at $200,000. However, at the lower merchandising levels these dollars must be translated into units of merchandise in order to be of value. For example, if a firm finds that its sales and inventories are well within the plan, its concern does not end there. Naturally, it would like to know whether or not most of the stock within the departmental inventory is in balance, that is, are there proper sizes, colors,

Balancing
Stocks
and the
Merchandise
Plan

299

materials, and styles for the customers. If not, this may well signal a store problem.

Assuming that a retail firm has made an adequate sales plan, the firm must then attempt to plan stocks that will achieve the sales goal and at the same time control the flow of this merchandise. Management must, therefore, look for guides for planning these stocks. Inventory turnover rates represent one such technique. However, even if the turnover rates are well planned there still remains the task of determining the proper amounts of merchandise to be carried in stock. It remains, therefore, for the lower echelon of management to actually list the basic stock items and the assortments of merchandise that must be carried in order to achieve the sales goal.

Last, the firm has the problem of keeping track of the number of items. That is, how many items were sold last week, how much should be ordered, and when will they be delivered? This problem requires an understanding of inventory control systems and the more recent developments in scientific methods of inventory control.

Stock Turnover

Stock turnover is used as a guide for determining how much a firm should carry. It is especially useful in planning the total size of the inventory. Stock turnover can be computed when planning in either units or dollars by the following formulas:

$$(1)\ \text{Planned rate of stock turnover} = \frac{\text{Planned number of units sold}}{\text{Planned average unit stock}}$$

$$(2)\ \text{Planned rate of turnover}^4 = \frac{\text{Planned net sales (in dollars)}}{\text{Planned average retail stock (in dollars)}}$$

Formula (1) is preferred. This method is unacceptable, however, unless a calculation is made for each type of merchandise.[5] Thus, if a firm planning to sell 100 radios during a year and 500 television sets maintains average stocks of 25 radios and 100 television sets, planned turnover rates would be 4 for radios and 5 for television sets.

Table 16-2 shows the variation in turnover rates among retail stores. Obviously, a sales plan of $100,000 sales for the next year for each of the stores included in the table requires an entirely different turnover ratio estimate. Indeed the turnover expected in a meat market would be considerably more, given the same sales volume, than that of a hardware store. More important, turnover is used as a guide for determining how well the stocks are in balance. Usually, a retail firm compares its total turnover with that of similar firms.

Using turnover data has severe weaknesses. Most of these failings revolve around the fact that a turnover is simply an average. Therefore, it is quite possible that though a firm's turnover may be in line, quite a number of departments may deviate considerably from this average. In the large firm, therefore, management will examine inventory turnover rates on a departmental basis.

---

[4] If records are kept on a cost basis the following formula is applicable:

$$\frac{\text{Planned cost of goods sold}}{\text{Planned average cost inventory}}$$

[5] William R. Davidson and Paul L. Brown, *Retailing Management,* 2d ed. (New York: Ronald Press Company, 1960), p. 265.

Appliance and radio-television dealers	4.2
Book stores	3.3
Children's and infants' wear stores (under $50,000)	2.1
Department stores (over $50 million)	4.1
Florists	24.9
Furniture stores (less than $250,000)	2.2
Supermarkets	19.4
Hardware stores ($50,000 to $100,000)	2.0
Meat markets	40.0
Men's wear stores (less than $100,000)	2.0
Music stores	3.4
Office supply and equipment dealers	3.5
Retail pharmacies	3.7
Service stations ($50,000 to $100,000)	17.3
Shoe stores	2.0
Sporting goods stores	2.8
Toy stores (over $60,000)	3.6
Variety stores	3.6

Sources: National Appliance and Radio-TV Dealers' Association; American Booksellers; Dunn & Bradstreet; Accounting Corporation of America; National Retail Merchants Association; Supermarket Institute, Inc.; National Retail Hardware Association; Men's Wear Magazine; National Stationery and Office Equipment Association; Eli Lily and Company; Footwear News; National Sporting Goods Association; "Playthings."

Table 16-3 demonstrates an additional guide used by management in the planning of stocks and sales. The formula:

Stock-Sales Ratio

$$\text{Stock-sales ratio} = \frac{\text{planned retail stock at a given period}}{\text{planned sales for the period}}$$

contributes a relatively simple guide to planning stocks. The ratio differs from the turnover ratio in that it is restricted to determining a figure on a monthly basis. In addition, the ratio is used mainly by a departmental group in formulating plans and determining if the merchandise plans are consistent with actual business experience.

The key to establishing stock sales ratios is to maintain past records of end-of-month or beginning-of-month stocks related to sales. With the past as a guide, the future sales (or goals and guides) can be readily established. As a simple example, if we accept the stock-sales ratio for boys' clothing in Table 16-3 of 4.7 in September as a worthwhile goal, and have planned sales in this same month of $5,000, planned beginning-of-the-month stock for this month should be approximately $23,500 (4.7 × $5,000).

Other Planned Guides

Sales and stock ratios, and turnover rates, are certainly the key to developing proper guides for the merchant. In addition, however, many large general

TABLE 16-3   Department Store Ratios of First of the Month Stocks to Sales

Sales $1-5 Million

Departments	Feb.	Mar.	Apr.	May	June	July	Aug.	Sept.	Oct.	Nov.	Dec.	Jan.
Piece goods	5.7	4.8	5.2	5.9	6.7	6.5	5.0	5.4	5.1	5.0	5.4	6.8
Cosmetics	5.6	5.4	5.3	5.1	5.5	6.5	6.1	5.2	6.2	4.9	2.0	6.7
Stationery, greeting cards and religious articles	3.8	4.5	4.3	4.4	3.9	5.3	5.2	4.9	4.6	3.5	1.7	4.5
Handbags & small leather goods	4.5	3.3	3.3	3.6	4.3	5.2	3.8	3.3	3.7	3.7	1.6	5.5
Corsets & brassieres	5.0	4.4	3.8	4.5	4.1	4.6	4.2	3.7	4.2	4.6	3.1	4.7
Women's & misses' coats	2.7	2.2	2.7	3.9	8.5	6.2	4.3	3.8	3.3	3.7	2.7	3.1
Junior dresses	3.3	2.3	2.1	2.2	2.6	2.8	2.4	2.8	2.9	3.5	2.2	4.3
Aprons, housedresses & uniforms	3.8	3.2	3.0	2.5	2.4	3.0	2.9	2.7	3.5	3.8	2.3	4.9
Teenagers' wear	6.1	4.3	3.9	5.6	4.1	4.3	2.8	4.0	4.9	3.4	2.6	7.8
Men's clothing	7.3	7.9	7.2	8.0	6.0	6.9	7.6	7.1	6.6	6.3	2.8	7.3
Boys' clothing	6.5	5.0	5.3	7.6	6.8	6.5	3.4	4.7	6.3	4.1	2.9	8.8
Lamps & shades	8.5	9.0	9.1	10.8	10.8	11.0	8.5	8.8	8.1	5.8	4.0	9.8

Source: *Departmental Merchandising and Operating Results of 1966,* Controllers Congress, National Retail Merchants Association.

merchandise firms plan other related statistics intimately connected with their firms. Among the most widely planned statistics are markdown, stock shortages, and employee discounts.[6] A number of firms, however, are reluctant to merchandise planned price reductions. Behind this reluctance is the belief that by planning reduction the buyer will tend to reduce prices simply because they are in the plan.

To the outsider the tendency on the part of retailers to plan markdown has always been a source of bewilderment. Some have interpreted this action to be a forecast of allowed "errors" in planning. This long-standing concept of planning has been the subject of debate among scholars. In its essentials, the question arises as to whether prices are not being set above economic levels if a firm must resort to a planned price reduction.

Stock Assortments

Once management has planned the size of its inventory, and has allocated it to the departments, one task remains. That is to divide the dollar stock into items of merchandise. This stock must be representative of its customers' needs. The first step, therefore, for the lower levels of the firm's merchandising staff is to divide

[6] See footnote 3, this chapter.

stock into meaningful categories. Among the most widely used criteria are the following:

303
Planning and Controlling Inventories

1. Basic Stock
2. New Items
3. Assortment Groups[7]

Basic Stock is, as its name implies, the basis of a retailer's business. In many cases, a store may do most of its business in this category of merchandise. In all cases, basic stock is merchandise that a customer would ordinarily expect to find in the store at all times. For instance, in a department store a consumer would ordinarily expect to find a white, button-down shirt in all sizes. In a food store, a customer would expect to find basic stock items: such as bread, milk, butter, vegetables, fruits, and meat products. In addition, the consumer would expect soap products to be offered. This item may be represented on the basic stock list by only a few soap products, produced by a few of the major soap manufacturers. And they may represent only a small proportion of the actual soap products carried on the shelf most of the time. However, management is thereby saying to the store head that at all times some soap products must be stocked. The firm carries, in addition, a wider assortment of merchandise than simply items of the basic stock list: this constitutes its *assortment group* of items.

Because of the nature of competition, the food retailer will find that over the years he will be continually forced to revise his basic stock lists. The scope of the problems faced by the food retailer can best be understood if we consider the observation of one analyst that food stores in the early 1960's carried six times as many items as in 1948.[8]

Management interpretation of the role of basic stocks and particularly brands can influence the attention paid to "always being in stock" by the lower levels of management. For example, the growth of new product classifications in supermarkets, such as diet and gourmet foods, cosmetics, and housewares, is seemingly a basis for revising a basic stock list. A firm's failure to revise can be attributed usually to a top-level failure to reevaluate basic stock lists regularly. The changing importance of product classifications can be gleaned when we consider that ten years ago baby powder would probably have qualified as a basic stock item in a drug store and possibly in a department store. Since then, however, supermarkets have added this item to their lists. However, even if baby powder were not considered to be a basic stock list item, it certainly represented *a new item* upon its introduction to the supermarket. Food stores always have a plentiful supply *of new items* that must be planned for in making up a merchandise plan.

How many branded items a firm should keep on the basic stock list suggests a question that can only be answered by top management. The recent growth of private brands, noted in a number of studies, suggests that retail management is questioning the value of stocking too many brands. As suggested by Professor

---

[7]John T. Padley, "Inventory Management Increases Store Profits," *Journal of Retailing,* Vol. 39, No. 2 (Summer, 1962), p. 5. Mr. Padley also lists "traffic items." However, we will assume in this section that basic stock price cuts will suffice in bringing in traffic.

[8]Henry L. Munn, "Should Retailers Reduce Number of Brands Stocked?" *Journal of Retailing,* Vol. 38, No. 4 (Winter 1962-63), p. 1.

Munn, in many cases "shelf and floor space opened up by the reduction in brand offerings can be more efficiently utilized in adding new product classes appealing to new specialized consumer demands."[9]

Table 16-4 demonstrates the type of considerations that must go into the planning of a stock assortment. This table shows the various areas where the typical customer spends her money. Almost $4 of each $100 goes for non-food items. In contrast almost $30 is spent on meat and over $40 on dry groceries. The range of these expenditure patterns obviously controls the stock assortment the typical supermarket must maintain.

TABLE 16-4 **How A Customer Spends $100 in a Super Market**

Meat	$28.27	Household supplies	$ .94
Produce	7.62	Jams, jellies, spreads	.92
Dairy	10.34	Juices & drinks, veg., fruit	1.28
Ice cream	1.13	Laundry supplies	.53
Frozen foods	3.36	Macaroni products, dry	.39
Bakery	4.95	Meat & prep. food	1.39
Dry grocery	40.54	Milk, canned & dry	.51
Baby foods	.48	Paper products	2.68
Baking mixes	.88	Pet foods	1.37
Baking needs	.45	Salad dressings	.60
Beer, wine, ale	2.75	Shortening & oils	.51
Candy, chewing gum	.95	Snacks	.81
Cereals	1.31	Soaps & detergents	2.05
Cigarettes, sm'kg. sp'ly.	4.80	Soft drinks	2.66
Coffee, regular	1.08	Soup, canned & dry	.95
Coffee, instant	.81	Sugar	.67
Condiments	1.65	Tea	.25
Cookies	.85	Vegetables, canned	1.88
Crackers, toast prod.	.40	Vegetables, dry	.26
Desserts	, .39	Diet meals, cookies	.05
Fish, canned	1.06	Non foods	3.75
Fruit, canned	1.29	Health & beauty aids	1.77
Fruit, dried	.12	General merchandise	1.98
Household clean. com'pd.	.63		

Source: *Progressive Grocer,* April, 1972, p. 83.

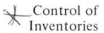
Control of Inventories

Though inventories do not fluctuate to any great extent over a long period of time, it is obvious that they can and do within a year's time. As a result, a buyer is faced with the problem of carefully balancing his inventory during the year in order to avoid being out of stock excessively — a situation that plays havoc with his sales in both the short and the long run. Conversely, the buyer tries to avoid carrying too many assortments over and above his needs which will eventually affect his profits.

This section will examine the means and techniques the retailer (either small or large) uses to control inventories and reorder the proper amount of stock items. In

[9]*Ibid.,* p. 60.

particular we will concentrate on the more recent "scientific" methods of control with special emphasis on inventory control formulas widely discussed in business journals.

The simplest technique of controlling merchandise, and one resorted to mainly by small retailers, is the *visual control system.* In effect, the retailer using this system simply takes account of what is left on his shelf or in his stock at regular periods of time. This system is a particularly useful one in small grocery stores, or in any type of outlet that tends to carry a large number of items stocked on open shelves or in display cases. This function can be performed simultaneously when merchandise is ordered directly from a visiting salesman. Typically, in a small grocery store a retailer may, for example, examine the soap shelves of his store when the soap salesman arrives. This means of ordering is not restricted to small stores; certain departments (i.e., cosmetics) in large stores rely on wholesalers or company salesmen to order merchandise based on visual controls. This technique avoids the heavy record-keeping techniques discussed in the following sections. It is, therefore, understandable that many "mama and papa" type outlets prefer to control their inventories in this manner.

Unit Control System

Unit control systems have as their goal the maintenance of a record of the sale of individual items of merchandise. In a large retail store, it is obviously impractical to keep records. The retailer, therefore, must resort to concentrating on only certain classifications of merchandise. In choosing the merchandise to set up under unit control, a retailer is usually guided by one or a combination of the following:

1. The unit cost of the item. The tendency is for a high unit cost to be controlled in this manner.
2. The characteristics of the item that make it easily identifiable.

Using these criteria, it is understandable, for example, that stores are likely to have dresses under unit control, but that the buyer does not maintain unit control records on needles.

Unit control systems are also quite flexible in the amount of information that can accrue to the buyer. In addition to the selling price and cost of the merchandise sold, the buyer can maintain records on color and style sales trends. With certain types of apparel, records can also be kept on the types of materials favored by the consumer.

Unit control systems are unique in that they maintain control of individual items rather than the dollar value of each unit of stock.

If used properly such a system should:

1. reveal slow selling merchandise
2. aid the buyer in making purchases
3. aid the buyer in making sales plans.

Open-to-Buy

✱   The open-to-buy system is one of the major techniques the buyer has for keeping his inventory under control. The center of this control is the buyer's ability to plan his sales, purchases, inventories, and price reductions over a specified period of time. The OTB system is usually the basis for control in the larger firms. In effect, this system is self-adjusting in that failure to meet specified sales plans results in an automatic reduction in future purchasing power and thereby reduces the inventory on hand.

A simple illustration is presented to demonstrate the mathematical computation of OTB in a hypothetical department.

Initial Plans

Stock on hand, March 1	$30,000*
Planned sales for the month	60,000
Planned stock, March 31	30,000

Status of Department on March 15

Sales to date	$25,000
Receipt of goods to date	20,000
Goods on order	15,000

*All figures at retail prices

Computation

I. Stock on Hand = Beginning Stock + Receipts of Goods – Sales to Date
     $40,000   = $30,000   + $20,000   – $25,000
     + Goods on Order
     + $15,000

II. Needed Stock = Planned Stock + Planned Sales – Sales to Date
                   (March 31)
     $65,000   = $30,000   + $60,000   – $25,000

III. Open to Buy = Needed Stock – Stock on Hand
     $25,000   = $65,000   – $40,000

Open-to-buy calculations are relatively simple, yet helpful. OTB is particularly useful when the firm has to consider its position in the middle of a planned period. It is something akin to taking a trip in a car over a stretch of road seven hundred miles long. At the beginning you are well aware of the seven hundred miles and have made plans concerning your rate of speed and the time it will take to get to your destination. However, after driving for eight hours, if asked where you now stand, or in other words, are you meeting your schedule, you would have to stop and think, and possibly make some calculations. For example, you would probably first start with your plan, determine how far you have gone, calculate how far you have to go, and derive the needed answer — namely, am I on schedule?

Open-to-buy systems have one major failing, in that they control total dollars but not units. Thus, the OTB could show a well-balanced stock position in dollars, yet the actual classification of goods could be in poor shape. For example, though the inventory in a shoe store could be within the goals set by management the actual makeup of the inventory could be such that the sizes, colors, and styles are missing. To remedy this situation management must usually combine OTB controls with unit-control systems that indicate the status of each merchandise classification unit.

With the advent of computers, however, many firms have established weekly OTB systems for major classifications. By narrowing the OTB calculation to groups of merchandise rather than a whole department, management can maintain a tighter control over its expenditures for inventories.

Across-the-Board Ordering by Chains

It may surprise the owner of a small store using simple weekly ordering techniques that many large retail chains use a variation of the same ordering techniques. That is, they review each item they sell weekly, examine their turnover goals, and eventually place orders to meet the needs of their customers. One author describes the "across-the-board" ordering techniques used by the J. C. Penney Company. In effect, the company reviews each item sold in its stores on a weekly basis:

> Inter-item differences in supply control levels and delivery time levels for the various items are not the same, however. The company has certain turnover rates which are considered attainable for various classes of items. Stock levels are set in such a manner as will bring about the proper rate of turnover. Such levels include safety allowances to allow for variations in demand or in delivery time; in fact, anything over and above one week's supply is a safety allowance in the above sense. These safety allowances are set without explicit consideration of the probability of depletion, the costs of depletion, carrying charges, etc.[10]

It was noted that the review at the Penney Company covered each of the firm's 25,000 items. It might be pertinent at this point to ask what costs are involved in reviewing each and every item sold every week. Additionally, we may also ask, does the across-the-board ordering, considering the costs involved, represent a questionable practice in retailing? Though in a previous section we considered the costs involved in placing orders, we can repeat that there exist many measurable and unmeasurable costs related to an across-the-board ordering system.

To begin with, simply assigning the inventory personnel this weekly task can be an expensive proposition, particularly if ordering need not be done on a weekly basis. In addition, it is improbable that each of the orders placed is at an economical level, from the point of view of taking advantage of consolidated transportation shipments, costs of actually placing an order, and the receiving and processing costs that seem to be a function of the number of orders placed. As nearly as we can determine, these costs can be considerable.

In answer to the second question we raised — Does across-the-board ordering make sense? — it seems probable that we can make an evaluation of this technique

---

[10]Thomas M. Whitin, *The Theory of Inventory Management* (Princeton, N.J.: Princeton University Press, 1953), p. 21.

by simply considering the assumptions that must be made about merchandise ordering if we use this approach. In other words, if we approve of the Penney technique of ordering merchandise on a weekly basis, we must agree with a number of the following statements:

1. All of the different items ordered have the same lag time. By lag time, we are referring to the time between ordering and receiving the merchandise. This time is greatly affected by the amount of time it takes to manufacture and ship the items.

2. All of the different items ordered have the same expected demand fluctuation.

3. All of the different items ordered are subject to the same depletion of price if ordering intervals are the same.

4. All of the different items ordered involve the same carrying charges, i.e., insurance, storage, damage, etc.

5. All of the different items ordered have the same quantity discounts.

6. All of the different items ordered have the same costs involved in placing orders.[11]

After considering all of these factors, we are in a position to make a decision and answer the question raised above: Is this system of ordering a questionable practice? Based on our knowledge of items sold in a store one can safely say that this across-the-board ordering system is a costly way of operating the department. We may therefore ask why it is that firms still use this system.

Though no exact answer can be given, it does seem that management has noted some advantages to this system. Seemingly the advantage of forcing the firm's buyers and control specialists to evaluate the present position of their inventories on a certain day every week may have the side value of spurring them into thinking about ways and means they can improve their merchandise assortments. In addition, it avoids the problem of scheduling reorder dates for the 25,000 items the firm keeps in stock.

Reordering weekly also avoids the crisis inherent in ordering at less frequent intervals, namely, that merchandise will turn over slower. Under ordinary conditions, it is a fact that the shorter the ordering cycle, the higher the turnover and the smaller the inventories relative to sales.[12] However, management's decision to use this technique substitutes faster turnover for a higher cost of operation.

More Sophisticated Management Control Systems

The above controls are basic to the operation of stores of all sizes. However, in recent years there has been a tendency to develop more sophisticated techniques for controlling both the size of inventories and what is eventually purchased. These systems take advantage of the trend toward automation by utilizing computer systems to help maintain inventory levels.

The many scientific systems which have been developed have similar characteristics:

1. They are governed by a statistical formula. Some simply utilize the relationship outlined above and add another dimension — the cost of carrying

---

[11]*Ibid.*, p. 20.
[12]*Ibid.*, p. 19.

inventory and the cost of ordering. Others are grounded in statistical theory, which has a basis in expected probability occurrences.

2. They are based on analyses of past trends or experiences.

3. They are best utilized in the control of staples, since regularity is the basis of their analyses.

4. They usually can be worked into a computer analysis.

Control Theory

Two fundamental questions that must be answered in controlling the replenishment of goods are *when to replenish* and *how much to reorder* for adequate replenishment.

In understanding the theory behind scientific inventory control development, the first principle is that we can never know enough about consumer demand to be able to predict with certainty what will happen next week, next month, or over the next six months. Therefore, any scientific inventory plan is based on *probability*, that is, the probability that consumers will only purchase six of item A over the next ten weeks, or twelve of item B over the same period. However (and this is the second principle), it is rarely profitable for a retailer to be in stock at all times. Therefore, one most conclude that all systems will be out of stock at some time. Hopefully, the system will be in stock most of the time — and certainly enough of the time to satisfy customers.

Being out of stock is, of course, a dangerous situation for a retailer. For it is rare that he has the opportunity to reorder and still retain the customer. And, as noted earlier when discussing the types of errors that occur when demand is not met, it can be critical to the continuance of a retail business.

Acceptance of Scientific Controls

There is good evidence today that retail management is slowly shifting away from haphazard methods of inventory management control to more scientific methods. This shift has been under way for a number of years, and there are many factors which account for it.

First, the slipping margins of retail firms during the postwar period caused greater interest in the use of less unscientific methods of control. Coinciding with this, markdowns have been increasing since end of the war. This has been particularly true among the large firms, especially large department stores.

Second, many retail stores, particularly discount competitors of these stores, have been relying more and more on the sale of merchandise that involves less of a risk and ultimately is less susceptible to markdowns. The loss of staple business by the traditional stores to these competitors is forcing them to rely more on their style and fashion appeal and hence the risk of markdowns in their case is even greater.

A third factor, the country's postwar reliance on electronics and the scientific approach to management, has spurred rapid advances in this area. In addition, one author has observed that throughout the depression years intensive research was conducted in the manufacturing field, which resulted in the development of formulas useful in the control of inventories.[13]

Fourth, the increase in the number of branches and outlets by most major firms (e.g. department store branches) has had a positive effect on the development of this approach. The growth of these new outlets has given management the problem of proper allocation of inventories in addition to the usual problems of how much and what to buy. The same is true for chain food stores, which have been growing equally fast throughout the same period.

Scientific
Methods of
Inventory
Control

How does a retailer keep from being out of stock? The most obvious way is to keep a large reserve on hand. The question of how large a reserve is, of course, the key to maintaining a proper inventory balance. Many of today's more sophisticated retail control techniques are based on determining the size of the reserve for each product in the store.

The growth of "scientific" techniques is easily understood if we consider how ineffective or risky a rule-of-thumb technique can be. Suppose we consider a product such as a candy bar that is selling at the rate of ten units per week. If the retailer maintains a "basic reserve low stock" of four units plus a week's sales for a reserve of fourteen, the total in stock may seem to be adequate. However, one author, versed in some of the more advanced techniques, dissected this problem (applying probability theory) and emerged with the astonishing discovery that this reserve level guaranteed that the firm would be out of stock once every thirty-eight years![14] Obviously, this is a reserve level too conservative for even the most traditional of firms.

What Inventory to Control

Most of the modern scientific techniques are concerned with the control of units of merchandise rather than dollars. It may be recalled that the previously discussed open-to-buy and planning techniques had as their major goal maintaining a fixed dollar budget. In other words, buying power was based on previously forecasted dollar goals. To illustrate this, consider a buyer with month-to-date sales of $100,000, a book inventory of $50,000, and a planned EOM inventory of $20,000 — with three days of selling remaining till the end of the month. Management, no doubt, considers this buyer to have overbought. However, if we were to examine his inventory, we would find that he has not only overbought, but his present inventory will not even meet the minimal demands of his customers. How can this happen in a retail store, we might ask. Many observers have blamed management's fascination with dollar aggregates as a major causal factor. Others have shown that if management were more concerned with units rather than dollars they would have the inventory position better attuned to their buying public.

---

[13]*Ibid.,* p. 6.

[14]Douglas J. Dalrymple, "Controlling Retail Inventories," *Journal of Retailing,* Vol. 40, No. 1 (Spring, 1964), p. 9.

To illustrate this point further, consider the following statement:

> Important items in a store are the twenty per cent of stock goods which produce about eighty per cent of your dollar sales. About fifteen per cent of your dollar sales come from fifteen per cent of your in-stock merchandise. In total, therefore, thirty-five per cent of your stock items produce ninety-five per cent of your sales. By simple deduction, we then conclude that sixty-five per cent of your stock items produce five per cent of your firm sales.[15]

Though we need not accept these figures as entirely accurate, it can be assumed that many firms find that a relatively few lines of products account for a large part of the firm's sales and, in cases where expenses can be determined, profits.

Now consider this equation:

> If dollar sales of your "important items" increased (important items equal twenty per cent of stock goods) by twelve-and-one-half per cent − the total store sales will increase by ten per cent. How much would sales of the low items have to increase to provide an increase in store sales of ten per cent? By the low items, we again refer to the sixty-five per cent of the items that produce about five per cent of the total sales. The answer is two hundred per cent or sixteen times the rate of sale of "important items."[16]

The significance of the above discussion has been recognized by those interested in applying mathematical techniques to retail inventory systems. It has been demonstrated that the large number of items sold in a retail store precludes the possibility of a firm maintaining a completely thorough control on all items. As a result, even in the most advanced stores, only limited monthly control records are kept on a large proportion of the firm's offerings. Where records are kept, they concentrate mainly on the best-selling items within the firm. With this in mind, we introduce some of the more recent thoughts and techniques for controlling inventories in the retail store.

Scientific Control Procedures

All scientific methods of inventory control start with the sales forecast. The purpose of the forecast is to establish the goals of the control techniques. In effect, the forecast shows management where it is going, and by a simple computation, how far it has already gone. This aspect of our planning procedure has been covered previously.

After making a sales forecast, the typical inventory system must then determine:

1. Lead time allowance, taking into consideration the time it takes to re-order the merchandise and actually receive it.

2. Allowance for the type of inventory count the store uses, i.e., if the store takes an inventory count once a month, the above re-order level must be adjusted to this fact.

---

[15]Padley, *op. cit.*, p. 2.
[16]*Ibid.*

3. The amount to be ordered, taking into consideration the safety reserve. This allows for any errors in our calculations and swings around the arithmetic mean.

Anticipating Sales Behavior

The key aspect to any scientific approach to inventory control is an understanding of the role of sales forecasting in the control of inventories. Previous discussions have shown us that forecasting takes into consideration past sales. In actual forecasting procedures, allowances are made for changes and any additional promotional activities of the firm. Though a retail executive may examine sales records and keep even the most minute detail records, his major problem is describing the future distribution of weekly sales. For, once he has accomplished this, he is then in a position to be able to estimate order and delivery dates of his merchandise in the quantities that are needed.

In using the scientific approach, management computes an *average sale per item*, based on previous sales records, and, of course, an evaluation of future demand for the product. As an illustration, let us assume that management maintains a stock of eight units per week at all times for a particular product. Management, of course, is concerned with the chances that sales will exceed this stock over a particular period of time. Based on experience, management is well aware that there will be weeks when sales will be less than eight items and other weeks when sales will exceed this amount. Stated another way, management's problem is to answer the question: What is the probability that sales will exceed eight items over a fifty-two-week period? This problem could be solved easily if management could construct a table showing the odds or chance that sales will exceed nine, ten, eleven, or twelve items per week. With this table, management would obviously have the ingredients needed to make a proper decision. In essence, the availability of this information would enable management to estimate the reserves and calculate the total quantity to be ordered. However, there are many problems connected with any attempt of this nature. The cost and the time involved are certainly two major drawbacks. From a more technical point of view, however, a major problem arises because the probability of the sale of an item in a retail store is slight when we consider the total audience of the store, the number of shoppers in a store on a given day, and the competing items on the shelves and counters throughout the store. In effect, the possibility that a consumer will purchase item X is rather remote. On the other hand, if the store sold only five varieties of candy bars at the rate of 100,000 per day, we could more easily predict the sales volume of this item (within reasonable error limits) over a period of a year.

It has occurred to management, therefore, that what is needed is a means of predicting improbable events. In this endeavor, statistics has dusted off a rarely used mathematical distribution that can trace its origins to 1837. In essence, this distribution, called the Poisson, if used accurately, can predict the outcome of such rare occurrences. One nineteenth-century example of its use was that by L. Von Bortkiewicz in 1898.[17] This noted statistician calculated the number of Prussian cavalrymen killed annually by the kick of a horse — certainly a rare occurrence. The

---

[17]Cited by John I. Griffin, *Statistics* (New York: Holt, Rinehart and Winston, 1962), p. 125.

actual tabulations for a number of corps, and his theoretical estimate for a twenty-year period are shown in Table 16-5. By examining this table we can see that this mathematical distribution appeared to be an excellent predictor of actual occurrences. The value of the Poisson distribution is that it is concerned mainly with averages. Once a retailer has established an average sale per unit of merchandise he can then make chance estimates of the weekly demand for his product based on these averages. The problem of the retailer, then, is to establish an average sale for his product. This, of course, is not possible in the sale of high-fashion merchandise. Since this type of merchandise has a short life cycle, we cannot depend on past experience for estimating by this technique a short unpredictable sales curve. Therefore, most applications have been in the grocery field where style or fashion do not play a major role. The cosmetic and houseware departments of a department store have also proved to be an excellent area for using this technique.[18] Fortunately for those interested in applying this distribution to inventory problems, a book of tables has been published for occurrences ranging up to average sales of one hundred items.[19]

Poisson Distribution for Cavalrymen Problem **TABLE 16-5**

Casualties in Year	Number of Occasions on Which the Annual Casualties in the Corps Reached the Figure in First Column	
	Actual	Predicted (Based on Poisson Distribution)
0	144	143.1
1	91	92.1
2	32	33.3
3	11	8.9
4	2	2.0
5 or more	0	0.6

The distribution in Figure 16-6 illustrates the probability of occurrence of an item with a mean average sale of eight. This figure shows that in about 2 per cent of the cases, sales will exceed fourteen items. In other words, if you were maintaining over a year period a stock of fourteen of an item whose expected sales should average eight per week, in about *one* of these weeks (2 per cent times fifty-two weeks) you will be out of stock.

Should the firm decide to maintain a stock of thirteen items at all times, the possibility of being out of stock increases to 3 per cent. Suppose, however, that our study of previous sales of the same item in the stores shows a sales average of only four units per week over the year. How many items would we choose to stock in order to be out of stock 3 per cent of the time? According to our distribution (Figure 16-6) eight items would have to be in stock to maintain this same

[18] See William S. Peters, "Control of Stocks in Grocery Retailing," *Journal of Marketing,* Vol. XXII, No. 2 (October, 1957), p. 148, and Joseph L. Buchan and Ernest Koenigsberg, *Scientific Inventory Management* (Englewood Cliffs, N.J.: Prentice-Hall, Inc., 1963), Chapter 2.

[19] See E. C. Molina, *Poisson's Exponential Binomial Limit* (New York: D. Van Nostrand, 1942).

FIGURE 16-6   Selected Poisson Distribution of Weekly Sales

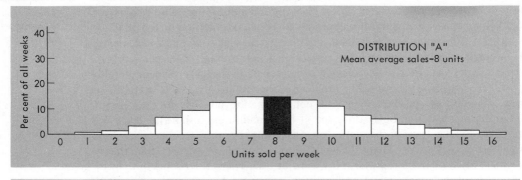

DISTRIBUTION "A"
Mean average sales–8 units

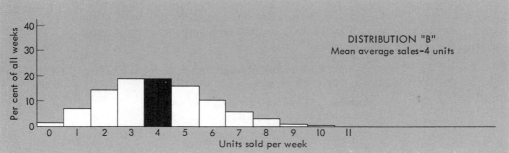

DISTRIBUTION "B"
Mean average sales–4 units

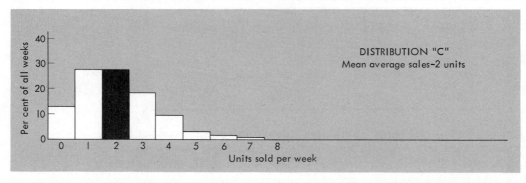

DISTRIBUTION "C"
Mean average sales–2 units

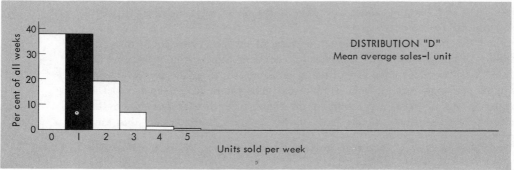

DISTRIBUTION "D"
Mean average sales–1 unit

Source: Edgar A. Pessemier, *The Management of Grocery Inventories in Supermarkets,* Bureau of Economic and Business Research, Bulletin No. 32 (April, 1960) (Pullman, Wash.: Washington State University), p. 19.

314

distribution. If only two items per week of the same unit of merchandise were sold on the average a control stock of seven items would have to be maintained (Figure 16-6). It should be noted that as the probability of occurrence declines, the ratio of stock to average sales must increase. That is, where sales are on the average two items per week, the protective stock exceeds three times the weekly sales. When sales average four items per week, the protective stock is only twice the sales rate. Lastly, a sales rate of eight items per week requires a stock of thirteen, or about 60 per cent of the rate of sale. Our rule, therefore, is that as the sale of an item rises, the coverage rate (sales plus protective stock equals coverage) declines.

The significance of these findings supports our belief that bigness in retailing pays off to an extent. In effect, the larger the sales per unit, the higher the turnover of merchandise and the less, proportionately, the investment.

The use of these tables places squarely in the hands of management the problem of determining the risk the firm will take. Referring back to Figure 16-6 we see that management has a wide choice of decisions. For example, if management wants to insure that the store will practically never be out of stock it can maintain a stock of eighteen items. However, by doing this, the firm will increase its inventory investment considerably, risk taking markdowns, and generally reduce stock turnover. Therefore, all decisions in this area are compromises with cost. Thus, in this case management may decide that maintaining a stock of fourteen units will serve the firm's purpose adequately, and, in effect, will represent the firm's endeavor to balance cost and sales losses.

Determining Order Size

Whether a firm relies on a basic stock list, the Poisson distribution, or dollar budgets as a means of controlling stock, at some stage in its control pattern the firm must place an order, either directly with the vendor or, as in the case of a food chain store, with a central warehouse. Though a firm may establish the size of a shelf inventory, it must still take into consideration many factors before setting the total amount of its orders. Some of these factors are the *lead time,* the *unit of safety reserve,* and the *delivery* and *processing time* of the vendor. Before discussing these factors it is worthwhile to remember that earlier we discussed costs traceable through inventories. Many of these costs, it will be remembered, are related directly to processing the merchandise and hence must be handled as economically as possible. These costs must be figured in all estimates of the economic order quantity (EOQ). More will be said on this aspect toward the end of this chapter.

Lead Time

One of the factors determining the size of the order is how long it will take to replenish the stock. Obviously, if it takes a retailer four weeks to obtain merchandise, the size of the order must be larger than when deliveries are more frequent. Therefore, a merchant must consider lead time in determining the size of his order. Lead time calculations must take into consideration:

1. The period between stock counts (that is, where ordering and receiving are not instantaneous)
2. The period required to place an order with a vendor (or warehouse)

3. The period required to receive delivery of the merchandise from the vendor (or warehouse)

4. The period required to process the stock into the department where it is displayed and sold

Lead time in retail stores varies considerably. The time that elapses between placing an order and receiving the merchandise in a chain grocery store may be as little as seventy-two hours. Even the independent grocery store may receive delivery within this time, particularly if the firm is associated closely with a cooperative warehouse. On the other hand, lead time on furniture, rugs, and some appliances in a department store may be considerably longer. In some cases where manufacturing is "to order," two to three months may be a typical lead time period.

In some firms the period between stock counts may be considerable. In others (such as food chains) stock counts may be on a biweekly basis. A chain shoe store may take inventory at the close of each day.

Processing the merchandise to the department after it is received in the store is a problem that must be considered by stores that pre-mark merchandise before it is put up for sale. In many cases, this processing may be as time consuming as delivery time. Making tickets for merchandise, attaching them to the merchandise, counting the items, and checking the invoices can sometimes be measured in hours, or this procedure may take days.

The significance of lead time is obvious. Reductions in lead time can have a significant effect on the maintained stock period. For example, if the firm cuts the order and delivery time in half, this will have two major repercussions on the firm's ordering process. First, it will automatically reduce the size of the order since the order placed will only have to cover half of the previous period. Second, since the store does not have to order as much as previously, the store stock is also reduced since the safety reserve becomes smaller as it protects against a shorter period of time. More will be said on this below.

Buffer or Safety Stocks

As we noted earlier, the Poisson distribution demonstrates that sales will fluctuate greatly above the average. Therefore, though a firm can make excellent forecasts as to the time period that needs to be covered and the units that should be ordered, our analysis tells us that sales expectations will often exceed estimates — in some cases by a considerable number of units.

Figure 16-7 illustrates this point. It shows that in two cases sales during the lead time period cut into the buffer stock. If the firm had not established a buffer stock the sales would have been lost. Further complicating the problem for the retailer is the fact that the lead time may vary considerably during the year. Though the firm in this illustration has equal lead times, it is generally conceded that during busy periods of the year deliveries from manufacturers are slower and store processing may also be much less efficient. It is clear, therefore, that in placing an order a firm using the newer inventory control system must estimate the lead times and then determine the size of the buffer and the average order.

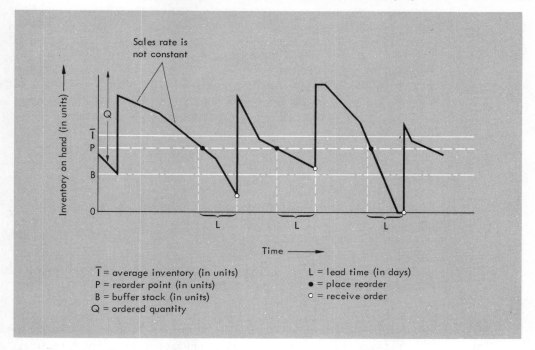

Source: Buchan and Koenigsberg, *op. cit.*, p. 6.

How Much Shall We Order?

In using the nonscientific methods, ordering is relatively easy (though not efficient) in that a buyer has a certain number of dollars to spend from his OTB account and proceeds to do so. The recent methods, however, are based more directly on the sales of individual units of merchandise (i.e., they are less concerned with aggregates) and are tied in closely with the cost of maintaining inventories and purchasing stock. All calculations of this economic order unit must therefore take into consideration the cost factor. In this discussion, however, the cost aspect will be ignored and we will simply show how the number of units to be ordered is determined.

Figure 16-8 illustrates the weekly sales of a unit of merchandise for a 100-week period. If this item averages four sales per week, what would be the EOQ and buffer stock? Let us examine this distribution. First we note that average sales are four items per week. So, if we had one weekly ordering time, we would consider four units as comprising our basic stock. However, we must also maintain a buffer stock since in 38 per cent of the cases sales exceed four items per week. Suppose we had a buffer stock of four items — Buffer (4) plus On Order (4) equal 8. How many times would sales exceed this amount? Referring again to our illustration we see that only twice in one hundred times would this amount be exceeded. Though determining reorder amounts is a little more complicated than this illustration, it nevertheless demonstrates the principles underlining the relationship between EOQ, lead time, and safety stocks.

317

FIGURE 16-8   Distribution of Weekly Retail Sales of One Item for 100 Weeks

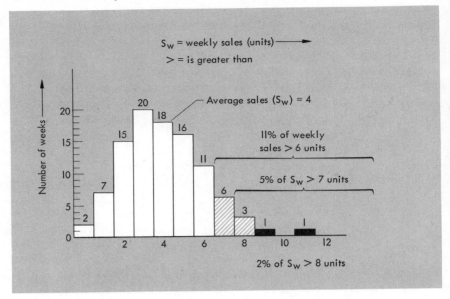

Source: Buchan and Koenigsberg, *op. cit.,* p. 8.

Counting the Inventory

Though the control techniques in a retail firm vary, management usually has a fairly good idea as to the size in dollars, or units, of its inventory. Nonetheless, at some point within the year an actual physical count of the inventory is made.

Possibly the reader may have experienced the often drearisome task of counting a firm's inventory. The first step is, of course, to sort and separate the merchandise and eventually divide the storage shelves into well-organized and easily recognizable piles of merchandise. If you were unlucky, the firm may have asked you to participate in the count, which included listing both the number and the cost or selling price per unit.

Taking a physical inventory to determine the status of the firm's investment in merchandise can be a costly proposition. In some cases, a firm may close the store for a day; in others it may take the count during a period when the store is ordinarily closed (usually the firm would incur additional wage costs), or take a count during the period when the store is open. This latter condition results in poorer service to the customer, and it is thought that it may actually lower sales.

Other costs are also incurred in the taking of a physical count. It is necessary, for example, to tabulate the results of the count, make various bookkeeping adjustments, and spend a good deal of time re-checking the accuracy of the entries. A number of years ago, J. C. Penney determined that the one-day cost of taking inventory exceeded $7,700 (without figuring the cost of closing down for the day).[20]

In addition to knowing how much inventory is on hand, the taking of a physical count is useful to a firm for two reasons. First, it establishes the value of the store's "inventory" assets. Second, it usually offers management an opportunity to

[20]Whitin, *op. cit.,* p. 25.

evaluate the firm's inventory in terms of its "age" (that is, the length of time most product classifications have been in stock), and its size in relationship to future planned business.

In spite of its usefulness from an accounting point of view, the physical inventory count is of little value in controlling the day-in, day-out flow of merchandise across the retailer's counters.

SUMMARY

The planning and control of the firm's inventory is a major function of management. The first step in planning inventories is to make a sales estimate. Sales estimates are made at two levels in large retail stores: among the top-level executive groups and the lower departmental or store levels. At the top level estimates are made either using the personal judgment of a reliable executive (or committee) or a more formalized approach. In the former case the persons making the judgment rely on past experience and intuition. In the latter an attempt is made to relate economic data to the firm's future sales, through the use of statistical tools. On the national level, the firm may relate personal income, business investment, or housing starts to a firm's retail sales. In addition, as firms do business in their local trading areas, local economic data may be a greater indicator of future retail sales.

Lower-level estimates though influenced by national indicators, are more likely based on what the sales trend has been in the past six months, related to departmental or store sales.

After establishing a sales forecast the firm next proceeds to establish a planned stock for the forthcoming period, by establishing a merchandise plan that includes planned sales, inventories, and retail reductions. In establishing a merchandise plan, informal or formal techniques may be used. Formal techniques include bottom-to-top planning, where the buyers make their forecasts and plans first; top-to-bottom planning, where the major merchandising executives set the plans first; or all-level planning, where both levels cooperate in establishing the merchandise plans.

Management strives to maintain the proper inventory levels as related to their sales and the proper number of units of stock on hand. To do this several techniques are used, including stock-turnover and stock-sales ratios in conjunction with retail reductions. Once the size of the inventory has been established the stock items must be selected. These are usually divided into basic stock, new items and assortment groups.

Within the planning period the retailer has to establish a system to control the size and replenishment of the stock. Several systems have been used for years, namely, unit control, open-to-buy systems, and across-the-board ordering.

In recent years, aided by the computer, retail firms have developed more successful procedures for controlling stock. These procedures take into account load time, inventory-taking procedures, and the safety reserve. The statistical formula usually used follows the Poisson distribution. In all cases and at some point in time the firm must take an actual inventory count to establish the size of the firm's investment in inventory and to determine the age of its stock.

Turnover

Stock turnover refers to the number of times that the average stock in a store is sold and replaced during a given period of time. Thus, a toy department with a stock turnover of 5 in effect has replaced its average stock five times during the year. If the average stock in this department is $20,000, then sales are about $100,000.

Two formulas apply to the determination of stock turnover:

$KNow$

$$(1) \quad \frac{Sales}{Average\ Stock\ at\ Retail} = Stock\ Turnover$$

$$(2) \quad \frac{Cost\ of\ Goods\ Sold}{Average\ Stock\ at\ Cost} = Stock\ Turnover.$$

Formula 1 is the most widely used by large stores, as inventory records are kept at retail. Thus, average stock divided into sales will give the firm a turnover estimate.

In formula 2 it should be noted that the average inventory at cost is not divided into sales but into the cost of goods sold.

Formula 1 is the most widely used simply because the data is easily available in stores where the retail method of inventory is maintained.

In determining the average stock several approaches can be used. A firm can add the beginning inventory to the ending inventory and divide the sum by two. However over a period of a year this may give an inaccurate average of inventory. Thus, most large firms add the twelve inventories at the beginning of each month and the inventory at the end of the last month and divide the total by 13 to compute the average inventory. Thus a firm with a fiscal year running from February 1 to February 1 of the following year would add the twelve inventories at the beginning of each month and add to them the inventory at the end of January for a total of 13. By dividing the sum by 13, they would compute the average inventory. Should they not use the thirteenth inventory, the first-of-the-month inventories would not cover the month of January. In some cases the average stock may be computed from either beginning-of-the-month inventories (BOM) or end-of-the-month inventories (EOM). You should be able to solve these problems:

1. A department in a store had a BOM stock of $5,000 and an EOM stock of $9,000 at retail for a recent one-month period. Net sales for the month totaled $24,000. What was the stock turnover for the month?

2. Compute the same department in Question 1, if all inventories were stated at cost value of 60 per cent of retail and the cost of goods sold was $13,000.

3. A buyer plans to have an average stock of $50,000 at retail during the next year. The stock turnover is planned at 4. What should be the buyer's planned sales?

4. The net sales in a department are planned to be about $200,000 during the Christmas season. As the planned stock turnover is to be 4, can one determine the average stock at retail?

5. A department had sales last year of $400,000. The stock turnover was 4. It is planned during the next year to increase sales by 10 per cent and reduce the average stock by the same percentage. What will be the new stock turnover?

The buyer's job requires that at any given time he know the exact status of his stock position. He is then in a position to determine the amount of units he can purchase over the following period.

As the buyer's stock is constantly undergoing change, primarily because of selling, reordering, and receipt of goods, his position at a given moment requires a careful computation. The most useful and widely used computation is called the open-to-buy report. These reports are based on sales and stock plans made by the buyer for the merchandising period.

The simplest way of expressing the open-to-buy report is to note that it produces two totals, namely, *total stock on hand* and *needed stock*. If the needed stock is greater than the stock on hand then the buyer has a favorable open-to-buy (referred to as OTB). The reverse means that the buyer is overbought and thus has no OTB.

The two totals that are necessary to make this computation are made up of the following items:

Total 1	*Total 2*
Needed Stock	Stock on Hand
Planned sales	Beginning stock
Planned markdowns	Goods received
Planned ending stock	Goods on order

Thus, OTB = Needed Stock − Stock on Hand
    (Total 1)   (Total 2)

Should the calculation take place during the month it is only necessary to subtract sales-to-date from Totals 1 and 2.

You should be able to solve these problems:

1. On June 1 a department had an inventory of $15,000 at retail and planned an inventory of $13,000 on June 30. Planned sales for the month were $7,000 and markdowns were estimated to be $700. On-orders were approximately $2,000. Calculate the department's OTB.

2. A buyer estimates that his December 31 stock of $180,000 will be the largest in the history of his toy department. Sales during the month are planned at $76,000. Stock at the beginning of the month was $200,000 and on-orders were $70,000. Markdowns are expected to be unusually heavy at $9,000. Is he overbought?

3. Calculate the OTB from Question 2 as of December 15, when sales to date are $49,000.

4. Find the OTB as of April 15 from the following data:

Planned sales April	$ 40,000
Actual sales as of April 15	37,000
Planned markdowns April	5,000
Goods on order April 15	15,000
Stock on hand April 15	75,000
Planned stock April 30	100,000

5. What would happen to OTB if planned stock in Question 4 was reduced by 60 per cent?

QUESTIONS

1. Discuss some major local economic indicators useful for making retail forecasts.

2. Why are forecasts so important in the retail store?

3. Discuss the importance of the merchandising plan. Why is it considered to be so important?

4. Discuss the organizational aspects of developing a merchandise plan.

5. Which of the above-mentioned organizational plans would be best:
   a. in a food chain?
   b. in a department store branch?

6. Discuss five major basic stock items for a:
   a. variety store
   b. men's wear store
   c. candy store
   d. restaurant

7. Define and relate to controlling inventories:
   a. open-to-buy
   b. unit controls
   c. across-the-board

8. What is meant by scientific inventory control?

9. In using a scientific system discuss the importance of:
   a. lead time
   b. inventory count time

10. In most cases why would the Poisson curve be a better estimate of retail sales than the normal curve?

11. What economic indicators would one consider in making a forecast for a:
   a. furniture store
   b. ice cream parlor
   c. appliance store

12. Table 16-2 indicates that the annual inventory turnover of supermarkets is six times that of a bookstore. Explain.

Store
Location

17

OBJECTIVES YOU SHOULD MEET

1. *Explain* how the octant and saturation methods can be used to evaluate a potential retail area.
2. *Indicate* the costs and demand estimates a firm must make to determine the possible profits of a particular location.
3. *Describe* the present state of the central business district in the city retail structure.
4. *Describe* the present state of the suburban shopping center.

Location cannot be discussed in isolation – any more than price setting can be understood without reference to the consumer. The present value of the location is determined by numerous factors of varying importance. A retail firm can enumerate the factors that are examined before a location is chosen. Many of these will be discussed in this chapter.

Yet a retailer, though understanding the importance of each factor by itself, may choose poor sites and make many errors. This usually happens because he must not only understand the factors, such as population, per capita income, etc., but must also have a theoretical grasp of their relationship in the retailing complex of a given city. Since World War II, retailers have had ample opportunity to apply this kind of knowledge. It is required for such decisions as: Shall I move my men's wear store to the suburbs? Shall I move my variety store into a shopping center? Or simply, shall I build up my downtown store?

Let us elaborate on this point. Consider this two-edged decision facing an integrated retailer. The firm, the Bethlehem Furniture Company, is a manufacturer of fine furniture with a major decorator outlet on Park Avenue in New York City (one of the world's largest furniture districts). Mr. Ted, the owner of this firm, has been invited to open a decorator showroom in a distant suburban shopping center. Prior to this offer, however, his firm was invited to move its present showroom to another expanding business district within the confines of this city.

At this point we might ask, What should Mr. Ted do? However, a better question would be, What should Mr. Ted know? The answer is obviously that Mr. Ted should know precisely how his firm fits into the existing New York City retailing complex. He should not, of course, consider the city location to the complete exclusion of the other sites. But first and foremost he should have an understanding of the type of merchandise he sells, the retail shopping patterns, and the competitive situation in New York City.

Retailing Complex   The casual viewer of the many retailing districts within the city usually concludes that retailing is in a chaotic condition. He may observe in one district two variety stores next to each other, empty stores interspersed throughout the district; eight or ten apparel chains scattered throughout; a photographic shop, three florists, etc. In another district, a few blocks away, this same group of stores may be duplicated. On the other hand, a few miles away, the observer may note a preponderance of food and candy stores, laundromats, liquor stores, and small apparel shops. In summary, the observer may consider the retailing complex in the city as being unplanned and scattered.

On the other hand, a trip to the suburbs may elicit the opposite reaction. The suburbs, to the casual observer, look well organized. The various shopping centers, with their highly organized highway arteries, grass malls, well-lighted thoroughfares, and blended architecture, may very well impress the first-time shopper. Orderliness seems to distinguish the suburbs, and the small suburban business district with its brick architecture, in keeping with the prevailing standards, appears to be a further indication of this orderliness. An observer may note that an older suburban area is facing the same problem of deterioration as the downtown business district. However, this is usually the exception. Also, closer study may reveal a developing hodgepodge of highway shopping districts, but again, he may choose to ignore this. The more analytical observer, however, will note elements common to both downtown business districts and the suburban areas. For example, he may observe that a large proportion of retail firms are located only in areas of heavy traffic or areas with an immediate supporting population. He may also notice that service stores are in plentiful supply in the older business districts and less plentiful in the newer ones.

If the observer is sufficiently alert and analytical, he may slowly become aware that retail trade is composed of many little islands of business throughout the city, with some parallelism among all of those observed. It is the purpose of this chapter to discuss in detail the interrelationships of the various "islands" within the city, and to analyze the various factors that must be considered in choosing a proper location — in other words, the *locational decision-making process* of retail management. This requires knowledge of the techniques of site selection and understanding of the different retailing areas within the city.

In choosing a location, management is faced with a decision, one that depends on an evaluation of economic factors and of their projection into the future. The locational decision management must make is concerned with the probability of the store's immediate success. An error at this point can be expensive. It is not unusual, for example, for a store to invest over $3 million in a new highway location. This cost may include investment in land, buildings, fixtures, inventories, and personnel. Or firm investment may be in the form of a long-term rental commitment rather than in land and buildings. The rental agreement can be especially costly if the firm is obliged to maintain its operation, even though this proves unprofitable. The author was recently exposed to the problem of a men's wear chain with eleven long-term rental contracts in a large metropolitan area. Eight of these contracts were for locations that had been unprofitable for years. Half of these contracts were for stores that were so close together that they actually competed. In 1963 these eight leases had an average of eight years to run!

The problem of choosing a site for a retail firm has become more difficult since the end of World War II. The shifting population mentioned earlier has certainly contributed to this difficulty. Even more important than the population shift to areas outside the city has been the increased reliance on the automobile as a shopping vehicle. The impact of the automobile on retailing is one of the most striking occurrences of this century. As early as 1940, one expert noted that automobiles had increased the radius of the city considerably over previous years. He noted that the typical trading range had increased from five to fifteen miles. Application of the radius formula (πR^2) indicated that the area of urbanization increased from about seventy-five to approximately seven hundred square miles.[1] Changes in these conditions have offered the retailer a tremendous challenge and have also made the selection of a retail site more precarious than formerly.

Site selection. Selecting a proper site for a retail store requires exact economic data. In most cases, a great deal of this information can be obtained from secondary sources. However, a firm will often find that these sources must be supplemented by field research, whether by consumer interviewing or estimating competition.

A First Step

Most of the analyses aim at estimating present and future demand for the firm's products and trying to ascertain whether the firm can make money at a particular site. The retailer has many different sites to choose from. Obviously, a site location in a downtown area will differ greatly from a highway location. In each case different variables are relied upon.

In addition to the location of the site, the retailer must take into consideration the types of products sold. If a firm is selling shopping goods (comparison goods), then location need not be prime. Conversely, a candy store must be located where a great deal of traffic will pass.

---

[1]Harland Bartholomew, "The Present and Ultimate Effect of Decentralization Upon American Cities" (Chicago, Illinois: The Urban Land Institute, 1940), p. 5.

It is clear, therefore, that site analysis varies according to the type of goods sold and the general location contemplated. Nothing can be done on this score until a management first decides the importance of these two factors. For example, there is a considerable difference between the Grand Union food chain contemplating building a downtown supermarket or locating at a shopping center. And after a choice is made as to the location, the firm must decide whether it is planning to establish the Grandway stores (a combination general merchandise discount operation and food store promoted by Grand Union) or a food store alone. Similarly, the department store planner must know whether or not planned branch stores will contain a bargain basement or only upstairs departments. These decisions affect the first step in the choice of any location.

Trading Areas — A Second Step

Before collecting economic data, a firm must then, as a second step, determine its trading area. Here there is a significant difference between the problem faced by the retailer and that of the manufacturer. An analysis of the manufacturer's market would be less concerned with the immediate area and more with the national or regional markets. Macro-analysis would be the technique that best describes methods used by manufacturers in analysing and delineating their markets. The retailer, on the other hand, is seldom interested in an area of more than a few miles surrounding the proposed outlet. Micro-analysis describes the retailer's approach to a site problem. As will be pointed out in the chapter on research, however, the availability of trading area data is limited and improvisation is the key to obtaining the needed facts.

What comprises a trading area? This is a question often put to retail management. In order to answer this question, the analyst must know the type of firm being considered. For example, the trading area of a downtown department store is certainly more extensive than that of a variety store. The very nature of the department store accounts for this. Besides the many first floor convenience departments, the department store contains departments featuring fashion merchandise or shopping goods (such as furniture) that attract consumers from great distances. On the other hand, few shoppers deliberately go downtown in order to patronize a variety store. If they include a purchase in a downtown variety store, it is probably incidental to the major intent and purpose of their trip. Again, the discount house with its price advantages over the traditional store may have a more extensive trading area than the variety store.

Each individual retailer must in effect determine his own market. A word of caution however. Professors Applebaum and Cohen believe that there are numerous quantitative and qualitative factors that can affect the size of the firm's trading area in addition to the type of store. These factors include location, population density, accessibility, natural and cultural features, competition, and store "personality" (image).[2] Isolating these factors is a very difficult task. Once isolated, the retailer has the additional problem of converting these measures into quantitative terms. Some, of course, can be separated in this manner. Others, such as store image, are

[2]William Applebaum and Saul B. Cohen, "Store Trading Areas in a Changing Market," *The Journal of Retailing,* Vol. 37, No. 3 (Fall, 1961), p. 22.

not easily measurable. On the other hand, it may be possible to develop a special study to measure the image of a store vis-a-vis its competitors. In most cases, those entrusted with the job of measuring trading areas prefer to concentrate on economic variables that can be obtained with a minimum of effort. Edna Douglas delineated some of the trading area characteristics of a large southern city years ago.[3] Some of her findings are shown in Table 17-1. From this table several conclusions can be drawn. First, and most obvious, the retailer draws a considerable amount of trade from areas outside the city limits. Second, this ability to attract trade varies by type of firm.

Total Retail Sales and a Summary of Estimates of Out-of-Town Sales, by Certain Kinds of Retail Businesses in Charlotte   **TABLE 17-1**

Kind of Store	Millions of Dollars	Approximate Per Cent to Out-of-Town Customers
Department	$ 7,046	40%
General merchandise and dry goods	387	10
Women's apparel	1,098	45
Men's clothing and furnishings	1,242	40
Shoes	775	25
Furniture	2,277	25
New cars	6,487	15
Used cars	197	25
Automobile supplies	1,407	5
Hardware	446	25
Drug	2,000	10
Jewelry	780	20
Office supplies	981	30
Total	$25,123	
Average		25
Average, excluding new cars		30

Source: Edna Douglas, *op. cit.,* p. 488.

Though this analysis is not exactly pertinent to an understanding of how a retailer chooses a retail site, it does offer us some theoretical guides that can be put to good use. In particular, the various ratios depicting the drawing power of each type of outlet seem to be especially useful.

It is interesting to note that in order to delineate the trading areas in this study the following methods were used:

1. Records of the city's credit bureau were used for obtaining sources and addresses of consumers.

---

[3]"Measuring the General Retail Trade Area — A Case Study: I," *The Journal of Marketing,* Vol. XII, No. 4 (April, 1949), pp. 481-497.

2. Checks deposited by several major department stores were used to determine the location of the bank against which they were drawn.

3. Traffic flow statistics from highway and public works departments were used to determine the flow between cities in the area.

4. Application of Reilly's Law was used to indicate the impact of population and distance on trading patterns.[4]

Over the years there has been a growing reliance on the use of formulas to segment the market and delineate the trading area accurately. Two methods will be discussed here. One dissects the trading area into many segments; the other treats the trading area as a whole. The former, for the purposes of evaluation, we shall call the octant method; the latter, the saturation method. A word of caution concerning reliance on formulas. Much of a firm's success may be attributed to what was called earlier the qualitative factors — factors which defy definition by mathematical means. Hence, the use of formulas is limited to this extent.

Octant Method[5]

The major device used in the octant method is illustrated in Figure 17-1. By simply scaling this drawing to a trading area site, management can neatly divide an area into segments and groups. Once this is done, an attempt is made to get data for the formula cited below. Of course, the firm need not superimpose this chart on the area, but can simply obtain data from census tracts, planning commission reports, or other governmental bodies (see chapter on retail research). On the other hand, it has been well recognized that breaking a decision into its component parts will be likely to result in a better decision being made, since small errors in a segment are less important relatively than one over-all error.

The formula for each segment is relatively simple. Ritland expresses it in the following manner:[6]

---

[4]Back in 1929 William J. Reilly formulated a way to delineate a trading area — to determine the pulling power of two shopping centers of different size. He reasoned that if two cities of the same size (A & B) were 30 miles apart, a person living halfway between would be equally likely to go to either. If one (B) were larger, the person would be more likely to go the larger center. The question then arose: From how many miles toward the smaller center (A) would the larger one attract trade? This would seemingly depend upon the relative size of the two cities. Suppose B were four times as large as A. Would this mean that customers living 6 miles from A and 24 miles from B would be equally likely to shop in either place? That is, would they go four times as far because the center and its assortments were four times as large? A study of actual shopping habits convinced Reilly that distance is more important than size, that a customer only 6 miles from A would *not* normally travel 24 miles to obtain four times as large a selection. He came to the conclusion that the ratio of the square roots of the size ratios would indicate the breaking point between the two cities. Thus with A's population as one, its square root is one and with B's population as 4, its square root is 2. Thus he concluded that A would pull in the ratio of 1 to 2, that is 1/3 of the 30 miles or 10 miles and that B would pull 2/3 of the 30 miles or 20 miles. Thus, a distance of 20 miles from B would be the limit of the normal trading area for B, since people living at that point would be just as likely to shop in A as in B. John W. Wingate, "Reilly's Law and Shopping Centers," *The New York Retailer,* April, 1957, p. 12.

[5]The method used in this study is based on an article by Ross W. Ritland, "New Methods of Estimating and Forecasting Retail Sales," *The Journal of Retailing,* Vol. 39, No. 3 (Fall, 1963), p. 1.

[6]*Ibid.,* pp. 2-3.

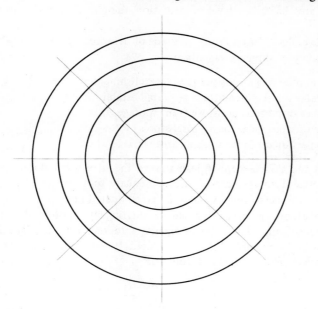

Source: Ritland, *op. cit.,* p. 3.

$$S = \sum_{1=i}^{n} [(P)(I)(x)(y) + T]$$

Where:

    P = Population spending units, or households

    I = Income per person, spending unit, or household

    x = Per cent of an individual's income spent at a particular store

    y = Share of the market of a store under consideration

    T = Sales made to transient personnel not living in the area being studied

    S = Total sales for store under consideration

    n = Number of segments into which market area is divided

    i = First segment

This formula includes most of the economic variables we would expect to find identified in a firm's observation of its potential in an area.[7] In actual fact, the formula would be applied to each segment of the octant. For convenience some segments can be combined.

Saturation Method

  Saturation measurements are usually used in reference to larger areas. By definition they include an evaluation of competitive facilities and their effective-

---

[7]The T factor will probably have to be developed on the basis of a direct consumer study, or empirically from previous studies.

ness. The theory behind the use of these measurements is simply that if the circumscribed area has a low level of saturation, the probability of a store's success is high.

Retailers have always used crude methods of determining area saturation. A few of the most widely used measurements are:

1. The number of persons per retail establishment
2. Available retail expenditures per retail establishment
3. Number of persons per store front footage
4. Ratio of store vacancies to total stores
5. Sales per square foot of selling area[8]

Applebaum and Cohen seem to lean toward the fifth method as being the most useful. In practice if an estimate of sales per square foot uncovers a high ratio, the conclusion is that understoring exists in the area under study.

A recent method of measuring and evaluating the potentiality of an area combines many of the above measurements into one formula. The formula as outlined below has been applied in the food field. It could quite easily be applied to other retail outlets. The formula is as follows:[9]

$$IRS_1 = \frac{C_1 \times RE_1}{RF_1}$$

Where:

IRS_1 = Index of Retail Saturation for Area One
C_1 = Number of Consumers in Area One
RE_1 = Retail Expenditures per Consumer in Area One
RF_1 = Retail Facilities in Area One

As can be seen, most of the data in this formula are readily available to the retailer. The number of consumers within his trading area can be derived from numerous governmental sources or local planning commission reports. Retail expenditures per consumer usually require the analyst to project or extrapolate national consumer data and apply them to the area under study. To determine the present retail facilities, however, is another matter. To attempt to obtain this information, one would be forced to take an actual count or, more accurately, to make an estimate based on observation.

Professor LaLonde offers an example of the development and application of this formula to a typical retail food problem in the following paragraphs:

Consider the following example in analyzing supermarket potential in Market A:

The one hundred thousand consumers in Market A spend an average of $5.50 per week in food stores. There are fifteen supermarkets serving Market A with a total of 144,000 square feet of selling area.

---

[8]William Applebaum and Saul B. Cohen, "Trading Area Networks and Problems of Store Saturation," *The Journal of Retailing,* Vol. 37, No. 4 (Winter 1961-1962), pp. 38-39.

[9]Bernard J. LaLonde, "The Logistics of Retail Location," Mimeographed paper presented to the American Marketing Association, December 27-29, 1961.

$$IRS_1 = \frac{100,000 \times 5.50}{144,000} = \frac{550,000}{144,000} = \$3.82$$

The significance of the $3.82 lies in its usefulness as a measurement of the sales per square foot of the current food stores. If, for example, a food chain contemplating entrance into this area knew from previous experience that sales at the rate of $5 per square foot were needed to maintain a profitable food store, they would probably not enter this market. On the other hand they still might make an affirmative decision if they felt that the location available to them would offer exceptional locational advantages. In either case this simple formula would give them the opportunity to make a decision based on valuable and useful information.

Other Variables

The previous formulas and accompanying economic variables do not by any means exhaust the actual number of variables used and evaluated by retailers in choosing locations. Per capita income, family income, automobile registrations, and retail sales by stores are just some of the variables that have attracted the attention of many analysts. On the other hand, the parameters previously discussed seem to be those most widely used by retailers. Nevertheless, attempts to uncover new measures go on. In the past few decades academicians have concentrated on the simple expedient of attempting to explain differences in retail sales in a city as a means of uncovering new variables. Most studies of this nature have concentrated on density of population and business establishments and/or family income (or total income) to explain these differences.

Final Step in Evaluating a Location

The last step in evaluating a location is always the determination on the part of management as to the possible profits of the eventual location. In order to do this, management must develop a *pro forma* profit-loss statement. This statement should reflect real estate cost estimates, merchandise costs, demand potential (reflected in sales estimates), and profit estimates. Real estate costs usually include the following items:

1. land
2. building
3. interest and amortization
4. insurance
5. repair and maintenance

In addition to these estimates, the retailer must take into consideration zoning requirements, condition of the present land for building purposes, estimated ratio of parking space (if parking is a planned consideration), and the interior embellishment required for this type of store.

The above outline assumes that a retailer will build his own store. In many cases, he may simply rent property or interest a developer in building a store at a guaranteed long-term rent. On the other hand, many retailers have recently become involved in setting up separate real estate corporations to deal specifically with these problems. This latter development stems from the recognition that picking sites and developing shopping centers or free-standing outlets is a complicated and dangerous business fraught with risks and requiring professional competence.

Rental Agreements

Rental agreements, where applicable, vary considerably.[10] Some, of course, are based on a flat rate. In recent years the shopping center's development has been keyed to rental contracts based on percentages of sales. The percentages vary for each type of store.

As would be expected, the more powerful the store is as a drawing device for the center, the lower the rental percentage. Conversely, the more the store depends on traffic already in the center, the higher the rental.

Tables 17-2 and 17-3, listing the high-rent and low-rent tenants in regional shopping centers, support this view.

Note, for example, that some of the major stores, which constitute an important drawing power for the centers, pay the lowest rentals per square foot. For example, department stores, variety stores, and supermarkets all pay under $2 a square foot of gross leasable space. In fact, among retail stores the department store ranks the lowest in rent.

Stores and outlets listed in the high-rental group can be generally characterized as "parasitic," in that they are not a drawing power but survive on the basis of the traffic developed by other major stores.

TABLE 17-2   High Total Rent Tenants in Regional Shopping Centers

Tenant Classification	Median Total Rent Per Square Foot GLA*
Key shops	$17.10
Carry-out	12.50
Hosiery	11.53
Watch repair	9.03
Tobacco	8.34
Costume jewelry	8.23
Candy, nuts	7.72
Optometrists	7.00
Millinery	6.91
Hot bakeries	6.14
Camera	6.03
Men's and boys' shoe	6.00

*Gross leasable area
Source: "The Dollars and Cents of Shopping Centers: 1972," *The Urban Land Institute,* 1972, p. 27.

[10]For an elaborate presentation of factors that determine store rentals see Saul B. Cohen and William Applebaum, "Evaluating Store Sites and Determining Store Rents," *Economic Geography* (January, 1960), p. 1.

Tenant Classification	Median Total Rent Per Square Foot GLA
Warehouse or storage	$1.19
Bowling alleys	1.39
Department stores	1.46
Car wash	1.74
Supermarkets	1.74
Hardware	1.96
Variety Stores	1.99
Junior department stores	2.00
Automotive	2.00
Post office	2.03
Drugs	2.25
Architect	2.36

Source: Same as Table 17-2.

Table 17-4 lists the rentals as a per cent of sales paid by some of the major tenants in regional shopping centers.[11] The national chains pay a lower rent than either the local chains or the independents. The range of rentals is also interesting in that they can range from a low of 2.70 per cent of sales for department stores in regional centers to a high of 10.54 per cent for a beauty shop.

City Retail Structure

Management's interest in choosing a location does not simply end with the choice of factors to be designated as the deciding criteria. The firm's familiarity with the various trading areas within the city will ultimately express itself in the choice of a site. Mr. Ted's problem as outlined earlier in the chapter is a direct function of the area of the city to which he contemplates a move. In making his decision, he will certainly examine the factors within the area he chooses. However, his ultimate choice as to the site depends on his analysis and understanding of the value of each business area within his own community. The number and complexity of these districts in a metropolitan area vary with the size of the city.

Central Business District

The Central Business District is the area in each city that contains the highest valued real estate, the largest concentration of retail stores, and the major office buildings. All city transportation has as its goal the accommodation of passenger service to this district.

---

[11]For a more detailed analysis of the latest shopping-center lease agreements see *Chain Store Age, The Executive's Edition,* Part 2 (May, 1972).

TABLE 17-4 Regional Shopping Centers: Median Operating Results of Selected National Chain, Local Chain, and Independent Tenants in the U.S.

	Square Feet GLA	Sales	Total Rent	Total Rent as a Percent of Sales
Ladies' wear				
National	6,600	$ 63.20	$3.19	4.97%
Local	4,151	69.17	4.23	5.93
Independent	2,800	70.88	4.59	6.02
Men's wear				
National	4,181	$ 70.40	$3.84	5.28
Local	4,058	92.69	5.00	5.89
Independent	2,704	94.65	4.80	6.01
Family shoe				
National	4,371	$ 55.00	$3.84	6.05
Local	4,227	60.11	4.00	6.00
Independent	3,218	93.44	4.35	6.01
Ladies' specialty				
National	1,850	$ 57.68	$4.50	7.23
Local	1,876	75.66	5.12	6.32
Independent	1,360	84.92	5.99	6.09
Cards and gifts				
National	2,324	$ 63.39	$5.00	8.01
Local	1,800	71.43	6.00	8.33
Independent	1,520	61.46	5.57	9.54
Ladies' shoe				
National	4,530	$ 50.91	$4.00	7.06
Local	3,032	76.20	5.35	6.01
Independent	3,124	80.34	4.87	6.95
Jewelry				
National	2,550	$ 85.11	$4.90	5.07
Local	2,079	111.00	6.31	5.75
Independent	1,714	122.89	6.54	6.00
Restaurants				
National	4,552	$ 62.83	$4.04	6.02
Local	3,945	75.64	4.47	5.96
Independent	3,432	72.85	4.49	6.66
Department stores				
National	130,000	$ 55.54	$1.42	2.70
Local	168,266	68.72	1.46	2.70
Independent	97,585	40.81	1.42	3.27

	Square Feet GLA	Sales	Total Rent	Total Rent as a Percent of Sales
Beauty shops				
National	1,879	$ 51.85	$4.44	10.54
Local	1,650	41.29	3.91	9.69
Independent	1,280	48.99	4.65	10.00
Music and records				
National	1,963	$ 79.83	$4.68	6.00
Local	1,850	103.15	5.50	5.30
Independent	1,809	100.50	4.85	5.94
Men's and boys' shoe				
National	1,527	$ 68.31	$6.00	6.75
Local	2,850	60.92	4.50	6.04
Independent	1,727	103.24	7.14	6.52

Source: *Urban Land Institute, op. cit.,* p. 207.

The United States Department of Commerce has been collecting data on retail sales in the CBD (Central Business District) for a number of years.[12] However, these statistics are not always comparable, since the CBD's in many cities have contracted their areas, or in many cases have increased their scope.[13] Nevertheless, analysts have been well aware that sales in these areas have been declining at a rapid rate, and have generally been shifting to the suburban areas. Though most economists point out that this sales shift has been especially pronounced since the end of World War II, Homer Hoyt noted that it was well under way even before that time.[14] He observed in his study that in 1930 about 90 per cent of all general merchandise sales (mainly variety store and department store sales) were made in the downtown areas of the United States. In contrast, his study of general merchandise sales in 94 metropolitan areas showed that in 1958 the sales in surrounding districts exceeded the sales in the Central Business District by 19 per cent.

Why this about-face in consumer shopping? Why the deterioration of the downtown area? There are probably many answers, most of which can be found in Chapter 5, where we discussed the population changes in the metropolitan areas of the country. In addition, the failure of public transportation, the further deterioration of the downtown plant, and the "automobile mania" of suburbia have further complicated this problem.

Many retailers, city planners, and real estate interests have attempted to alleviate this situation, but they have met with only minimal success as the sales pattern indicated above continues. At this stage, however, management is still faced with

---

[12] For a sampling of this information, see Chapter 20.

[13] For a complete analysis of the problems faced in delimiting the boundaries of the CBD, see Raymond Murphy and J. E. Vance, Jr., "Delimiting the CBD," *Economic Geography,* Vol. 30, No. 2 (July, 1954), p. 189.

[14] "Sales in Leading Shopping Centers and Shopping Districts in the United States," *Urban Land,* September, 1961, p. 3.

two problems, both of which would help Mr. Ted solve his aforementioned dilemma. The first and most important is, Should a retailer attempt to rehabilitate downtown and, in particular, refurbish his own plant? This question cannot be answered easily. However, many retailers are beginning to agree that a retailer should follow the population shift. That is, if a movement to the suburbs persists, then he should move to the suburbs also. This does not necessarily mean that the retailer should close down his CBD store. However, it does mean that he should probably set up an additional outlet in view of the shift. Whether or not he maintains his outlet depends on his answer to our second question; that is, Does the type of merchandise that he sells still have adequate support in the downtown area? Here again is the crux of the problem for Mr. Ted. Yes, the population in his city is moving to the suburban area; nevertheless, it may be wise to stay in the city if the consumers who shop downtown still purchase most of their furniture in this area.

To make this decision Mr. Ted must know consumer shopping habits as related to the CBD "islands." In more exact terms, it means that management must have a clear understanding of what the consumer hopes to find in his downtown shopping — specifically, who shops downtown and what types of stores the shopper expects to find.

Downtown Shopping

Many studies have been made of the consumer shopping preferences in the Central Business District. Some of these studies have determined specific preferences for certain types of outlets, and others have been more concerned with views about improving transportation facilities or aiding the planning commissions of the local government bodies. Our purpose is not to summarize all of these findings but to offer general conclusions that seem to characterize downtown shopping.

Downtown shopping in most cities has taken on a distinctive role. In particular, downtown seems to be the place to shop for fashion merchandise and home furnishings. It is also the belief of many retailing executives that downtown has also been able to attract the bargain hunter. This latter statement is disputed by analysts.[15] On the other hand, in a number of cities, this may still be the case. For instance, William Filene and Sons in Boston, Massachusetts, is an excellent example of a store that has developed a basement operation to a remarkable level. This basement is located in the downtown area of the city. Another example is the basement of the J. L. Hudson Company in Detroit. Again, the success of this operation seems to indicate that shoppers can still be attracted to downtown by a bargain. Nevertheless, the major role of downtown still seems to be to sell merchandise that consumers are willing to spend time and effort to purchase.

The makeup of the downtown populace is also changing. A good deal of the shopping audience still consists of workers who are employed in the business district and ordinarily reside in the nearby suburban areas. This aspect has tended to restrict the busy hours of the retail firms to lunch periods and the few hours following the end of the work day.

---

[15]See, for example, Stuart U. Rich, *Shopping Behavior of Department Store Customers* (Boston, Mass: Harvard Business School, Division of Research, 1964), p. 229.

In addition, the economic composition of the city has changed, particularly of those who live around the business district. In recent times, we find that either low-income groups or high-income groups reside within these confines. The so-called "middle class" seems to be mainly residing in the suburban areas of the city.

Suburban Shopping

The suburban shopping pattern revolves around the shopping center or free-standing highway location. The former has been of particular interest during the postwar period.

In 1956, Paul Smith estimated that there were about two thousand shopping centers already built.[16] The rapid development of these centers is seen in the fact that in 1963 a shopping center directory lists 7,411 centers of all types throughout the United States and Canada.[17]

Though their size varies considerably, shopping centers have had a major effect on the tendency of retail sales to shift in the suburbs. As early as 1958, Homer Hoyt counted 110 of these centers with a volume of sales exceeding $10 million.[18]

Many types of centers have developed during this period. The *B* part of the following list represents one division of the planned shopping centers.[19]

A. Unplanned Business Districts
1. *Central Business District.*
2. *CBD String Stores.* Adjoin the CBD.
3. *Secondary Business District.* Serves portions of a central city or a suburb.
4. *Secondary String Stores.* Adjoin secondary business districts.
5. *Neighborhood Stores.* Occur in small clusters or in isolation.
6. *Outlying Highway Stores.* Occur in strings or in isolation.

B. Planned Shopping Centers
1. *CBD Planned Shopping Center.* Arise through urban renewal.
2. *Regional Planned Shopping Center.* In strong competition with CBD.
3. *Community Planned Shopping Center.* In competition mainly with secondary business districts or with the CBD in smaller cities.
4. *Neighborhood Planned Shopping Center.* Frequently called neighborhood "strip."
5. *Outlying Planned Shopping Center.* Draws, in part, upon the passing parade of highway traffic.

Of this list, three types have prevailed since the end of World War II. The most prevalent in the suburban areas of the city are the so-called neighborhood centers,

---

[16] *Shopping Centers* (New York: National Retail Merchants Association, 1956), p. 18.
[17] *The Directory of Shopping Centers* (Chicago, Ill.: National Research Bureau, Inc., 1963).
[18] *Urban Land,* September, 1961, p. 3.
[19] William Applebaum and Saul B. Cohen, "Store Trading Areas in a Changing Market," *Journal of Retailing,* Vol. 37, No. 3 (Fall, 1961) p. 20. *op. cit.,* p. 20.

which consist of about a dozen convenience and service-type stores. This center is specifically developed in order to service the immediate trading area.

The most expensive type of center found in the suburban areas is the so-called regional shopping center. This development includes about fifty to one hundred stores of all types. Usually it contains a branch department store (one or two), variety chains, food supermarkets, and dozens of specialty stores.

There are many variations of the above types. One in particular that is thriving at many metropolitan areas is the "free-standing" highway outlet (categorized in the above list as Outlying Planned Centers), featuring ample parking facilities. Variations of this center include the smaller two- or three-unit centers which contain a food supermarket, variety store, or discount house. The latter is almost always omitted from the regional shopping centers.

The elaborate nature of the centers governs their cost. For example, some centers contain parking accommodations at the rate of four or five feet per square foot of store space. In addition, other centers contain public auditoriums, malls and gardens, children's playgrounds, and other non-selling extras. Cost of construction of centers can range from a low of $18 to a high of $30 per square foot. In comparison, the less elaborate highway centers may cost as little as $8 per square foot to construct.

The breakdown of costs of a shopping center includes both the original cost of the land and the off-site and on-site improvements. The latter include the grading and construction of curbs and gutters and the many electrical controls and walkways necessary to complete the center. These costs approximate 20 per cent of the total cost of the center. In addition the developer must construct the building shell and the malls. He is also obligated to make certain improvements for the benefits of the tenants in the building shell. These costs may run somewhere in the vicinity of 75 per cent of the total cost of the center. The balance of the construction charges and promotional expenses include architectural and engineering fees, interest and financing, leasing costs, legal fees and the over-all cost of administrative overhead and construction supervision.[20]

The tendency in recent years is to construct enclosed malls in large regional centers. For instance, in a survey of 25 regional centers constructed in the past three years, 23 centers featured enclosed malls.[21]

The enclosed mall is obviously more expensive to build, yet the trend is continuing in all sections of the U.S. The reasons vary by area. In the South, as many malls are constructed to project the shopper from the hot weather, they are practically always air-conditioned. In the North the enclosed malls are heated in the winter and usually air-conditioned in the summer.

This type of consideration attracts the shopper by offering protection from the elements. One center, The Galleria, in Houston, Texas, uses the mall effect to protect its indoor skating rink as a major area attraction.

Location Within a Center

Recently, great interest has been developing concerning location strategy within a center. Should an independent retailer locate next to a department store? Should

---

[20]Urban Land Institute, *op. cit.,* p. 190.
[21] Urban Land Institute, *op. cit.,* p. 199.

a baker locate near a food store? Answers to questions such as these are what retailers are looking for.

Another question that requires consideration by management as this stage of retail development is, Should a firm invite a traditional competitor into the center? Or, even more of a problem, Should a traditional store invite a discount competitor into a center? The answers to these questions are not easy to obtain, and opinions are mixed. For example, in recent years Macy's invited its arch competitor, Gimbels, into its Roosevelt Field (Long Island) shopping center, for the avowed purpose of creating more interest in the center. In addition, it was also the purpose of this move to establish a better flow of traffic within the center, because it had been discovered that though a major department store in a center can create traffic and conduct a profitable business, the other stores in the center may not be able to do so. Therefore, the interest of shopping-center developers has turned toward analyzing traffic flow within the center itself. The addition of another major outlet seems to be part of the answer. In effect, they have found that the addition of another store increases the drawing power of the center and, just as important, increases the flow of traffic within the center.

Adding a low-margin discount store to a traditional shopping center is another means of carrying out a locational strategy that is also under consideration. The present growth of highway discount firms has been a cause of great concern to shopping centers in recent years. For example, a large regional shopping center, Cross County (located in Yonkers, New York), contains both Gimbel Brothers and Wanamakers department stores, as well as a variety store and numerous specialty stores. In spite of the successful development of this center, three major discounters have built profitable highway outlets within two miles of this center. The growth of discount outlets has been a source of concern for all centers. To combat this problem Stern Brothers, situated in a major New Jersey center directly across the highway from the E. J. Korvette discount house, built a walkway directly connecting both stores.

The above-mentioned Roosevelt Field shopping center invited Alexander's, a New York discount apparel firm into their center, though it is anchored by Macy's and Gimbels, two traditional department stores.

Location within a center has become a source of consternation to all developers. In recent years, many theories have been put forth as to the proper strategy to be used in considering the placement of operations within the center. Richard L. Nelson has put forward the following locational and parking considerations for a shopping center developer.[22]

1. The food market should be at one end or off by itself or situated so that the parking facilities near it are not taken for long periods of time by shoppers in the mercantile stores.

2. The bakery must be next to the supermarket, and any other specialty food stores should be nearby. Drug, hardware, liquor, and most personal-service stores should also be in the same general area, though this requirement is not very strict — almost any location with some prominence is good for them all.

---

[22] Richard L. Nelson, *The Selection of Retail Locations* (New York: The F. W. Dodge Corporation, 1958), pp. 103-104.

3. A drug store that intends to keep longer hours than the other stores in the center should, if possible, be located in an end position and relatively near the highway, so that it will not be surrounded by a number of dark stores at night.

4. Apparel and shoe stores and other mercantile types should be located as close to the major generator (the department store) as possible. If there are two department stores, they should be located between them. If there is only one department store, the best location would be between that store and a chain variety store.

5. Personal-service stores need not be located in prominent positions.

6. The only concerns the owner of a department store should have are that there be adequate parking in his immediate vicinity, and that the balance of the center be rented to compatible and noncompetitive stores. The department store should not be located next to the food market, but if it has no food-serving facilities itself, a restaurant makes a very good neighbor. If there are two department stores, there should be a direct walk between them, and they should not be too far apart. A prominent position and adjacency to other self-generators is desirable.

7. *In small convenience centers* the supermarket should be in a position where shoppers at other stores will not occupy parking places next to it for long periods of time. The drug store should be at one end. Aside from these criteria, the exact location of stores of stores in these small strip centers is not very important as long as the compatibility groupings are observed.

The most numerous tenants found in regional shopping centers are of course apparel firms. Table 17-5 lists the ranking of various types of stores found in a survey of regional centers. Note should be made of the fact that the first four stores in terms of ranking are apparel. This finding coincides with results of a study of five regional shopping centers by Barry Berman, which indicated that about 42 per cent of the stores in these centers fall into the classification of clothing, accessory, and shoe stores.[23]

One should also note that in Table 17-5 medical and dental offices rank fairly high on the list of frequent tenants. This would seem to indicate that the regional center has perhaps become a center for services as well as goods.

SUMMARY

Location can not be discussed in isolation. In considering the value of any location, its population factors and its relationship to the total retailing complex in the area must be considered.

In selecting a site the first consideration is the general type of location (downtown or highway) and the type of products being sold. As a second step the firm must determine the extent of the trading area. Over the years several mathematical techniques have been developed to identify a trading area accurately. The octant method and the saturation method are two such techniques.

---

[23]"Locational Analysis Within Regional Shopping Centers," in David J. Rachman (ed.), *Retail Management Strategy, Selected Readings* (Englewood Cliffs: New Jersey, Prentice-Hall Inc.), p. 271.

Tenants Most Frequently Found in Regional Shopping Centers   TABLE 17-5

Tenant Classification	Rank
Food and Food Service	
Supermarket	16
Specialty foods	18
Candy, nuts	9
Restaurant	10
General Merchandise	
Department store	11
Variety store	19
Dry Goods	
Yard goods	15
Clothing and Shoes	
Ladies' specialty	4
Ladies' wear	1
Men's wear	2
Family shoe	3
Ladies shoe	6
Men's and boys' shoe	14
Other Retail	
Drugs	20
Jewelry	7
Cards and gifts	5
Music and records	13
Offices	
Medical and dental	8
Services	
Beauty shop	12
Barber shop	17

Source: Urban Land Institute, *op. cit.,* p. 26.

The last step in selecting and evaluating a location includes real estate cost estimates and sales and merchandise costs; in effect, a *pro forma* profit-and-loss statement may be constructed. Assuming the retailer decides to rent his store rather than build, he must consider the location and its value. In recent years he has probably been considering moving into a shopping center. Rentals at these centers are based on the drawing power of the store.

The city retail structure includes the Central Business District (CBD), an area that has been declining in the recent decade, and the suburban shopping area. The suburban shopping development has been aided by the growth of the planned shopping center. This development has caused the retailer to consider not only the costs of operating in such centers but the need to carefully select a location.

1. From your experience point out the ways in which downtown shoppers differ from suburban shoppers in terms of:

    a. types of goods they shop for in each of their areas

    b. economic characteristics that can affect their shopping patterns

    c. the types of stores they patronize

2. How does the octant method differ in concept from the saturation method of choosing a retail location?

3. Describe the variables measured by Reilly's Law. If you were arguing against the value of this measurement, what arguments would you use? If you took the opposite position, what would be your arguments?

4. Suppose you are entrusted with making a decision on locating a men's wear store within a large regional shopping center. You have the option of locating on either side of a department store, variety store, food chain, or directly alongside a competitive men's wear store. Which would you choose and why?

5. Why have shopping centers grown in such numbers in the postwar years? Why would a department store prefer the confines of a shopping center rather than building a free-standing highway outlet?

6. United Films, a local downtown movie house, is offered an opportunity to build a theater in a large suburban shopping center. Discuss the pros and cons of such an opportunity.

7. In locating a supermarket what economic variables would seem to be the most pertinent? Name a qualitative factor that would be a consideration and relate it to the choice of a location.

8. Of what importance is the CBD to the total retail structure in the city? Why is it that large department stores are fighting furiously to maintain their stores in these sections of the city?

9. How significant is the choice of a prime location in the building of a:

    a. furniture store

    b. variety store

    c. shoe repair shop

    d. television repair shop

    e. gasoline station

    f. women's specialty dress store

10. From observation in your city, discuss the reasons for the growth of a great many free-standing highway retail outlets. What types have grown most in the past few years?

11. How does a free-standing highway outlet usually differ from its counterpart located in the downtown business district?

12. Student A says that from a competitive point of view the growth of the suburbs has decreased competition because only the large downtown stores can afford to come to the suburbs. Student B says the movement has actually intensified competition. Support B's argument.

13. The lowest-rent tenant listed in Table 17-3 is the warehouse or storage. Explain why this tenant has a lower rental than the major retailers.

14. Among the newer shopping centers the enclosed mall is becoming the most popular. Offer some reasons why this type of center is growing in popularity.

15. Why are apparel stores the most plentiful in the large regional centers?

16. Why are supermarkets among the least frequent outlets in regional shopping centers (see Table 17-5)?

CONTROLLING
THE FIRM

IV

It has been clearly demonstrated in the preceding chapters that the retail firm has a whole host of alternative ways by which to select the proper retail mix for the store. How management can monitor and control its organization, an important aspect in the management of any enterprise, will be the subject of this final section.

Basically, there exist two major means of controlling the retail firm. The first is the use of financial controls, requiring an understanding of the profit and loss statement and the balance sheet.

The second is the use of research and secondary data information.

Management Control

18

OBJECTIVES YOU SHOULD MEET

1. *Summarize* the various ways sales are used as a financial control device.

2. *Illustrate* the difference between profits measured as a return on sales and profits measured as a return on investment.

3. *Explain* the relationship of the key components of a profit and loss statement.

4. *Discuss* the retail method of inventory.

5. *Illustrate* clearly how a profit and loss statement can be computed from a book inventory.

6. *Contrast* the classification of operating expenses based on a natural division with their classification based on profit centers.

7. *Define* assets, liabilities, and capital.

8. *Discuss* the control techniques used to evaluate the individual buyer.

As noted in Chapter 2, a major task of management is to maintain control over the firm and readjust its operations and plans. This chapter will identify the controls that management uses to monitor the store's present position.

Figure 18-1 outlines the management control process. As a first step the retailer *identifies the objectives* of the firm and *establishes plans* to accomplish its objectives. He *implements the plans* through a strategy that adjusts the mix of the basic factors: goods and services, communication, and physical distribution. He constantly *monitors the results* of this activity. On the basis of this monitoring, *he adjusts his objectives, his plans, or his implementation* of the plans.

Management controls are necessary for several reasons. At any given time management must know exactly where the firm stands and be in a position to take any necessary action. In addition, by establishing a control system the firm can be *accurately* informed of its position and locate its problems more easily. *Identifica-*

FIGURE 18-1   Management Control Process

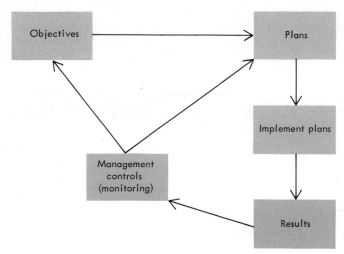

tion of problem areas is perhaps one of the major concerns of top management. Last, the installation of management control systems enables management to make plans on the basis of accurate historical information.

Controls can be classified as either *financial controls,* by far the most important, or *research controls,* which include retailing research and secondary sources of information. This chapter will discuss financial controls in detail. Chapters 19 and 20 will discuss research controls.

Financial
Controls

The retailer, like any other businessman, maintains records that allow him to determine the status of his business at any given time. Much of his information is in the form of accounting records such as profit and loss statements and balance sheets.

In today's rapidly changing environment firms are also in need of systematic ways to determine the status of the firm on a weekly or perhaps even a daily basis. Because the preparation of accounting statements requires time and effort, it has always been the retailer's practice to maintain in addition a flow of daily or weekly information that will keep him abreast of the firm's current operation. The official profit and loss statement published by the firm covers a longer period.

The firm usually develops guidelines that can be applied to the financial statements to measure the firm's progress and compare it to the achievements of other firms.

In the following sections these measurements will be discussed with particular emphasis on the over-all firm measurements used by top management. The concluding section of this chapter will discuss the measurements used to evaluate the individual buyer.

Over-all Company Measurements

The two major measurements of how a retail firm is doing are *sales* and *profits.* However, neither of these measurements is used solely by itself, but rather both are related to various other measurements of the firm's characteristics. For instance, sales in most firms are related to space, and profits to the firm's investment.

In addition to watching sales and profits figures, the firm studies the *profit and loss statement* and the *balance sheet* as a means of control. In the former, store expenses and income are usually under scrutiny; in the latter, financial ratios measuring the ability of the firm to meet its obligations are presented.

All these measurements are used to evaluate not only the total firm but also the individual department run by a buyer. Many of these measurements are interrelated, and few firms make a judgment based on only one guideline.

Sales Volume

An increasing sales volume is an important measurement of the well-being of a retail store. Though it is almost a platitude to say that sales volume indicates growth, volume is a doubly important factor in retailing. This observation is based on our knowledge that the typical retail store has a high labor cost, and sales increases reflect to a great extent the productivity of labor. Conversely, though all business organizations strive for higher sales, moderate increases may be more palatable than in the retail organization. For example, if the United States Steel Company experiences a sharp drop in sales, it can adjust to this decline by reducing the size of the workforce. Retailers are rarely in a position to do the same, as the size of a store and the hours it must be open command a minimum number of sales people. The steel company also has the advantages of being able to completely shut down a plant when demand is at a low level and of deriving more benefits from automation (with its resultant reduction in labor costs) than the typical retail store. In addition, in a retail firm sales per worker is an important measurement since little of the increase in sales can be credited to capital investment on the part of management. Those familiar with the contract negotiations in the steel industry are aware of the endless controversy over determining the relative contributions of capital investment and labor to increasing productivity in the industry. Retail negotiations do not revolve around these points of contention.

Retail management therefore keeps a close eye on sales reports. There are three basic measurements of sales: sales measured against the previous year's sales; sales measured against stores in the same general area; and standards of measurement based on national surveys.

There is a strong tendency for the retail firm to measure its sales against the performance of the previous year. On an annual basis, and allowing for catastrophic circumstances (such as a labor strike) or an unusual phenomenon (such as an inflation), this measurement is considered to be a valid one. The firm must make an adjustment, however, for the addition of new selling space in the form of renovating current properties or the building of branch stores. When the firm makes measurements on a month-to-month basis, however, this measurement is less than adequate. Comparing sales in the month of March with sales of the previous March may give a false impression unless adjustments are made for shifts in the calendar. As a simple illustration, the time at which Easter occurs can have an important effect on the weeks prior to the holiday and in some instances on the weeks that follow.

Aside from sales measurements of this nature the firm in some instances has an opportunity to compare itself with other firms either in the same industry or in the same city. These measurements will be discussed in greater detail in Chapter 20.

Other Sales Measurements

Though increasing its sales is a major goal for the retail firm, sales volume is also used to measure other relationships. Among these are sales per square feet and sales per employee.

Sales per square foot. The well-known relationship between sales and space within the store is used in many ways, for instance, in designing a food supermarket.

One of the major control measurements used in the retail firm is annual sales per square foot of store space. By dividing the sales for the year by the square footage of a store one can compute the sales per foot. In Table 18-1 one can see the sales per square foot of the Federated Department Store chain over a ten-year period. Though slight variances exist from year to year, the trend is obviously in an upward direction. In effect, the firm has increased its sales per square foot more than $25.

TABLE 18-1   Sales per Square Foot for Federated Department Stores 1962-1971

Year	Sales per Square Foot
1971	$96.20
1970	89.16
1969	88.19
1968	85.10
1967	81.88
1966	80.58
1965	81.36
1964	81.01
1963	69.76
1962	69.82

Source: Computed from Federated Department Stores, Inc., *1971 Annual Report.*

The significance of this figure can be seen in several ways. It is management's view that an increase in the firm's sales per square foot indicates that its merchandising operations are becoming more efficient. In the case of Federated over this ten-year period, the firm has increased its square footage from approximately 13 million to over 24 million square feet. This figure tends to support the view that an increase in sales per square foot suggests an increase in productivity and efficiency in the firm.

Many firms use sales per square footage as a goal in making their long-range plans. For instance, Thalhimer Bros., a chain with headquarters in Richmond, Virginia, reported sales per square foot of $48 and announced its intention of increasing this figure to $60 by 1975. The firm reported that it would place strong emphasis on high-fashion merchandise and pay closer attention to lease operators, who account for 5 per cent of the firm's total sales. In the latter case, it planned to reexamine leases in light of the leasee's sales per square foot.

Sales per employee. Space in its relationship to sales is not the only measurement of the productivity of the firm and its operation. Another seemingly related measurement is sales per employee. Figure 18-2 indicates the annual sales per full-time employee in a supermarket from 1961 to 1971. The average full-time supermarket employee produced over $73,000 of sales in 1971, contrasted with $55,000 ten years earlier.

The increase in sales per employee would seem to indicate that the supermarket is getting more productivity from each employee. However, the analyst must be cautioned that some of the increase in sales is due to price increases attributable to the general inflation in our economy. Thus any attempt to measure this increase in efficiency must first deflate the sales figures.[1]

Annual Sales per Fulltime Employee in Supermarkets   **FIGURE 18-2**

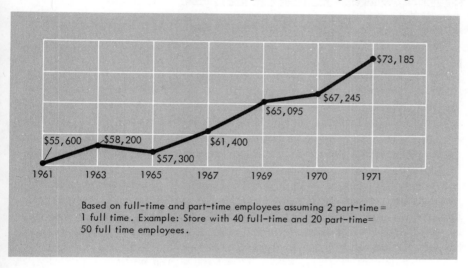

Based on full-time and part-time employees assuming 2 part-time = 1 full time. Example: Store with 40 full-time and 20 part-time = 50 full time employees.

Source: *Progressive Grocer,* April, 1972, p. 82.

Profits

Though a firm finds sales data a fairly reliable measurement of the firm's tendency to grow, it is possible, nevertheless, that in spite of the fixed nature of most retail costs, the firm's sales could be increasing at a less than profitable rate. It is, therefore, incumbent upon management not only to observe sales but to develop a measurement of profits. Two profit measurements are relied on: profits as measured against net sales and profits as a return on investment.

The following formulas are used to compute each:

---

[1] The deflation process was discussed in Chapter 5.

$$\text{Return on Sales} = \frac{\text{Net Profit}}{\text{Net Sales}}$$

$$\text{Return on Investment} = \frac{\text{Net Profit}}{\text{Net Worth (or owner's equity)}}$$

The first measurement is the most widely used. In Table 18-2 it can be observed that food chains, representing some of the largest firms in retailing, earn lower profits as measured against sales than many of the general merchandise or mail order firms shown. Does this mean that food firms are less profitable than general merchandise stores? The answer is "No" and will be discussed below in greater detail. Stores in collecting this data usually rely on published studies for comparisons among related stores.

Using this measure, however inadequate, still gives the firm an indication as to how it is meeting the needs of the consuming public. For we know that profits, whether measured as a ratio of sales or by other means, do vary considerably over a period of time. In Figure 18-3 we see the profits of some major department stores charted and compared to changes in the postwar business cycle. This seems to indicate that, aside from the firm's ability to meet consumers' needs, profits in retailing are strongly affected by the business cycle.

Though profits measured as a ratio of sales are widely used as guides, during the postwar period it became recognized that another measurement was needed. This measurement, called "return on investment," showed profits as a ratio of the firm's equity or investment in the business. It was first widely disseminated in the so-called Harvard Studies published during the 1930's. Its use, however, was limited until the postwar expansion took place. As a result of the expansion many firms were faced with the problem of evaluating the operations of individual stores over far-flung areas of the United States. They were also aware of the fact that though a firm turned in a high ratio of profits to sales, it required a great deal of inventory investment and labor to do so — the idea being that sometimes lower profits as measured against sales can actually be higher in terms of the amount of investment the firm has in the store. This concept is demonstrated in Table 18-2, where it can be seen that the stores with the highest ratio of *profits to sales* do not necessarily have the highest ratio of *profits to investment.* Conversely, many of the firms with the lowest ratio of *profits to sales* achieved the highest *profits on investment.* A glance at the food chains bears out this observation. One food chain, for example, with a profit to sales ratio of 1.9 per cent earned about 26.8 cents on each dollar of investment. To many observers this latter measurement is a good indicant of the firm's ability to balance costs and consumer demand.[2]

Profit
and Loss
Statement

All firms at some point in their planning period compute a profit and loss statement, which always encompasses the total firm. In many firms it is also computed by department: The buyer of handbags, for example, will receive a statement, usually on a monthly basis, of his profits and losses for each month and to date. This statement is used by the buyer in evaluating his present position in the planning cycle.

---

[2] For a more detailed discussion of return on investment see E. Beekman, "Problems of Calculating Return on Investment," *Journal of Retailing* (Summer, 1968), p. 3.

TABLE 18-2 Sales, Profits, and Net Worth Ratios of Major United States Retail Firms for the Year 1972, by Type of Store

Retail Firms	Sales 1972	Profit Before Taxes 1972	Net Worth 1972	Profits Before Taxes Per Cent of Sales	Profits Before Taxes Per Cent of Net Worth
Apparel Chains					
Alexander's	$ 325,896,000	$ 3,050,000	$ 53,520,000	0.9%	5.7%
Lane Bryant	277,475,000	18,243,000	62,406,000	6.6	29.2
J. W. Mays	161,450,000	6,326,000	25,224,000	3.9	25.1
Department and Specialty Stores					
Allied Stores Corporation	1,482,955,000	50,580,000	335,672,000	3.4	15.1
Associated Dry Goods	1,130,004,000	79,624,000	368,068,000	7.0	21.6
Broadway-Hale Stores	931,049,000	70,921,000	268,181,000	7.6	26.4
Buffum's	39,793,000	2,155,000	13,288,000	5.4	16.2
Carson, Pirie, Scott and Company	289,912,000	12,292,000	60,975,000	4.2	20.2
Elder Beerman	75,279,000	3,357,000	17,160,000	4.5	19.6
Federated Department Stores	2,665,148,000	203,573,000	826,376,000	7.6	24.6
Garfinckel, Brooks Bros., Miller & Rhoads, Inc.	197,556,000	15,554,000	66,618,000	7.9	23.3
Gimbel Bros., Inc.	812,184,000	25,312,000	230,343,000	3.1	11.0
Goldblatt Bros., Inc.	246,794,000	4,511,000	43,528,000	1.8	10.4
Higbee Company	149,472,000	6,097,000	45,941,000	4.1	13.3
Holmes (D. H.), Ltd.	73,096,000	3,674,000	19,720,000	5.0	18.6
Macy (R.H.) and Company	1,041,122,000	52,169,000	271,402,000	5.0	19.2
May Department Stores, Inc.	1,467,930,000	91,508,000	461,024,000	6.2	19.8
Mercantile Stores Co., Inc.	458,328,000	39,156,000	139,647,000	8.5	28.0

TABLE 18-2 Continued

Retail Firms	Sales 1972	Profit Before Taxes 1972	Net Worth 1972	Profits Before Taxes Per Cent of Sales	Per Cent of Net Worth
Department and Specialty Stores (cont.)					
Penney (J.C.) Company	$ 5,529,600,000	$ 311,195,000	$1,138,027,000	5.6	27.3
Rich's, Inc.	260,670,000	22,857,000	89,933,000	8.8	25.4
Food Chains					
Acme Markets, Inc.	2,025,300,000	4,301,000	187,288,000	0.2	2.3
Daitch Crystal Dairies, Inc.	182,751,000	2,094,000	39,909,000	1.1	5.2
Food Fair Stores, Inc.	1,980,458,000	17,369,000	134,506,000	0.9	12.9
Grand Union	1,379,681,000	15,677,000	151,387,000	1.1	10.4
Great Atlantic and Pacific Tea Co.	6,368,876,000	105,277,000 (loss)	599,301,000	-1.7	-17.6
King Kullen Grocery Co., Inc.	126,628,000	1,079,000	13,605,000	0.8	7.9
Kroger Company	3,790,532,000	33,213,000	353,360,000	0.9	9.4
Lucky Stores, Inc.	1,988,376,000	57,434,000	154,882,000	2.9	37.1
National Tea Company	1,089,752,000	11,275,000 (loss)	92,908,000	-0.1	-12.1
Safeway Stores, Inc.	6,057,633,000	176,271,000	606,304,000	2.9	29.1
Stop and Shop Inc.	994,469,000	10,803,000	66,751,000	1.1	16.2
Waldbaum, Inc.	365,117,000	6,841,000	25,547,000	1.9	26.8
Winn-Dixie	1,833,572,000	72,164,000	198,623,000	3.9	36.3
Mail Order					
Marcor Stores, Inc.	3,369,321,000	132,052,000	957,214,000	3.9	13.8
Sears, Roebuck and Company	10,991,000,000	1,030,157,000	4,515,414,000	9.4	22.8

TABLE 18-2 Continued

Retail Firms	Sales 1972	Profit Before Taxes 1972	Net Worth 1972	Profits Before Taxes Per Cent of Sales	Per Cent of Net Worth
Discount Stores					
Caldor, Inc.	$ 132,473,000	$ 8,914,000	$ 26,400,000	6.7	33.8
FedMart Corporation	213,726,000	5,170,000	21,409,000	2.4	24.1
Friendly Frost, Inc.	32,466,000	349,000	5,838,000	1.1	6.0
Masters, Inc.	47,994,000	2,167,000	13,379,000	4.5	16.2
Sage International Inc.	14,171,000	392,000	2,663,000	2.8	14.7
Vornado, Inc.	755,597,000	18,619,000	141,735,000	2.5	13.1
Zayre Corporation	939,710,000	17,250,000	99,539,000	1.8	17.3
Drug Chains					
Begley Drug Co.	14,391,000	1,103,000	6,438,000	7.7	17.1
Cunningham Drug Stores, Inc.	90,690,000	1,561,000	38,137,000	1.7	5.5
Gray Drug Stores, Inc.	203,671,000	7,463,000	32,715,000	3.7	22.8
People's Drug Store	238,103,000	2,346,000	34,773,000	1.0	6.7
Walgreen Company	863,334,000	19,507,000	108,608,000	2.3	18.0
Variety Chains					
Grants (W.T.) Company	1,644,747,000	58,421,000	334,338,000	3.6	17.5
Kresge (S.S.) Company	3,836,826,000	200,187,000	779,726,000	5.2	25.7
McCrory Corporation	1,226,845,000	44,830,000	98,950,000	3.7	45.3
Woolworth (F.W.) Company	3,148,108,000	93,886,000	891,331,000	3.0	10.5

FIGURE 18-3   Quarterly Cyclical Behavior of Seven Department Store Chains

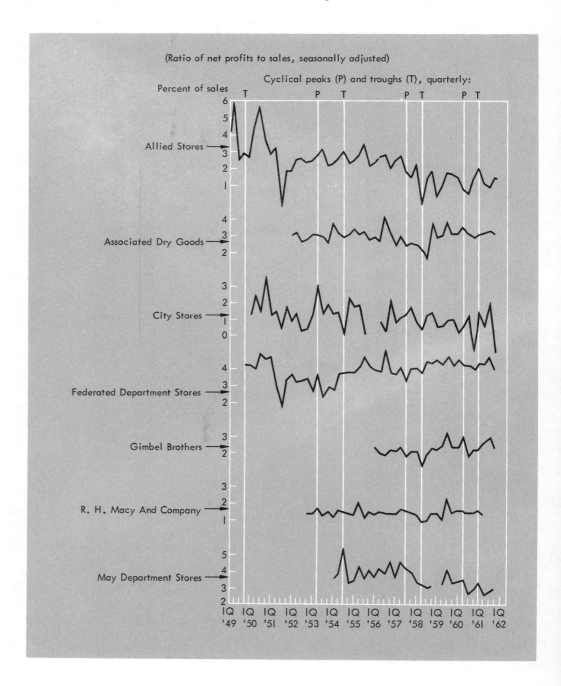

Source: David J. Rachman, "Postwar Cyclical Behavior of Department Store Chains," *Journal of Retailing,* Fall, 1962.

The small retail firm resorts to a rather simple method of calculating a profit and loss statement. A preliminary statement is shown in Table 18-3. In effect, Net Sales minus the Cost of Goods Sold equals Gross Margin. By subtracting his operating expenses from the gross margin, the retailer determines his net profit before income taxes.

Operating Statement as of March 31, 1973   TABLE 18-3

	Dollar Amounts	*Per Cent to Sales*
Net sales	$100,000	100
Cost of goods sold	45,000	45
Gross Margin	$ 55,000	55
Operating expenses	40,000	40
Net profit before taxes	$ 15,000	15

The small retailer can readily obtain most of these figures from his records. Net sales, for example, are the firm's retail sales minus the returns by customers. Thus, if sales are $205,000 and customers' returns are $5,000, net sales are $200,000. In a small firm gross sales can be obtained from cash register receipts, and returns can be recorded separately as credits are issued to customers.

Operating expenses in the small store can be calculated from the firm's checkbook, as most payments for expenses and bills are paid by check. A tabulation of these checks can be used to calculate this figure.

The major obstacle the retailer encounters is to compute the *Cost of Goods Sold* for his firm. The computation of this figure is as follows:

Open inventory at cost, January 1, 1973	$21,000
Purchases at cost	40,000
Freight	1,000
Cost of goods handled	$62,000
Closing inventory at cost, March 31, 1973	17,000
Cost of goods sold	$45,000

C+G HANDLED

Consider that the retailer had an opening inventory of $21,000 at cost, and during the three-month period he made purchases of $40,000 and incurred freight charges on these purchases of $1,000. Totaling these three figures one arrives at a total of $62,000, which represents the *Cost of Goods Handled*. This figure represents the cost value of all merchandise handled in the store during this period and, in effect, the amount of merchandise available for sale to the customer. By subtracting the firm's closing inventory of $17,000 from this figure, one arrives at what was actually counted the *Cost of Goods Sold*. This figure represents the cost value of the goods sold during the three-month period. The difference between the cost value of these goods and the net sales represents the *gross margin,* out of which the firm must pay all of its expenses and, one hopes, earns profits.

Large Firm's Report

One should note that in order to make its cost and profit computations the small retailer must take a physical inventory at cost. Taking inventory is necessary because the retailer has no way of estimating his closing inventory.

As most large retail firms need estimates of their profit situation at regular intervals (usually monthly), an accounting system that requires a physical inventory is not practical. Large retailers usually take inventories at least twice a year and make a calculation similar to the small retailer's.

However, the problem of the large retailer is to calculate the inventory during the year from the book records, for which he maintains a *retail method of inventory* throughout the year. The large retailer records a cost and a retail price on all merchandise purchases. As a practical matter a buyer purchasing 100 handbags at $5 a piece enters on his accounting records the following line:

	Cost	Retail	Retail Markup Per Cent
100 handbags @ $5	$500	$1,000	50

Using the retail method of inventory it is *not* necessary for the retailer to enter the cost price on the price tickets of each piece of merchandise on the floor. It is necessary only to list the retail price.

Calculation Based on Physical Inventory

Should the large retailer wish to determine the cost of the closing inventory he can use the retail conversion method. Under this system the inventory is taken at retail price, because all merchandise is marked with the retail figure.

Consider the retailer who has the following position as of a given date:

	Cost	Retail
Opening inventory	$40,000	$ 80,000
Purchases	50,000	70,000
Total merchandise handled	$90,000	$150,000
Closing inventory at retail (physical count)		$ 30,000

In order to determine the cost of goods sold, the retailer must determine the cost of the closing inventory. To make this calculation he simply notes that the cost of the merchandise handled approximates 60 per cent of the retail price (90,000 ÷ 150,000 = 60 per cent). Assuming that the same relationship applies to the closing inventory, the cost value of the inventory is 60 per cent of its retail value or $18,000. Once the retailer has this cost value he can compute his profit and loss statement on the same basis as the small retailer.

The book inventory calculation of a closing inventory and the subsequent calculation of a cost of goods sold is used by firms that require a continuing statement of profit and loss (usually monthly). This calculation is made without an actual physical count, in the following way:

	Cost	Retail
Opening inventory	$ 40,000	$ 80,000
Purchases	70,000	130,000
Total merchandise handled	$110,000	$210,000

Total Merchandise Deductions

Sales	$100,000
Markdowns	8,000
Employee discounts	1,000
Estimated shortages	4,000
Total merchandise deductions	$113,000

The cost of the total merchandise handled is determined by dividing $110,000 by $210,000, which gives a cost percentage of 52.4 per cent.

At this stage the book inventory is customarily calculated, taking all deductions from the retail value of the merchandise handled. The merchandise deductions include all transactions that reduce the retail value of the total merchandise handled. That which is left over represents the store's inventory. What reduces the total merchandise handled at retail? The answer is sales, markdowns, employee discounts, and estimated stock shortages. In this case they amount to a total of $113,000. Reducing the retail value of the merchandise handled by this amount leaves us with a *retail* book inventory of $97,000 ($210,000 − $113,000). To determine the cost value of this inventory, one simply applies the cost percentage of 52.4 per cent to the retail inventory, getting a product of $50,828.

Once the inventory cost has been determined, a relatively simple calculation will determine the gross margin and the net profit, as follows:

Sales		$100,000
Total merchandise handled	$110,000	
Less ending inventory, at cost value	50,828	
Cost of goods sold		59,172
Gross margin		$ 40,828
Less operating expenses		20,000
Net profit before income taxes		$ 20,828

Thus, without taking a physical inventory count the large retail firm can determine its profit and loss for the period under study.

Operating Expenses

As a matter of routine the managers of a retail business carefully analyze the expense ratios in their business, as a rise in one item can cause a reduction in profits or perhaps even a loss.

Table 18-4 lists a composite operating statement for men's wear stores as reported for 1970. It should be noted that the gross margin of these stores approximates 37.5 per cent, while the operating expenses average slightly over 34 per cent.

TABLE 18-4   Operating Experiences of Men's Wear Stores, 1970

	Stores Handling Men's Wear Only (170 Firms)	
	Range of Common Experience	*Median Store*
SALES		
1. Net sales, excluding leased departments, per cent of total net sales	93.6% to 100.0%	100.0%
2. Net sales of leased departments, per cent of total net sales	4.0 to 9.0	6.6
COST OF GOODS SOLD (Per cent of net sales excluding leased departments, except as noted.)		
3. Beginning inventory at cost	18.6 to 33.2	25.6
4. Net purchases at cost including transportation charges	58.3 to 65.9	61.8
5. Cost of total merchandise handled	78.9 to 95.8	87.2
6. Ending inventory at cost	19.5 to 34.6	26.3
7. Gross cost of merchandise sold	57.7 to 63.6	60.2
8. Cash discounts earned	0.7 to 1.3	0.8
9. Net workroom costs	1.4 to 3.3	2.1
10. Total cost of merchandise sold	59.2 to 64.5	62.0
11. Gross margin, excluding leased department income and sales	35.5 to 40.8	38.0
12. Gross margin, including income from leased departments, as a per cent of total net sales	35.0 to 40.3	37.5
OPERATING EXPENSES (Per cent of total net sales.)		
13. Payroll (total)	15.6 to 20.2	17.8
a. Payroll of owners and officers	4.0 to 9.2	6.3
b. Selling payroll	7.2 to 11.0	9.2
c. Non-selling payroll	1.6 to 4.9	2.8
d. Sick leave, holiday, military leave, and severance pay	N.A. to N.A.	N.A.
14. Advertising	2.0 to 3.5	2.7

15. Taxes (total)	1.1	to	2.0	1.5
a. All state and local taxes with the exception of payroll taxes and Federal income taxes	0.4	to	1.0	0.7
b. Social security and unemployment taxes	0.7	to	1.1	0.9
16. Supplies (total)	1.1	to	1.2	1.6
17. Services purchased (total)	0.5	to	1.6	0.9
18. Unclassified (total)	0.2	to	1.0	0.5
19. Traveling	0.2	to	0.6	0.4
20. Communications	0.3	to	0.7	0.5
21. Pensions	0.4	to	1.4	0.8
22. Insurance (total)	0.7	to	1.6	1.1
a. Workmen's compensation insurance, sickness, accident, group medical, group hospital and life insurance premiums	0.4	to	1.0	0.6
b. All other insurance premiums	0.4	to	0.9	0.6
23. Depreciation	0.5	to	1.4	0.9
24. Professional services	0.2	to	0.5	0.3
25. Donations	0.1	to	0.3	0.2
26. Bad debts	0.2	to	0.7	0.4
27. Equipment costs	0.2	to	0.7	0.4
28. Real property rentals	2.0	to	4.5	3.0
29. Total expenses	30.4	to	36.5	34.2
NET GAIN (Per cent of total net sales, except as noted.)				
30. Operating profit, including income from leased departments	1.2	to	6.4	3.3
31. Net other income and expenses	-0.2	to	1.6	0.7
32. Net profit, before Federal income taxes	1.2	to	7.1	3.4
33. Net profit before Federal income taxes as a per cent of net worth	4.8	to	23.3	12.4

Source: Men's Store Operating Experiences, *Annual Business Survey, 1970,* Menswear Retailers of America.

In the sample statement from the men's wear stores it should be noted that the payroll expenses represent over half of the store's expenses. The selling payroll represents over half the total payroll. Only advertising and rent seem to be of any major significance in the total picture. It goes without saying therefore that the management of a men's wear store will watch the payroll rather carefully.

Table 18-5 lists a compilation of operating expenses of food chain stores in a recent year. Though the gross margin in a chain store is almost half that of the men's wear store, it is notable that the payroll cost represents over half of the total expenses of the firm, even though the chain food store is a self-service operation.

TABLE 18-5   Composite Food Chain Store Operating Expenses (1970-71)

Gross margin	21.39%
Expenses	
Payroll	11.09
Supplies	1.01
Utilities	.74
Communications	.07
Travel	.11
Services purchased	1.31
Promotional activities	1.32
Professional services	.10
Donations	.02
Insurance	.60
Taxes and licenses (except on income)	.92
Property rentals	1.49
Equipment rentals	.12
Depreciation and amortization	.85
Repairs	.59
Unclassified	.68
Credits and allowances	(−.54)
Total expenses before interest	20.47
Total interest	.73
Total expenses including interest	21.20%
Net operating profit	.19
Other income or deductions	
Credit for imputed interest	.58
Cash discounts earned	.58
Other revenue, net (including profit or loss on real estate)	.38
Total net other income	1.54
Total net earnings before income taxes	1.73
Total income taxes	.87
Total net earnings after income taxes	.86
Earnings as a percentage of net worth after-tax earnings	8.88
Number of stockturns	12.51

Source: *Progressive Grocer,* April, 1972, p. 75.

The most elaborate expense classification system can be found in department stores. The various breakdowns can be seen in Tables 18-6 and 18-7. In Table 18-6 one finds the natural classification of expenses, categories recommended for most retailers because they comprise most of the natural expenses incurred by most stores.

Expenses by Natural Division   TABLE 18-6

Payroll (01)
Advertising (03)
Taxes (04)
Supplies (06)
Services purchased (07)
Unclassified (08)
Travel (09)
Communications (10)
Pensions (11)
Insurance (12)
Depreciation (13)
Professional services (14)
Donations (15)
Bad debts (16)
Equipment costs (17)
Real property rentals (20)
Expense transfers (91)
Outside revenue and other credits (92)
Gross operating expense
    Less: accounts receivable handling charges
Net operating expense

Source: National Retail Merchants Assocation

Expenses Classified by Expense Center   TABLE 18-7

Expense center
110 General management
210 Accounting and data processing
310 Accounts receivable
320 Credit and collection
410 Sales promotion
510 Service and operations
550 Telephone and other utilities
570 Cleaning
580 Maintenance and repairs
610 Personnel
630 Supplementary benefits

TABLE 18-7   Expenses Classified by Expense Center

720	Maintenance of reserve stock
740	Receiving and marking
750	Shuttle service
810	Selling supervision
820	Direct selling
830	Customer services
860	Wrapping and packing
880	Delivery
910	Merchandising
920	Buying
930	Merchandise control

Source: National Retail Merchants Association.

A much more elaborate system of expense classification is found in Table 18-7, which classifies expenses by expense centers. This classification is used as an addition to the natural expense classification. It offers the retailer an opportunity to measure the productivity of each expense center in his store. For example, by combining all expenses related to *direct selling,* the retailer is in a position to calculate the cost per sales transaction or the cost of each dollar of sales. Ordinarily, such a detailed classification system is used only by large department stores.

Balance Sheet

The balance sheet, outlined in Table 18-8, shows the financial position of the firm in terms of its assets and liabilities. *Assets* are what the business owns, and *liabilities* are debts that the business will have to pay at some future date. *Capital* (also called Net Worth) is the stockholders investment in the firm and any earnings that have not been withdrawn. In essence the balance sheet represents an equation: Assets = Liabilities + Capital.

To measure the financial position of the retail firm, many balance-sheet ratios are computed by analysts. Some of the most widely included are the following, computed here from the figures in Table 18-8:

$$\frac{\text{Current Assets}}{\text{Current Liabilities}} = \frac{\$55,400}{\$19,500} = 2.8 \text{ to } 1$$

Known as the *current ratio,* this ratio of assets to liabilities is an important test of the ability of the firm's liquid assets to meet debts due within the current period.

$$\frac{\text{Net Sales}}{\text{Working Capital}} = \frac{\text{Net Sales}}{\text{Current Assets} - \text{Current Liabilities}}$$

$$= \frac{\$188,000}{\$55,400 - \$19,500} = \frac{\$188,000}{\$\ 35,900} = 5$$

[3]Small Business Reporter, *op. cit.,* p. 8.

(Name of Business)
BALANCE SHEET
December 31, 1970

1.	**ASSETS**			
2.	Current assets:			
3.	Cash		$ 8,000	
4.	Accounts receivable	$22,400		
5.	Less allowance for bad debts	(1,000)		
			21,400	
6.	Inventory (valued at cost)		26,000	
	Total current assets			$55,400
7.	Fixed assets:			
	Fixtures and equipment	$13,000		
	Truck	3,200		
			$16,200	
8.	Less accumulated depreciation		(3,880)	
	Total fixed assets			12,320
9.	Total assets			$67,720
10.	**LIABILITIES AND CAPITAL**			
11.	Current liabilities:			
12.	Notes payable (due within 1 year)		$ 3,500	
13.	Accounts payable		15,300	
14.	Accrued expenses		700	
	Total current liabilities			$19,500
15.	Long term liabilities:			
16.	Notes payable (due after 1 year)		2,400	
17.	Total liabilities			$21,900
18.	Capital			
19.	Owner's capital, January 1, 1970		$45,120	
20.	Profit for period	$17,930		
21.	Owner's withdrawal	(17,230)		
22.	Undistributed earnings		700	
	Total capital, December 31, 1970			$45,820
23.	Total liabilities and capital			$67,720

Source: Small Business Reporter, *Retail Financial Record,* Bank of America, 1971, p. 5.

This ratio, known as the *turnover of working capital,* indicates how actively business cash is being put to work in terms of sales. The greater the turnover, the more active the cash.

Though much of what has been said applies to an evaluation of the total firm, management must also maintain control over the buyer and his merchandising efforts throughout the year; it therefore applies many of the same over-all firm controls to individual store departments.

Evaluating the Buyer

363

One of the basic devices used to evaluate the buyer is the merchandise plan illustrated in Figure 18-4, in which the firm keeps a continuous record of the buyer's department. In this case the merchandise plan is for a dress-goods department. It indicates to management that the buyer met the sales plan for the month of February; in fact, sales exceeded the plan by $361. Markdowns were $10 under the plan, as was the stock position of the department. This latter figure was offset by the fact that purchases were considerably over the plan for the month. Other important measurements used in the plan include initial markup, gross margin, and retail advertising. The following summary includes the most common measurements for judging the buyer:[4]

FIGURE 18-4   Season Merchandise Plan

MERCHANDISE PLAN   STORE NO.____ LOCATION *N.Y.*

FROM *August* 19__ TO *February* 19__ DEPT *Dress Goods* NO____

	% INITIAL MARKUP	% MARKDOWNS	% SHORTAGE	% GROSS MARGIN	% DISC. EARNED	STOCK TURN WITHIN THIS PERIOD
PLAN	35.0	3.0	1.5	34.0	1.9	.93
ACTUAL LAST YR.	34.2	5.0	1.6	31.7	1.8	.88

		SPRING FEB. (FALL AUG.)	MAR. SEPT.	APRIL OCT.	MAY NOV.	JUNE DEC.	JULY JAN.	TOTAL	% INC
SALES	ACTUAL 19__								
	ACTUAL 19__	2207	3666	4321	2917	1824	1275	16,210	9
	PLAN	2420	4030	4750	3200	2000	1400	17,800	10
	ACTUAL	2781	4311						

								STOCK*	AV. STOCK
STOCK (B.O.M.)	LAST YR.	17,695	20,923	21,032	19,061	17,692	16,530	15,876	18,404
	PLAN	18,700	21,250	21,650	20,080	18,250	17,550	16,500	19,140
	ACTUAL	18,509	21,576	21,147					

								TOTAL	% TO SALES
REDUCTIONS	LAST YR.	37.	172	194	211	133	65	812	5.0
	PLAN	70	120	140	100	60	40	530	3.0
	ACTUAL	60	198						

								TOTAL	% M.U.
PURCHASES (RETAIL)	LAST YR.	5472	3947	2544	1759	795	706	15,223	34.2
	PLAN	5040	4550	3320	1470	1360	390	16,130	35.0
	ACTUAL	5908	4080						

		SALES	ADV.	SALES	ADV.	SALES	ADV.	SALES	ADV.	SALES	ADV.	SALES	ADV.	TOTAL	% TO SALES
NEWSPAPER ADV. (% TO SALES)	ACTUAL 19__														
	ACTUAL 19__	70	3.2	104	2.8	115	2.6	86	2.9	55	3.0	40	3.1	470	2.9
	PLAN	78	3.2	117	2.9	133	28	96	3.0	64	3.2	47	3.4	535	3.0
	ACTUAL	84	3.0												

		SALES	ADV	SALES	ADV	SALES	ADV	SALES	ADV	SALES	ADV	SALES	ADV	
% TO SEASON TOTAL	ACTUAL 19__													
	ACTUAL 19__	14	15	23	22	27	24	18	18	11	12	7	9	100
	PLAN	14	15	23	22	27	24	18	18	11	12	7	8	100
	ACTUAL													

PLANNED PURCHASES ADJUSTED

PLANNED PURCHASES	5040	4550
PLUS OR MINUS STOCK VARIATIONS	+191	−326
TOTAL	5231	4224
LESS UNFILLED ORDERS B.O.M. DELIVERY THIS MO.	3200	2561
OPEN TO BUY DELIVERY THIS MO.	2031	1663

APPROVED_____ BUYER   APPROVED_____ MDSE. MGR.

* STOCK END OF SEASON

Source: Wingate and Friedlander, *op. cit.*, p. 166.

[4] John W. Wingate and Joseph S. Friedlander, *The Management of Retail Buying* (Englewood Cliffs, N.J.: Prentice-Hall, Inc., 1963), pp. 19-20.

1. *Sales results:*
   a. In dollars.
   b. In units of merchandise sold or in number of sales transactions.

Sales results include a comparison with the previous year and the plan for the season under control. In some cases, because of the impact of inflation and the need to deflate sales figures, management may also examine either the number of units sold or the sale transactions.

2. *Inventory results as revealed by:*
   a. Stockturn.
   b. Proportion of old stock carried over at the new planning period.

Inventory is controlled in terms of stockturn and the ratio of old stock just discussed. The view of management is that if either ratios or proportions are out of line the buyer may be forced to increase his markdowns in the near future to reduce his slow-moving old stock.

3. *Margin results:*
   a. Initial markup (aggregate original retail prices less aggregate invoice costs).
   b. Gross margin realized (final selling price less cost of goods sold).
   c. Controllable profit (gross margin less direct departmental expenses).
   d. Operating profit realizes (gross margin less all expenses chargeable to the department).

The evaluation of margin results is based on the amount of control the buyer has over his own department. If the buyer is not involved in budgeting the expenses of his department, he is usually judged on either his ability to maintain a suitable initial markup or a gross margin figure.

If the buyer controls the budgeting of advertising, sales people, delivery, and other direct costs in his department, the controllable profit (i.e., gross margin less direct expenses) is usually the criterion. This latter technique is usually referred to as the *contribution* plan, as only direct department expenses are charged to the department and the remaining profit used as a contribution to the store's overhead – top management salaries, rent, light, heat and power, and other storewide costs. Firms using this technique assume that all chargeable expenses are controllable by the person responsible for the department.

In some stores the firm charges each department with overhead expenses and then judges the department's performance by the operating profit realized. The department is charged with its direct expenses and alloted a share of the overhead expenses such as rent, management salaries, and similar items.

This seemingly useful means of control suffers from several limitations, especially the problem of determining the criteria to be used to allot overhead expenses to a department. For instance, how should a store allot rent? The most widely used technique seems to be to charge the department for the space occupied. Thus a department occupying 5 per cent of the store's space would be charged 5 per cent of the store rent. A major limitation of this technique is that the importance and productivity of space is dependent not so much on the amount of space occupied as on its location. Thus a department that occupies 5,000 square feet of first-floor space is using prime space in contrast to a department that has the same amount of space on the fifth floor.

It is even more questionable to allot rent to a department on the basis of the sales volume the department generates. For instance, a department that accounts for ten per cent of the store's volume would be charged under this system for ten per cent of the store's rent. Here again one runs into problems. Many departments attain a high volume because of the nature of the merchandise they carry; however, they may take up little store space. Thus a television set sold in an appliance department by the simple expedient of carrying a sample on the selling floor may create a lot of sales volume in a minimum of space.

As one can see, the latter control device is questionable. It is understandable that most firms prefer the controllable-profit approach.

SUMMARY

Management needs to monitor and control the firm's total effort, by both financial and research controls. The financial controls are discussed in this chapter.

Sales and profits are two key control items used by top management to judge the progress of the firm. Sales volume is usually compared to previous years' sales or measured against other stores in the same general area or, where relevant, on a national basis. The important relationship between sales and space in the store creates interest in the sales per square foot ratio widely used as a measure of the efficient use of space in the firm. Similarly, sales per employee over a period of time indicates the efficient use of manpower in the store.

The most widely used measurement of profits is relating the profits to sales. However, this measurement does not take into consideration the relationship of profits to the firm's net worth or investment. As can be seen in any study of these operating criteria, firms with a high profit-to-sales ratio do not necessarily return a high profit on the net worth of the firm. As a matter of fact, one cannot be sure that the two ratios go together.

In constructing a profit and loss statement for the small firm, a physical inventory must be taken in order to compute the cost of goods. However, in the large retail firm a profit and loss statement is needed at least monthly. As taking a physical inventory is too costly and impractical, firms rely on the retail method of inventory. By recording both the cost and the retail price of all purchases, the large retailer is able to estimate a closing inventory at cost and thus construct a profit and loss statement similar to that of the small retailer.

Retailers must carefully watch their operating expenses, and operating expenses are usually classified in a routine manner. However, in department stores several types of classification systems are used, namely the natural classification system and the system that divides expenses into expense centers. The latter system is widely used to measure productivity in large stores.

Another financial tool used in the firm is the balance sheet. The equation governing entries in the balance sheet is Assets equal Liabilities plus Capital. Several important ratios are applied to the balance sheet to determine the financial position of a firm; they include the current ratio and the turnover of working capital.

Aside from evaluating the total firm, management also monitors the performance of the individual buyer with the same over-all store controls, including sales volume, inventory ratios, and margin results.

QUESTIONS

1. In what two major ways can management control its firm?

2. Discuss the major items a small retailer must know in order to construct a profit and loss statement?

3. How would your answer to Question 2 differ for a large store?

4. What is meant by the *retail method of inventory?*

5. How often is it necessary to take a physical count of the stock in a store?

6. What are merchandise deductions?

7. Discuss the relationship between the formula that relates profits to sales and that relating profits to net worth?

8. If the ratio of profits to sales is high it follows that return on investment will be high. True or False? Discuss.

9. What expense items are typically found in the profit and loss statement of a store?

10. The contribution plan is the most widely used measurement of a department's profitability. Why?

11. A store had the following information available at the end of a year.

	Cost	Retail
Purchases	$100,000	$150,000
Beginning Inventory	$ 60,000	$100,000

At the end of the year a physical count of inventory was $40,000 (at retail), and it was estimated that $3,000 worth of merchandise was worthless. Determine the cost of goods sold.

12. Suppose sales in Question 11 were $180,000 and expenses $50,000. Can you calculate the profits before taxes?

13. Compare the operating statistics presented in Table 18-4 and Table 18-5. How do you account for the difference in the profits, return on net worth, and gross margin?

14. Make a list of the five best-known retail chains found in Table 18-2. Compare their profits to sales and return on investment ratios to the average in their category. How do they rate? Comment on this statement: "The best-known firms are always the most profitable!"

15. A recent advertising campaign by a major food chain emphasized the fact that the after-tax profits of the firm amounted to only one cent out of every dollar the consumer spent in the store. Comment on this campaign.

16. List the five most profitable department-store and specialty-store chains in Table 18-2. How do they compare with the top five discount houses? List the top three food chains and compare them with your discount-house list. Examine the significance of your findings.

Reducing Retail Risk: Adding the Research Dimension

19

OBJECTIVES YOU SHOULD MEET

1. *Define* retail research in your own words.
2. *Cite* a useful theory that could develop from a research study.
3. *Describe* the three general approaches to conducting a research project.
4. *Specify* the major types of studies that can be conducted using these three approaches.
5. *Outline* some of the limitations of these approaches.

One of the early retailing entrepreneurs, John Wanamaker, was said to have stood at his door and personally greeted many of his customers. Probably many of his customers appreciated his thoughtfulness, and no doubt he had this reaction in mind. However, by engaging in pleasantries of this sort, Wanamaker was also gaining information about his customers' needs and wants.

Mr. Wanamaker was fortunate in this respect. He had one store, few entrances, and evidently enough time to talk to consumers. Today's retail management is not so fortunate. The Chairman of the Board of Macy's has 14 stores in New York City, and every day an estimated 200,000 customers enter his downtown store alone. Therefore, management has to depend on research.

Research is a sort of buffer zone between the consumer and the management decision-making apparatus of the retail firm. In a sense it is a useful control and monitoring device for the firm. Possibly the best way to consider the research function is to recognize its value as a consumer feedback device of management. We can think of this feedback device also as offering management a second dimension to the decision-making process. Consider, for example, this business decision: With sales falling the controller of a department store considers releasing a few merchandise adjustments clerks. These clerks handle merchandise returns by customers, and according to the personnel records there are twenty employed in the store's main downtown location. A decision to reduce this staff by two might be called a one-dimension decision, simply because it is based on the internal needs of the firm to reduce the total store expenses. This is a rather easy decision to make since there is a direct relationship between the number of people employed in that department and its total expense. However, there is another dimension to this decision that has nothing to do with the expense budgets of the store: it is the consumer's reaction to a slower handling of customer returns. Knowledge of this reaction (through feedback) adds a new dimension to the controller's decision. He now has all the information necessary to make a decision: impact of a cutback in personnel on the expense structure of the firm and, more important, its impact on the consuming public. Where does he get this feedback information? One source, discussed in a later section of this chapter, is a continuing program of customer walkout studies. By examining these studies, the controller may find that one of the major consumer complaints about his store is its slowness or general ineptness in handling merchandise returns. A decision by the controller which disregards this finding may adversely affect the store's sales curve.

It is not always necessary for the controller to conduct special studies or have an elaborate budget to attain this second dimension. If, for example, he is concerned with the fact that discount firms are a growing competitive threat, then he can avail himself of numerous studies of the discount-house consumer. Many of these studies report that the consumer regards the liberal return policy of discount stores as a major advantage in their competition with traditional stores. Again, the point is that the budget-minded controller can add a new dimension to his decision making through research. If he then decides, for example, in the instance cited above, to reduce the number of employees in his adjustment department, he will have made a decision based on all the relevant facts.

Despite the obvious advantages of research as a basis for decision making, retailers traditionally spend less money on research than do manufacturers. In recent years, however, several major retailers have developed large and sophisticated research departments. Numbered among this group are Penneys, Sears, and Federated Department Stores. Most business managers know that even huge expenditures of money on research does not guarantee success. The continued failures of new products in the "soap" industry with its highly developed research techniques point to the fact that research is still very much more of an art than a science. Nonetheless, research does improve the chances of success in the marketing of products and does give management an opportunity to make a decision with some facts in hand. The expenditures of manufacturers on this aspect of their marketing program attest to a fair measure of success.

If we ask why most retailers have not developed a continuing research program and have spent a relatively small amount on this function, one obvious answer is that retail firms are often too small to support a research program of their own. The "mama and papa" grocery store would certainly not require, and could not afford, a research director or a trained sampling consultant. However, "papa" — if he is alert — does conduct research in the tradition of John Wanamaker. Small stores, with forward-looking management, can develop an adequate research program of their own as described in the following article.

DOING YOUR OWN RESEARCH[1]

T. D. Ellsworth

Small Gift Shop

One young man to whom research brought rich reward was the owner of a small gift shop, which he had taken over from his parents at a time when he had had little practical business experience. He had completed an intensive course of instruction in store management and operation, however, and was resolved to put his theoretical knowledge to an immediate and thorough test. He resolved, that is, to make no business decision without having all pertinent facts at hand, and thus he became the official researcher for his store.

As a starting point for his experiment, he selected the silverware department because of its small size and the relatively staple nature of its merchandise. He began his analysis of this department by investigating its sales history for the preceding two-year period. He compared its sales to corresponding figures for other stores of the same general merchandise classification in his Federal Reserve District. He concluded that, based on his December dollar sales, he could almost double his annual silverware sales figures if he could attain the same monthly percentage distribution of sales as the other stores in the Federal Reserve District.

He next analyzed his previous six months' silverware sales by selling price. This analysis indicated that the department had a total of sixty-one individual prices ranging from $1.50 to $50.00. A further breakdown revealed that seven regular prices had accounted for 31 per cent, and one promotional price had accounted for another 17 per cent of the department's unit sales. At the other extreme, there were ten prices that had accounted for only one sale each, and sixteen prices at which no sales had been made. In view of these findings, he decided to eliminate a total of twenty-eight selling prices. His final pricing plan included twenty-two regular and eleven special prices, grouped into four price zones. He found that the new price schedule not only made it easier for his customers to select the items they wanted but also enabled him to make a material dollar reduction in his silverware inventory.

He then made a vendor analysis. This revealed that his firm had made no more than one purchase each from a number of resources during the preceding six-month period. Further investigation showed that two of these concerns had supplied the firm with exceptionally good-selling promotional items. He decided that he could eliminate the remainder of the resources in this group without injury to his business. In fact, he found that by concentrating his purchases with a relatively few key resources he could reduce office clerical work, shorten the receiving room operation, cut shipping charges, and be in a better position to obtain necessary quantities of promotional merchandise at favorable prices during off seasons.

It would be repetitious to report each of the remaining steps in his step-by-step analysis of the silverware department. He stated emphatically, however, that his effort earned a rich dividend for his firm in the form of increased sales and profits and a greatly reduced dollar

---

[1] Excerpts from *Journal of Retailing,* Vol. XXXIV, No. 2 (Summer, 1958), pp. 63-66.

inventory investment. In addition, he gained valuable experience in solving problems in an orderly, systematic manner and in being his own researcher. In his words, "research can pay rich rewards for a relatively small investment of time, effort, and money."

Suburban Lamp Store

Dr. Lawrence C. Lockley, Dean of the School of Business Administration, University of Southern California, uses the following case to illustrate how a small retailer can be his own researcher. It concerns an ex-G.I., who opened a lamp store in a suburban area. This enterprising young man imported vases, electrified them, and drew prospective customers into his store through attractive window displays. But he faced a problem that confronts many retailers: would he saturate his market?

In other words, how many lamps are enough for a household? If he were saturating the homes of the residents of his trading area with lamps, then he could anticipate a dwindling business, with new sales mostly dependent on new families moving into the neighborhood.

His problem was to find an answer to this sixty-four-dollar question. He and his co-operative wife invested many evening of work in finding its solution. Together, they studied sales for the two and a half years he had been in business, separating customers into groups according to the number of lamp purchases each had made. Then they studied the interval between purchases of the customers who had been in several times. As a result, he discovered that he had a sizable group of customers who had apparently either bought lamps as gifts or as replacement items. He judged that repeat purchases would keep him in business, but that growth and greater profit would have to come from broadening his merchandise offerings, or his trading area, or from community growth.

When this enterprising young man had completed the analysis of his past sales, he probably could not have reported any very exact figures on his findings. He did know in a general way, however, the facts on which he would have to plan his future as a merchant. This was good research.

He continued the study of his business just as any merchant can. He began to chat with shoppers as they circulated about his store. He asked them, informally, whether they gave lamps as gifts, whether their purchases of lamps were related to home decoration, how they had happened to come into his store. Once more, he did not accumulate any precise figures but he did gather a fund of general information which helped him to interpret his previous findings. In this, he again demonstrated that he had learned one of the most valuable facts about research. It is useless to spend either time or money collecting more precise facts than you require.

Small Retail Chain

The president of a chain of small general stores in the Midwest insists that each of his store managers knows both the extent and the intensity of coverage of the area being served by his store.

How are the store managers supposed to obtain this information? The answer is easy. Each store manager is requested to procure a large, detailed street map of the community in which the store he manages is located. His next job is to obtain the names and addresses of all persons making purchases in his store during various fortnightly periods, distributed throughout the year, and to note these home locations on his area's map with colored pins.

This relatively simple procedure enables each store manager to define his market area in a surprisingly short time. The information makes it possible for him to concentrate his promotional efforts on weak spots in his market.

Small Dress Shop

Finally, there is the case of the merchant who operated a small dress shop in a Southern city. He wanted to realize the full potential of his very excellent pedestrian traffic location. This meant that he would have to make maximum use of his windows. He was torn between the need to maximize his sales, however, and the desire to build a reputation for carrying prestige merchandise.

How did he resolve his problem?

He conducted an experiment to determine whether it was more profitable for him to display popular-priced or prestige merchandise in his street windows. Based on his findings, he set a policy of using his windows to display popular-priced merchandise with the price plainly marked on each item. He backed his window displays with interior departmental displays and adequate stocks of these items.

The second reason offered by retailers for not conducting retail research derives from the belief of many that *they buy and sell merchandise* only; if a product line fails to sell in a profitable manner they can either reduce the price or return the merchandise to the manufacturer. Stated another way, they consider themselves the showcase of the manufacturer's wares: if the manufacturer's product doesn't sell, it will eventually be discontinued. This argument shows a lack of understanding of the role of the retailer in a community. A retailer is not only a showcase. As one retailer noted: "Every town has a showcase; it is called the museum. Rather than by merchandise managers it is run by curators. My store has one purpose in mind — to sell merchandise!" Though this retailer's stated purpose of only selling merchandise may be a simplification, nevertheless his analysis may be quite accurate. In order to obtain merchandise, retailers buy from all types of manufacturers, both large and small. In the case of the latter, few have adequate research facilities or the personnel to judge consumer demand for their product. Moreover, even a well-conducted and tested manufacturer research program may be inadequate for the needs of a particular store located in a particular area of the country. For example, prices suggested by manufacturers (based on their research) must be applicable to New York retailers as well as to those located in Tupelo, Mississippi.

Many retailers believe that the role of the retailer is to be a true merchant; that is, to develop his own products and rely as little as possible on the manufacturer. Few firms have attained this stage; however, some, through the stocking of private brands, have taken a giant step in this direction. The growth of the jet age has shrunk the foreign markets and has therefore made it much easier for the retailer to develop his own sources of merchandise.

Another major argument advanced by the retailer as an excuse for not developing a research department is that *retailers have many more products than the manufacturer to concern themselves about*. They claim that it is literally impossible for them to be concerned with the total output of the retail store. This argument has a great deal of validity. The typical supermarket, for example, displays over 5,000 different food items. It has been estimated that the typical department store stocks as many as 213,000 items of merchandise.[2] These facts, however, do not negate the need for an adequate research program. Research, as we shall see in the following pages, need not concern itself with the sale of a product; it may deal with changing markets, store locations, or even the acceptance by the consumer of a major classification of products; for example, the consumer's attitude toward buying meat in a supermarket. This has been noted by Professor Cassady who believes consumers do not buy meats in these stores as readily as other products — a finding that has been of major concern to the management of the food chains.

The last argument put forward is that the *retailer is concerned mainly with the local area surrounding his store*. Therefore, so the argument runs, national, regional, or even citywide statistics and studies are for all practical purposes useless. Here again, we are faced with a half-truth. Many retail firms *are* local in nature and their horizon may not extend beyond a mile or two around their store. However, it has been observed that few retailers are totally unaffected by what is happening in the total market area. For example, we have all observed the impact which the suburban movement has had on the downtown location, and the changing demands of the suburbanite in terms of the types of merchandise wanted — problems, incidentally, of sufficient importance to attract the interest of a research-minded management.

To sum up: Inasmuch as vital decisions must be made by the retail firm, it would seem that they are made better with the aid of research.

Defining Retail Research

Defining retail research is a perplexing matter; in fact, the definition offered usually reflects the attitude of the researcher. If we define research as "fact finding" it broadens the area of research and accounts for practically all activities of management. For example, counting the number of employees entering a store ten minutes after opening time can be considered, under the above definition, to be research. Listing the trend in gross margin of the store's hosiery department would also be research, as would investigating the high cost of delivery and formulating a program for its reduction.

We can see then that it is not feasible to consider every function of management as research. What is needed is a definition that reflects the *consumer-oriented approach* that must govern retailing management — one that obtains knowledge about the consumer and guides management in adjusting its three submixes. Let us consider this definition of retail research: *the systematic collection of market information pertaining to the future strategy of the retail firm with the idea of*

---

[2] Barkev Kibarian, "Why Department Stores Can Meet Discount House Competition," *Journal of Retailing,* Winter, 1960-1961, p. 205.

reducing the risks involved in altering the three submixes of the store, namely, the *goods and services, communication, and physical distribution mixes, to the* *demands of the consumer.* The term "systematic collection" refers to an organized method of obtaining information. This is in contrast to the usually more subjective approach of the manager who announces that, on the basis of his floor experience, his department is meeting the demands of the consumers. Though the judgement of the manager may be quite accurate it is nevertheless dangerous to assume that his sampling of observations is representative. It is therefore a first rule in research that the collection of data be systematic. This requires the use of appropriate sampling techniques and of organized data collection forms. For example, an inquisitive research man may wonder how the manager can reconcile declining departmental sales with the conclusion that his department is meeting consumer demand. If he carries his curiosity further, he may find that the manager is only observing consumers on Friday and Saturday; the other days of the week he spends either in his office performing routine duties or in the merchandise markets buying for the department. In addition, he may rarely converse with consumers and may take two hours for lunch.

"Reducing the risks" — to continue with the major components of the definition — is of course the major reason for conducting research. Business decisions are always made in the face of uncertainty concerning the future and particularly the whims of consumers. Building a branch store in a certain section of a metropolitan area is a risk, for even if we predict through research that there will be an immediate demand for the store's products, what about the demand ten or more years from now? Obviously in constructing a branch store costing millions of dollars, long-term considerations are of major concern. Long-range planning involves determining not only whether or not a market will remain in this area but whether the store can handle the projected business growth. The site must also remain superior in terms of traffic patterns and ease of shopping. Not all of these problems can be solved by research. However, a research approach to some of these questions will reduce uncertainty. It seems obvious that decisions made on the basis of purely subjective predictions are less valid and have less chance of success.

As we pointed out in an earlier chapter, management is continually faced with altering the three mixes of the firm. Our research definition must, of course, take cognizance of the fact that research needs to help management adjust these mixes.

Business Theory

Though research has the immediate benefit of helping management make decisions in the face of uncertainty there is an unmeasurable long-run benefit that is usually not associated or at least credited to a continuous performance of the research function. We are referring to the development of theories that can be applied to solving everyday business problems. Theory development concerning business decisions is usually thought of as being based on past experience rather than on an accumulation of understanding through many years of studying business reports and research findings. However, it is obvious that theories are developed on the basis of both reports and experience. Unfortunately, however, the word "theory" may have the same effect on a businessman as the red flag has on the bull.

Few businessmen talk in terms of theories; they are concerned only with facts, as they are quick to let you know. In reality, however, you will find a typical everyday business conversation filled with theories. The higher the level of management the more prone managers are to discuss theories since they have little "day in — day out" routine to discuss with the passerby.

The following may very well be a record of a typical conversation between a buyer and his merchandise manager:

> *Merchandise Manager:* "Why are you taking such a high markup on this order for the new white shirts?"
> *Buyer:* "They are good values and the consumer is unaware that they can be sold for less."
> *M.M.:* "Why not sell the shirts at a lower price? Won't you sell more?"
> *B:* "I don't believe so; the consumer who purchases this shirt is in the high-income group and the one-dollar price reduction would mean very little to him."

Careful study of the brief conversation above will show that the buyer has espoused the following theories:

1. Consumers cannot recognize apparel values as clearly as they can other types of merchandise values.

2. High-income consumers are unconcerned, to some extent, with an extra charge of one dollar on a white shirt. Implied here is that the demand for white shirts is unaffected by a reduction in prices. Additionally, the buyer also implies that only high-income consumers purchase this product.

Closer study of this brief conversation will no doubt uncover other theories concerning the consumer. But if we interviewed the buyer, he would tell us in no uncertain terms that he is opposed to professors and their set theories. Nevertheless, a retail business operates on many theories mostly revolving around the interpretation of consumer actions. Most of these theories have been developed on the basis of previous experience and may be entirely unsupported by empirical data, although they may accurately portray the whimsical behavior of the store's consumers. However, the economic changes that have been described in previous chapters suggest the inherent dangers of operating a retail firm on the basis of past experience or guesswork. Hence, a number of more forward-looking firms are turning to research as a basis for developing theories and adjusting their retailing mixes in the development of market strategy.

The Research Department

What types of research projects does a retail firm engage in? It may be recalled that our definition of retailing research precludes the inclusion of internal analysis. Nevertheless, a retailing research department does engage in a great deal of internal evaluation of expenses and personnel. This facet of its operation is of little concern to those saddled with the responsibility of developing a retailing strategy based on evaluation of each of the firm's submixes in a particular market.

The research function, if it is to fit into today's modern concept of business, must concern itself mainly with the consumer; and it should not be too concerned with past problems but rather with the present status of consumers and particularly with their future status. A typical sales forecasting problem demonstrates this point.

While a sales forecast would start with an evaluation of the *past,* this may have little to do with the present economic or consumer environment. For example, if two major discount stores opened in a trading area within the past year, this could have a serious effect on the sales forecast of any nearby traditional retail operation. It could also upset the pricing policies of the traditional outlets and cause a reduction in gross margin estimates and demand projections. Thus, in making a sales forecast, the research department must evaluate the possible effect of a low-margin discounter on the sale of merchandise at the traditional outlet.

The research department may not actually go out and conduct a consumer survey in making these forecasts. However, it does have to have knowledge of consumer reactions to new low-margin outlets in order to make an accurate estimate. In addition, the research department must be able to evaluate not only immediate effects on sales but their long-range impact. For example, if the store developing a sales forecast for the next year is a department store, the consumer interest in low-priced merchandise must be known. In actuality, the new discount houses may immediately affect the department store's basement store operation and yet have little impact on the sales of the upstairs fashion departments. In any case, a knowledge of consumers' reactions to the discount house will determine the accuracy of the forecast.

Sales forecasting, though an important factor in store planning, may not be performed by the research department. It may be handled instead by the store controller. Nevertheless, the research department should be able to perform many tasks and aid in reducing errors in sales forecasting. A study of the types of research reports available to the management of the Kroger Company, a national food chain, lends some support to the theory that research departments do engage in a great deal of varied activities. The following types of reports were prepared for management over a two-year period.

1. Merchandising: Twenty reports. Aimed at improving varieties and types of products carried.

2. Premiums: Seventeen reports. Checked consumer responses or attitudes toward certain types of premiums.

3. Customer attitudes: Ten reports. Based on surveys of consumers' opinions of Kroger and their competitors.

4. Competition: Eight reports. Based on surveys of competitors' activities.

5. Advertising: Eight reports. The effectiveness of radio and newspaper advertising was tested in a number of communities.

6. Promotions: Four reports. These examined the results of price promotions.

7. New merchandise lines: Twelve reports. These dealt with the desirability of adding new types of merchandise in various stores.

A few studies outside of the usual scope of the department were also conducted during the two-year period.[3]

---

[3]David J. Luck, Hugh G. Wales and Donald A. Taylor, *Marketing Research,* 2nd ed. (Englewood Cliffs, N.J.: Prentice-Hall, Inc., 1961), pp. 484-485.

Note that all of these reports are based on consumer reactions toward and knowledge of Kroger and its competition. Research projects 1 and 7 directly affect the goods and services mix. The retailer is always looking for reactions of consumers to his present assortment of merchandise and, if possible, to his planned merchandise assortments.

Projects 2, 5, and 6 are concerned with the communication mix of the firm. Information concerning the reactions of consumers to advertising expenditures are of major interest, and are of special importance to large retail firms. The size of the advertising expenditure makes it imperative that management have some knowledge of consumers' reactions to their programs. For example, a typical department store with a volume of sales exceeding $50 million will spend approximately $1.5 million of its own money and the same amount of a manufacturer's money on newspaper advertising.

Projects 3 and 4 can relate to any of the three mixes. Consumer opinions may be solicited concerning the offerings of the Kroger firm, and the answers derived may affect the goods and services mix. Consumer attitudes toward store locations may affect the physical distribution mix of the firm. Information concerning competition may force Kroger to increase its offerings of non-foods (a distributive trend in today's food retailing) and may affect the goods and services submix. Thus all aspects of the alternatives available to management can be explored by properly constructed retailing research.

Conducting the Research Project

After making a preliminary analysis of the problems involved, management may find in many cases that the problem requires further research and analysis. In retailing, the formal research project usually takes the form of (1) observation of consumers, (2) a direct contact survey, and (3) an in-store experiment. In addition, we may add a fourth category of research techniques, the collection of secondary data. This technique may serve as a basis for background information for the other research techniques or it may, if conducted in sufficient depth, be considered a technique in itself. This latter technique is covered in Chapter 20.

Observation
Method

Though a manufacturer has little opportunity to observe customers in action, the retailer is constantly exposed to them. Therefore, observation studies of consumer habits and actions can be conducted easily in a store. Of the various types that can be conducted in a retail store, two seem to be most prevalent: those conducted for the purpose of: (1) determining consumer traffic patterns; (2) observing consumer reactions to merchandise and displays.

One of the basic tenets of the observation study is to watch consumer actions carefully but remain inconspicuous. As one astute research director noted, "A competent person conducting an observation study should be able to arrest at least two shoplifters a day!" Though this may be an exaggeration, it does make the point that an observer should remain as inconspicuous as possible. By not communicating with the consumer or interfering with the natural buying patterns the sample retains a higher degree of validity than would otherwise be the case.[4]

The numerous observation studies that have been conducted have yielded a great deal of meaningful store information. The most widely used type of observation study is the "traffic count." This technique is used both inside and outside of the store by almost all types of retailers. For example, it is used as a basis for locating a gasoline station, a franchised ice cream parlor, or practically any type of outlet where success or failure hinges on a steady flow of customers. The location of the gasoline station obviously depends on a count of passing automobiles; the location of the ice cream stand can be chosen on the basis of either a pedestrian or automobile count, depending of course on the type of site under consideration.

Departmentalized stores take traffic counts both within and outside of the store to develop many different types of consumer information. For example, it would seem to be of interest to the store management to know the direction or flow of traffic within the store in order to maximize the exposure of departments that sell impulse goods. Again, a department store is interested in the traffic flow outside of its store in order to determine the types of window displays and entrance accommodations needed. We recall one particular store which, after simple observation, noted that about a third of its customers were entering the store completely unaware of the major promotions featured in the store windows. By the simple expedient of including an entrance window in the total window display arrangement the store was able to expose this group to the current campaign under way.

In actual practice, counting traffic can be a very complex operation. It is complicated by the fact that all types of people pass with the result that there is much duplication of traffic. When conducting a project of this type, the retailer must ask himself: Whom shall I count? Shall I count children, for example? – Shall I count the same person passing twice? – Shall I count teenagers? – What day should I choose?[5]

Observation studies, however, need not be restricted to the taking of traffic counts. Observation studies can be used in combination with other forms of surveying; for example, a traffic count may be done in conjunction with consumer interviewing. In addition, the observation study can be done under controlled conditions (a subject discussed later in this chapter).

In one study conducted in a department store, it was found that consumers tend to notice mannequins presented against a scenic background more readily than unadorned. The study was conducted over a two-week period under controlled conditions.[6] The subject matter consisted of three mannequins adorned with dresses from a "better dress" department; during half of the experimental period a display backdrop was used. Three types of consumers were observed and counted under

---

[4]An innovative technique for measuring in-store customers is discussed in Donald H. Granbois, "Improving the Study of Customer In-Store Behavior," *Journal of Marketing* (October, 1968), p. 28.

[5]Regarding the complexity of this form of research, see Saul S. Sands, "Improving the Accuracy of Pedestrian Traffic Counts," *Journal of Retailing,* Vol. 37, No. 2 (Summer, 1961), p. 33.

[6]Leslie Schuller, "Scenic Background Increases Response to Dress Display," *Journal of Retailing,* Vol. 38, No. 3 (Fall, 1962), p. 5.

both conditions: (1) those that passed without observing the display, (2) those that passed but "looked" and (3) those that "stopped" and "looked." Comparison of the findings under both conditions were supplemented by personal interviewing of a sample of passers that "stopped." One of the weaknesses of this type of study is that in-store traffic may vary considerably over the period of the study. In order to minimize this variable, the study was conducted during a week that was divided into two parts; that is, on Monday to Wednesday embellished displays were used and on Thursday to Saturday, unembellished. The following week the procedure days were reversed.

Through simple observations of this type it is possible to learn something about the preferences of shoppers. For example, one intensive group of display studies showed that women shoppers favor store windows featuring fashion displays. Windows featuring products and furnishings for the home ranked much lower.[7]

Retailers, on occasion, conduct direct contact surveys in order to collect direct merchandising information. Data collection of this type uses one of three forms: mail questionnaires, telephone interviews, and personal interviewing.

Direct Contact Survey Method

Mail Surveys

Retail firms, by the very nature of their business, usually have access to mailing lists. Since the first principle of conducting a meaningful mail survey is to obtain accurate up-to-date mailing lists, it would seem that they are particularly fortunate in this respect. Where there are installment credit or charge accounts, these lists offer stores an excellent way of sampling their customers. Besides being up-to-date, such mailing lists assure a sampling of people who are acquainted with the store.

There is, however, a disadvantageous aspect to using a retailer's list. Since it includes only those who are customers of his store, he may not be able to learn anything about those consumers who are still within his trading area but buy elsewhere. Also, use of a charge account list ignores what may be a large segment of potential customers, namely, those who pay cash at all times. Therefore, at some time or other, a retailer is forced to consider obtaining outside lists of consumers in order to gain adequate data.

Mail surveys have many advantages and disadvantages, and it is always up to management to weigh the values against a cost measurement. Probably the least obvious disadvantage is the low rate of return that seems to be typical of mail surveys. However, though the rate of return per dollar expended may be low in most surveys, the retailer can still expect by this method (provided he uses his charge list) a return that would exceed simple random sampling of families in the area.

With all of its possible drawbacks the mail survey of consumers should not be overlooked by management as a source of meaningful consumer information. One such study based on sampling of charge account lists obtained much useful information that sometimes supported and sometimes refuted some of the pet

---

[7]"Surprising Reactions of a Shopper," National Association of Display Industries, New York City.

theories of management. It was found, for example, that few consumers were "basement only" shoppers. Most preferred shopping in both the upstairs and downstairs stores. Thus, this study seems to contradict the widely held belief of store executives that the basement customer is entirely different from the customer who shops in the upstairs store. It was also noted that higher-income charge customers are more likely to shop around than the low-income groups. In addition, the higher-income groups, though they spend more money in total, actually spend it in more stores than do lower-income consumers. Therefore, the study found that a consumer from a lower-income group, though she may spend less money altogether, may be a better customer for a store than a higher-income shopper.[8]

Though we are not concerned in this book with the statistical aspects of sampling to any great extent, it is worthwhile to point out that the use of charge accounts as the sampling universe offers management an easy method for obtaining the parameters needed for determining a reasonable size sample. The two statistics that must be obtained in order to estimate the sample size are the standard deviation and the allowable error. Since most credit departments have available the dollar range of charge accounts, these estimates can be made easily.

Mail surveys are also useful as a means of keeping in touch with customers who use store home services. For example, a store that repairs home appliances, offers rug cleaning services, or repairs or installs upholstery can keep in contact with consumers through the use of a follow-up mailing card. Sending a postcard a few days after a consumer has used a store home service will help management obtain information concerning the level of customer satisfaction.[9] Not too long ago, the author was witness to the writing off by a major department store of bad debts exceeding $750,000 for a store food freezer plan. Most of this loss was attributable to an overzealous sales force representing a lessee. As was determined at the "inquest," salesmen signed up many poor credit risks, made dubious promises, and offered long-term return guarantees, the latter without the consent of the store. It has occurred to the author that a simple postcard mailing to a sampling of the early purchasers would have alerted management to the problem.

Telephone Interviewing

Telephone interviewing as a technique of collecting research information has the major advantage of being quick and relatively inexpensive. One of the disadvantages of using the telephone is that the interview must be kept quite short. Since sampling from phone books is a fairly simple procedure and since only a few families are without telephones, the tendency is to rely on their use. However, some experts have noted that, increasingly, high-income families are maintaining unlisted telephones. The practice has become so prevalent that in many states the telephone company is charging an additional fee for maintaining an unlisted number. The knowledge that a simple random sampling of the phone listing will not produce enough high-income respondents may not be a problem to a store with only a

---

[8]D. F. Blankertz, "Shopping Habits and Income" and "The Basement Store Customer," *Journal of Marketing,* Vol. XIV, No. 4 (January, 1950), and Vol. XV, No. 3 (January, 1951).

[9]In addition, the card serves a public relations function of informing the consumer of the store's interest in her welfare.

limited number of customers in these income groupings. On the other hand, a high-fashion specialty shop or exclusive department store may find this drawback more serious and therefore may consider the possibility of stratifying the sample in some way in order to reach higher-income groups.

Stores may also conduct a telephone survey of their present customers based on their charge account lists. This technique requires extra work since the compilers of the list must obtain the telephone number separately. And this technique has the shortcoming common to all charge account lists — they exclude the cash customer.

Personal Interviewing

Personal interviewing, though not always practical, is usually the best way to conduct a survey. Collecting information in this manner affords a retailer an opportunity to interview customers in a shopping environment or, as has been demonstrated in many studies, in the act of buying.

Probably the most widely used technique is to interview consumers leaving a store. This type of survey, known as a *walkout study,* affords the retailer an opportunity to have the consumer reconstruct his whole shopping adventure. With a steady flow of customers leaving a store, interviewing can be done on a production line basis and consequently at a minimal cost per interview. Properly used, walkout studies can aid management considerably in making changes and adjustments in their product mix. For example, one statistic compiled on the basis of walkout interviews is the purchasers versus the non-purchasers. It becomes a matter of great significance to management to know that only 10 per cent of all potential purchasers bought what they had planned to upon entering the store.

One of the major problems in conducting an analysis of this type of survey is to establish rigid definitions of what management considers to be a shopper, purchaser, non-shopper, and walkout customer. Though on the surface these definitions may seem simple, in actuality they are quite complex. As an illustration, suppose we have just completed an interview of a female shopper who has told us in our sidewalk interview that she has just purchased a blouse. We found in the interviewing that the shopper had not had a blouse purchase in mind when she entered the store. She recalled for us that she intended to purchase a sweater she had seen in our newspaper ads but the store did not have it in stock; however, when she was in the store, she passed the blouse counter and decided to make a purchase; in addition, she ordered a set of dishes to be sent to her home. Should we classify her as a purchaser or non-purchaser, and in any case, after we decide, we must ask what we learned from this interview? Obviously since the shopper did purchase merchandise, we must consider her as a purchaser. The store, however, cannot help but be concerned with the fact that she did not find the merchandise she intended to purchase. The situation is particularly significant in that the merchandise she did not find was advertised. In one sense, therefore, she is a non-purchaser, if we define a "non-purchaser" as a consumer who does not find the merchandise that she had originally intended to buy. Management would be interested in more details on why she could not purchase the merchandise she originally intended to buy. For example, the store may not have had her size, color, or style. On the other hand, the possibility exists that she could not find a sales person to wait on her.

It must be remembered that some retail outlets by the very nature of the goods they sell may have a high walkout ratio. For example, a furniture store will have a high walkout ratio since the product sold is shopped for in more than one store and, more important, the decision to buy is usually a family decision. On the other hand, a children's apparel store will have a lower walkout ratio.

In food stores, personal interviewing is used to determine in-store customer demand or, more specifically, impulse buying habits of food customers. One type of study that has been used widely is the so-called "shopping list" study. The technique used is to record a customer's shopping list before she enters the store. The list may be in written form or, if not, the customer may be asked to list those items she expects to buy. After she completes her shopping, her omissions, substitutions, and additions are noted.[10] Obviously this type of study has many limitations. In particular, where the housewife does not have a shopping list, the value of the "mental list" is at best questionable.

Figure 19-1 is a typical questionnaire used as a data collection form for a department store walkout study. Note the questionnaire carefully, particularly its brevity. As a general rule, walkout questionnaires should be brief since shoppers are quite busy and usually can be detained for only a few minutes. This is especially true if we are interviewing in the downtown business district where many of the shoppers are also working. On the other hand, the length of the interview can be extended if the study is being made at a suburban shopping center. Interviewing people at these centers as they are entering their autos or just arriving has been found to be especially effective, and the consumers are more receptive to long interviews.

The walkout questionnaire shown in Figure 19-1 was used in interviewing 2,654 shoppers leaving a store. Management in this study was looking for information concerning the store image and, if possible, wanted to pinpoint weak merchandise areas. Tabulation of the findings showed that 24 per cent of the consumers had bought at the store; 48 per cent had not and the rest were passing through. The walkouts, it was discovered, were concentrated in the ready-to-wear departments. Unattractive styling seemed to be the predominant reason given for not buying. Without belaboring the study's findings, management soon learned that the store had a weak style image. In effect, therefore, management now had a good deal of customer feedback information from which a well-managed organization could take appropriate action resulting in an improvement in the store's position among consumers.[11]

Motivation research. Motivation research is a relatively new technique for obtaining useful marketing information by direct contact with consumers. It can be defined as *a research technique that attempts to delve into the psychological attitudes of the consumer through the use of projective tests or techniques.* The well-known "ink blot" test, "sentence completion" and "word association" tests are widely used in motivation research.

Though an attempt to understand the psychological orientation of the consumer may be a worthwhile goal for a firm interested in selling products, there has been a

---

[10]William Applebaum, "Study of Customer Buying Behavior in Retail Stores," *Journal of Marketing,* Vol. XVI, No. 2 (October, 1951), p. 178.

[11]Robert H. Myers, *op. cit.*, p. 129.

<u>Questions Asked of Brant Walk-Outs</u>

Pardon me . . . I am making a consumer survey for Brant's.

1. Did you buy anything at Brant's today? ___ Yes ___ No ___ Just passing through

   If respondent answers "yes," thank her for her patronage and tell her that

   the study you are making does not involve Brant customers.

   If she is just passing through the store, thank her for this information.

   If her answer is "no," go ahead with the rest of the questionnaire.

2. What departments at Brant's did you visit (indicate department and floor)?

3. Would you mind telling us your reason for not buying anything at Brant's?

Item	Didn't have what I wanted (size, color, brand, style, etc.)	Price too High	Salesperson not helpful	Out of Stock	Just looking	Other, specify
a)						
b)						
c)						
d)						

4. When you think of Brant's what is the first thing that comes to your mind?

Classification data –

   What part of town are you from? (Eastland, Riverview, etc.)

   Do you work downtown?   Yes   No

   Age (to be estimated by interviewer)   Under 30   30–44   45 and over

   Man   Woman

   Date and time

Store entrance (circle one)
   Walnut Street Cosmetics   Walnut Street Men's Furnishings   Walnut Street Blouse
   Euclid Street Purses   Euclid Street Hosiery   Main Street
   Euclid Street Men's clothing

Source: Robert H. Myers, "Sharpening Your Store Image," *Journal of Retailing,* Vol. 36, No. 3 (Fall, 1960).

great deal of adverse criticism of this technique. Possibly the major criticism of "psychological research" is that the exposure of the mental illnesses of a minority of the population is of minimal value to marketing people selling to a mass market. A second major criticism has to do with the use of small samples to gain information; as a practical matter, the use of these techniques is limited to small samples mainly because of the high cost per interview caused by the need for highly skilled interviewers. Users of these techniques find that the cost of interpreting the findings is also well above that of the typical research study. On the other hand, motivation research has uncovered some valuable marketing data. The question to be answered, however, is, would other less expensive techniques have unearthed the same information?

Motivation research has rather limited value for retailers since most of the early developments in the use of this technique have dealt with the attitudes of consumers toward products. However, one author noted that motivation research can possibly offer some retailers information regarding consumer attitudes toward shopping in supermarkets. He quotes Dr. Ernest Dichter, who notes that to the housewife the supermarket is an extension of her pantry. Dichter suggests, therefore, that a white supermarket convinces her that the company believes "her pantry was just as white and gleaming and clean at home." This implication flatters her, of course. This finding, according to Dichter's study, has implications for checkout counters, where the supermarkets have been aware of a problem. Since, as Dichter notes, the supermarket is considered by the housewife to be an extension of her pantry, she has a resentment against the checkout girl when she realizes that she has to pay for what amounts to merchandise from her own pantry. Hence, the consumer also exaggerates waiting time at the checkout counter; it was found that waiting time has been estimated to have been as much as 40 minutes when in actual fact it was less than three minutes.[12]

Of course the major problem connected with this type of study is, how do we implement the information it has given us? Assuming that in some way we can accomplish this, the next question that needs to be answered is, Is it possible to obtain the same information through simple direct interviewing techniques?

Though no comparable study of the "pantry-shopper" has been published by a non-motivation research firm, it is interesting to note that unconscious resentment against a retail firm was brought out in a study of shoppers in the San Francisco area.[13] In this study 400 consumers were asked to estimate the traveling time and distance in miles they had to travel to reach a local discount store and a department store. A comparison of the findings with the actual time and distance involved showed that consumers considered the department store to be closer to their residence than was actually the case. The author in this instance points out that "subjective distance" may be an important basis for measuring a consumer's reaction to a location. He suggests that the generally poorer displays and fewer services offered by the discounter influenced the consumer's estimate of traveling time and distance. Thus, this study demonstrated that it is possible for research to uncover subjective and psychological reactions of consumers without resorting to

---

[12] W. G. McClelland, *Studies in Retailing* (Oxford: Basil Blackwell, 1963), pp. 47 and 48.

[13] Donald L. Thompson, "New Concept: Subjective Distance," *Journal of Retailing,* Vol. 39, No. 1 (Spring, 1963), 5.

motivation techniques. In any case, the worth and application of psychological research in making business decisions are still unproven at this stage.

In-store Controlled Experiments

The complaint about most experimental marketing tests is that the environment is always changing and hence it is not possible to conduct two experiments under similar conditions. Though this statement accurately reflects research opinion, it is nevertheless true that the retail store offers an opportunity to conduct "controlled" experiments under better-than-average conditions.

Controlled condition experiments are more meaningful if the tests are conducted in more than one store or location. However, experiments have been conducted using only one location but varying the test props. As a general rule, it is also better to vary only one condition when comparing experiments, since a change in more than one condition can result in a confusion of causal factors. Earlier in this chapter we referred to a study of consumer reaction to display mannequins in a controlled experiment. This was an attempt to control conditions by using only one test area.

An example of rigid control technique used in a number of food stores is presented in Table 19-1. This study shows the increased sales that result from prepackaging a fresh vegetable. The table demonstrates that a 30 per cent increase resulted in the five test stores, whereas under the same conditions, without prepackaging, sales in the five control stores increased by only 7.8 per cent. If the test and control conditions were kept the same, the only variable being the packaging, then management can assume that the prepackaging of vegetables resulted in a 22.2 per cent net sales gain.[14]

Example of Results of Prepackaging Experiment   **TABLE 19-1**

	5 Test Stores			5 Control Stores		
	Pre-Test 4 Weeks	Test* 4 Weeks	Per Cent Change	Pre-Test 4 Weeks	Test 4 Weeks	Per Cent Change
Store sales	$300,000	$306,000	+ 2.0	$298,000	$304,000	+2.0
Fruit and vegetable sales	$ 44,000	$ 45,100	+ 2.5	$ 44,400	$ 45,300	+2.0
Sales of tested vegetable	$ 2,000	$ 2,600	+30.0	$ 2,040	$ 2,200	+7.8
	25,000†	32,500†	+30.0	26,500†	22,500†	+7.8

*During these 4 weeks the vegetable tested was sold prepackaged in the 5 test stores only.
†In pounds
Source: William Applebaum and Richard F. Spears, "Controlled Experimentation in Marketing Research," *Journal of Marketing,* Vol. XIV, No. 4 (January, 1950), p. 511.

This type of experimentation, if carried on continuously, can yield valuable information not readily available from pure observation. In addition to packaging information, by using this technique a store can obtain information concerning display, pricing, promotion, new products, and the operation of store equipment.[15]

---

[14] William Applebaum and Richard F. Spears, "Controlled Experimentation in Marketing Research," *The Journal of Marketing,* Vol. XIV, No. 4 (January, 1950), 505-517.

[15] *Ibid.*, pp. 512-515.

Unfortunately, however, this type of research has many limitations. The major one is its expense. Conducting a project of this scope properly requires a great deal of personnel. Maintaining the same conditions in all stores is another major problem faced by those conducting this type of study. Throughout the study, steady communications with personnel must be maintained. In addition, supervision must be thorough and particularly alert to changing conditions. Those who have attempted to control conditions in more than one store can attest to the various problems. In the previously mentioned mannequin study the supervisor ran into a major crisis when a part-time sales girl unknowingly sold a dress off one of the test mannequins!

Maintaining the same conditions in all areas or stores under study is not only a problem of controlling personnel but also of determining the time period of the study in all stores under control. The time period refers not only to the time of the day, which can be equalized simply by limiting the study to 9 to 5, but, more important, the day of the week. A relatively new technique for determining the time periods has recently become available. Called the Latin Square design, this technique is simply a method of randomization. First presented by R. A. Fisher, the Latin Square design has been used in solving pedestrian sampling problems and, most widely, in controlled experimental studies by the Department of Agricultural Economics of Cornell University. In one particular study,[16] the purpose was to measure the consumer reaction to a sample of different quality labels on the egg containers in a number of Grand Union supermarkets, e.g., grade A, extra large; grade A, large, and so forth. The action of the consumers in each case was carefully observed and recorded by the enumerator. Eight stores were chosen from which to conduct the experiments. As in most controlled experiments, four stores were paired in each group and the merchandise was displayed differently in each of the two paired groups. The major technical problem faced by the enumerators was how to give equal weight, by hours and day, to each store, and in what store and at what hour to sample consumers to assure themselves of randomization?

Table 19-2 demonstrates this sampling plan for the four weeks under study. Note that they are using a four-by-four Latin Square design that gives equal weight to all four stores. Each letter represents a time period during which the store will be surveyed. For example, this table shows that store 4 will be sampled during the first week during time "C" (1:30-3:45). During the second week, sampling will be conducted during time "D" (3:45-6:00).

Table 19-3 demonstrates the sampling plan during one of the weeks of the time study. Again we see that store 4 is sampled during five time periods as is every store in the study. Note that since on Fridays the store maintains longer hours, separate provision was made for this day.

In actual practice the stores were sampled during only one-half of the listed time periods in order to allow the enumerators enough time to "service" the displays and travel between the stores. This points up one of the major values of this research design: it allows one enumerator an opportunity to survey a number of stores and

---

[16] See *Egg Merchandising Studies in Supermarkets, Part I:* "Consumer Response to Egg Quality," A.E. 923, Department of Agricultural Economics, Cornell University Agricultural Experimental Station, September, 1953. Also see Ronald Gatty, "Statistical Models for Experiments in Merchandising," *1965 Proceedings of the Business and Economic Statistics Section,* American Statistical Association, p. 227.

Four-By-Four Latin Square of Time Period to be Sampled in Stores 1 Through 4   TABLE 19-2
on Mondays, Weeks 1 Through 4 (A, B, C, D, = time periods)

	Stores			
Week	*1*	*2*	*3*	*4*
1	B	D	A	C
2	A	B	C	D
3	D	C	B	A
4	C	A	D	B

Source: *Egg Merchandising Studies,* op cit.

Example of a Sampling Schedule Used by Enumerators in Making Observations in   TABLE 19-3
Stores During One of the Four Weeks Covered

		Time Periods		
	A	*B*	*C*	*D*
Day	*9:00-11:15*	*11:15-1:30*	*1:30-3:45*	*3:45-6:00*
		Stores		
Monday	1	2	3	4
Tuesday	1	3	2	4
Wednesday	1	3	2	4
Thursday	2	1	4	3
Saturday	2	4	1	3
		Time Periods (Friday Only)		
	A	*B*	*C*	*D*
	9:00-12:00	*12:00-3:00*	*3:00-6:00*	*6:00-9:00*
Friday	3	4	1	2

Source: *Egg Merchandising Studies,* op. cit.

hence reduces the cost. If the study were made by continuous sampling during all hours at all eight stores, the cost would be prohibitive and there is little indication that the results would be any more accurate than by the Latin Square design.

Determining the Priorities for Research

As noted earlier, research expenditures are still relatively low in retailing, although in recent years many of the major retail organizations have spent considerable funds in developing research departments. This raises the question of how management can properly evaluate these research expenditures. No doubt judgment and intuition play the biggest part in evaluating the research costs in relation to benefits.

Whenever the uncertainties, a research budget must be drawn up and project priorities established. The size of the budget is usually based on the previous year's expenditures plus the outlook for the coming year. The allocation of budgeted funds and additional monies takes place on the basis of the priority of needs, for one must assume in retailing that research funds are not sufficient to provide money for all contemplated projects.

Though suggestions have been made as to how to establish priorities in terms of return on investment, the fact is that it is almost impossible to quantify this approach properly.[17] The most likely technique is simply to attach priorities on the basis of (1) the size of the firm's investment in the problem studied; and (2) the estimated importance of the problem in terms of reaching the firm's profit objectives.

On this basis, it is clear that site *location* research of a new branch store would receive top priority primarily because it represents a huge investment in inventory, plant, and people; it would seem to offer a prima facie case for research in terms of expenditures measured against the value of the return. Other studies of secondary importance would be the attitudes of customers toward a store and changes in the buying behavior of consumers.

Thus priorities are allotted according to management's judgment as to the effect that solving the research problem will have on its total effort.

SUMMARY

Research is a sort of buffer zone between the consumer and the management decision-making apparatus of the firm, yet retailers spend less money on research than do manufacturers. Several answers are to this puzzle are offered, namely:

1. Retail firms are usually too small to afford research.

2. Retailers, as they only buy and sell merchandise, can eliminate unprofitable lines and thus have little need for research.

3. The sheer number of products carried makes it more difficult for the retailer to research products.

4. As the retailer is concerned mainly with the local area around his store, secondary statistics that cover larger areas are not useful for most retailers.

All of these objections can be answered by noting that inexpensive research studies can be done by even the smallest stores, that research need not concentrate on an individual product but can look broadly at product areas, and that all major changes in the retailer's environment affect all sizes of retailers.

Retail research is defined as the systematic collection of market information pertaining to the future strategy of the retail firm, to reduce the risks involved in altering the three mixes of the store, namely, the goods and services, communication, and physical distribution mix, to meet the demands of the consumer.

One important side benefit of research to management is the development of theories that can be applied to decision making. The research department engages in studies that include most areas of decision, such as merchandising, customer attitudes, promotional activities, and competition.

---

[17]For a criticism of the return on investment approach in market research, see Ralph L. Day, "Optimizing Marketing Research Through Cost-Benefit Analysis" *Business Horizons,* Vol. 9, No. 3 (Autumn 1966), 50, 51.

In conducting a formal research project the firm can use three general approaches: observation, direct contact, or an in-store experiment. A fourth method is the collection of secondary data. This latter technique is covered in Chapter 20.

Observation methods include the determination of consumer traffic patterns and the observation of consumer reactions to merchandise and displays.

Direct contact survey methods usually include mail surveys, telephone interviews, and personal interviews. The latter would include walkout studies and perhaps motivation research.

In-store controlled experiments usually involve a careful control of environmental conditions. If the experiment covers more than one store a Latin Square design may be resorted to, in order to control the possible variables among the stores.

The three-part table indicates the possibilities and applications of retail research.

A. Observation Studies

Management Needs	Techniques	Limitations
Traffic flow to determine maximum location of merchandise.	Consumer traffic patterns	Defining who is a customer and double counting; many stores have numerous entrances.
Maximizing consumer reaction to displays.	Observing consumer reactions to in-store merchandise displays	Requires that store displays remain the same over a reasonable period of time.

B. Direct Contact Survey

Management Needs	Techniques	Limitations
Measuring consumer attitudes and shopping behavior.	Mail surveys	Low rate of return; lists usually limited to charge customers and firm's own customers.
Measuring consumer attitudes and shopping behavior.	Telephone surveys	High- and low-income groups are not represented adequately in the phone book; short interviews only.
Measuring consumer attitudes and shopping behavior.	Personal interviews	Costlier than above methods; require trained interviewers to to avoid bias.
Measuring consumer attitudes and shopping behavior.	Motivation research	Extremely costly since only trained psychologists can be used; small samples not representative.

C. In-Store Experiments

Management Needs	Techniques	Limitations
Measurement of product's sale due to price and packaging changes.	Controlled experiments	Environment difficult to control.

QUESTIONS

1. What is an observation study? What type of observation study could you conduct for a chain grocery store?

2. How does an observation study differ from an in-store controlled experimental study?

3. Define retail research. How does it differ from the following definition: Retail research is "finding facts for management's use."

4. Describe a type of inexpensive research study a small corner drugstore might conduct.

5. Distinguish between the research needs of a manufacturer and a retailer.

6. Describe a few situations where a department store might conduct a motivation research study.

7. What are the advantages and disadvantages of conducting a mail survey to obtain customer information about credit account customers for a department store.

8. Can a telephone survey be substituted for a mail survey in all cases?

9. Write instructions for a research worker who is assigned the task of counting pedestrians passing a drugstore. (*Hint:* Who is to be counted? Who is a potential customer? Where should they stand?)

10. List five types of information that can be obtained from conducting a walkout study.

11. The walkout ratio in a hosiery store is 60 per cent. Is this high? Why?

12. The same 60 per cent ratio is determined in a furniture store. Is this high? Why?

13. List five possible studies a research department might conduct for a mail order firm.

14. Your firm has 10 stores scattered throughout the country. You are assigned the task of sampling the consumer reaction to a new packaged toy product. List the problem you will encounter in designing the study.

Secondary
Sources

20

OBJECTIVES YOU SHOULD MEET

1. *Define* secondary sources.
2. *Identify* an internal source of research information in a department store.
3. *Identify* several major sources of government data.
4. *Distinguish* between government and private studies.

Though the retailer can gain a great deal of insight into the attitudes of consumers and the position of his firm in his market area, it does not necessarily follow that he needs to conduct surveys. The retailer can rely in many cases on the plethora of secondary-source information. Secondary sources refer to information gathered from published or internal store records. The retailer has many types of information of this sort, the most important being his own internal sales records. In addition, there is a myriad of government data, local and national, as well as private studies, some of which are published regularly.[1]

The very nature of a retailer's business, which encompasses numerous transactions while dealing directly with consumers, affords him an opportunity to acquire meaningful consumer information. For example, if a retailer conducts a credit or charge account department, he has a natural source of consumer data. In other firms where credit information is unavailable, such as food chains, contest records or simply customers' names on file for reference in cashing checks serve a similar purpose. Another source of information may be mail or telephone orders received by the firm as a direct result of their regular promotional campaigns.

Internal
Records

[1] A publication for retailers outlining the types of information available is found in *Government Statistics Handbook,* National Retail Merchants Association, 1969.

The opportunities to convert these sources into useful consumer information are many. For instance, by simply plotting on a map the residences of a sampling of consumers, a store's promotional manager can ascertain the gaps in his trading area. If he finds that the gaps represent income groups that the store should be reaching, he may decide that something is wrong with either the merchandise selection or the media being used to reach this market. A comparison of the data with either city planning maps or Census Tracts published by the local or federal government (discussed below) can give the firm detailed information about the economic status of the consumer in these areas.

A retailer can learn a great deal about his customers from a sampling of sales checks. In one instance, a firm conducted a price line analysis of a sample of its sales checks in order to answer the question: if a consumer spends $100 on a man's suit, how much can the firm expect him to spend for a shirt, tie, shoes, and other accessories? From this analysis the firm learned that a number of departments stocked large quantities of higher-priced merchandise that had only a limited appeal to its customers. Had it wished to, the firm could have learned from a mail questionnaire where else these customers spent their apparel dollars and the prices they paid for the other items they purchased.

Drawing samples from sales slips or charge records is a relatively simple technique. The systematic sampling methods based on the experience of auditors are most useful. To randomize selection samples are drawn by choosing every nth card or using a table of random numbers.

Government and Private Studies

Government and private publications provide most of the sources of secondary information for the retail firm. Occasionally, a retailer may find a study by a university or other academic institution to be relevant to his problems.

Difficulties in Using Government Data

One of the difficulties a retailer faces in using government data is that most retail markets are either local or regional in scope. For example, R. H. Macy, which is New York based, has outlets in only a few other cities. On the other hand, Sears, Roebuck, which is truly a national firm, until a few years ago was represented by only a few stores in the confines of New York City. An example of a regional food chain is Kroger, with well over 1,400 food stores located mainly west of the Mississippi.

Retailers are aware that national statistics as used by manufacturers have limited relevance to their store problems. However, retailers do find a great deal of local data in government sources that can help them evaluate their competitive position and their relationship to the buying public.

Census Data

The Census of Retail Trade published during the postwar years of 1948, 1954, 1958, 1963, and 1967 contains a great deal of information that can help the retailer determine his relative position, and in some cases the relative position of the types of merchandise he sells. For example, an examination of the statistics from several

Retail Census studies for Rochester, New York (see Tables 20-1, 20-2, and 20-3), shows the following information.

In Rochester, chain stores seem to be increasing their share of the market (Table 20-1). This trend is particularly noticeable among apparel stores. We might ask, Since chains increased their share of the apparel market between 1958 and 1967, would we expect to find more or fewer stores per 10,000 persons in Rochester? The answer to this question is supplied by statistics presented in Table 20-3. This computation gives management an indication of the saturation level of Rochester. It can be seen that the number of apparel stores per 10,000 population in Rochester declined considerably in the nine years under study. Therefore, an additional question may be asked by the analyst: If the number of stores declined in relation to population, how did the chains increase their share of the market in view of the fact that apparel sales in Rochester increased by 24.5 per cent from 1963 to 1967 (see Table 20-2)?

There are two possible answers to this question. We could speculate that the number of non-chain apparel stores declined and therefore the additional apparel sales went to the chains. In Table 20-1 we see that the number of non-chain stores did not decline. However, we also see that the number of chain stores also increased. We can therefore conclude that the true answer to the growth of the chain may *not* be found in our tables.

The answer is to be found in what is happening in the apparel business in terms of the size of each outlet. By now we should be well aware that there is a relationship between the size of a store and its ability to generate sales. Thus in Rochester, over the four-year period, the stores being added by the chains are much larger and thus are able to accommodate many more customers. Unfortunately, the Census studies do not show us either the footage represented by the stores in each Census group or the number of stores added and dropped. The change represents simply a net figure. Therefore, a personal knowledge of the changing apparel outlets in Rochester is needed by management to make a complete analysis of this situation.

Though a firm can measure its market position by comparing its sales to the reported census sales, there are many pitfalls in relying completely on these findings. One of the major failings of Census figures is that they are concerned mainly with numbers of stores and sales rather than the above-mentioned size or the different products they carry.

To further develop this point, let us give consideration to the problems faced by a department store. Let us suppose that one firm found that, based on its analysis of the Census of Business in both 1963 and 1967, its share of the department store market has increased by 10 per cent. The store management may therefore be tempted to applaud its record, and to the unsophisticated this increase in share may serve as an indicator of the total department store position in the city, it may represent a misleading picture of how the store is faring within the product lines they offer. For example, though the department store may have experienced a substantial increase in drug sales, the food chains in the same city may have actually experienced a much more sizable increase in drug sales over the same period of time. However, since food chains are not included in the "department store" sales figure in the Census of Business (they are included in the store grouping "food

TABLE 20-1 Selected Retail Stores and Volume of Sales, 1967 and 1958, by Metropolitan Area

Rochester, N.Y.

Type of Business	Number of Stores		Sales (In Millions)		Percentage in Sales, Chain Stores and Non-Chain Stores / Share of Market	
	1967	1958	1967	1958	1967	1958
Retail trade — total:						
All stores	5,808	4,983	1,495	707	100	100
Non-chain stores — total	5,550	4,411	811	418	54	59
Chain stores — total	824	572	684	289	46	41
2 or 3 stores	206	187	141	64		
4 to 10 stores	130	93	79	22		
11 stores or more	488	292	464	204		
Apparel, accessory stores:						
All stores	399	374	77	49	100	100
Non-chain stores — total	288	274	28	22	36	45
Chain stores — total	111	100	49	27	74	55
2 or 3 stores	19	28	13	12		
4 to 10 stores	25	14	18	2		
11 stores or more	67	58	18	13		
General merchandise group stores:						
All stores	173	134	230	100	100	100
Non-chain stores — total	95	87	7	4	4	4
Chain store — total	78	47		96	96	96
2 or 3 stores	7	8	*	*		
4 to 10 stores	4	7	*	*		
11 stores or more	67	32	174	*		
Food stores:						
All stores	1,071	1,044	344	178	100	100
Non-chain stores — total	875	907	128	68	37	38
Chain stores — total	196	137	215	110	63	62
2 or 3 stores	35	30	14	5		
4 to 10 stores	18		14			
11 stores or more	143	107	187	105		

*Withheld to avoid disclosure.
Source: *Census of Business, Retail Trade, 1967 and 1958.*

stores") the management of the department stores may not be aware of the competition of the food chains, except through consumer surveys or by simple observation of their competition. It is also worthwhile to note that the reverse, of course, also occurs. For example, a men's wear specialty store may find that its sales record compares favorably with other men's wear stores. However, it may be losing ground to the department stores' men's clothing department.

Retail Stores Sales and Per Cent Change in Sales, 1963 to 1967, Central Business District of Rochester, the Entire City, and Rochester Standard Metropolitan Statistical Area   TABLE 20-2

| | Per Cent Change | | | 1967 | 1963 |
| | Central Business District | City | Standard Metropolitan Statistical Area | Sales ($1,000) | Sales ($1,000) |
Kind of Business					
Retail stores, total	5.5	19.7	31.3	1,426,968	1,087,066
Building materials, hardware, and farm equipment dealers	− 37.8	32.4	36.3	72,188	52,973
Hardware stores	(D)	− 3.3	17.2	10,260	8,751
Other	− 42.6	40.8	40.0	61,928	44,222
General merchandise group stores	13.5	25.0	50.8	229,847	152,369
Department stores	14.4	26.7	47.9	183,323	123,919
Variety stores	− 8.8	34.2	57.7	27,530	17,452
Miscellaneous general merchandise stores	49.9	− 1.6	72.7	18,994	10,998
Food stores	− 10.1	15.9	31.4	343,602	261,395
Automotive dealers	5.7	5.0	20.3	287,410	238,932
Gasoline service stations	32.4	46.6	39.5	82,534	59,142
Apparel and accessory stores	6.7	18.1	24.5	77,281	62,069
Women's clothing, specialty stores, furriers	11.8	19.8	21.0	31,294	25,862
Women's ready-to-wear stores	27.1	34.0	39.7	29,071	20,804
Other apparel and accessory stores	1.5	16.1	27.0	45,987	36,207
Furniture, home furnishing, and equipment stores	− 2.9	33.7	32.8	68,303	51,441
Furniture stores	− 62.2	36.7	37.9	26,946	19,537
Home furnishings stores	164.1	11.5	9.8	8,167	7,436
Household appliance, radio, television, and music stores	42.9	35.4	35.6	33,190	24,468
Eating and drinking places	2.8	42.8	43.5	111,935	78,002
Eating places	3.3	55.3	53.6	86,097	56,038
Drinking places (alcoholic beverages)	1.3	15.7	17.6	25,838	21,964
Drug stores and proprietary stores	− 3.2	31.2	43.8	50,454	35,085
Miscellaneous retail stores	− 12.1	7.5	8.1	103,414	95,658

395

TABLE 20-2   Continued

Liquor stores	− 32.1	33.6	35.3	19,535	14,438
Sporting goods stores, bicycle shops	3.6	53.7	57.5	4,845	3,076
Jewelry stores	35.2	61.2	50.8	7,690	5,098
Florists	− 3.5	−24.8	− 6.5	4,683	5,011

Source: *Census of Business, Retail Trade 1967.*

TABLE 20-3   Number of Retail Establishments per 10,000 Population Rochesters SMSA, 1967 and 1963

Kind of Business	1967	1963	Change
All Retail Trade	68.4	78.5	−13%
Food stores	12.2	14.7	−17
Eating, drinking places	15.7	16.4	− 4
General merchandise stores	2.0	1.9	+ 5
Apparel stores	4.5	5.7	−21
Furniture, household appliances	4.0	4.2	− 5
Automotive group	4.3	4.6	− 7
Gas service stations	7.0	8.1	−14
Lumber, building material, hardware	3.8	5.0	−24
Drug stores	2.1	2.4	−13
Other retail stores	12.8	11.5	+11
Non-store retailers	4.0	4.0	−

Source: *Census of Business, Retail Trade,* 1967.

Large stores, however, can adjust many of the census figures in order to gain a clearer picture of what is taking place in their particular city. One of the adjustments made by department stores and other stores selling a wide variety of merchandise for the family is called the "GAF," which is simply the pooling of various categories of stores to represent what management considers to be their total market. In Table 20-2 we see a typical listing of census store figures from 1963 to 1967 for the Rochester Standard Metropolitan Statistical Area. A department store wishing to measure its total market would probably combine the total sales for General Merchandise Stores, Apparel Specialty, and Furniture outlets.[2] If, for example the department store had a sales volume of $37 million it would find that its share of the listed total market in the city was about 10 per cent of the total "GAF" sales ($230 + $77 + $68 = $375 million). Other firms selling a less broad-based group of merchandise might use different classifications.

---

[2] The word "GAF" derives from the first letters of the major categories of stores, namely, General Merchandise, Apparel, and Furniture.

The central business district (CBD) is the area in each city that contains the real estate of highest value, the largest concentration of retail stores, and the major office buildings. All city transportation is designed to accommodate passenger service to this district. Retail firms with sites in the downtown area are of course interested in business trends in this section. The United States Department of Commerce has been collecting information on retail sales in the central business district for a number of years.

Table 20-2 shows some of the tabulations made by the government for the central business district in Rochester. The table shows that though retail sales increased in the entire standard metropolitan statistical area by 31.3 per cent from 1963 to 1967, sales in the central business district increased by only 5.5 per cent. Of the major groups, food stores experienced a sharp decline in CBD sales during the period under study. The postwar shift of retail sales from the downtown areas of the city to the suburban fringes of the metropolitan area have made these statistics particularly important to management.

In addition to data on shifts in retail sales in central business districts, the government has made available figures on the number of establishments and the percentage of convenience and shopping goods being purchased in this area. In its most recent census, the government also collected data on what is known as the major retail center (MRC), which is located outside the central business district but within the metropolitan trading area (see Table 20-4). MRC's include either suburban shopping centers or blocks that contain major shopping centers. They are similar to census tracts (discussed below), except of course that they identify total retail trade.

In the Table 20-4, twenty-two establishments are identified. Six of these stores are clearly identified as selling convenience goods and ten sell what is classified as shopping goods. The most numerous outlet in this shopping area seems to be the apparel outlet.

Census Tract Data

The Census of Housing and Population which has been conducted at ten-year intervals since the end of World War II contains information that can be used by retailers attempting to evaluate smaller sections of their local market.

The smallest land area for which information is available is the city block. Most of this information is gathered in cities with populations exceeding 50,000. Where block data are not available, enumeration districts are tabulated by the Census Bureau. These districts vary in size from one to ten blocks. Both city block and enumeration district studies publish data on the age, education, occupation, and income of the residents of these blocks. However, both reports are of limited value to retailers because the areas covered are too small.

There is, however, another type of area data available that can be of inestimable value to retailers interested in determining the characteristics of certain areas in their market. These studies called "census tracts," are available in 180 major metropolitan areas. Census tracts are defined as small areas into which metropolitan

TABLE 20-4   Retail Stores: 1967 — Major Retail Center No. 1 in the Rochester Standard Metropolitan Area

MRC No. 1 includes the planned center known as "Culver Ridge Plaza" and establishments on Ridge Rd. E. from Culver Rd. to Forest Ave. (Monroe Co.)

Kind of Business		Total
Retail stores, total:		
Number		22
Sales	$1,000	13,326
Convenience goods stores:		
Number		6
Sales	$1,000	4,926
Shopping goods stores (GAF):		
Number		10
Sales	$1,000	7,178
All other stores:		
Number		6
Sales	$1,000	1,222

Number of Establishments	Number of Establishments
Retail stores, total	22
Building materials, hardware, and farm equipment dealers	1
Hardware stores	—
Other	1
General merchandise group stores	3
Department stores	1
Variety stores	2
Miscellaneous general merchandise stores	—
Food stores	3
Automotive dealers	1
Gasoline service stations	1
Apparel and accessory stores	6
Women's clothing, specialty stores, furriers	3
Women's ready-to-wear stores	2
Other apparel and accessory stores	3
Furniture, home furnishings, and equipment stores	1
Furniture stores	—
Home furnishing stores	—
Household appliance, radio, TV, music stores	1
Eating and drinking places	2
Eating places	2
Drinking places (alcoholic beverages)	—
Drug stores and proprietary stores	1
Miscellaneous retail stores	3
Liquor stores	1
Sporting goods stores, bicycle shops	—
Jewelry stores	1
Florists	—

Source: *Census of Business, Retail Trade, 1967.*

areas have been divided for statistical purposes. These tracts are available in the decennial censuses, so that continuity has been maintained. The size of the areas covered makes these studies useful to the retailer. For example, within the city of Rochester, New York, the 1970 census of Population and Housing lists 91 tracts with a population ranging from a low of 34 persons to a high of 6868. Census tracts provide data on contract rent, place of work, automobile ownership, the year families moved into place of residence, and other information widely referred to by retailers.

As noted earlier in the chapter, this type of information is useful when combined with samplings of customer lists in order to determine the quality of the market a retailer is reaching. In addition and possibly more important, these data when compared with previous census figures indicate trends in income or other quantitative factors. For example, one particular firm located in a large metropolitan area was interested in the number of years families in their marketing area had been living at their present address. It was thought that this knowledge could be valuable in determining whether an area was undergoing a change, and if so, the quality of this changing market (as measured by income). With a little imagination census tracts can be used to advantage by retail firms interested in expanding their market or picking new retail sites.

Other Government Retail Reports

Though the Census of Retail Trade, described earlier, is of major interest to retailers, it is valued as a historical document rather than an up-to-date measure of competition. This is because the census figures are only available every four or six years and are published in many cases years after the census has been completed. Therefore, retailers turn to the Department of Commerce monthly and annual retail trade tabulations to determine their competitive position.

The Retail Trade Annual Report and the Monthly Retail Trade Reports are both published by the Bureau of the Census and contain sales by census regions and kinds of business. They also contain various merchandising ratios usually representative of key operating ratios of value to management. Their major value, however, is as an indicator of consumer demand.

The Census of Business, Retail Trade, has made available market data for most retail establishments in many of the metropolitan areas of the country. Table 20-5, for example, shows the changing proportion of sales by merchandise lines by the retail outlets. Thus we see that department stores in 1963 in metropolitan Houston increased their share of women's and girls' apparel by 11.8 percentage points over 1948. In contrast, the women's ready-to-wear stores had a comparable loss in proportion of business in the same period of time.

In addition, a retailer can determine the types of outlets that sell his product in a given area. Table 20-6 shows the great variety of stores reporting sales of footwear in a recent year. By watching the share of the footwear market change for each of these outlets over a period of time, a retail firm can gain a keener insight into its competition.

| Kind of Establishment in which Sales Reported | Per Cent of Total | | | |
| | West South Central States | | Metropolitan Houston | |
	1948	1963	1948	1963
Department stores	30.9	37.8	37.8	49.6
Dry goods, general merchandise	15.8	8.7	7.8	3.2
Limited variety	3.7	5.8	3.6	4.9
General stores	.9	——	——	——
Men's & boys' clothing stores	.1	.3	——	——
Family clothing stores	11.6	14.7	14.6	14.8
Women's ready-to-wear stores	35.8	26.4	34.6	23.6
Women's accessory stores	——	2.8	——	——
Women's & girls' shoe stores	.8	.6	1.6	.9
Family shoe stores	.4	.3	——	——
Shoe stores	——	.9	——	1.0
Food stores	——	.9	——	1.3
Other retail stores	——	.8	——	.7
	100.0	100.0	100.0	100.0

[1] Exclusive of Footwear

Source: John R. Young, "The Growing Strength of Department Stores," *Journal of Retailing,* Vol. 42, No. 1 (Fall, 1966), 47.

Published Consumer Reports

Retailers have always had difficulty in evaluating a national study concerning consumer actions and relating it to their local business. Their opinion is that consumer studies of other cities cannot be applied to their trading area. Nevertheless if one were to examine all metropolitan areas, the following characteristics would emerge.

1. A population shifting to the outer fringes of the city.
2. A shifting population consisting mainly of white-collar home owners.
3. A shifting population that is mobile in the sense that it relies more on the automobile to get around than do other groups.
4. A shifting population that is causing a deterioration of the central business district.
5. A rapid development of suburban retail outlets.

This similarity of population and retail sales movements within all metropolitan areas of the United States provides a valid basis for efforts by the retailer to apply studies of other areas to his own city. Though there are literally hundreds of these studies available, only two will be cited here. They are chosen because they represent two completely different retail outlets — department stores and food chains — and also because they seem to be statistically reliable.

Hardware stores
General merchandise group stores
    Department stores
    Limited price variety stores
    General merchandise stores
    Dry goods stores
Home and auto supply dealers
Apparel and accessory stores
    Men's and boys' apparel stores
    Men's and boys' clothing and furnishings stores
    Custom Tailors
    Women's Clothing Specialty Stores
    Women's Ready-to-Wear Stores
    Women's Accessory Specialty Stores, Furriers
    Hosiery Stores
    Apparel, accessory, other specialty stores
    Furriers, fur shops
    Family clothing stores
    Shoe stores
    Men's shoe stores
    Women's shoe stores
    Children's juvenile shoe stores
    Family shoe stores
    Children's infants wear stores
Drug stores
Other retail stores
    Second hand stores
    Sporting goods stores
    Bicycle shops
    Luggage stores
    Hobby, toy, game shops
Non-store retailers
Mailorder houses
Direct selling organizations

Source: *Government Statistics Handbook, loc. cit.*

Rich Study[3]

Typical of the many studies available to management is the study by Professor Rich of the general merchandise shopper in the cities of Cleveland and New York. It was based on thousands of interviews with both suburban and central city shoppers out of which developed a great deal of statistical data.

[3]Stuart U. Rich, *Shopping Behavior of Department Store Customers* (Boston: Graduate School of Business Administration, Harvard University, 1963).

Rich's study is particularly important in that it focuses on the discount house shopper and the suburbanite's attitude toward downtown shopping. It was completed during a period when retailers were re-evaluating the downtown retail situation and the future growth of their suburban branches and shopping centers. The study did throw a great deal of light on this situation. For example Rich criticized the retailer's belief that consumers come into the downtown business district to obtain bargains. In effect, he found that consumers buy downtown when they are looking for fashion merchandise and at times when they are interested in a large assortment of home furnishings. This finding has implications for large department stores, particularly for those stores that are considering whether to build a basement in their newest branch.

Dillon Study

Studies by trade magazines are also available to the retailer. One of the most widely used series of studies of demand in a food supermarket are those available from *Progressive Grocer Magazine.*

One study contains an analysis of sales by lines of good (and non-food) products in the Dillon chain over a period of 16 weeks. Some of the findings are shown in Figure 20-1. In effect, the retailer is in a position to determine demand and its relationship to profit in many of the lines of merchandise offered in these stores. Not shown in this table are the many display tests run under controlled conditions during the period under study.

SUMMARY

Though the retailer can conduct surveys of his market he does not necessarily have to resort to such research to gain information. Many firms rely on secondary sources of information, which can be secured from published or internal store records. These records include important government studies and private studies. Internally the firm can use information derived from the firm's sales checks and charge accounts.

In using government information the retailer may find it difficult to relate the data directly to the firm's market, because government data is collected on the basis of either political subdivisions or wide-ranging trading areas.

The most useful source of information can be found in the Census of Retail Trade. Here the firm can examine changes in retail composition over a period of time. In addition, areas within a major trading area can be examined such as the central business district or the suburban areas of this same city. Census tract data within the major metropolitan areas can give the retailer important information concerning the demographics of his market. Much of this information is derived from the Census of Population and Housing. In addition, the Census of Business now supplies data on merchandise lines, showing the types of stores selling a particular line of merchandise and associating a sales volume with each type of outlet.

Studies issued by private organizations such as colleges or trade associations also can supply the retailer with useful information. Such studies show important

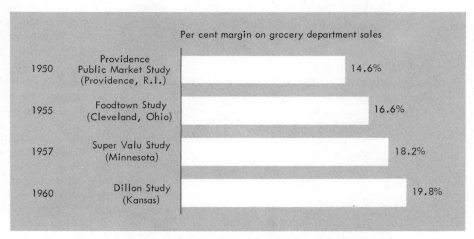

Per cent margin on grocery department sales

1950 — Providence Public Market Study (Providence, R.I.)	14.6%
1955 — Foodtown Study (Cleveland, Ohio)	16.6%
1957 — Super Valu Study (Minnesota)	18.2%
1960 — Dillon Study (Kansas)	19.8%

CHANGES IN MARGINS BY PRODUCT GROUPS IN GROCERY DEPT.

	1950	1955	1957	1960
Cigarettes	5.75%	5.8%	6.0%	5.5%
Canned Vegetables	19.38	20.8	21.4	21.3
Soaps and Detergents	6.27	8.4	10.5	10.4
Flours, Mixes	13.52	12.9	17.5	15.2
Crackers, Cookies	20.25	23.5	25.3	27.0
Candy, Gum, Nuts	22.30	24.1	25.5	25.8
Sugar	9.09	6.2	8.0	7.6
Canned Dried Milk	7.97	8.5	13.5	11.0
Canned Fruit	16.02	18.1	21.6	22.4
Canned Fish	15.99	14.1	19.4	22.3
Paper	22.61	23.9	23.4	25.3
Household Supplies	23.60	28.4	28.3	32.2
Soups	11.13	11.6	15.1	12.5
Canned Juices	16.20	18.2	19.4	21.1
Canned Meats	14.48	13.3	21.0	20.2
Salad Dressing, Oils	17.28	16.0	15.5	16.8
Cerals	11.89	13.3	18.1	17.8
Mac. and Spag.	13.38	19.9	18.8	21.4
Spreads	20.87	21.4	23.6	23.4
Pickles, Relish, Olives	21.03	28.1	26.7	28.3
Pet Foods	13.31	17.9	20.2	19.1
Condiments	21.37	24.2	18.4	21.7
Desserts	11.80	14.3	16.7	16.3
Potato Chips	23.88	22.2	23.9	23.8

Source: "The Dillon Study," Editors of *Progressive Grocer*, May, 1960.

changes in the metropolitan areas and movements in the types of products sold in stores that are undergoing changes.

DISCUSSION QUESTIONS

1. Comment on the following quote: ". . . the type of mind best suited for executive work often differs greatly from the type of mind producing the best results in analytical research work." H. Pasdermadjian, *Management Research in Retailing* (London: Newman Books, 1950), p. 13.

2. The Macy Corporation recently announced the development of a branch store to be located in Rego Park, a section of the Borough of Queens. The space available for this branch was limited, and the firm soon discovered that the usual large parking lot could not be built. As a result of a great deal of analysis, the firm decided to develop circular indoor parking ramps around the store. This innovation would make it possible for a consumer to park his car right at the department or at least the floor in which he planned to shop.

    a. What types of problems do you believe will face the Macy branch in terms of consumer convenience? Can you visualize other problems that will eventually occur?

    b. What type of research would you recommend that management conduct:

        (1) while the store is still being planned?

        (2) after the store has been opened?

3. Department Store A, located in a large city in Ohio, submits the following facts:

    a. Analysis of the 1967 Census of Business showed the store had attained 80 per cent of all department store sales.

    b. Analysis of the 1963 Census of Business showed that the firm at that time was doing 75 per cent of all department store sales.

    What conclusions can we come to on the basis of the above facts?

4. Recently, the J. L. Hudson Company, located in Detroit, noted that in spite of the rapid influx of discount stores into the Detroit area, their firm has been able to increase their share of "GAF" sales. Can you refute this statement? If so, what additional facts would you need to carry out this task?

5. If you were recently appointed research director of a major department store in your city, what research projects would you suggest that you conduct this year? Would the projects change if you held a similar position with a major apparel chain such as Robert Hall?

6. What major sources of internal information are available to a:

    a. major department store.

    b. chain food store.

    c. "mama and papa" grocery store.

7. Evaluate the Dillon Study report as shown in Figure 20-1 on the basis of:

    a. the products you would be most likely to stock.

    b. the products that would require further consideration.

    What products would you consider dropping from your store based on this study?

8. Of what value are Retail Census studies of the government?

9. What conclusions can be drawn concerning Table 20-5 showing the important changes in the sale of women's and girls' wear in:

1. large stores.
2. chain stores.
3. specialty stores.

10. In Table 20-6 identify the top three potential competitors of a department-store footwear department.

CASES

Matrix of Cases by Chapter

Case Number	Part I Introduction Chapters		Part II Uncontrollable Factors Chapters					Part III Controllable Factors Goods & Services Chapters				Communication Chapters			Physical Distribution Chapters			Part IV Controlling the Firm Chapters		
	1	2	3	4	5	6	7	8	9	10	11	12	13	14	15	16	17	18	19	20
1	✓	✓																		
2			✓									✓	✓							
3	✓	✓																		
4	✓								✓											
5	✓												✓							
6			✓	✓					✓											
7							✓		✓					✓						
8												✓	✓							
9												✓	✓							
10								✓	✓											
11				✓	✓				✓	✓										
12									✓	✓	✓									
13				✓	✓													✓		
14									✓	✓	✓									
15								✓	✓	✓										
16			✓					✓	✓	✓	✓								✓	
17									✓	✓	✓							✓	✓	
18						✓													✓	✓
19																✓				
20															✓			✓	✓	
21																		✓	✓	
22																			✓	✓
23								✓							✓	✓		✓	✓	
24															✓	✓		✓	✓	
25																✓	✓	✓		

In the second section of a local newspaper Jacob Schlanger saw a small article that caught his attention and fancy. The headline read: "Coming Soon: The superstore." The article predicted: "shopping in 1982 will be done at a "superstore" in which customers can not only buy groceries but also complete a host of routine chores such as banking and fueling the family car.

"That's the prediction," the article continued, "of a four-member research team from the Marketing Science Institute, as released at the 34th annual meeting of the National Association of Food Chains.

"In a trend paper released yesterday, the team said the superstore will take its toll among conventional supermarkets and discount stores that resist change. The situation will be comparable to the havoc wreaked by the development of supermarkets on family-owned groceries in the 1930's, the researchers said."

Schlanger cut out the article and tucked it into his pocket. He walked briskly, soon arriving at his destination. Barging into his house, he burst in on his wife who was just baking his favorite cake. Smacking his lips with relish, he exclaimed, "It must be my lucky day." "Why is that?" asked his wife. Jacob showed her the article, which she read with anticipation. "I know what's on your mind, Jacob. As usual you want to be three steps ahead of everyone: Just how do you intend to create a superstore?" "Well, with your help, my ingenious wife, we will think of something."

Being the owner of Schlanger's Supermarket on Main Street gave Mr. Schlanger a strong push. Although his store was quite successful, Jacob continuously experimented with new innovations and ideas. Some attributed his success to his willingness to try something new.

1

Schlanger's
Superstore

Schlanger sat down to the problem, tackling it head-on. He decided that his superstore would allow him to reduce grocery space, offer a greater variety of fruits and vegetables, open a book shop, a branch for the local bank — facilitating the banking procedure for customers — and a drugstore with a prescription counter. For his customers he will install gas pumps in the immediate area of the store with a mechanic at hand.

Jacob Schlanger assumed that this superstore would be a large investment that would definitely pay off in the long run. He proceeded to buy land and to negotiate with the various concerns, hopefully to create a new entity, "Schlanger's Superstore."

1. Do you believe that the "Superstore" is coming? Elaborate.

2. Is it advisable for Schlanger to make this large investment, especially as he is presently successful?

2

The Mod Cycle Shop

The Leatherneck Cycle Shop scored great success in the Southern Los Angeles area. The plan to attract the motorcycle gangs worked like a charm.

Neal Notis, owner of the Leatherneck, decided to enlarge his business and open a new motorcycle store. With the Leatherneck running smoothly, Notis was able to take time to scout areas for a new store. After checking various neighborhoods, Notis selected a store in what he hoped would be a promising site, near the campus of San Fernando University. The immediate area was a college town, and Neal Notis decided that if he could appeal to the college community, his motorcycle shop would be a success.

Realizing that the university clientele would be radically different from the Leatherneck customers, Notis decided on a completely different image for the college area. Following the "Mod" trend of today's colleges, Neal Notis decided to call his store the "Mod Cycle Shop."

Deciding on a full-fledged advertising campaign to make his shop known to the University community, Notis banked on the following strategy. He printed large posters showing "mod" couples riding motorcycles. On some of the posters boy and girl cyclists were shown. Others portrayed a couple together on a scooter. Realizing that collegians prefer scooters, he offered a 10 per cent discount on all motor scooters during his opening week. Clearly depicting the San Fernando University emblem on the shirts of the cycle riders on the posters, he felt, would act as a subconscious link to the university community. Notis went further by naming a popular model the "SFU" — for San Fernando University. He bought prime-time advertising slots on WSFU, the college station, and full-page ads in the college newspaper.

His next step was to install a motorcycle parking lot to further the impression of cycle pre-eminence in the San Fernando University community.

Feeling great confidence in his advertising campaign, Neal Notis opened the Mod Cycle Shop assured that this addition to his motorcycle business would be a successful and lucrative move, indeed.

1. What possible problems could Mr. Notis encounter in starting his new store?

3

Hechter Baking Company

The Hechter Baking Company is an 84-year-old baking company that specializes in selling packaged bread, cake, and other baked goods to food stores in the New York area.

A favorite for many years, it recently has run into financial trouble. In 1971 the Hechter Baking Company suffered a deficit of approximately $100,000 because of high union costs and unprofitable delivery routes.

Recently a driver-salesman strike immobilized the company and forced it into an unwilling but necessary decision.

At a press conference at the Belmont Plaza Hotel New York City, Morton Hechter, the president of the Hechter Baking Company announced his decision to close his plant for good. The closing of the plant, which employs 250 persons, was forced by the 17-day strike by its driver-salesmen, coupled with the $100,000 deficit in 1971.

Hechter was one of eight bakeries struck by Local 802 of the Teamsters Union. Eleven other bakeries shut down at the same time in a unity move.

Morton Hechter, who said his company grossed $7 million last year but ran $100,000 in the red, said he could not afford to meet the union's pay demands.

Under the old contract, Hechter said, his driver-salesmen earned an average of $350 a week, including a 9 per cent commission on gross sales over $650 per week. On top of salaries, Hechter said, the company paid $35.50 a week per driver into the Teamsters welfare pension fund.

The conference was attended by the heads of several bakeries, all of whom said they were on the verge of also going out of business. The bakers pointed to what they termed inflexible union work rules that have prevented them from eliminating unprofitable routes.

Further, the struck bakers charged that bakeries in New Jersey, using Teamster drivers, were supplying New York restaurants and stores with baked goods during the walkout.

The mood of the conference was summed up by a spokesman for one bakery, who said: "It's a crazy world, with a crazy economy and crazy unions."

1. Criticize Mr. Hechter's views.

4

Leatherneck Cycle Shop

The Leatherneck Cycle Shop is situated in downtown Los Angeles. It is a privately owned store that buys all types of motorcycles and scooters directly from manufacturers. They offer all the brand names such as Yamaha and Honda but also stock other, lesser-known makes.

The Leatherneck Cycle Shop is "smack in the middle" of Hell's Angels territory. It is known as Hell's Angels territory because of the supremacy of that feared gang in the area. When a few members appear in a street, roaring through on their heavy-duty motorcycles wearing fearsome-looking black leather uniforms and swinging chains in their hands, the inhabitants know what to do — and they do it. The street clears immediately, because each person knows if he gets in the way of the Hell's Angels he may not live to regret it.

Neal Notis, the owner of the Leatherneck, was two steps ahead of everyone. He realized that he must gear his cycle shop to the Hell's Angels to enjoy a safe and lucrative business. He offered a special discount on a new motorcycle to the Commander of the Angels, in return for his support. The Commander gladly accepted Neal Notis' offer and kept his part of the bargain. He sent all his friends to the Leatherneck to buy their new cycles from Neal.

Notis further decided to lure these heavy-duty gang customers by offering them free service and repairs on their motorcycles. He figured it would be a harmless offer on his part for a number of reasons: (1) As the motorcycle gangs ride their cycles very roughly, the offer of free repairs would greatly influence a prospective buyer to obtain his motorcycle at the Leatherneck. (2) Neal knew that a gang motorcycle in need of repairs is in many cases "unfixable" — the incidence of motorcycle crashes among gang members being very great. Thus Notis further ingrained his popularity among the Hell's Angels at no major expense to himself.

Another reason for his courtship of the Hell's Angels was his realization that the Angels, the major gang in the area, by showing satisfaction with his cycles and service, would automatically lead numerous other gangs and even private cyclists to buy at the Leatherneck. Sort of a status symbol — We get our cycles at the Hells Angels Shop!!

1. Do you agree with Notis' strategy?
2. Suggest alternate or additional ideas to boost his sales.

Fancy Hatters is a hat store on Fifth Avenue. Living up to its name, it specializes in all types of men's hats and headwear. Sheldon Fancy, the owner, deemed it proper to call his store "Fancy Hatters" for two obvious reasons. First, as the hats he sells are expensive, he wanted to get that message across in the name of the store. Second, he "fancied" seeing his name in lights. His wife pointed out that the "untrained" observer would think the store high-class but would not associate the name "Fancy" with anything but the hats — never as the name of the owner. Sheldon Fancy concurred with his wife's observation, "You know, you're right, as usual. Maybe I should call it the 'Sheldon Fancy Hat Store' instead," he remarked. "No," said his wife. "If you do that, everyone will think your last name is Sheldon and that's one last name I don't want." Mr. Fancy asked, "What about the 'S. Fancy Hat Store'?" "No," answered his wife, "then people will say S. stands for "especially" fancy hats, and no one will come to buy the hats because we will be too forbiddingly exclusive." "Well," answered Sheldon, crestfallen, "I guess we will stick to our original choice of "Fancy Hatters," and I will have to forget about having my name in lights." "Don't be upset, darling," comforted his wife, "your name will still be in lights — but you'll be the only one who knows it."

5

Fancy Hatters

1. What should Fancy do?

6

Assemblyman Mark Harder

Assemblyman Mark Harder had just finished a meeting with several consumer groups at his state capital. Mr. Harder had served in his state assembly for eight years. He noted that in the past two years more and more consumer groups had been forming and making their opinions known to those in the state legislature, a refreshing change from previous years in which members of the legislature were constantly harassed by lobbyists representing companies and industries.

The groups he met this morning were particularly adamant about a piece of legislation they advocated. The assemblyman admitted that their position seemed particularly strong. The groups' asked that the state repeal Bill No. A431, passed in 1947. The bill made it illegal for any pharmacy in the state to post prescription prices. The groups have heavily criticized this law, feeling that it forces consumers to pay higher prices because they have no opportunity to make price comparisons, as they would on most consumer goods. For example, they noted that in drugstores and discount houses the same merchants post prices on all non-prescription prices in their store, enabling the consumer to make legitimate comparisons. Though they recognized that a consumer could ask a druggist to quote a price on a prescription drug, they felt that many consumers were reluctant to do so. They strongly suggested that, with rising drug costs and other inflationary pressures, the present would be an excellent time for the assembly to take a strong stand on their behalf. They were particularly interested in Assemblyman Harder's position because he headed up the Health and Welfare Committee that had to introduce such legislation.

During the previous week the assemblyman had heard from two lobbying groups in his state who opposed any change in the law.

The first was the State Retailers Association, which pointed out that the repeal of the law would cause the closing of hundreds of small drugstores throughout the state. They also noted that since one of the most important functions of a drugstore was to fill prescriptions when people were ill, the public would encounter severe problems in case of such closings. In addition, the large chains would capture most of the drug business and eventually would raise prices simply because there would be less competition. Last, the closing of so many stores would result in vast unemployment among pharmacists and cause the state's major pharmaceutical college to close down.

The assemblyman was also briefed by the representative of the American Pharmaceutical Association, who stated that increasing the demand for drugs through promotional activities served no useful purpose. In addition, the association supported the view of the State Retailers Association and also suggested that the pharmacy profession would lose its professionalism and would perhaps sink to the level of a firm selling commercial goods, whereas the profession should be respected because a close relationship between the medical doctor and a professional pharmacist is necessary to the health of the patient.

1. What should Assemblyman Harder do?
2. How would you judge the two contrasting opinions?

7
R. H. Macy

R. H. Macy boasts that it is America's largest store. In the past decade the firm has been concerned with a problem faced by all major department stores, namely, what should be the role of the buyer. Traditionally, the buyer has been the "kingpin" of the department, that is, he has been completely in charge of buying the merchandise for the downtown store and all of the branches. In addition, he had helped the salespeople in the downtown store perform efficiently by supervising them and educating them on the major selling points of any new merchandise brought into the department. This dual role is carried out in the downtown store for several reasons. The first and most obvious is that the buyer maintains his office in the downtown store and thus spends most of his time at that site. Second, because of the growing number of branches he finds it almost impossible to visit outlets in the outlying areas with any consistency.

Though management is well aware of the buyer's contributions to merchandising, they have noted for many years that his relationship with the salespeople has caused problems, simply because the salesperson has another manager, a department or section manager, who is always on the floor. This manager has several duties in relation to the salespeople. For one, he is in charge of scheduling their regular and lunch hours on a daily basis. He is also charged with the task of handling any problems with a sales transaction or customer complaint.

Macy's has noticed that as a result of this duality, the orders of the sales supervisor in some departments are often countermanded by the buyer. They have also noted that in some departments the older and wiser salespeople have a habit of playing one "manager" off against another when a particular order does not suit them.

Macy's management has been considering an important organizational change in recent months that they believe could eliminate this problem. As the buyer buys merchandise for the branches without engaging actively in managing the salespeople, a similar role could be fashioned for the downtown store. Management was well aware that such a change could cause some difficulty, as the buyer was stationed in the downtown department. However, management was determined to alleviate a deteriorating situation.

To accomplish this, management considered sending out a notice to all buyers that henceforth the Macy's buyer was not to give orders to any of the salespeople, nor was he to spend any sizeable amount of time on the sales floor.

1. Discuss the implications of this change.

8

Jason Supermarkets

Jason Supermarkets have been in the supermarket business for twenty years. Sales in their three stores in Saginaw, Michigan, exceeded $4 million last year.

In recent weeks the management of the firm has been considering dropping trading stamps. The most pressing reason seems to be the continuing food inflation that has raised prices to a level where consumers are resisting buying more expensive cuts of meats and vegetables. In fact, in recent months the share of the business of each of these profitable groups has dropped by five per cent.

The management feels that the dropping of stamps at this time would be appropriate, as in their view most customers believe that stamps are one of the major causes of high prices.

From the firm's point of view, stamps are costly. In the latest year, the firm has noted, stamps cost the company over $80,000. This saving would accrue to the company immediately. The firm also felt that if stamps were dropped the advertising department could promote this happening as a saving to the customers through the general lowering of prices. In this inflationary era, this move should cause an upsurge in business.

Of major concern, however, was the reaction of the consumer presently saving the firm's stamps. How badly would this customer resent the dropping of stamps and the lost opportunity to buy the gifts listed in the firm's stamp catalog?

1. Should Jason's drop stamps?
2. What are their alternatives?

9

Enders Department Store

Albert Cummings, the advertising manager for the Enders Department Store, was discussing with the major CBS outlet in his market area the possibility of the firm's using television commercials as part of its over-all promotional plan in the coming year.

The station representative pointed out to Cummings that a major competitor of Enders, the Lynch Company, had already committed itself to television advertising. He strongly suggested that Enders should not let its major competitor gain an advantage for too long, as a certain amount of experience is necessary to produce effective television commercials. He also called to the attention of Cummings that Sears and J. C. Penney were effectively using television to the benefit of all of their outlets, four of which were located in this market area.

Aware of this trend, Cummings had discussed using television with the merchandise staff only the past week. The response had been somewhat negative. All of the merchandise managers preferred to continue with papers, as they felt they would get the most immediate response from ads in this media. Although all seemed willing to try television advertising, they suspected that its immediate effect on sales would be negligible.

Cummings agreed with the merchandise people but was also aware that television's greatest impact seemed to be in its ability to develop a favorable image for a firm, a strategy that required a long-range outlook on the part of management. He was also aware that the necessary investment was high. For instance, a television commercial had to be produced, at a cost that usually ran between $20,000 and $30,000. It was true that some commercials could be produced for less, but in his opinion they looked unprofessional when positioned alongside national commercials produced for manufacturers.

Once the commercials were produced, the firm still would have to buy time. The tendency among most local retailers was to spend their money on cheaper nonprime hours. He also noted that with this huge investment in production costs the commercials should be general so that they could be used over and over again, in order to gain the maximum benefit from the initial investment.

1. Should the firm go into television advertising?
2. If they eventually do, what benefits should accrue to the firm?

10
Wards Supermarkets

Every Monday morning the buying committee at Wards Supermarket meets at the company headquarters in Boston. This committee is made up of all the major merchandise people, the advertising manager, the controller, and seven operation executives.

Wards is a fifty-store chain that has been growing rapidly throughout the New England area. In recent years, the firm has been opening stores at the rate of one a month and intends to increase that number within a few months.

It is the belief of top management that the firm has grown so rapidly because of good management, a management that weighs and measures all decisions carefully. The buying committee is thought to be a living example of this management in action.

On this particular Monday morning the buying committee, as usual, was considering several new products offered by manufacturers. The committee is constantly aware that a decision to add a new product automatically affects products now carried in their stores, because of limits on space. For example, last week when the decision to add a new line of soup was made, it was agreed that all present lines would be reduced in terms of space by 20 per cent.

The first item considered on this Monday morning was a new shampoo offered by Lever Brothers. This shampoo, according to the company, contained an effective dandruff agent that would make the product superior to all other shampoos on the market. This agent had been carefully tested by a major research organization, and the result would be published in a major advertising campaign starting the next month. In addition Lever Brothers would offer a large advertising allowance to those firms that committed themselves to buy 500 bottles per outlet three weeks before the campaign was to begin.

Wards was carrying 28 brands of shampoo, four of which were Levers' own brands. The largest-selling three brands accounted for 32 per cent of all shampoo sales.

The second request of the morning was from Clyde Chemical Company. The firm has been supplying Wards with baby food for the past ten years, under the brand name of "Baby Talk." Because of the national decline in the birth rate, the firm has decided to find other markets for their food products. As a result of several years research, they have determined that similar products can be produced to appeal to the geriatric market. After several months of testing, the firm planned to launch a full line of canned vegetables and desserts in the New England market. The products would be backed by a strong advertising campaign, and a strong cooperative advertising effort would be available to cooperating retailers.

1. What should the buying committee do?
2. What decision-making criteria should they establish?

11

Terminal Book Shop

The Terminal Book Shop, a small overcrowded bookstore, is located in the George Washington Bridge bus terminal in Washington Heights. The bus terminal itself is used by many hundreds of commuters travelling to all parts of New Jersey, over the George Washington Bridge (for which the terminal is obviously named). The Terminal Book Shop carries a huge amount of reading material, both on the store floor and in its stockroom. Despite the large stocks of literature and the constant flow of commuters and neighborhood visitors, sales are declining.

The Terminal Book Shop is part of a chain of transportation-depot bookstores with outlets in all the major bus and train terminals in the metropolitan area. Aware of the sliding sales, the management of the chain first asked the manager of the Terminal Book Shop to offer a solution. This being of no avail, management decided to replace the manager with a young college graduate. Steven Langer had graduated from college with a major in film-making but had at one time owned a small bookstore. His experience and imagination would come in handy, the chain owners felt, and offered him the job. He readily accepted, seeing himself involved in a creative challenge.

Mr. Langer felt that the bookstore's major drawback was the overcrowding and overstocking of books. In his view one could literally "drown" in a sea of books. Even the walls seemed made of books; behind the shelves were more books, and there were more in the stockrooms.

Steven Langer now feels he has the problem solved. "It took two or three months, but all is running smoothly," he noted recently with satisfaction. Langer's plan of attack was as follows: He took an inventory of the entire bookstore. He cleared the aisles of all books, keeping only relevant and attractive books on show. He got rid of the overstock on the walls and shelves, changed the wall paneling to a lighter color, and installed stronger lights. All this produced a strong impression of airiness and elbow room. "A prospective customer likes browsing leisurely," said Langer. "If he trips over piles of books blocking the aisles, he will leave the book shop angry and definitely won't come back again. If he is satisfied, he will come back again."

1. Evaluate Langer's plan.
2. Suggest alternate or additional plans.

12
Stereo Sound Music Shop

The Stereo Sound Music Shop in downtown San Francisco is a quality music store. Its owner, Leonard Ward, specifically designed his shop to attract high-income buyers who were, as he termed them, "music nuts." They looked for precision and quality in sound, with all the possible conveniences a stereo could offer. They were able to pay for their desires, and Leonard Ward made sure to supply them with top-quality stereo sets. He advertised only in quality magazines, thus furthering his image. To induce his potential buyers further, he offered a liberal repair service, assuring them that the stereo sets were of such a high quality that repairs, if any, would be practically nonexistent.

With the great rock-and-roll revolution sweeping the country and San Francisco being especially affected, Mr. Ward decided to investigate that market. He wanted to determine what effect rock-and-roll had upon the style, quality, price, and customers of stereo sets. He was especially concerned with the higher-income bracket as his business depended on these consumers.

He surveyed the San Francisco area and discovered that the rock-and-roll music shops seemed to be doing well. These shops usually specialized in selling musical instruments such as guitars (folk and electric), amplifiers, and stereo sets of lower quality than the type he sold. The store owners told him that the young generation immensely enjoyed loud, blaring music with good sound, but were not interested in purchasing high-quality stereo sets. Furthermore, they were attracted to music shops with a mod layout, with such drawing features as rock-idol posters given with each purchase and rock music amplified onto the street. These stores also advertised in magazines of interest to teenage girls and boys. The firms also put on promotional campaigns in local schools, hanging posters featuring their products. Another important factor was the price. One store owner emphasized, "You got to give these kids something they can afford." Continuing on to higher-priced music stores, Mr. Ward discovered that they seemed less successful. Usually they complained of old customers now buying cheaper equipment, a fact that indicated a startling change in taste among higher-income music lovers. They, too, seemed "turned on" by the "rock revolution." Touring the other higher-priced stores he realized that a trend was forming – a gradual turnabout from the more expensive, high-quality music equipment to the middle- and low-priced types. Profoundly concerned, he realized that he faced a challenge and must move quickly to avoid a seemingly inevitable business loss.

1. What are Mr. Ward's alternatives?
2. What alternative should he pursue?

13

Opticians Ltd.

Opticians, Ltd., a large retail firm selling contact lenses, has been dismayed by consumer aggravation over contact lenses. Checking their records they discovered that more than 50 per cent of their customers discontinued wearing lenses after a short period of time even though it meant reverting to glasses. This trend has seemed to increase, and Opticians, Ltd. feels that their business is threatened if the trend continues.

Recently the board of directors met to discuss the issue and find a solution. It was decided to appoint Vice President Henry Grimes to investigate the matter and to offer a solution. Mr. Grimes was given enough manpower and financial support to allow a thorough investigation and decided to interview other opticians who recently had discontinued contact lenses.

After an intensive survey, he discovered that (1) Many felt that the amount of pain and tears one had to suffer to adjust to the contact lenses was not worth the convenience of the lenses. (2) As the lenses don't cover the cornea of the eye completely, eyeglasses function better. (3) The risk of losing lenses is great and costly.

Mr. Grimes presented the survey results to the board of directors. He then recommended to the board that a committee of opticians should scientifically try to correct the flaws in the contact lenses. Mr. Grimes was of the opinion that as soon as the physical solutions were solved, the other problems would be easily overcome. The net result, he felt, would be that the majority of ex-contact-lens wearers would return to the fold and thousands of wearers of eyeglasses would turn to contact lenses.

1. Evaluate Mr. Grimes' technique in uncovering the problem with contact lenses.

2. Do you agree with his suggestion?

3. Can you offer alternate suggestions to solve the problem of Opticians, Ltd.?

A large department in downtown Dallas had a strict policy on payment for purchases. The Lone Star Department store had consistently refused to join the credit and charge trend in the United States. "Our policy is that what you pay for you get, otherwise come back tomorrow," said the president of the store.

After a number of years the board of directors voted to change policy and install a credit system, using charge accounts. They realized this would increase certain expenses but hoped that this convenience would push sales upward.

Reviewing sales and performance the following year the board of directors were gratified to see a 100 per cent jump of sales. "We definitely can attribute that sales increase to our introduction of the credit and charge policy," noted the chairman of the board with satisfaction.

The next year the board reviewed the situation and came to the following conclusion: Sales were approximately $6,400,000 per year. Of that volume, half were charge sales. Billing and collecting procedures took 3 or 4 weeks, and 20 per cent of the charge account customers paid their bills 2 or 3 months late. The firm estimated that costs of maintaining charge accounts were 6 per cent of the charge volume, equalling $192,000. The board decided to hire a credit and charge firm to handle their charge accounts rather than having the store manage the charge accounts. They received an offer of a 4 per cent charge on the accounts receivable of the store, payable as a deduction from the total amount of charges due the store. At the present volume, this fee would equal $128,000. The firm taking over the charge accounts simply deducted the 4 per cent charge from bills paid to the store. If the charge-account bills equalled $30,000 for one week, the credit firm would receive $1200 and pay Lone Star $28,800, the remainder. In order to profit from the charge accounts, the credit firms would charge a 2 per cent service charge for any accounts overdue after 30 days.

In a midyear board meeting the secretary notified the board that the store was receiving a deluge of mail condemning the extra charge for lateness with a substantial number of charge-account cancellations. Realizing the possibility of reduced sales volume the board was forced to make a decision regarding the charge accounts.

1. What would you decide if you were chairman of the board?

2. Should the company absorb the cost of late payments for the goodwill of the customers?

15

Joe's
Liquor Store

Joe's Liquor Store is located on a main street in Glens Falls, N.Y. The owner, Joe Manning, has been in business for several years. In recent years Joe has experienced a decline in earnings because of several factors.

The first and most important reason for the decline in profits was the ending of price controls in New York State. Though the legislature substituted a minimum markup law (12 per cent) for liquor, Mr. Manning finds that this markup is not enough to maintain his business at the previous profitable level.

The second reason, in the opinion of Manning, for his declining profits is his inability to offer the consumer a reason for shopping exclusively in his store. In his opinion, most liquor purchasers are price conscious and rarely loyal to one store.

Though he felt he could do little about the dropping of effective price controls in New York State, Mr. Manning believed that he could take several steps to differentiate his store and thus develop a loyal patronage. He noted several successful operations in Syracuse, N.Y. In one store he visited, most of the sales were not in liquor but in wine. Wine in New York State is still under price control and thus can be profitable to the retailer. Wine is, however, a specialty product that appeals to a small segment of the market.

In another major store in Syracuse, Mr. Manning noted a strong emphasis on private brands. The owner of the store informed him that 35 per cent of the firm's business was in private brands, a particularly effective means of establishing a loyal customer because he could find your private brand only in your store.

The establishment of a private-brand business seemed to be relatively easy. All Manning had to do was contact a wholesaler who would obtain liquor with "Joe's Liquor Store" labels printed on each bottle, which could be accomplished quickly. The problem arose in making the price of such bottles attractive. Almost by definition, a private brand must sell for less than a national brand. As most of the cost of a bottle of liquor is made up of federal, state, and local taxes, the retailer would have difficulty finding a private-brand liquor that would cost less than the national brand. In addition, since price controls had been dropped, the prices of national brands had declined substantially. By offering private brands at a lower price the retailer would be almost forced to take a lower markup on these items than on national brands. Nevertheless, Mr. Manning felt that by offering a private brand he would develop loyal customers.

In his opinion the chance of developing a wine business was practically zero, as the people presently coming into his store and living in the immediate area were not interested in wine.

1. What should Mr. Manning do?

John Britman, the divisional merchandise manager of dresses of the Kern Brothers Department Store in San Francisco was becoming concerned about their popular-price dress department. He had noted a substantial decline in profits from this department even though sales had been increasing. In the past three years profits had declined by 24 per cent while sales increased by 6 per cent.

Mr. Britman and the firm's research director decided that the firm should do some customer interviewing to determine what was going wrong.

The research director proposed that the firm interview approximately 25 to 30 customers regarding their attitudes toward Kern's and the six other major stores in the bay area. The number of interviews was limited by the amount of research funds available and by the fact that the director felt that an in-depth study would elicit more detailed information.

After constructing a questionnaire, the research department interviewed 30 women shoppers and tabulated the data. One questionnaire was discarded because the answers were considered unreliable. The researchers made the following report:

Appearance of Departments
Shoppers are unanimous in praising the attractiveness of your department. They like the decoration, lighting, furnishings, and the "air of gracious ease," due to its orderly appearance and absence of crowding. One shopper stated, "To me Kern has a charm and dignity in appearance no other store has." "It is new and modern, well lighted, and has easy and comfortable chairs and couches, upholstered to carry out department decorations." Considered *best-looking* department of seven stores shopped.

Fitting Rooms
Comments on our fitting rooms are *virtually all favorable*. They were described as large, clean, well lighted, and "so nice that you feel like buying the dresses you try on." The mirrors, allowing a good view of back as well as front, received special praise. Minor criticisms were (1) absence of shelf for bag and accessories and (2) lack of pins and of hangers for customers dresses.

Contacting the Salesperson
Although most comments were favorable, there were too many uncomplimentary statements (11 out of 29). Lack of floor supervision is the outstanding fault reported. No one greets customer when she enters department. Some salespeople seemed inattentive and uninterested; there are not enough salespeople. Several instances reported of loud talking and quarreling among salespeople.

Salesmanship
Majority of comments on this point were *unfavorable*. Out of 29 reports, 14 were unfavorable, 4 partly favorable. Repeated instances of customers kept waiting in fitting room for long periods. Salespeople left to wait on other customers and in some cases did not return at all. Some girls in the department use excessive make-up. Many were inattentive and uninterested.

One shopper reported, "I spent 15 minutes in there (fitting room) trying on without any assistance. She (the saleswoman) had excused herself, saying she was occupied with another customer. I might have walked out with any of the dresses, as no one even looked at me as I left the dressing room."

Merchandise Assortment

Your dress assortment ($9.00 to $20.00) was *sharply criticized.* Out of 29 reports, 18 were unfavorable, 6 partly favorable. Assortment rated *next to last,* of 7 rated stores. *Insufficient* stock for adequate selection was chief objection.

Styles were criticized because they were not "snappy" enough. But dresses were well made and of good materials. As one woman said, "the dresses were good value, the right colors and fabrics, but the styles – the good looking ones – were not unusual."

In small misses' sizes, selection was exceptionally poor. In junior department, no styles are suitable for small women who are not juveniles. Another common objection was the lack of dark summer dresses suitable for street and business wear before July. Shoppers stated that white and pastel shades were not suitable for spring wear.

One shopper suggested a separate maternity department. A minor suggestion was to cover dresses with cellophane protectors instead of muslin.

1. What action should Mr. Britman take?

17
Hawthorne Discount House

The Hawthorne Discount Store has been in business for over ten years. Located on the Veterans of Foreign Wars Highway south of Boston, the store has been a profitable operation from practically the day it opened.

In its most recent year this 50,000 square-foot unit attained a peak volume of just under $2.5 million. Like most such stores in this area it carries all kinds of staple goods, auto accessories, toys, sporting goods, drugs, jewelry, appliances, and cameras. In addition, the store devotes 8,000 square feet of its space to a supermarket.

In a recent survey of the discount industry by the *Discount Merchandiser,* a trade publication, it was noted that discount stores attained the following sales per square foot:

1968	$70.52
1969	68.22
1970	67.37
1971	66.96

Richard Minor, the president of the firm, noted that Hawthrone had sales per square foot of only $50 ($2.5 million ÷ 50,000). Though the trend of the averages as reported by the magazine was definitely downward, Hawthrone had managed to increase its sales per square foot slightly during this same period.

Nevertheless, Mr. Minor suggested that something must be wrong if the national averages were so much higher. To find out what, he hired an outside consulting firm from the Boston area to advise him on the action he should take to improve the store's sales per square foot.

1. Do you agree with Mr. Minor's evaluation?
2. Did he take the proper action?

A team of research people in the Department of Agricultural Economics at the University of Hawaii came up with an idea to aid consumers that appealed to the head of the department. It was their view that consumers were ignorant of price differentials among stores, not because of laziness or illiteracy on their part but simply because of logistics. Consumers cannot shop in all the stores in their cities and make price comparisons. Even if the consumer could overcome the logistics problem, price comparisons would be impractical because the stores carry too many products.

There was great interest in food-store prices in Hawaii, as the cost of living in this state was ranked among the highest of the fifty states. For example, in 1970 the U.S. Labor Department reported that a four-person family living in Honolulu needed $12,776 in order to live modestly. This figure exceeded that for all other cities in the U.S.

It was the research team's view that the school should supply the consumer with the necessary price information to make a proper judgment. It was proposed that the school collect such information on a regular basis and publish it either in the newspaper or in releases to the public.

To test the validity of collecting price information in food stores, the research group collected the following preliminary information:

EXPLANATORY NOTES ON THE OAHU FOOD PRICE STUDY. ON APRIL 7/8 1971 THE PRICES OF 85 ITEMS WERE OBSERVED IN THE FOLLOWING STORES:

TIMES SUPERMARKET MCCULLY
STAR SUPERMARKET MOILILI
FOODLAND MARKET CITY
FOOD CITY BERETANIA
SAFEWAY BERETANIA
HOLIDAY MART ALA MOANA
PARKVIEW-GEM KAPALAMA

18

University of Hawaii

GIBSON DISCOUNT CENTER
SHOPPING BASKET KALIHI
KALIHI QUEENS SUPER MARKET
CHUNHOON SUPERMARKET
P AND P SUPER FOODS
ZANES 9TH AVENUE MARKET
A AND M SUPERMARKET
MELS MARKET WAIMANLO
SHIMAS MARKET WAIMANLO
DOTES SUPERMARKET KANEOHE
LINDYS I G A HAUULA
HALEIWA I G A SUPERMARKET
KITS SUPERMARKET HALEIWA
BIGWAY SUPERMARKET WAHIAWA
NAKATANI SUPERMARKET NANKULI
TAMUAR SUPERETTE WAIANE
CORNET GROCERY WAIANE
JET SUPERMARKET WAIMALU

All items were selected from comparable grades and brands, specified in the following list. Items in each store that were marketed at the low price are marked with an *.

Each item was assigned a weight as a measure of its importance in the marketbasket. Weighted subtotals and a total were computed for each store by summing the products of the weights and item prices. The median price was substituted for all item prices labeled "No Data", allowing the stores to be compared. The stores were ranked on the basis of these weighted subtotals and totals. In addition to the brands listed, many stores carry private brands of similar quality that may offer a further saving.

Sample findings, for bakery goods and cereals in nine of the stores, are shown in the table on page 427.

1. Discuss the research technique used in the study.
2. How would you interpret the findings?

19

Cater Brothers

Cater Brothers, a family shoestore located in downtown Dallas, has been in business for over 20 years. Recently they noted that many of their downtown competitors have been successfully opening branches in the outlying suburban areas. As a result the family decided to look actively for a site in a suburban shopping center.

The firm was invited by the Alco Company to move into a center it is developing in the northeast suburbs of Dallas. The Alco Company has been developing shopping centers throughout Texas for the past ten years. In the

Retail Food Prices on April 7/8, 1971 – OAHU

	Times	Star	Foodland	Foodcity	Safeway	Holiday	Gem	Gibson	S. Basket
Bakery and Cereals									
Bread, White 1 lb. Holsum, Loves	0.28	0.27*	0.27*	0.27*	0.27*	0.28	0.27*	0.27*	0.27*
Bread, Wheat 1 lb. Holsum, Loves	0.36	0.34	0.34	0.35	0.33*	0.35	0.34	0.35	0.35
Donuts 8 ct. Holsum, Hostess	0.44	0.43	0.45	0.42	0.43	0.43	0.41*	0.41*	0.45
Cookies Cream									
Sandwich 15 oz. Hydrox, Oreo	0.55	0.53	0.53	0.53	0.54	0.55	0.53	0.53	0.49*
Corn Flakes 12 oz. Kelloggs	0.43	0.46	0.43	0.43	0.47	0.45	0.43	0.41	0.41
Soda Crackers 10 oz. Diamond	0.39	0.37	0.37	0.36	0.37	0.39	0.36	0.36	0.37
Flour,									
All Purpose 5 lb. Any Brand	0.59	0.63	0.59	0.59	0.55**	0.59	0.59	0.69	0.59
Pancake Mix 40 oz. Bisquick	0.59	0.59	0.59	0.59	0.60	0.69	0.59	0.55	0.59
Rice Calrose									
U.S. 1 10 lb. Extra Fancy	1.29*	1.29*	1.29*	1.29*	1.29*	1.29*	1.29*	1.29*	1.29*
Subtotal	4.92	4.91	4.86	4.83	4.85	5.02	4.81	4.86	4.81
Weighted Subtotal	4.31	4.25	4.23	4.20	4.24	4.33	4.18	4.18	4.18
Store Rank	9	8	6	4	7	10	1	3	2

past two years this firm has developed two successful centers in Houston and Austin.

Cater Brothers, after weeks of discussion with the developers, selected a 3,600-square-foot store located in an area that contained two other family-type shoestores. After carefully planning the fixtures and displays to be included in the store, management determined that the store would have 2,600 square feet of selling space, the rest to be used for office space, stock rooms, and a receiving dock.

The firm estimated that sales volume for the first year would approximate $300,000, close to the sales volume of the downtown store. However, the downtown store was approximately 2,000 square feet larger and contained larger stock areas.

The firm was concerned, however, with the rental terms proposed by the Alco Company. The leasing department of the developers proposed a minimum rental of $28,700 per year. This rent would remain at the minimum until the sales volume exceeded $400,000 annually. At that point it was proposed that the rental would become 7 per cent of all sales.

From the sales estimate, Cater Brothers realized that its rental expense would approximate 9 per cent of sales. Their downtown store had a rental agreement that was less than half the cost of the proposed shopping-center lease.

After a period of negotiation the firm was convinced that this agreement was the best they could get. The only concession they appeared to receive was the offer of a ten-year lease with an additional ten-year option, as most small firms moving into the center were offered only 20-year leases.

1. What should the firm do?
2. How can one justify such a rental difference between two stores?

20

Enson's Shoe Store

Harvey Enson, the owner of Enson's shoestore, took an inventory of his stock on December 25th and found that it amounted to $40,000 at retail. He was interested in determining the cost of this inventory. As he had taken inventory simply by writing down the retail prices of the merchandise, he knew he must convert the retail inventory to a cost figure.

Going over his records, he determined that his purchases during the year had amounted to $75,000 at cost. Calculating the retail value of all these purchases, he determined that the $75,000 in purchases represented $125,000 in retail value.

He reasoned that as both the purchase cost and their retail value were known to him, then by simply calculating his average markup during the year and applying its complement to his ending inventory he could determine the cost value of the inventory.

He then made the following calculation:

retail value: $125,000
cost purchases: $75,000

$75,000 ÷ $125,000 = 60% (cost of inventory)
$40,000 (ending inventory at retail) X 60% (cost) =
$24,000, cost value of ending inventory

1. Do you agree with the approach by Mr. Enson?
2. What alternative did he have?

Two brothers, Sam and Greg Lancaster, inherited a liquor store from an uncle who passed away after quite a long illness. Their uncle had built it up into a popular shop, and sales were usually brisk. But understandably, as the uncle's health failed so did the liquor store's. The Lancaster brothers faced a challenge with great potential. The store had proved itself profitable, and it was up to them to return the store to its former glory.

Being both successful businessmen with little spare time, the Lancasters decided to hire a manager to run the liquor store, at a $10,000-a-year salary for a three-year experimental period. After three years they felt they would be able to judge if the liquor store was a worthwhile business venture or if they should sell it and salvage what they could.

The manager, a middle-aged man with some retailing experience, was hired with the hope that he would facilitate the store's profit. At the end of three years the Lancaster brothers reviewed the performance of the store, shown in the following figures:

21

**The
Lancaster
Liquor Store**

	Year 1	Year 2	Year 3
Sales	$59,000	$62,000	$64,000
Cost of goods sold	32,540	34,190	36,180
Gross margin	$26,460	$27,810	$28,320
Operating expenses	13,800	14,630	16,320
Profit (before tax)	$12,660	$13,180	$12,000

The Lancasters were disappointed in the drop in profits in the 3rd year.

1. What would you conclude from the data presented?

22
Miles Stores

Dr. David Rachman
Bernard M. Baruch College
17 Lexington Avenue
New York, New York 10010

Dear Dr. Rachman:

When your recent book arrived here, I was appalled to read your definition of retail research as it appears in Chapter 19. After reading it, I immediately drafted this letter. My disagreement is with your first eleven words, namely "Retail research is the systematic collection of market information pertaining to. . . ."

First, I looked at your definition from the point of view of management, and I found myself imagining a situation where the performance of the research function would be based on your definition — particularly the "systematic collection" part. I looked at my desk piled high with papers, charts, and expense plans — and then I looked at my files and found an array of information, advice, ideas, statistics, and other data. In many folders, all of these were mixed together under one subject heading, while in others — the fatter ones — greater separation and division was possible; one thing was certain — it was not systematic collection (at least if it was, the system was not visible to management). Furthermore, something else about research appeared to be more important to management.

Next, I considered your definition from my point of view as Director of Research for a group of department stores in the Southwest. Six of our recent projects were examined, and the time spent on each was analyzed. Each project was divided into three work-parts. First, Research — the process of gathering facts, interviewing, digging, and checking. Second, Analysis — reviewing the facts found, forming and testing conclusions, choosing those which appear pertinent. Third, Presentation — the preparation and layout and presentation of researched material, the process which will make the results of two weeks' hard work completely understandable in less than ten minutes to somebody who has never seen it before. The result of our analysis is shown below.

Percent of time spent on each segment

Research	10%
Analysis	15%
Presentation	75%

Each part of our work is considered equally important, but perhaps we give more attention to presentation, because we know we are dealing first with people.

I am not sure if you would consider some part of research more important just because people spend more time doing it, but it does seem to me, Dr. Rachman, that there is far more to research than you have stated in your definition.

Yours sincerely,

Alfred Carr
Director of Research
Miles Stores

AC:bgc

1. Is the research procedure described by Alfred Carr "systematic"?

The buyer of men's shirts for the Long Department Store in Columbus, Ohio, was presented with the following operating statement at the end of a recent three-month period.

Sales			Percentage
Gross sales		$110,000	
Less returns and allowances		10,000	9.09
Net sales		$100,000	100.00
Cost of Sales			
Inventory — first of period		20,000	
Gross purchases (billed cost)	$73,000		
Less returns and allowances	4,000		
Net purchases		69,000	
Transportation charges		1,000	
Total merchandise handled		$90,000	
Inventory — end of period at cost or market		25,000	
Gross cost of merchandise sold		65,000	65.0
Cash discounts earned		3,000	3.0
Net cost of merchandise sold		62,000	62.0
Net alteration and workroom costs		1,000	1.0
Total merchandise costs		$63,000	63.0
Margin and Expenses			
Gross margin ($100,000-$63,000)		$37,000	37.0
Operating expenses		30,000	30.0
Operating profit		$7,000	7.0
Other Income			
Miscellaneous other income	2,000		
Deductions from other income	1,000	1,000	1.0
Net profit before federal income tax		$8,000	8.0

Though the department showed an $8,000 profit the buyer was aware of the fact that he had told management that by the end of the year his profits would be closer to 10 per cent of sales.

It was the buyer's view that in order to accomplish his goal he would have to increase his gross margin from 37 per cent to at least 38 per cent.

1. How can this goal be accomplished?

24

Pratt Men's Wear

David Pratt enjoyed his daily work. It really kept him on the go and always furnished new challenges. Mr. Pratt owned a men's wear shop in midtown New York City. Located at Fifth Avenue and 42nd Street, Pratt Men's Wear was in the midst of the hustle and bustle that is Midtown, New York City; and Pratt enjoyed every minute of it.

Pratt Men's Wear was a medium-sized store well known in the business area it served. The owner prided himself on constantly being on top of the ever-changing fashion scene. The store offered a large variety of clothes to its customers, from conservative suits to the latest sports clothes. Pratt's not only offered suits, jackets, and slacks but also carried a complete line of shirts, ties, belts, and other men's accessories.

David Pratt had an excellent taste in men's clothing, which his customers valued and appreciated. His expertise in choosing clothing and matching colors and styles was enhanced by his eagerness to assist his customers. As far as purchasing the clothing, Dave Pratt kept up with all the new trends, closely watching the world fashion centers and men's fashion magazines. He took pleasure in going to the market to purchase his stock.

Mr. Pratt was very disturbed over the fact that his stock position worsened every year; while his turnover decreased, his inventories of merchandise increased. The past four years had produced the following records:

	1969	*1970*	*1971*	*1972*
Beginning stock at retail	$ 9,000	$ 21,000	$ 32,000	$ 53,000
Purchases during year at retail	112,000	128,000	153,000	180,000
Total stock at retail	$121,000	$149,000	$185,000	$233,000
Sales	94,000	110,000	125,000	152,000
Markdowns and shortages	6,000	7,000	8,000	8,000
Stock at end of year at retail	$ 21,000	$ 32,000	$ 53,000	$ 73,000

Mr. Pratt disliked record-keeping and planning. He bought instinctively, acquiring what he thought he could sell and only estimating his current stock. As his business grew, his investments grew. He had no control except his own judgment on what the store had and needed. Old goods remained on his shelves for years, without any plans for markdowns to clear them from stock. Because it lacked proper planning and control, Pratt Men's Wear was in serious trouble.

1. Do you agree to the statement of the problem?
2. How would you correct the situation?

Mr. Stewart opened a small watch repair shop in the downtown section of Chicago. As a youth he had been an apprentice to a watchsmith and now, growing older and more mature, he felt that he could finally start off on his own. He had intentions of enlarging his shop and possibly adding a jewelry line, but that seemed to be a while away.

Being an independent young man, James Stewart decided to do everything on his own. He asked more experienced people for advice in running his business affairs but made all decisions himself. He also took a few courses in accounting to be able to conduct his money matters fairly proficiently.

After some time, Stewart enlarged his watch repair shop. As he originally anticipated, he entered the jewelry line, combining it with his watch repair shop. His line of jewelry offered a limited number of items to his customers. He felt that he should start small and only if successful expand his business in jewelry products.

As the value of Mr. Stewart's jewelry inventory remained the same from year to year, he decided to use the cost method of valuing his inventory. Stewart marked the unit cost of each item in code, and whenver he took a physical inventory, he recorded the cost price for each item.

After a while, Mr. Stewart felt the time was ripe for expansion. He enlarged his store and added many new jewelry items. Although his store was not over-large, Stewart decided to departmentalize his store into various small departments, such as watches, rings, necklaces, bracelets, and repair.

Of course, with this enlargement, Mr. Stewart realized a revision of his inventory method might be necessary. A financial expert suggested to Stewart that he switch from the cost method to the retail method.

1. Do you agree with the proposed change?

Selected Bibliography

Possibly the best way to study each of the topics in this textbook is to examine the footnoted references in each chapter. To supplement this reading, individual bibliographies can be consulted.

The bibliography below lists only major books that are available in most business libraries. It does not pretend to be complete but should meet the needs of most students interested in the study of retailing.

Books for Further Reference

Douglas J. Dalrymple and Donald L. Thompson, *Retailing: An Economic View,* New York: The Free Press.

Delbert S. Duncan, Charles F. Phillips, and Stanley C. Hollander, *Modern Retailing Management* (8th ed.), Homewood, Ill.: Richard D. Irwin, Inc., 1972.

Ronald Gist, *Basic Retailing: Text and Cases,* New York: John Wiley and Sons, Inc., 1971.

Fred Jones, *Retail Management* (rev. ed.), Homewood, Illinois: Richard D. Irwin, Inc., 1967.

Rom J. Markin, *Retailing Management: A Systems Approach,* New York: The MacMillan Company, 1971.

John W. Wingate and Joseph Friedlander, *The Management of Retail Buying* (3rd ed.), Englewood Cliffs, N.J.: Prentice-Hall, Inc., 1963.

John W. Wingate, Elmer O. Schaller, and F. Leonard Miller, *Retail Merchandise Management,* Englewood Cliffs, N.J.: Prentice-Hall, Inc., 1972.

Books of Readings

Gist, Ronald (ed.), *Management Perspectives in Retailing* (2nd ed.), New York: John Wiley and Sons, Inc., 1971.

Markin, Rom J., Jr. (ed.), *Retailing: Concepts, Institutions, and Management,* New York: The Macmillan Co., 1971.

Rachman, David J. (ed.), *Retail Management Strategy: Selected Readings,* New York: Prentice-Hall, Inc., 1970.

Ryans, John K., Jr., Donnelly, James H., Jr., and Ivancevich, John M., (eds.), *New Dimensions in Retailing,* Belmont, California: Wadsworth Publishing Co., Inc., 1970.

Index

A

C

R

Race, as factor in consumption, 79
Rachman, David J., 7*fn*, 76, 182*fn*, 188*fn*, 262, 340*fn*, 354
Rack jobber, 154, 156-57
  and trade discounts, 165
Radio advertising, 244
Rate structures, challenged by consumer, 61
Ray, Royal H., 232*fn*
Regional shopping center, 337, 338
Reilly, William J., 328*fn*
Reilly's Law, 328
Religion, as factor in consumption, 79
Rent:
  as fixed expense, 190
  as overhead expense, 365-66
Rental agreements, range of, 332-33
Reorder source, as wholesaler's function, 154
Resale price maintenance, manufacturer's and retailer's views, 26, 54
Research:
  determining priorities for, 387-88
  dimensions of, 368-69
  direct control survey methods, 379-85
  general concerns, 372-73
  observation study, 377-79
  types of reports, 376
Research department, functions of, 375-77
Research project, elements of, 377-87
Residence, as customer characteristic, 111
Restraints (*See* Legal restraints; Social pressures)
Restraints Upon Retail Competition, 48*fn*
Restrictive laws, 51-59
Retail advertising (*See* Advertising, retail)
Retail Advertising and Sales Promotion, 249*fn*
Retail decision-making, general outlines, 8-14
Retail Distribution, 4*fn*, 201*fn*
Retail entry and concentration, 32-34
Retail environment:
  choices for control of, 6
  controllable mix, 8-11
  uncontrollables, 8, 11-14
Retail firms:

sales, profits, and net worth ratios, 351-53 (*T*)
scope of, 3
Retail grocery store, acquisitions, 1949-1968, 35 (*T*)
Retail inventories (*See also* Inventories)
  fluctuations in, 279-80
Retail management:
  functions of, 18-23
  locational decision-making process, 324
Retail Management Strategy, Selected Readings, 340*fn*
Retail method, of inventory, 356
Retail Outlook 1964, The, 292*fn*
Retail reductions, 215, 295, 295*fn*
  definition, 210
  formula for estimation of, 210
Retail research (*See also* Research)
  definition, 373-74
  possibilities and applications, 389-90
Retail sales, as variable in site selection, 331
Retail salesman, relationship to consumer, 268
Retail selling (*See also* Selling)
  barriers to, 262-65
  as communicative function, 258
  organizational problems, 267-69
  positive aspects of, 265
  sources of wages, 265-67
  by telephone, 269-70
Retail selling function, 259-65
Retail trade, reported sales of apparel, 400 (*T*)
Retail Trade Annual Report, 399
Retailer-owned cooperatives, 157-58
  sales changes, 159 (*T*)
Retailers:
  concerns of, 24-25, 372-73
  contrasted to manufacturer, 24-27
  descriptive criteria, 5
  impact of legislation on, 50-51
  as own researcher, 370-72
  place in distribution system, 23-24
  services offered by, 167, 168 (*T*), 169 (*T*)
Retailing:
  differentiation, 43-44
  and energy shortage, 68-69
  firm size, 39-42
  functions of, 4-5
  general approaches, 3

U

V